{ **The Civil War in the West**

THE
LITTLEFIELD
HISTORY OF THE
CIVIL WAR ERA

Gary W. Gallagher and T. Michael Parrish, editors

SUPPORTED BY THE LITTLEFIELD FUND FOR SOUTHERN HISTORY, UNIVERSITY OF TEXAS LIBRARIES

The Civil War in the West

Victory and Defeat from the

Appalachians to the Mississippi

Earl J. Hess

The University of North Carolina Press
Chapel Hill

Set in Miller and Clarendon types

by Rebecca Evans

Manufactured in the United States of America

The paper in this book meets the guidelines for permanence
and durability of the Committee on Production Guidelines for
Book Longevity of the Council on Library Resources.

The University of North Carolina Press has been a member
of the Green Press Initiative since 2003.

Library of Congress Cataloging-in-Publication Data
Hess, Earl J.
The Civil War in the West : victory and defeat from the
Appalachians to the Mississippi / Earl J. Hess.
p. cm. —(The Littlefield history of the Civil War era)
Includes bibliographical references and index.
ISBN 978-0-8078-3542-5 (cloth : alk. paper)
ISBN 978-0-8078-7231-4 (large-print pbk.)
1. Southwest, Old—History—Civil War, 1861–1865—Campaigns.
2. Mississippi River Valley—History—Civil War, 1861–1865—Campaigns.
3. United States—History—Civil War, 1861–1865—Campaigns. I. Title.
E470.4.H47 2012   973.7′34—dc23   2011035950

16 15 14 13 12   5 4 3 2 1

For Pratibha and Julie, with love

{ Contents

} Map and Illustrations

Map

Illustrations

Preface

Today, it is difficult to imagine how much Civil War America was defined by regional aspects of geography and culture. The United States was a continental nation loosely held together by a handful of key political concepts, a common language, and a vision of destiny. The secession of eleven Southern states indicates how loosely those ties held the multiregional nation together. While the ties that bound the West and the East were stronger because of the absence of slavery, even the inhabitants of West and East were keenly aware that the differences between those two Northern sections were significant.

Westerners, especially, realized that their conduct of the war against the Confederacy was unlike that of their national partners in the East. Geography, more than any other factor, made the Civil War in the West unique. The Western states of the Confederacy embraced an expansive and varied territory, with a large population and many difficult topographical features to bog down Union offensives. Merely supplying a Federal column as it tried to penetrate the deep territory of the Western Confederacy was a huge problem. Dealing with guerrilla attacks on extended transportation lines, with recalcitrant civilian populations and thousands of refugee slaves, accentuated the difficulties of Federal commanders in the West.

Geography further divided the West into several subregions. The Upper South consisted of Kentucky and Tennessee, while the Deep South comprised Mississippi, Alabama, and Georgia. The Appalachian Highlands cut across parts of the Upper South and the Deep South to embrace the mountainous areas of Kentucky, Tennessee, Georgia, and Alabama. The Gulf region stretched across the coastal lowlands of southern Louisiana, Mississippi, Alabama, and Florida. But in many ways the most important subregion was the Mississippi River, which connected the western portions of Kentucky, Tennessee, and Mississippi in a waterborne network of commerce.

The Federals won the war in the West despite the enormous difficulties posed by geography and the fierce opposition of Confederate forces in that region—and not just because the Union side had more men, guns, and ships. The Federals made more astute use of their available resources for war making than did their opponents, they developed an advantage in morale early on in the conflict, and they were able to take advantage of some geographic factors that facilitated deep penetration of the Confederate land mass in the West. Rivers and railroads helped them to invade and conquer Rebel territory, and defeating Confederate opponents led to a self-confidence among average Northern soldiers that gave them an edge on the battlefield. Southerners often suffered not only from shortages of manpower and resources, things they had little control over, but also from poor management of whatever resources they did possess. The Federals overcame problems posed by geography by dint of extreme effort, ingenuity, and persistence, while the Confederates failed to utilize the advantages nature had given them and too often frittered away opportunities for a variety of reasons.

It should not be assumed that Union victory in the West was guaranteed, for there were real limits to Northern resources and transportation capacity. The Federals had what was needed to conquer the Upper South and the Mississippi River, both of which they had accomplished by the end of 1863. But their ability to penetrate the Deep South was severely limited. Major General William Tecumseh Sherman was barely able to feed and supply his huge army group during the Atlanta campaign, and he recognized that it was impossible to go farther south once that city had been captured. Federal commanders were forced by dint of logistical realities to experiment with something Confederate general Braxton Bragg had done in the Kentucky campaign: move an entire field army rapidly through contested territory without a secure line of communications. Only in this way could the Federals more or less dominate the Deep South in the last few months of the war.

Moreover, even though there was a great deal of friendly competition between the Western Federals and their comrades in the East, the war in the West was won in part by a good deal of support between the two Northern sections. New England troops provided most of the manpower in the Gulf region, capturing New Orleans, Baton Rouge, and Port Hudson, Louisiana. Two divisions of the Ninth Corps were shifted from the Army of the Potomac to Kentucky and Mississippi, where they helped to win Vicksburg and eastern Tennessee. The Eleventh and Twelfth Corps also were shifted from the Eastern army to help secure Chattanooga in late 1863 and continued with Sherman's army group throughout the remainder of the war.

Westerners also helped to fight the war in Virginia. Many Western states sent newly raised regiments to the East early in the conflict. While the first installment of Western generals to go east, in the summer of 1862, proved unable to engineer victory, Ulysses S. Grant took several Western subordinates with him to assume important command positions in the Virginia theater in 1864. Many black regiments raised in Kentucky in 1864 were shifted to the Army of the James, and the Twenty-third Corps was transported from the West in the winter of 1864–65 to help conquer North Carolina. Finally, Sherman's sixty thousand men—all veterans of successful Western campaigns—zeroed in on Robert E. Lee's Army of Northern Virginia to help end the war in the East by April 1865.

The West and the East had a vital if contentious relationship during the Civil War, characterized by a good deal of frustration as well as genuine cooperation. The Rebel government also sought to use its transportation network to invigorate its war effort with transfers east and west. So many regiments were shifted from the West to Virginia early in the conflict to protect the Confederate capital at Richmond that the Army of Northern Virginia wound up having units representing every state in the Confederacy, making it a truly national field army. The same was to a lesser extent true of the Army of Tennessee—the Confederacy's major field army in the West. But that army rarely possessed the manpower resources enjoyed by Lee, even though two divisions of Lee's army were temporarily attached to it under James Longstreet in 1863. Field commanders such as Joseph E. Johnston and P. G. T. Beauregard were shifted between the two theaters of operations as well, but the Confederates could never match their opponents in interregional cooperation because of the sorry state of their rail network and shortages of manpower.

In the end, mobility was the key to the Union triumph in the West. Whether it was expressed in a logistical network of steamboats and railroads that could transport troops and supplies, or in adapting operations to suit limited logistics, the Federals learned the lesson better than their opponents and persisted in applying the results until the Southern Confederacy was no more. To a large degree, the Union victory in the Civil War was a Western victory in more than one sense of the term. Despite the enormous amount of attention paid to the political center of the conflict—the 100-mile stretch of ground that separated Richmond from Washington, D.C.—the heartland of the Confederacy lay in the West. That heartland was subdued first, and decisively, before the East caved in.

This volume of the Littlefield series is devoted to the land and river campaigns that took place in the Western theater of operations—from the Mississippi River eastward to the Appalachian Highlands. It is a book about how the North won the Civil War in the West, one that also gives significant attention to the South's efforts to maintain control of the area. I summarize the flow of events during the Union conquest of the Western Confederacy, but also look at the logistical and transportation aspects of those campaigns. In addition, this volume briefly covers the many problems Union commanders faced in the West as they sought ways to deal with rebellious civilians and guerrillas, and to provide for thousands of blacks who chose to leave their plantations, seeking freedom under the Stars and Stripes. The desperate Confederate effort to fight an increasingly losing war in the West is also a subject of discussion here. In many ways, this book looks at the ways in which the Union won and the Confederacy lost the expansive landscape that stretched for 450 miles east to west and 600 miles north to south; this region constituted the most important territory of the nascent slave nation.

The emphasis placed on what was happening behind the lines helps us to recall that warfare took place on many other fields than battlegrounds. Federal forces had the job not only of pushing back Rebel forces from contested territory, but also of reclaiming populations that lived in the area. That job proved to be more complex and difficult than defeating enemy troops on the battlefield, and Federal commanders never came up with a consistently winning strategy to accomplish it. Until Abraham Lincoln's emancipationist policy went into effect by the midpoint of the war, the most troubling aspect of occupation remained the thorny question of what to do with runaway slaves. By 1863, what had been a problem was now viewed as an opportunity. Federal officials strove to employ the black population of the seceded South as soldiers and, more importantly, as laborers.

Commanders on both sides of the war also confronted problems arising from their own troops, for neither army rations nor transportation networks consistently afforded men in either blue or gray enough to eat. Many other factors influenced a general theme; soldiers on both sides plundered food and many other items from local civilians whenever they had an opportunity, even if they were not starving. Civil War armies ate their way to either victory or defeat, devouring resources like swarms of locusts and depriving friends and foes alike of their means of living. From the start of the war to the last, the Western armies of both the Union and the Confederacy tended to exceed the plundering done by those of the East, and it was not primarily a political phenomenon designed to punish the enemy or undercut their ability to resist armed force. Taking, using, or destroying material resources became a complex, important element of the war in the West, and therefore it has a significant role in this book.

If there was a Western way of war in the Civil War, a system governing military operations that was distinctive to the Western theater, then it is necessary to begin understanding what that "way" consisted of. This book will serve as a first step toward that goal.

I am grateful to Gary Gallagher and Michael Parrish for inviting me to contribute this volume to the Littlefield series, and for their support in its writing. The trustees of the Littlefield Fund deserve a large vote of gratitude for sponsoring this series. Michael Parrish and Thomas Cutrer shared significant sources with me, and the staff at the University of North Carolina Press did their usual thorough, professional, and supportive job of producing the book.

Most of all, I give thanks to my wife, Pratibha.

{ **The Civil War in the West**

1 } Spring and Summer 1861

The secession crisis inspired confused reactions among people across the Northern states that lay west of the Appalachian Highlands. Promises of a peaceful separation of the seven Deep South states had lulled many Northerners into the idea that breaking up the country might be inevitable, or even helpful in settling controversies concerning the spread of slavery in the Western territories. Others were more reluctant to countenance the destruction of the political unity that had been maintained through a system of compromise on that issue for eighty-five years. Most Northerners, however, simply did not know what to make of the newly created Southern government in Montgomery, Alabama, its pretensions to independence, or its future. Secession created a malaise among many in the free states, unresolved by the tempering stance of the outgoing James Buchanan administration and the incoming Abraham Lincoln regime.[1]

But the Confederate bombardment of Fort Sumter on April 12–14, 1861, altered everything. As John Sherman of Ohio put it, Sumter touched "an electric chord in every family in the northern states" and changed "the whole current of feeling." Sherman admitted that he was shocked by feelings of "surprise, awe and grief" by the act of violence, but later thought: "It brings a feeling of relief; the suspense is over." Benjamin Scribner of Indiana felt "animated with patriotism, for "the flag of the Union was to me a sacred object." For many across the North, the key issue lay in a respect for law and order, which the new Confederate government had demonstrated it did not possess. Federal authorities could not afford to look the other way at this forcible seizure of a U.S. government installation. "There would be no end to it," thought Walter Q. Gresham of Indiana, "and in a short time we would be without any law or order. We must now teach the Secessionists a lesson." For Gresham, it was "all bosh and nonsense to talk about the North making war on the South. The South rebelled against the laws and makes war on the government."[2]

Newspaper editors of all political leanings beat the tocsin of war by interpreting the firing on Sumter as an unpardonable act of violence to settle an issue that should have been handled through negotiation. It was both a threat and an insult to the government. "On one side stands rebellion, treason, anarchy," declared the *Chatfield (Minn.) Republican*, while "on the other the government, patriotism, law and order." Everything undemocratic was vested in the seat of government at Montgomery, while the principles of the founding fathers of the nation were vested in the hands of Lincoln's new administration in Washington. The *Indianapolis Daily Journal* believed that "We are fighting for the existence of our own Government," more than for "the destruction of that at Montgomery."[3]

For some of the more progressive-minded citizens in the North, there was gratitude for what happened at Sumter. The overt act of violence and lawlessness taught Northerners what they could expect from a slave Confederacy on their border. College professor and Republican state senator James Garfield of Ohio hoped the war would not end until the Confederacy was blotted out of existence, along with the institution that underpinned its economy, society, and culture. Another member of the Ohio Senate, Jacob Cox, vividly recalled how news of Sumter was announced during a session of that august body, causing "a solemn and painful hush" until a well-known abolitionist in the gallery shouted "'Glory to God!'" Cox, along with most of the other legislators, could not share such enthusiasm for the moral redemption of the nation, but he steeled himself for the war by thinking that the sacrifice could only be justified by preserving thereby "the right to enforce a fair interpretation of the constitution through the election of President and Congress."[4]

Whether Northerners welcomed Sumter because they saw that it foretold the death knell of slavery, or simply viewed it as an alarm for the defense of fundamental values held dear by the country, the firing on the fort solidified a common cause among Northern residents. Support for making war on the Confederacy was nearly universal, grounded on the need to defend the flag and all that it symbolized. Only the bombing of Pearl Harbor eighty years later had a similar effect on the American people, dispelling lingering feelings of isolationism and forming a mighty consensus in favor of war to the end.

There was an issue that quickly emerged among Northerners as another motivation for fighting. In fact, for many in the upper Mississippi Valley, it was as important as the motive to preserve the Union. This issue involved possession of the Mississippi River, a vast artery of commerce and communications. It had been in full possession of the common government since 1803, at enormous expense to the nation to secure its citizens full control not only of the waterway but also of New Orleans, the major port whereby

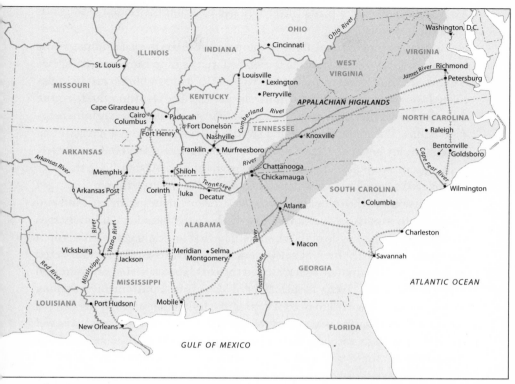

The Western Theater of Operations

Western farmers offered their products for shipment outside the country. Many Northerners wondered what secession would do to their historic right to navigate and use the great river, for it seemed to portend a reversion to the old days when Spain and France alternately possessed New Orleans, as well as the vast, undeveloped Louisiana Territory that stretched west of the Mississippi.[5]

Since 1803, technology had made the river far more important as a trading artery than it had ever been. The first regular steamboat travel on the Mississippi began in 1812, with increasing numbers of craft plying the turbid waters every decade. The steamboat era reached its peak in the 1850s, the same decade that cotton production soared to its height in the Deep South. In 1859–60 more than 2 million tons of goods were shipped to New Orleans from the extensive watershed of the Mississippi, amounting to nearly $300 million worth of property. From Cincinnati, 206 steamboats put into New Orleans that year; 172 arrived from Louisville, 110 from Memphis, and 526 from Pittsburgh. From St. Louis, the second most important trade city in the

Mississippi Valley, 472 boats traveled to the Crescent City laden with goods from the upper valley.[6]

The Mississippi drained about 40 percent of the territory encompassed by the nation's forty-eight states, a region as large as nine European countries combined. The Northern half of the river, with its high bluffs, needed relatively little improvement to support navigation. The Southern half, on the other hand, was broader, deeper, and had long stretches of nearly imperceptible banks. The most troublesome stretch of the river, from a navigational viewpoint, lay between Cape Girardeau, Missouri, and the Gulf of Mexico. While these two points lay only 600 miles apart on a straight line, the river meandered so much that a boat needed to travel more than 1,100 miles to get from one point to the other. Moreover, this region's deltalike mix of land and water led to expansive overflows on a yearly basis that affected landscapes many miles to either side of the channel. The first levee along the Mississippi River was built with the first settlement of New Orleans; it was completed in 1727 to protect that low-lying city on the east bank, situated one hundred miles north of the river's mouth. More levees were built northward along whichever bank seemed to need it during the following years. By the time of the Civil War, a fairly good system of embankments lined long stretches of the river, although with significant gaps. The majority of the levees, mostly constructed in the 1850s, were relatively low—only three or four feet tall.[7]

Steamboat commerce could be dangerous. The boats had a tendency to explode, hit snags, or burn because owners were free to build them to any standards they wished. It has been estimated that by 1860, 299 riverboats on the Western waters were damaged and another 120 totally destroyed. *De Bow's Review* calculated that more than 1,800 people had been killed in steamboat accidents, and another thousand injured, up to 1848.[8]

Ironically, the decade of steamboat ascendancy also witnessed the fast rate of growth for a major competitor of the boats. Developed in the 1820s and 1830s, railroad technology took off in the 1850s with thousands of miles of track laid, mostly across the Northern states. Major trunk lines began to link the Northwest with the Northeast, beginning to divert commerce to a West-East orientation rather than West-South. Canals had also begun to do this as early as the 1830s, but the railroad was a far more potent competitor of the steamboat. While 58 percent of Western produce was shipped through New Orleans in 1820, that figure dropped to 41 percent by 1850 and decreased even more by the time of the Civil War. Though many Northerners were not aware of it, the importance of the Mississippi River as the linchpin of Western commerce had declined. It retained its regional and local significance, but in a larger sense could lay claim to sharing the national flow of goods between the Northwest, the South, and the Northeast. Even so, it had proportionately come to serve Southern interests as much as Northwestern by the 1860s, for many Deep South planters invested so heavily in large-scale cotton production that they did not grow enough food to feed their slaves. The Northwest readily satisfied this deficiency.[9]

Questions of future sovereignty over the Mississippi River surfaced long before the firing on Fort Sumter. As soon as South Carolina seceded in late December 1860, Northern editors asked if their readers could trust the Southern Confederacy's promise to keep the river open to their navigation and trade. Even if they honored their pledge, Andrew Johnson of Tennessee pointed out, later generations of Southerners might not do so. William T. Sherman was certain that the temptation to tax Northern commerce on the river was so great as to be irresistible. "Collisions are sure to follow secession," he wrote his wife, "and the states lying on the upper Rivers will never consent to the mouth being in possession of an hostile state."[10]

Northern doubts about the Southern government's policy exploded when Governor John Jones Pettus of Mississippi constructed a few gun emplacements at Vicksburg on January 12, 1861, only three days after the state seceded. Pettus acted on rumors that the North was sending a party of armed men down the river to reinforce Federal forts and arsenals in Louisiana. Pettus called out the militia, but the scare evaporated by January 15. This act inflamed opinion among many Northerners against secession, as threats of war emblazoned newspaper headlines across their section. "The Northwest will be a unit in maintaining its right to a free and unobstructed use of the Mississippi river," proclaimed the *Cincinnati Daily Gazette*. Newspapers in Iowa, Illinois, and Minnesota claimed as much right to free navigation of the great river as Mississippi or Louisiana. "It is *their right*, and they will assert it to the extremity of blotting Louisiana out of the map," threatened the *Chicago Daily Tribune*.[11]

Many editors in the Northeast recognized the vitality of Northwestern interest in free navigation of the Mississippi and predicted their sister section would go to war with the Deep South over that issue alone, even if the Federal government made no move in that direction. The *Buffalo Morning Express* had predicted, even before Pettus's action, that "a tornado of indignation" would result from any Southern effort to "cut off from the commerce of the world" the farmers and tradesmen of the Northwest. Even Massachusetts newspaper editors suggested that the coming contest between North and South would be decided in the valley of the Mississippi, and the *Pitts-*

burgh Evening Chronicle warned the South that no one "who is acquainted with the robust character and resolute daring of the Western people can doubt the result of such a struggle."[12]

Southerners could read Northern newspapers too, and they made strenuous efforts to assure Northwesterners of their good intentions. The Louisiana secession convention passed an ordinance of secession and a resolution guaranteeing free navigation of the Mississippi on the same day, January 26, 1861. The newly formed Confederate government in Montgomery moved forward along the same line, passing a bill to establish free trade that President Jefferson Davis signed on February 25. A trade bill, passed on February 18, and a tariff bill, passed on May 21, established a Confederate policy of prohibiting taxes on imports of agricultural products. Even so, Southerners expressed fear that the thorny issue might derail secession altogether by creating an implacable animus against dividing the length of the Mississippi between two sovereign states.[13]

A few dissenting voices in the North pointed out that the river no longer held the preeminent place in national commerce it once possessed. The *Cincinnati Daily Commercial* noted that four major railroad lines and the Erie Canal linked the Northwest with the Northeast and could completely supplant the Mississippi while forging an even tighter unity between two sections that shared much more in common than either shared with the South. The Confederacy could only hurt itself, the editor believed, if it blocked navigation on the Mississippi. He noted that, apart from purely economic considerations, there was a mystic character about the Mississippi and its commercial significance that had not faded, despite the new economic realities. Many people still believed it was important, because it was a view handed down to them by previous generations. But Abraham Lincoln, speaking for those who understood the new economic realities, still thought saving the Mississippi River was important enough to go to war for. A product of the Western frontier who had taken boatloads of agricultural produce down the river to New Orleans in 1828 and 1831, Lincoln pointed out that Northwesterners could not accept any limit to their commercial opportunities and would not be content to rely solely on the railroads and canals. They wanted "access to this Egypt of the West, without paying toll at the crossing of any national boundary."[14]

Some Northerners interpreted the river navigation issue as far more significant than mere commerce. They took a geopolitical view of the controversy, noting that the Mississippi stretched "its branches into the heart of the continent," carrying the melted snow of the Rockies to the Gulf of Mexico. The river created a "physical unit" that was destined to be controlled by one government. Sherman fully agreed with this point, noting that the river and its branches made separation of North and South impossible. The Mississippi River was a symbol as well as an avenue of trade—a symbol of progress, regional pride, and national sovereignty that physically tied the North and the South. While it was an intensely Northwestern issue, the feeling was understood and supported by the Northeast and taken seriously by the South. The Northwesterners shared their sectional neighbors' reaction to the firing on Fort Sumter, but they had a special reason, in some ways more important than Sumter, for making war on the Confederacy.[15]

Kentucky Neutrality

Lincoln's call for troops on April 15, 1861, was rejected by many in the Upper South slave states. Supportive of the right to secede, but having decided that the election of a Republican president had not been a justified cause of it, those residents now refused to support Lincoln's efforts to use military force to restore the Union. Four more states seceded (Virginia, North Carolina, Arkansas, and Tennessee), constituting a formidable bulwark against Federal invasion of the Deep South. The northern border of the growing Confederacy now rested against an additional tier of slave states for most of its length. These border states (Maryland, Kentucky, and Missouri) remained in the Union because public opinion was so deeply divided on the national crisis that a legitimate secession movement proved impossible.[16]

The border states represented the threshold between contending sections, with important ties to both of them. While the Federal government took halting but effective steps to secure them in 1861, Kentucky adopted a unique approach to the sectional crisis that inhibited both belligerents from setting foot on its soil for several months. Governor Beriah Magoffin defended slavery as well as the right of secession, and he rejected Lincoln's call for troops. Though many Kentuckians agreed with his stand, they argued that the state ought to reject Confederate attempts to woo Kentucky into the Southern camp as well. A group of Kentucky politicians, comprising the State Rights Party, advocated secession, but they were not strong enough to sway the state in that direction. Although he cooperated with key secessionists to form Kentucky's policy of armed neutrality, Magoffin genuinely believed that the state could honor its commitment to take no sides. The legislature supported the move, passing resolutions on May 16 and 24, bracketing Magoffin's proclamation of neutrality on May 20.[17]

While many Northerners did not take Kentucky neutrality seriously, believing that such a stand was tantamount to support of the Confederacy, there is plenty of evidence that the position was genuinely endorsed by the state's most influential residents in the late spring of 1861. Northern predictions that neutrality would break down, however, began to prove true before summer's heat warmed the area. Unionist sentiment grew in the southern, central, and northeastern parts of Kentucky, while secessionists became dominant in the western part of the state. In the Bluegrass surrounding Lexington, the oldest, richest, most culturally influential region, pro-Confederate sentiment at least equaled devotion to the old Union. A number of factors, including the level of slave ownership and commercial ties to the Deep South, influenced which section leaned in which direction. "In this end of the State we are entirely Southern," wrote a resident of Murray in northwestern Kentucky.[18]

Unionism began to be dominant in Kentucky by summer's end, however; when elections for the legislature took place on August 5, pro-Federal candidates won a majority of seventy-six seats compared to twenty-four in the house, and twenty-seven compared to eleven in the senate. Now there was a split within the state's political leadership, with the legislature favoring Northern goals and the governor clinging to the outmoded policy of neutrality. Pro-Union candidates also won nine of Kentucky's ten U.S. congressional seats in August. The legislative election was the turning point in shifting Kentucky to the side of Abraham Lincoln, a native son, against the side of Jefferson Davis, who also had been born in Kentucky. In the words of Richard W. Johnson, a Kentucky native who became a Union general, the election "fixed the popular mind against the rebel cause."[19]

Nevertheless, for the time, both belligerents respected the state's neutral stand. Tennessee's Governor Isham G. Harris, as active a supporter of the Southern cause as one could find in Kentucky's sister state, assured everyone that he had no intention of interfering in his neighbor's policy, but he offered to send troops to help if Magoffin called on him. Nevertheless, Harris was concerned that the Mississippi River might enable Yankee gunboats to sail past Kentucky and attack Memphis. He knew that the best defensive ground south of Cairo, Illinois, was Columbus, on the Kentucky side of the river, and that high ground was denied to Confederate forces as long as Kentucky remained neutral. For his part, Lincoln tried to woo Simon B. Buckner, whom Magoffin had appointed commander of the state army, by offering him a brigadier general's commission in the Union forces. Buckner, a sincere advocate of neutrality with strong leanings toward the Southern cause, refused the offer. Although the tide was shifting toward Unionism, both sides continued to court friends in Kentucky and wait for a plausible excuse to break the state's neutrality.[20]

Defense of the Mississippi

As Isham Harris pointed out, Kentucky neutrality was a roadblock to important Union and Confederate strategic objectives in the West. "There is a great fear at present in this Country of invasion down the river," Charles J. Mitchell of Richmond, Louisiana, wrote Jefferson Davis. It was widely known that little had been done to construct defenses by late April 1861, which "produced a sense of insecurity here." That sense of insecurity was intensified by rumors of Northern plans to send troops downstream "to burn our cities and devastate our country," according to Confederate secretary of war Leroy P. Walker.[21]

Josiah Gorgas, acting head of the Confederate Engineer Bureau, swept aside mere rumor and warned that the Federals were massing upward of forty thousand troops at Cairo for the obvious purpose of descending the river, using a fleet of steamboats to support the men, and laying siege to the two masonry forts that guarded the approach to New Orleans south of that port city. The only way to save the river was to build fortifications at Columbus to stop this column before it went too far. Gorgas advocated a large, entrenched camp on the high ground, guarded by thirty thousand men. A number of other Southerners also supported plans for using Columbus as the key to stopping a descent down the river, despite Kentucky's neutrality. "Self-preservation demands it," wrote observer William W. Lee.[22]

Other Southerners advocated an aggressive course of action to save the Mississippi River, urging that the Confederate army move north and seize Cairo as a preventive measure. Memphis residents especially saw the value of this move as the best way to protect their city if Columbus was not within reach. The levees now became an object of military strategy. Reacting to rumors that the Northerners would recruit two hundred saboteurs to secretly travel south and cut levees to allow spring floods to injure Southern resources, an anonymous writer urged Davis to do the same to the levees that barely protected Cairo from both the Ohio and Mississippi Rivers and "drown out the rats."[23]

Officers of Tennessee's fledgling army pointed out that river batteries alone would not suffice. Gideon J. Pillow, commander of the state's armed force, noted that the Federals could pass east of any gun emplacements on the bank of the Mississippi and invade western Kentucky and western Tennessee; he did not have sufficient force to counter an inland move. Residents of Memphis and New Orleans alike complained that the government did not seem alive to the importance of the Mississippi River in Confederate strategy. Several concerned citizens in New Orleans argued that it was "the key to the Southern Confederacy" and vulnerable to a Federal seaborne invasion, given Davis's complete lack of a navy early in the war.[24]

The Confederate government could only try to allay such fears, expressing "deep solicitude in relation to the defenses of the Mississippi," and pointing out, as Davis did to a correspondent, that the Northerners "have so great a dread of our climate that they could not be prevailed on to march against us" during the summer months. But assertions like this persuaded few residents of the valley. They noted, in particular, the lack of a river fleet to supplement shore batteries. Even by November 1861, the pace of Confederate defense planning on the river exasperated many in the valley. Ordnance officer J. T. Trezevant argued that the Federals would "make most desperate efforts to cut their way down this river," and the fall of key cities would impel the collapse of the whole region. "With Memphis goes the valley, so far as the towns and plantations on the river are concerned." Trezevant belittled the importance of Virginia by arguing: "Where there is one life and $1 involved on our side in the triumph of the enemy on the Potomac, there are five lives and $5 in their triumph down this valley." For contemporaries and historians alike, Confederate defensive preparations along the river "resembled a perilously thin, hollow shell."[25]

The fears of contemporaries were well grounded in fact. The North had possession of a civilian fleet of steamboats that could carry troops and supplies anywhere that prewar commerce had taken them. Chief Engineer Joseph G. Totten reported in early June that at least 250 steamers, capable of carrying about seventy-five thousand men, were available on the Ohio River alone. At St. Louis, an additional 150 boats could be used. Two hundred freight barges and 400 coal barges were also available at both locations. Totten suggested that a fleet of 10 to 20 gunboats was needed to support operations on the river system. The gunboats would be owned by the Federal government, but the civilian steamers needed to transport troops and supplies could be used through contracts with their civilian owners. One of Totten's subordinates noted, however, that such contracts would have to be negotiated carefully, "for I have no doubt the boatmen and shippers will be ready to ask the full value."[26]

General in Chief Winfield Scott proposed to strangle resistance with minimal loss of life by using this unique river-borne resource. A seacoast blockade, proclaimed on April 19, would cut off the Rebels from outside help while "a powerful movement down the Mississippi to the ocean" would sever the new nation in half. Scott believed that by reopening communications down the Mississippi, he could, in conjunction with the seacoast

blockade, force Confederate authorities to negotiate an end to hostilities "with less bloodshed than by any other plan." Scott anticipated that up to twenty-five steam-powered gunboats would spearhead a fleet of forty riverboats carrying sixty thousand men; he hoped to begin the expedition by November 10, 1861. He envisioned the commander dropping off garrisons to hold key points along the river.[27]

Scott's famous Anaconda Plan never became a blueprint for all commanders to follow, in the twentieth-century sense, for regional commanders did not need a directive from Washington to tell them how to reopen navigation. They were fully aware of the political and military significance of the river. "After all the Mississippi River is the hardest & most important task of the war," declared William T. Sherman. Governor Richard Yates of Illinois agreed with Sherman and with Wisconsin governor Alexander W. Randall in telling Lincoln that the Western war would be centered on the river system to cut off trade to the rebellious states, to maintain commerce among the Northwestern states, and to "reach a vital part of this rebellion" in order to destroy it.[28]

Moreover, there was some fear among Northerners that the Confederates might use the river to attack free territory. Cairo and other ports on the Mississippi and the Ohio were vulnerable, and prominent residents of Chicago protested the sending of so many Western regiments to Virginia early in the war. All Westerners believed that "the true line of military operations is through the Valley of the Mississippi," asserted the Union Defense Committee of Chicago.[29]

Westerners could not help but view the river as the key to their war effort. Governor William Dennison of Ohio proposed organizing all Union troops into two regional armies, one centering its operations on Washington, D.C. in the East, and the other centering its movements along the Ohio and Mississippi Rivers. Republican state senator James Garfield brought this idea to Governor Oliver P. Morton of Indiana and Governor Yates of Illinois, and received their enthusiastic endorsements of the scheme.[30]

Breakdown of Kentucky Neutrality

Despite the fact that both belligerents pledged to respect Kentucky neutrality, both North and South secretly undermined it for their own purposes. As a result, Magoffin's policy crumbled before the end of the summer, throwing the state fully into the sectional contest.

As early as mid-May 1861 Lincoln authorized the secret shipment of arms to loyalists in his native state, justified, he thought, by numerous requests from the Unionists themselves. The Northern president reserved the right to send Federal troops into the state if it became necessary to preserve the Union. By late June, Secretary of War Simon Cameron authorized the recruitment of Union regiments from Kentucky and Tennessee as well. News of the Federal defeat at Bull Run on July 21 "intensified feeling on both sides" in the state, but prominent Unionists such as William Nelson continued to funnel arms to their compatriots in defiance of the growing concern of Governor Magoffin.[31]

Nelson even established a Union recruiting rendezvous in Garrard County, called Camp Dick Robinson, after the legislative elections created a Unionist majority in the state house in August. Buckner negotiated with Major General George B. McClellan, commander of Ohio's state forces, and with Governor Harris of Tennessee, in an effort to obtain assurances that both sides would continue to respect the state's neutral policy. Magoffin approached Lincoln and Davis for similar assurances. The Confederate president offered to respect Kentucky neutrality for the while, assuring Magoffin that the troops massed in northern Tennessee were meant merely to defend the Confederate border. But Davis warned Magoffin that he reserved the right to intervene if the Federals did so first. Lincoln forthrightly declined to curtail Union recruiting on Kentucky soil, claiming that it was done "upon the urgent solicitations of many Kentuckians." In effect, the Northern president told Magoffin that the governor and his colleagues no longer represented the popular mood of the state.[32]

Lincoln recognized that the tide of popular opinion was in his favor. Kentucky Unionists reported increasing interference from Tennessee to strengthen the secessionists of Kentucky, "making this State a feeding trough for treason," as a Unionist in Louisville put it. But Lincoln also was aware that Kentucky unionism was vulnerable. When Union general John C. Frémont issued a proclamation emancipating slaves in Missouri, there was a severe reaction against the U.S. government among many Kentucky loyalists who valued their slave property as much as they were devoted to the Union. Lincoln forced Frémont to rescind the proclamation.[33]

In the end, the Confederates made the first move to shatter Kentucky neutrality once and for all. That neutrality more seriously hampered their strategic goals than those of the Federals. Governor Harris began to prohibit commerce north of the Tennessee-Kentucky border on the Mississippi River soon after Gideon Pillow began to move men up to New Madrid, Missouri, on the west bank of the river and near the same border. Pillow aimed to strike deeper into the border state of Missouri in order to hinder Union plans to descend the Mississippi, hoping to attack Cape Girardeau a bit upstream from Cairo. Limited Confederate resources prevented Pillow from following through, although he began to see Island No. 10, a few miles up-stream from New Madrid, as a feasible place for Confederate batteries. The Southern high command estimated it would take at least thirty thousand men to do more than merely alarm the Yankees at Cairo, and it did not have such an abundance of troops.[34]

Frustrated by his failure to defend the valley by taking the offensive, Pillow argued that he needed to occupy Columbus, Kentucky, as the only true strongpoint for the defense of the Mississippi. Low-lying New Madrid and Island No. 10 paled in comparison with the high bluffs at Columbus, but the state's neutrality precluded the establishment of a Confederate battery there. Pillow aggressively argued with Confederate lieutenant general Leonidas Polk that Kentucky was "now a boiling cauldron" that threatened to spew forth a mass of Lincolnite troops to invade Tennessee. "Kentucky neutrality is no longer regarded, if indeed it ever was." Pillow was willing to take full blame for invading Kentucky to preempt a Union move to seize Columbus, but Polk refused to let him take that chance. Born in North Carolina and a graduate of the West Point Class of 1827, Polk formed an enduring personal friendship with Jefferson Davis even though he resigned from the army soon after graduation to serve as an Episcopalian minister and bishop of the Southwest. Davis appointed Polk commander of Confederate forces on both sides of the Mississippi River, and he kept minutely informed of developments in Kentucky so as not to lose an opportunity to seize Columbus.[35]

A short time later, Davis appointed General Albert S. Johnston overall commander of Confederate forces in the West, further consolidating the Rebel command structure in the valley. At the time, Johnston was widely regarded as the most prominent commander in the nascent Rebel army. Born in Kentucky and a West Point graduate of 1826, he saw service in the Black Hawk War before resigning from the army and going to Texas to join in that region's revolt against Mexico. Johnston served as general and secretary of war for the Republic of Texas, fought in the Mexican-American War, and led a U.S. Army expedition against recalcitrant Mormons in Utah in 1857. He also commanded the 2nd U.S. Cavalry. His credentials and his potential seemed impressive.[36]

Many Northern authorities also concluded that civil war in Kentucky was inevitable and made preparations to enter the state. Many felt that the Confederates were poised to move north from Tennessee. "If we lose Kentucky now, God help us," warned Jeremiah T. Boyle, a slaveowning Unionist who was soon to become a Yankee general. In mid-August the War Department in Washington created the Department of the Cumberland, which included Kentucky and Tennessee even though neither state yet had been occupied by Federal troops. In a similar vein as their Confederate counterparts, Union commanders argued that they could not conduct operations down the Mississippi without violating Kentucky neutrality, and seizures of steamboats on the Ohio River by both sides demonstrated that the state's policy of neutrality complicated peaceful commerce and navigation on the rivers as well.[37]

The Federal counterpart to Gideon Pillow, in terms of his efforts to take the offensive along the rivers, was Ulysses S. Grant. Born in Ohio and a graduate of the West Point Class of 1843, Grant had performed well in lower-level commands and as a staff officer during the Mexican-American War. Under a cloud for a drinking problem, he resigned from the army in 1854 and had difficulty crafting a civilian career until the Civil War offered the opportunity to return to uniform. Grant won promotion to the rank of brigadier general of volunteers and was appointed commander of the District of Southeast Missouri. He tried to drive pro-Confederate state forces under M. Jeff Thompson from that quarter of the state, but his efforts to coordinate the movement of several columns fell apart when Benjamin M. Prentiss refused to obey his orders, believing his own commission predated Grant's.[38]

Nevertheless, as part of his offensive, Grant sent Colonel Gustave Waagner with the 12th Illinois by boat to Belmont, a low point on the Missouri shore opposite Columbus, to destroy Confederate fortifications reportedly located there. When Waagner arrived on September 2, he found no works but reported a Confederate flag flying at Columbus. Grant ordered Waagner to return to Cairo and recommended to General Frémont that the Federals invade Kentucky to take Columbus, assuming the Rebels had already entered the town. Frémont did not hesitate to authorize Grant to do so, directing him to seize Paducah on the Ohio River first, then, if possible, move down both sides of the Mississippi. Neither Waagner, Grant, nor Frémont knew that the flag flying over Columbus on September 2 had been raised by civilians and did not signify Rebel occupation of the place.[39]

But the Confederates acted quickly in response to Waagner's reconnaissance, assuming the Federals intended to take Columbus. Polk sent Pillow by an overland route to get there first, on September 4, the same day that Grant recommended Federal seizure of the place. Davis endorsed the move, declaring that "The necessity justifies the action." The citizens of Columbus itself also thanked Polk for his action. The Federals began to seize all vessels on both rivers bordering Kentucky and sent a column of eighteen hundred men to take Paducah on the morning of September 6. "I never after saw such consternation depicted on the faces of the people" of this pro-Southern port city, Grant recalled. "Men, women and children came out of their doors look-

Ulysses Simpson Grant. (Library of Congress, LC-DIG-cwpb-07310)

ing pale and frightened at the presence of the invader." Rebel flags were flying from several houses in expectation of a Confederate column approaching
from Columbus, which reportedly stopped a mere sixteen miles away on
receiving news of the Union occupation. The Federals took possession of
wharf boats at the river landing, public buildings in town, and the funds
in Paducah's banks. But Grant also issued a proclamation to calm civilian
fears and charged the commander of the post to carefully avoid offending
innocent residents. "Exercise the strictest discipline against any soldier who
shall insult citizens or engage in plundering private property," he directed.[40]

By the time the dust settled, the Federals managed to occupy two-thirds
of Kentucky and the Confederates the Southern one-third—all without firing a shot. Rebel troops took possession of Cumberland Gap, where the state
lines of Kentucky, Tennessee, and Virginia met in the Appalachian Highlands, plus Bowling Green in the south-central part of the state, in addition
to Columbus. Later, they established a fortified camp on the north bank of
the Cumberland River near Mill Springs, about one hundred miles west of
Cumberland Gap. They also pushed forward with fortifications on the Tennessee and Cumberland Rivers just south of the Tennessee border, which
they had begun to construct before the breakdown of Kentucky neutrality.
This patchwork line, consisting of detached strongpoints, now became the
bulwark of Confederate defense in the Western theater.[41]

Initially, Governor Harris of Tennessee was concerned that Confederate
occupation of southern Kentucky would harm the Southern cause. He suggested that Polk and Pillow pull out. In fact, Secretary of War Judah P. Benjamin ordered Polk to evacuate on September 5. Initially, Simon Buckner
felt the same way and offered to negotiate with the Federals to get them out
of the state as well if the Rebels retreated. The Kentucky legislature demonstrated its leanings by urging Magoffin to order Confederate troops off
Kentucky soil, but it refused to demand the same of Federal troops. When
the legislators repassed this resolution over Magoffin's veto, the governor
was forced to comply.[42]

Confederate officials refused to honor Magoffin's request. Polk responded
by listing all Yankee transgressions on the state's neutrality. He was convinced that his occupation of Columbus saved what was left of Confederate
support there. "Kentucky was fast melting away under the influence of the
Lincoln Government," he told Davis. This viewpoint was shared by many
other observers. As Johnston boldly informed the Confederate president,
"The troops *will not* be withdrawn." Davis needed little convincing, having supported the move from the beginning. With the Confederate presence
an accomplished fact, Buckner now swerved entirely toward the Southern

cause, declaring that the state legislature had been "faithless to the will of the people."[43]

The Confederates now had a much stronger defensive system along both their northern border and the Mississippi River. Thus the breakdown of Kentucky neutrality can be said to have rebounded to the benefit of both sides. While Southern soldiers dug in at Cumberland Gap, Mill Springs, Bowling Green, Forts Henry and Donelson, Columbus, and Island No. 10, Northern troops established posts and fortifications at Paducah, Lexington, and numerous other places across the wide breadth of the state. The battle lines in the West had been firmly drawn.[44]

P reparations for war dragged on much longer than anyone on either side anticipated. Rather than a quick solution to secession, the fall of 1861 witnessed little more
than the consolidation of opposing positions in Kentucky and along the Mississippi River, in addition to
seemingly endless work to organize, train, and supply regiments for
service in the field. Both belligerents also wrestled with the thorny
problem of how to treat people within their zones of control.

The Confederates were disappointed with their reception in
Kentucky. Not long after occupying the southern one-third of the
state, Albert S. Johnston complained that they joined his colors in
such small numbers as to restrict his ability to push northward.
"They appear to me passive, if not apathetic," he wrote. Although
there was considerable sympathy for the Southern cause among the
residents, there was no "concert of action." James L. Alcorn had to
give three speeches a day to persuade even a few men to enlist at
Hopkinsville. Another Rebel commander, Wirt Adams at Bowling
Green, was disgusted enough to believe that Kentucky could only
be secured "by the mailed hand and not by argument or interest,"
because most of its residents viewed "this great struggle with stupid
indifference." Adams characterized them as "ignorant, mercenary
and base." In fact, many Kentuckians refused to accept Confederate
currency when selling provisions to Johnston's command. Secretary
of War Benjamin refused to let Confederate officers use any other
currency, or to discount the value of Confederate notes in order to
entice Kentuckians to accept them. He preferred instead that Johnston's men seize supplies.[1]

Even so, Governor Isham Harris was delighted that Kentucky
rather than Tennessee now appeared to be the future battleground
of the Civil War. In early May the General Assembly of Tennessee
had issued a formal invitation to the Confederate government to
locate the national capital at Nashville. Such a move would have
ensured adequate military resources to protect the city. Soon afterward, however, the Confederate Congress decided to move from
Montgomery, Alabama, to Richmond, Virginia.[2]

Harris now urged President Davis to push deeper into Kentucky, all the way to the Ohio River and even to St. Louis, to give additional security to his state's northern border. Harris also wanted to threaten the Northwestern states, disrupting their preparations for war and disheartening their will to fight. "It is the West that sustains the Federal Government in prosecuting the war," he wrote. "If able to take such positions as will command that section the East becomes powerless."[3]

Not everyone believed that Tennessee was secure enough to allow the meager Confederate army to strike out northward on an offensive campaign. Gideon Pillow continued to worry about the state's frontier. Only Fort Henry stood guard on the Tennessee River against the approach of a Union fleet. Tennessee had already sent several regiments to the Confederate army in Virginia and needed more guns, men, and supplies to adequately defend itself. Columbus, Kentucky, was the key, in Pillow's view; if it fell, the entire Mississippi Valley would be lost, "with all its untold wealth." As General John P. McCown put it, "This is a war of defense (on our part)"; there should be no talk of taking St. Louis when the homeland's defenses were yet ill-formed. Madison Peoples of Carter County, Tennessee, spoke for most residents of his state when he pleaded with Judah Benjamin for more help. "If we are invaded, every Southern man will be taken a prisoner or else murdered in the night-time. Our very existence depends on Mr. Lincoln's ability to invade the State."[4]

At Columbus, the linchpin of all hopes for defense of the valley, Leonidas Polk wrestled with the problem of supplying his garrison. To accumulate provisions for a long siege, he temporarily stopped every shipment of food from the surrounding area by civilians. Then he sent officers out to negotiate contracts for "wheat, corn, hay, and salt" and lifted the ban when he felt he had arranged for all possible supplies.[5]

The Confederates may have been disappointed in the benefits they reaped from their occupation of Kentucky, but the Federals had every reason to rejoice in their share of the state. By the end of 1861, nearly twenty-seven thousand Kentuckians had enlisted in the Union army. The Confederates were so jealous that they eagerly believed every report of discontent among those Kentucky soldiers, ascribing the dissatisfaction to signs of an abolitionist policy by officials in the Lincoln government. The Confederates sought ways to entice these Kentucky Unionists to desert and join the Confederate army instead.[6]

On October 29–30, 1861, Confederate sympathizers in Kentucky met at Russellville, where they issued a call for a convention to take place one month later. Delegates assembled at Russellville on November 18–20 to declare Kentucky free of association with the United States. They created a provisional state government, headquartered at Bowling Green, and requested admission to the Confederacy. Richmond admitted the state on December 10. The new governor, George W. Johnson, also served as a volunteer aide on Albert S. Johnston's staff at Bowling Green. The legality of the Russellville proceedings was questionable, and it is impossible to argue objectively that the delegates truly represented majority opinion in the state. The old government of Kentucky continued to meet at Frankfort, and Magoffin carried on as governor until he resigned in August 1862.[7]

The Confederates remained fully aware that the river system of the West offered the Federals their best opportunity to penetrate the porous frontier. A river pilot with experience navigating the Tennessee and Cumberland Rivers was detained by authorities at Clarksville. He could not explain why he was in the city, and officials feared he might be scouting the rivers in preparation for an ascent by Yankee gunboats.[8]

The Federals had every intention of taking advantage of their superiority in assembling boats and building new, protected warships to use the rivers as avenues of invasion. In the summer of 1861 they converted three civilian craft into wooden gunboats, named the *Tyler*, *Lexington*, and *Conestoga*. Engineer Samuel Pook also designed shallow-draft wooden gunboats with plates of iron for protection, their guns housed in casemates. By October 1861 James B. Eads constructed seven of these "Pook Turtles" in boatyards near St. Louis and at Mound City, Illinois, at a cost of $89,000 apiece. In addition to these craft, Eads converted a former government salvage boat into the ironclad *Benton* and a ferryboat into the ironclad *Essex*. Both of these powerful vessels were ready by January 1862. John Charles Frémont, the Union commander headquartered at St. Louis, also initiated the construction of thirty-eight mortar boats, which were completed by March 1862.[9]

Captain Andrew Hull Foote took charge of the developing Mississippi Flotilla in September 1861, but the boats were the responsibility of the army, not the navy. Washington wanted to ensure close cooperation of river-borne resources and the land force. The government hired pilots for the warships from the prewar pilot's union, which was also their source of all pilots for civilian-owned transport ships chartered by the Federals for war service.[10]

Belmont

When the gunboats were almost ready for service, Union commanders began to test Confederate river defenses. Grant regretted that his meager force at Cairo did not allow him to move sooner down the river to attack

Columbus. He had enough strength to threaten the Rebels and divert them from Frémont's major drive into southwestern Missouri that fall and thus organized three columns. While one Federal force moved west from the Mississippi into southeastern Missouri and another marched from Paducah toward Columbus, Grant put three thousand men on steamers, protected them with two gunboats, and headed down the Mississippi to destroy the Confederate camp at Belmont, Missouri, across the river from Columbus.[11]

Grant landed his men upstream of the camp on November 7 and led them across the bottomland, taking the Confederates by surprise and driving them from the encampment. But Polk shifted reinforcements across the river to launch a counterstrike that drove the Federals from their prize. This seesaw battle nearly ended in disaster for Grant; he hastily reembarked his command, protected by the fire of the gunboats, and beat a hasty retreat. Federal losses amounted to six hundred men and the Confederates lost slightly more, yet Belmont ranked as a small battle by later Civil War standards. Grant interpreted it as a success, for he accomplished his objective and correctly argued that there was no utility in holding Belmont unless he also could hold Columbus. Moreover, the battle gave his raw recruits much-needed combat experience, which would stand them in good stead during future operations.[12]

The battle of Belmont increased Confederate fears for the safety of Columbus. Polk intensified efforts to turn that place into the Gibraltar of the Mississippi, planting underwater mines in the river and stretching a chain across the stream to snag Union boats. The defenses at Island No. 10, downstream, also received additional attention in late 1861 as a secondary line of defense along the great river if Columbus should fall. Perceptive observers were not satisfied, noting that both banks of the Mississippi should be fortified to the full, as well as Memphis and Vicksburg. But Confederate resources were already stretched too thin to accommodate such a plan.[13]

The Confederates attempted offensive actions to disrupt Union plans, but they amounted to little. In late December M. Jeff Thompson took a small force from New Madrid to Commerce, Missouri, on the west bank of the Mississippi some distance south of Cape Girardeau. He rounded up the males of the village to prevent them from spreading word of his presence to the Yankees, looted clothing from stores owned by Unionists, and prepared to bombard the steamer *City of Alton*. Women in Commerce, however, managed to signal the boat before it reached the bank; the Confederates fired their muskets but could not damage it. Thompson quickly evacuated the town before trouble arrived from Cape Girardeau, hauling his loot back to New Madrid.[14]

Eastern Tennessee

Compounding fears for the security of Tennessee's northern frontier, the residents of the mountainous eastern part of the state rose in revolt against Confederate authorities in the fall of 1861. Trouble had been brewing for sometime because the mountain counties were filled with people who retained a traditional loyalty to the U.S. government. They also had little faith in slavery or the cotton aristocracy it supported. The same was generally true of all the Appalachian regions of Kentucky, Alabama, Georgia, the Carolinas, and Virginia, but loyalist sentiment burned far more deeply in eastern Tennessee than anywhere else. Robert Jefferson Breckinridge, a Kentucky Unionist, accurately warned Southerners that the mountaineers would be a source of disunity within the Confederacy.[15]

As long as the loyalists expressed their views peacefully, through political means, Governor Harris had little to worry about. They voted against secession on two occasions, then petitioned to separate the mountain counties from the rest of Tennessee after the state left the Union. That petition was ignored, of course, but Unionist sentiment increased in vigor during the early fall. The loyalists intimidated pro-Confederates in eastern Tennessee by strength of numbers. Support for secession appeared mostly in areas linked by the construction of a rail line between eastern Tennessee and the cotton economy of the Deep South. Knoxville, the major city in this section, was deeply divided in its loyalties. Worried about the safety of the railroad, Harris encouraged the dispatch of Rebel troops to occupy key locations in eastern Tennessee, which started a trickle of refugees making their way into Union-held Kentucky.[16]

Federal authorities sought a way to disrupt the important rail link between Virginia and the Deep South that went through Knoxville, but there were no good avenues of invasion from Kentucky into the Tennessee River Valley. Cumberland Gap, a historic pass through the mountains located where the state lines of Virginia, Kentucky, and Tennessee met, was an obvious portal through which to penetrate eastern Tennessee, but the roads leading to it, like all mountains roads, were unreliable for the supply of sizable numbers of troops. Nevertheless, as the plight of the loyalists became more widely known in the North, Lincoln and others in Washington became anxious to offer relief to their most visible group of supporters in the Confederacy. "East Tennessee is anxiously looking and listning for the sound of old Abes Horn," wrote a loyalist to Tennessee's Andrew Johnson, the only senator from a seceded state who remained loyal to the Union.[17]

There were, in short, two strategic reasons for the Federals to push a column into eastern Tennessee, despite the difficulties of managing the movement. The military reason tended to be overshadowed by the political-humanitarian one, but Lincoln used both in efforts to cajole commanders in Kentucky to act. Brigadier General William T. Sherman succeeded Robert Anderson as commander in that state. Born in Ohio, Sherman had graduated from West Point in 1840 but had missed the action during the Mexican-American War. He entered the banking and law professions after resigning from the army and served as superintendent of a military academy that would later become Louisiana State University. Sherman commanded a brigade at First Bull Run before being sent to Kentucky, but he found his resources far too limited to embark on a risky venture into the difficult terrain of eastern Tennessee. Sherman also was under a dark cloud because he told Secretary of War Simon Cameron and Adjutant General Lorenzo Thomas that he would need two hundred thousand men to hold Kentucky and invade the mountains. The remark was bandied about in the press as if Sherman were crazy for making such a wild comment.[18]

This incident occurred at a time when Reverend William Blount Carter was deeply involved in a plan he had brought to Sherman and Brigadier General George H. Thomas. Carter proposed to round up a group of daring loyalists behind Confederate lines and burn several bridges on the railroad through eastern Tennessee as a prelude to a Union strike to free Carter's homeland. "This whole country is in a wretched condition," Carter wrote Thomas. "A perfect despotism reigns here. The Union men of eastern Tennessee are longing and praying for the hour when they can break their fetters." Thomas was willing to cooperate, but Sherman gave only his half-hearted consent. Carter went to Washington and received the support of the president and General in Chief George B. McClellan. Then the daring minister disappeared into the mountains without a trace.[19]

On the night of November 8, Carter's conspirators attacked bridges all along the line of railroad through eastern Tennessee. They caused alarm and panic for Confederate officials and sympathizers alike. "Civil War has broken out at length in eastern Tennessee," declared A. G. Graham of Jonesborough, who urged President Davis to drive the families of loyalists from the area. In four counties, the bridge burnings were followed by the appearance of hundreds of loyalists who assembled into military groups and skirmished with Confederate troops. Harris promised to send ten thousand troops, and Richmond officials authorized the dispatch of regiments from Virginia and Alabama. Richmond also sent Colonel Danville Leadbetter, the head of the Confederate Engineer Bureau, to repair the nine bridges that had been destroyed.[20]

William Tecumseh Sherman. (Library of Congress, LC-DIG-cwpb-06584)

Unfortunately for the bridge burners who had risked their lives, the Federals did not move. Sherman assumed responsibility for that decision. Based on his knowledge of Confederate troop strength at Bowling Green and Hopkinsville, he could not spare Thomas's troops for a risky venture into the mountains, especially near the start of winter. Sherman gave top priority to Kentucky rather than eastern Tennessee. Although a severe disappointment to the loyalists, his reasoning would hold sway with other Union commanders in the region for a long time to come.[21]

The bridge burners were now at the mercy of an enraged occupying power. Secretary Benjamin authorized their trial and execution, adding: "It would be well to leave their bodies hanging in the vicinity of the burned bridges." Davis supported Benjamin's decision. Although some of the raiders were wounded in the attack, none had been killed. Many were rounded up, and five of them were hanged.[22]

In the wake of this tragic miscalculation, Confederate authorities clamped down even harder on the loyalist population. Many thousands of Unionists fled their homes and trekked toward Kentucky. The anti-Confederate feelings intensified among those who remained, and Leadbetter was convinced that three-fourths of the residents would "rise in arms to join them" as soon as Union troops crossed the state line. The governors of North Carolina and Georgia were relieved when signs of similar loyalism failed to appear in their own mountainous counties, indicating how unique was the intensity of this phenomenon in eastern Tennessee.[23]

Sherman felt burdened by the knowledge of what happened to the bridge burners and his role in the failure to help them, but he was relieved of command in Kentucky because he was generally unable to cope with the myriad problems in the area. Major General Don Carlos Buell replaced him in November. Born in Ohio and a graduate of the West Point Class of 1841, Buell fought in the Second Seminole War and was badly wounded in the Mexican conflict. In the 1850s he served mostly as a staff officer. Buell was widely respected for his intellect and professionalism. In Kentucky, he received an avalanche of pleas to move into eastern Tennessee before it was too late. George McClellan sided with Lincoln and the exiled loyalists in urging Buell to do so, suggesting he send fifteen thousand men into the mountains and fifty thousand toward Nashville. McClellan admired the loyalists as "noble fellows" and the Union's "gallant friends," but he also wanted to snip the Confederate rail link through eastern Tennessee. If logistics was the major problem, Lincoln proposed using Federal government funds to construct a railroad from some convenient railhead in Kentucky through Cumberland Gap to Knoxville. Nicholasville was selected as the best place to start such an enterprise, but War Department advisers pointed out the obvious: the length of time required to build this railroad would to make it useless for the invasion of the mountains.[24]

Though fully aware that eastern Tennessee "was all the talk in Washington," Buell agreed with Sherman that advancing on Bowling Green was the right course to pursue. In fact, Buell informed McClellan that he considered this obscure railroad town in south-central Kentucky "the most important strategical point in the whole field of operations." Buell was willing to send twelve thousand men into the mountains but warned that they would need at least twelve hundred wagons to supply their basic wants and much additional manpower to guard the extended line of communications. Moreover, he could not pinpoint a date for the departure of this column.[25]

Buell's delay intensified frustration among those politicians who yearned for relief of the loyalists, and Lincoln was increasingly pressed to do something during the winter months. McClellan continued to push for the invasion, believing that political concerns were becoming more important than military issues; he hinted that his own offensive plans in Virginia might have to be changed if Buell could not cut the rail line running through Knoxville. The news that Buell did not have his heart in the proposed incursion greatly affected Lincoln. The president wrote that he would rather invade eastern Tennessee than capture Nashville and pinpointed his deepest distress as the knowledge "that our friends in eastern Tennessee are being hanged and driven to despair." Yet Buell clung steadfastly to his judgment, based on military necessity. Sherman put it succinctly when he acknowledged the emotional value of invading eastern Tennessee, but he argued that there simply were not enough men available to do it and to protect Kentucky at the same time, or to advance along the Bowling Green corridor. As a result, the loyalists had to suffer and endure for nearly two years before a Yankee column approached their mountain homes.[26]

Occupation

Thorny problems associated with the population of territories occupied by both armies loomed ever larger in the fall of 1861. They would only increase as the war progressed, especially for occupying Federal troops, and their solution bedeviled commanders.

Ironically, Confederate commanders also had to face the dilemma of dealing with a hostile population in their own country. By early January 1862, Danville Leadbetter was holding 130 political prisoners at Knoxville for trial by a military court. In some ways, it was difficult to know what to do with civilians held by the army. After his unsuccessful expedition to Wild Cat

Mountain, where his forces fought a small battle with Union troops on October 21, Brigadier General Felix K. Zollicoffer found himself in control of twenty-five Kentuckians and six Tennesseeans, plus a slave taken "from his master." He regarded the Kentucky men as prisoners but did not know what to do with the Tennesseeans or the slave. Normally commanders had to improvise solutions to questions like this; Johnston created a board consisting of a civilian judge and a Confederate provost marshal to examine the cases of citizens held by his forces at Bowling Green.[27]

One of the more complex problems confronting the Federals was trade. Northerners were eager to resume commerce with the South as soon as possible—most importantly, to extract cotton for the northeastern and English markets. Secretary of the Treasury Salmon P. Chase did not see how it was possible to resume "safe intercourse" between the loyal states and the disputed land of the South; he could only suggest that Lincoln "establish the power of the Government" and then "to let Commerce follow the flag." But working out the details of such a vague strategy would be troublesome, because any commercial contact near the military frontiers gave the enemy an opportunity to obtain needed material. The Mississippi River was a natural and compelling avenue of commerce, in war as well as in peace. Grant instructed his post commander at Cape Girardeau to stop all boats going south that were not under government contract and to search them for contraband of war. The Union general was well aware that contraband trade took place well north of Cape Girardeau. Civilian steamers loaded supplies on the river bank above Cairo, where Confederate sympathizers living in southern Illinois secreted them for transport across the Ohio River. Grant admitted it represented a small amount of goods, but it is ironic that he had to be concerned with such a problem to his rear as well as to his front.[28]

Grant's views on relations with the civilian population, and how those relations affected Union policy toward slavery and the war effort, gradually changed in a way that probably mirrored the views of many soldiers and civilians of the North. Initially he believed the war would be of short duration, decided by a couple of major battles, and then the two sections would "settle our difficulties." According to one source, Grant told Confederate officers in a conference held to discuss prisoners of war right after Belmont that his initial aim in the conflict was to restore the navigation of the Mississippi River. By late 1861, Grant felt that the Southern effort to achieve independence was more "formidable" than he had imagined, and he began to envision larger measures to achieve a Northern victory. Though his initial preference had been to respect the institution of slavery as a constitutional right of the Southern states, he now felt that it should be destroyed if that was a prerequisite for destroying the Confederacy. Until such a policy was adopted by the president, however, Grant did not want to see his officers surreptitiously helping slaves to escape their masters, or conversely to return runaway slaves to their owners, especially if the owners were hostile to the Union. Grant sought to find a delicate middle ground during those early months of the war until national policy might clarify the relationship among Federal soldiers, slaves, and slaveowners.[29]

Most Union commanders wanted to rehabilitate the civilian population of the South and resurrect a constructive loyalty to the flag. In some areas that was easy, but in other places it was almost impossible. Paducah, Kentucky, like many river towns, had been intimately linked to the cotton economy of the Deep South before Fort Sumter; its population now deeply resented the garrison of Yankee troops. Hardly a month after taking control of Paducah, Charles F. Smith felt compelled to clamp down on the residents, requiring passes to screen the flow of people and goods into and out of town.[30]

In contrast, when Richard J. Oglesby led an expedition out of Birds' Point, on the west bank of the Mississippi River opposite Cairo, to find Jeff Thompson, he believed the residents of southeastern Missouri were becoming sick of the Confederates, who harassed them for supplies and offered worthless currency as payment. The residents would be willing to return their loyalty to the Union if they could be guaranteed protection. Grant also noted a phenomenon that would continue throughout the war in the West: deserters from the Rebel army who claimed to have been pressured into Confederate service. Some of them wanted to enlist in the Union army, but most intended to go North. The Federals treated such men leniently, usually believing their intentions to be genuine. Grant even requested permission to provide transportation for them to their Northern destinations.[31]

As the months ticked by that autumn, Union attitudes tended to harden. Grant reacted harshly when civilians shot some Union soldiers near Birds' Point. He directed the post commander to establish a zone six miles around the place and warn the residents that any suspicious person within it would be shot on sight. He did not want to harass peaceful civilians, but patrols should make an impression on everyone to prevent a repetition of the incident. The post commander put this order into effect immediately. Grant also took action against other civilians in western Kentucky and southern Illinois whom he believed were trying to funnel supplies to Confederate forces. He arrested six "very dangerous men" and sent them to Fort Lafayette in New York Harbor. They were among a group of thirty-six political prisoners who signed a loyalty oath nearly two months later, promising never again to proffer aid to enemies of the U.S. government.[32]

Similar problems cropped up in the Department of the Ohio. Former Kentucky commander Robert Anderson had established a policy whereby the army would arrest civilians only for actively aiding the rebellion, not "for mere opinion's sake." Subordinates apparently did not take this seriously, for Anderson's successor, William T. Sherman, had to reiterate the directive. Sherman worried that Kentuckians who wavered or who had decided to put aside their former sympathy for the Confederacy might become enemies of the Union because of arbitrary arrests. He found that so many citizens had been arrested for slight cause, and after improper gathering of evidence, that he could not physically hold all of them. Sherman asked a civilian judge to head a commission to handle their cases.[33]

With the Federal army firmly in control, it was easy for Kentucky Unionists to throw their weight around. The acting editor of the *Louisville Courier* was arrested for publishing "most treasonable" editorials and sent to Fort Lafayette and then Fort Warren. He was released three months later after petitions in his favor were submitted to the authorities, but he was compelled to take an oath of allegiance to the U.S. government. The telegraph operator of the Associated Press in Louisville was apprehended for using his job to help secessionists. He refused twice to take the oath as a precondition for release. Charles S. Morehead was seized by a U.S. marshal on a warrant issued by the justice of the peace of Jefferson County, Kentucky, for "being actively engaged in stirring up and promoting rebellion." After four months in prison, Morehead agreed to a parole on the condition that he never enter Kentucky again, but he refused to take the oath of allegiance to the central government. In September 1861 Federal patrols arrested several men who were either recruiting for the Confederate army behind Union lines or were on their way to join the Rebels at Bowling Green. These men were treated as prisoners of war even though they had not yet been formally mustered. More typically, William Nelson arrested seven men in October who were believed to be "active secessionists." Although no formal charges were ever filed, the men spent a couple of months in prison before they agreed to take the oath and promised to amend their conduct.[34]

Ironically, during his short tenure in Kentucky, Sherman became more and more oppressed by the problems associated with military-civil relations. In reports to Washington he painted a gloomy picture of the population of Kentucky filling the space around army camps with spies. He had far too few troops to adequately control the state and feared for the safety of his railroad supply lines if he undertook an advance.[35]

Because of his inability to deal with the myriad challenges of improvising the war effort in Kentucky, Sherman was replaced by Buell in early November. In giving Buell his instructions, McClellan urged him to act with moderation so as to conciliate, not antagonize, the residents. He warned against the tendency of subordinates "to make vexatious arrests on mere suspicion." Kentucky was second in importance only to Virginia as a target of the Union war effort, and the inhabitants had to be convinced that Federal authority would guarantee the security of their persons, property, and local institutions. Buell understood the message. Like Anderson and Sherman before him, he reiterated McClellan's guidelines to his subordinates not to pay too much attention "to mere expressions of disloyalty."[36]

None of the Kentucky commanders knew how to deal with an integral problem of Union occupation—what to do with runaway slaves. The fugitives often claimed that their masters were pro-Confederate, or were serving in a Rebel force, and many subordinate officers were reluctant to send them back into slavery. Sherman intended to stick to the letter of the law and return them if the owners made a request to that effect. "We have nothing to do with them at all," he informed Alexander McDowell McCook, "and you should not let them take refuge in camp." He was sure it would hurt the Union cause among sensitive Kentuckians to give the impression that Federal troops were helping slaves escape from their owners.[37]

Eastern Kentucky

The broad band of Kentucky counties that lay within the Appalachian Highlands presented special difficulties for both belligerents. Even more sparsely settled than the mountains of eastern Tennessee, this region produced no spontaneous uprising against the Confederacy or a well-organized movement in favor of the Union. The isolated settlements seemed oddly quiet, but both North and South were interested in controlling the mountainous counties.

The Federals moved into this zone first; it had remained unoccupied since the breakdown of Kentucky neutrality. In early November 1861 William Nelson took up a position near Prestonsburg and called on the citizens to remain at their homes and live in peace. He also encouraged the county courts to hold regular sessions. But Nelson's efforts were disrupted when Confederate brigadier general Humphrey Marshall moved into eastern Kentucky. Marshall replaced the small Federal force at Prestonsburg and sought "to teach" the mountain people that the Confederate army was among them to protect their "constitutional rights." He tried to reform local governments in the region as a way of weeding out pro-Union magistrates, clerks, sheriffs, and judges by forcing all to take an oath of allegiance to the Confederate government. After barely a month of occupation, Marshall had to admit that his policy was not working. The residents refused to cooperate, they resisted efforts by the Rebel army to collect food, and barely one regiment's worth of sympathizers were willing to join the Southern cause. Marshall had to use his own soldiers to harvest and grind corn, and his commissary predicted that all available food supplies in the area would be exhausted in a couple of weeks.[38]

Marshall's incursion sparked a more serious Union effort in the developing struggle for control of the Kentucky hills. Colonel James A. Garfield mounted an offensive with 3,000 men, nearly half of them organized as a column to approach Prestonsburg from the west, while Garfield led the rest southward along the valley of the Big Sandy River. Marshall could muster only 1,967 men to oppose this force. He retreated toward the Virginia border, but Garfield caught up with him in the valley of Middle Creek on January 10, 1862. Though the battle that followed was little more than a heated skirmish by later Civil War standards, Garfield was able to punish the Confederates and send them quickly on their way. "I have come among you to restore the honor of the Union," he proclaimed to the inhabitants. Like so many occupying commanders, Garfield sought to make it clear that anyone who resisted Union authority would be treated harshly and those who cooperated would be protected. "The Army of the Union wages no war of plunder," he concluded, "but comes to bring back the prosperity of peace."[39]

Garfield next fixed his view on eastern Tennessee. He aimed to snip the railroad that ran through Knoxville, but the Confederate positions at Cumberland Gap and Mill Springs blocked the way. General Zollicoffer had established his main force on the north side of the Cumberland River near Mill Springs, about one hundred miles west of Cumberland Gap, to enable the Confederates to strike northward and attack Federal troops gathering near Somerset under George H. Thomas. Like Marshall and Garfield, Zollicoffer sought to mollify local citizens, assuring them that he was at Mill Springs to drive the hated Northerners away and protect civilian property. "We have come to convince you that we truly respect the laws, revere justice, and mean to give security to your personal and property rights." He also sought to encourage enlistments and promised that the Federals would "soon be driven across the Ohio."[40]

Those same Federals, however, moved first, and drove the Confederates across the Cumberland River in a midwinter campaign. It was the first Union victory against Johnston's defensive posture in southern Kentucky. Major General George B. Crittenden had arrived at Mill Springs to assume command of Zollicoffer's men, and on the night of January 18, 1862, he moved out of the Confederate fortifications that protected the crossing of

George Henry Thomas.
(Library of Congress,
LC-DIG-cwpb-03079)

the river to strike at the Yankees. George Thomas's troops had advanced to a point only a few miles away at Logan's Crossroads. The two forces clashed the next morning, January 19, in the hardest fought battle thus far in the West. Zollicoffer was killed in the seesaw fight that could have gone to either side. By noon, the Federals managed to place more regiments into action and handled them better than their opponents. Both sides had about 4,000 men involved; Thomas lost 248 and Crittenden 434.[41]

The Federals pursued the Rebels to the earthworks at Beech Grove, north of the Cumberland River, and secured an advantageous hill from which to bombard the fortifications. Dusk caused Thomas to postpone an attack until the next day, which gave Crittenden an opportunity to evacuate Mill Springs that night, crossing the river on one steamer and two flatboats. Despite his enemy's escape, George Henry Thomas had achieved a significant victory that gave the lie to any lingering doubt that this Virginia-born officer's loyalties lay with the Union. A West Point graduate of the same class as Sherman's, Thomas had seen extensive combat in the Mexican-American War and had commanded a brigade in Virginia in 1861. He would make his mark on the Western course of the Civil War.[42]

Confederate authorities reported that Crittenden's army was "utterly routed and demoralized," causing shock among Southern sympathizers in the region. Nothing seemed to bar the way to a Yankee invasion of eastern Tennessee except "bad roads and natural obstacles." The Federals were quite proud of the "little victory we have gained on the cumberland," and Tennessee loyalists were jubilant at the prospect of a Union drive through Cumberland Gap. Tennessee Unionist Horace Maynard urged Thomas to push on "until Knoxville is in your possession and that line of railroad in your grip." But hopes for a quick thrust soon soured as Buell pointed out the logistical difficulties of supplying Thomas in the mountains during winter. He noted that Thomas needed eighteen rather than the anticipated ten days to move from Lebanon to Somerset in early January; the last forty miles of that march devoured eight days alone. The problems associated with bad roads under winter weather would only increase as he approached Cumberland Gap. The message was clear; no one need expect a Union relief column in eastern Tennessee just yet.[43]

3 } Fort Henry to Corinth

rant proposed moving against the Confederate posture in the West as early as January 1862. He suggested shipping his men up the Tennessee River to strike at Fort Henry and use it as a base to operate toward Columbus or Memphis or up the Cumberland River. "It will besides have a moral effect upon our troops to advance them towards the rebel states," he added. Grant's superior, Major General Henry W. Halleck, had suggested the same thing to the general in chief several days before Grant wrote his recommendation. Few other West Pointers could boast of such intellectual accomplishments as Halleck, who had graduated third in the Class of 1839 and who had rich experience in all manner of army work before the Civil War. Halleck saw the Tennessee and the Cumberland as "the great central line of the Western theater of war," given that the Confederate guns at Columbus blocked a major push down the Mississippi. In early January Halleck had shared his views with Sherman, who completely agreed with Halleck's assessment that advancing up the Tennessee or the Cumberland could turn the Rebel position at Columbus. Buell was ready to postpone the invasion of eastern Tennessee even further in order to cooperate with Halleck's move in western Kentucky, and one of Grant's subordinates, Brigadier General Lew Wallace, was sure that the Federal gunboats could deal with any Confederate fortifications found on the way.[1]

Fort Henry

No more than thirteen steamers were available for Grant's expedition, forcing him to transport seventeen thousand infantrymen in two stages. Four ironclads and two timberclad gunboats accompanied the first wave as Grant landed troops on the east bank of the Tennessee River a short distance downstream from Fort Henry on February 5. As the infantry sought to cut off the small garrison by land, the gunboats approached to bombard the fort. The Confederates gave a good account of themselves, badly damaging the *Essex*, but the Tennessee was on the rise and began to flood Fort Henry. Rebel engineers had located it on the bottomland of the river be-

Henry Wager Halleck.
(Library of Congress,
LC-DIG-cwpb-04718)

cause better ground downstream lay on the Kentucky side of the state line, and they had honored that state's proclamation of neutrality. Most of the defending force evacuated, but the Federals captured seventy-seven men when they entered the work on February 6. Even though poorly located, Fort Henry was impressive to those Yankee soldiers who saw it. "Many a poor fellow would have lost his life in trying to take it by storm," thought George Carrington of the 11th Illinois.[2]

The fall of Fort Henry demonstrated the advantage the Federals held in their control of the river system, offering the opportunity to penetrate Confederate territory. Three gunboats immediately steamed up the Tennessee all the way to Florence, Alabama. They met no opposition. Local communities sent delegations to meet the boats and seek assurance that their people and property would be safe. "I told them that we were neither ruffians nor savages," reported Lieutenant Commander S. Ledyard Phelps, "and that we were to protect them from violence and to enforce the law." Moreover, there were widespread expressions of loyalty to the U.S. government among the northern Alabama communities. While some residents fled before the arrival of his boats, many others flocked to the river bank to cheer the flag and complain of persecution at the hands of Confederate authorities.[3]

In the area around Fort Henry, Grant found that the "scare and fright of the rebels up here is beyond conception." He already anticipated that the Treasury Department might want to open trade in the newly conquered territory, but he also had to deal with a disturbing problem in his own ranks. Up to three hundred men of John Cook's brigade roamed the countryside near Fort Henry on February 9, "robbing and plundering most disgracefully." Grant warned Cook to clamp down on such gross violations of discipline.[4]

Fort Donelson

Buoyed by the easy victory at Fort Henry, Grant planned on striking Fort Donelson—sixteen miles away on the Cumberland River—very soon. He envisioned an easy capture followed by the return of his men to Fort Henry, which he intended to make his base of operations. Grant's plan to move against Fort Donelson on February 8 was motivated by an assumption that General Albert S. Johnston would heavily reinforce that place, and it could take up to fifty thousand Federals to capture it if he dawdled for a month. But rains delayed his move, and Captain Andrew H. Foote needed to take his gunboats down the Tennessee and up the Cumberland Rivers to cooperate with the infantry. As a result, Grant did not set out until February 12.[5]

The attack on Fort Donelson proved to be anything but easy. In fact, the Federals tackled a job that was far more difficult than taking Fort Henry. Closing the land routes to the fort, the Federals launched three small-scale probes on February 13 that resulted only in casualties. On the fourteenth Foote steamed up the river to bombard the fort's water batteries, which were located on high ground at a bend of the channel. The Confederates pummeled his boats badly. The craft steamed as close as 350 yards from the guns, but all four ironclads were damaged and had to fall back. Worse still, on February 15 the Confederates launched a counterattack on land, taking the Federals by surprise and opening a line of retreat to Nashville. But the Rebel commanders foolishly dawdled rather than take advantage of their opportunity to save the garrison, allowing Grant to organize counterstrikes to recover his position. While reinforcements moved forward to reoccupy the road to Nashville on the Confederate left, Charles F. Smith's division successfully attacked the fort's outer defenses on the Confederate right.[6]

Disconcerted and weakened by their defeat, the Confederates surrendered on February 16. Their commander, Brigadier General John B. Floyd,

Water battery at Fort Donelson. This view demonstrates the advantage the Confederate heavy guns obtained over the Federal gunboat fleet during the attack on February 14, 1862. (Earl J. Hess)

did not want to be taken prisoner for fear of retribution because of his pro-Southern actions while serving as secretary of war in the Buchanan administration. Consequently, Floyd took several regiments of his Virginia brigade by steamer up the Cumberland River. His second in command, Tennesseean Gideon J. Pillow, went along. Abandoned by their frightened commanders, the Rebels gave up under Simon B. Buckner, who manfully shouldered the responsibility for negotiating with his prewar acquaintance. Grant, however, had no intention of entertaining negotiations. He sent a stern message to Buckner that he would accept only unconditional surrender, a message that intensified public admiration for Grant's management of the first major Union victory of the war. Up to fifteen thousand gray-clad prisoners and seventeen heavy guns fell into Federal hands that day. More importantly, the Confederate defensive stance in the West had been shattered beyond repair.[7]

In the wake of Grant's important victory, many Federals assumed the war would end soon. They still hoped that the Confederacy was a balloon, easily deflated once its outer shell was penetrated. "Great numbers of Union people have come in to see us," Grant reported to Halleck's headquarters, "and express great hope for the future. They say secessionists are in great trepidation." On February 28 Lincoln partially restored the opportunities for commerce between Northerners and residents of the rebellious states, subject to regulations promulgated by the Treasury Department. Because slaves had helped to construct the earthen walls of Fort Donelson, Grant issued a general order in his district forbidding citizens from entering the Union lines to look for their runaways.[8]

Grant's victorious troops seem to have considered the captured Rebel property at Fort Donelson as free to the taker. An enormous amount of plundering took place following the fall of the fort—so much so that news of it reached faraway Washington. Grant tried to explain that certain civilians and officers exaggerated these reports because he had prevented them from taking part in the thievery, but the true extent of the problem was bad enough to cause Grant much trouble. He detailed an infantry company to search steamboats for the purloined property and discharged a captain of the 52nd Indiana for attempting to ship material north. Grant also clamped down on soldier depredations against civilian property in the area near Fort Donelson, and he instructed his subordinates to prevent their men from leaving the confines of the regimental camps. Grant found enough captured supplies at the fort to support his command for twenty days but refused to let his men use any of it for "private purposes."[9]

The first large catch of Rebel prisoners during the war fell into Federal hands at Fort Donelson. Grant found it difficult to guard the lot and find enough shipping to transport them north. Eventually, they were sent to several army camps in the North, where room was made to accommodate both the prisoners and Union soldiers. Out of 1,400 Confederate prisoners housed at Camp Chase near Columbus, Ohio, about 100 were black slaves. The Federals considered them prisoners of war for the time being and treated them as they did the white prisoners. Many of the Donelson captives, especially members of Tennessee regiments, were willing to take the oath of allegiance to the U.S. government to secure their release. Those from eastern Tennessee claimed they had been forced into Rebel service against their will, and members of the Irish 10th Tennessee also expressed a readiness to serve in the Union army. Many Federal officers commented that the Rebel rank and file, once removed from the South and the influence of their officers, appeared "entirely harmless."[10]

Halleck put together a board to examine the prisoners and recommend a course of action. The officers who served on the board explained to the prisoners at Springfield, Illinois, that they would need to post a $1,000 bond as security and would not be allowed to cross Union lines, yet 1,640 of them applied to take the oath and promised to obey these rules. The great majority were from Tennessee and Kentucky. The board therefore recommended that they be trusted, but that the same offer not be made to the relatively few prisoners from Alabama and Mississippi who applied for release. Prominent spokesmen for the eastern Tennessee loyalists supported their countrymen and urged the War Department to release them as soon as possible after taking an oath of allegiance to the Federal government. When he became military governor of Tennessee, Andrew Johnson insisted that he be responsible for judging which Tennessee prisoners should be released. It would "exert a powerful influence throughout the state in our favour," he argued. By late August 1862, Union officials became convinced of the cogency of these arguments and authorized Johnson to take special charge of dealing with Tennessee prisoner oaths. They also empowered military prison officials to offer parole to any other Confederates willing to take the oath of allegiance and "discharge them." Parson Brownlow made the rounds of Federal prisons in an effort to talk eastern Tennessee Rebel officers into defecting, and some of them did. An officer of the Confederate 10th Tennessee estimated that two hundred of his men took the oath of allegiance to the U.S. government while held at Camp Douglas, near Chicago, and were set free.[11]

After Donelson

Grant was naturally jubilant over his great victory at Donelson. "My impression is that I shall have one hard battle more to fight and will find easy sailing after that," he informed his wife. But this could occur only if the Confederate will to resist collapsed, and quite the opposite took place. Southerners were astounded by the fall of Fort Donelson. Union possession of middle Tennessee directly threatened Deep South states "of sparse white and dense black population," where the demographics seemed to favor Federal success. Rather than give up, however, most Confederates were energized to make a renewed effort to save their fledgling nation. "We must defeat the enemy somewhere to give confidence to our friends," wrote General P. G. T. Beauregard as he prepared to assume a new command in the West. "We must give up some minor points and concentrate our forces to save the important ones." Five regiments, dispatched when the threat to Fort Donelson became apparent, were already on their way from New Orleans. Mansfield Lovell, the commander at the Crescent City, had suggested as early as February 12 that Confederate forces in the West concentrate at Corinth, Mississippi. It was the junction of important north-south and west-east rail lines and lay one day's march southwest of the Tennessee River. Everyone in authority agreed that defense of the rail system supporting Confederate positions in the Upper South should be the top priority.[12]

But those communities along the Mississippi River did not want to be left out of the strategic picture. The residents of Memphis, in particular, were in a panic after hearing of Donelson's fall. Their mood could not have brightened at word that Confederate authorities planned to evacuate Columbus without a fight, considering that Grant's victory had outflanked the position and its garrison was too valuable to lose. For the time, Island No. 10, New Madrid, and Memphis were still to be held. General William T. Withers of the Mississippi state forces was encouraged by reports that the Donelson batteries had repulsed Foote's gunboats, however, and argued that this could be done elsewhere as well. Withers shuddered at the thought of what would happen if Yankee warships were allowed to steam the entire length of the Mississippi unimpeded. He advocated using slave labor to construct heavy fortifications at Helena, Vicksburg, Natchez, Baton Rouge, and New Orleans.[13]

Other Confederate officials were thinking of taking the offensive against their enemy as the best way to counteract the effect of Donelson's fall. Gideon Pillow, who contributed to that disaster on the Cumberland, called for draining troops from the seacoast areas and driving the Yankees out of Tennessee and Kentucky. He then anticipated a Confederate invasion of Ohio and Indiana. "If we do not relieve heart of the country," he warned the secretary of war, the "Mississippi River will be opened, and then cause of South is desperate." Braxton Bragg, who commanded troops along the Gulf Coast at Pensacola, advocated a similar strategy, although he envisioned no more than a drive into Kentucky rather than a strike onto Northern soil. Albert Johnston could not seriously entertain such visions. He could only strive to concentrate units scattered by his own defensive plan in the West and hope to counterattack at some point to blunt the Union offensive. Johnston urged Jefferson Davis to travel west to take command of the troops, or at least to make an inspirational visit to encourage civilians and soldiers alike. It was not until early March, nearly a month after the surrender of Donelson, that Johnston felt that the tone of his troops, those from Tennessee especially, had been restored.[14]

Before he could concentrate his scattered units, however, Johnston had to retreat from Bowling Green to Nashville in the wake of the disaster at Donelson. The state capital seemed "indefensible" to him, due to the topography around the city, and Johnston had but eleven thousand men to contend with Grant, Buell, and George Thomas. On February 17–18 the Confederate general moved most of his men to Murfreesboro, leaving behind a rearguard consisting of Floyd's Virginia Brigade. Floyd evacuated the capital on February 23 and headed for Chattanooga. Johnston briefly debated whether to make his stand in middle Tennessee or the Mississippi Valley. He quickly chose the valley as an area of "paramount importance." Dispatching eight regiments to hold eastern Tennessee, Johnston headed west, leaving local commanders to fend for themselves as he proceeded with his offensive.[15]

The residents of Nashville were shocked that Johnston gave up their city without a fight. Many of them had formed companies to help the Confederate troops, but all organizations broke up when word spread that the city would be left to the Federals. Many citizens fled rather than endure occupation. By March 8 John Floyd reached Chattanooga, securing that vital rail link between East and West which also served as a portal to the Deep South. McClellan envisioned the seizure of Chattanooga and eastern Tennessee following Donelson, but his subordinates in the field had other ideas. It soon became evident that the Federals intended to operate in the Mississippi Valley, so for the moment Chattanooga, along with eastern Tennessee, seemed safely in Confederate hands.[16]

The Federals indeed were aiming at the great valley as their primary target while following up the Donelson victory. Oddly enough, huge swaths of Rebel territory became no-man's-land during the ensuing weeks, as the Confederates evacuated large areas to concentrate in front of them and the Federals failed to send troops into those abandoned regions. Both sides were concentrating, and the river system was the key. Another gunboat expedition up the Tennessee as far as Eastport, Mississippi, again elicited signs of latent Unionism among the residents. The gunboats took away some refugees—seventeen men willing to enlist in the Union army—and warned secessionists along the river not to molest loyalists or suffer the consequences. Frequent gunboat trips up the Tennessee seemed to indicate considerable Unionist strength nearly everywhere along the stream.[17]

The story was different along the Cumberland River. When Foote visited Clarksville, only fifty miles downstream from Nashville, he found that two-thirds of the residents had fled in panic. Foote issued a proclamation to calm those who remained, assuring them he would not seize their private property. "The rebels all have a terror of the gunboats," he reported.[18]

Military Rule

Nashville, the first Confederate state capital to fall into Union hands, also underwent a period of dread as its residents tried to adjust to Federal control. Halleck correctly predicted that Johnston would abandon the city, and Buell marched in without incident on February 25. Buell assured the residents that he had no intention of taking their property as long as they remained peaceful, and he created a board of army officers to determine cases where the loyalty of residents was in doubt. Another task of the board was to find out what property was owned by the Confederate government and what was owned by private citizens.[19]

Buell hoped that the easy capture of Nashville would lead to a great increase of Union feeling in Tennessee. Impressed by the loyalists who remained in the city, he urged that Lincoln move forward quickly with a lenient course of action, so as not to antagonize them, as he reconstructed "the machinery of the General Government" in the state. Brigade commander Jacob Ammen was also gratified by the Unionists when he entered Nashville. They welcomed his column, informed on pro-Rebel neighbors, and told him where the Confederates had hidden food and valuables. Buell hoped to use these people, although in a minority, to re-create civil government in Tennessee, but Lincoln felt the need to appoint a military governor instead. Two weeks after Nashville fell, the U.S. president named Andrew Johnson to fill that position, giving him a commission as brigadier general to add teeth to his title. Unfortunately, Lincoln did not establish clear lines of authority between Johnson's field of power and the responsibilities of the army, leading to much confusion and working at cross-purposes. Johnson seemed an attractive candidate to Lincoln because of the East Tennesseean's strong support of the Union. Furthermore, he represented the kind of Southern loyalism that Lincoln and many other Northerners hoped would undermine the Confederate war effort. But Johnson was a controversial figure among Middle and West Tennesseans. Lincoln invested him with almost dictatorial powers; he could suspend the writ of habeas corpus, establish state offices, and run Tennessee solely under the authority of the president.[20]

Before the Federals could move farther south, they had to deal with civilians in their newly conquered territory. Grant imposed martial law over all western Tennessee and vowed to lift it only when "a sufficient number of citizens of the State return to their allegiance to maintain law and order." "'Secesh' is now about on its last legs in Tennessee," he told his wife after hearing that two hundred residents of Clarksville wanted to confer with him for assurances of protection. Halleck issued a general order urging his men to comport themselves well in captured territory so that Southerners could see the Union army intended only "to crush out rebellion and to restore to them peace and the benefits of the Constitution." He did not want them to encourage slaves to seek safety in army camps, for the civil courts, not the military, had to decide the future of relations between slave and owner.[21]

Moving South

How to follow up the capture of Fort Donelson was a matter of some discussion. Halleck preferred that Grant send an expedition up the Tennessee River to cut rail lines near Corinth, Jackson, and Humboldt, but Grant had to prepare slowly for any move because a shortage of transports hampered his ability to use the river system. He also detached hundreds of men to garrison various places and counted up losses due to illness. Meanwhile, the Confederates evacuated Columbus and Union cavalrymen entered the "boasted "Gibraltar of the West'" on March 3. Halleck suggested that Buell go west to join Grant so the combined forces could operate against Memphis or any number of other cities in the Mississippi Valley.[22]

At the time that Columbus fell, Grant and Halleck had a falling out due to a mysterious breakdown in communications. Grant traveled to Clarksville and then on to Nashville; the ultimate purpose of his short trip was to coordinate lines of authority with Buell and ensure that no important points in middle Tennessee were left unattended. His messages to Halleck failed to arrive at their destination, and the theater commander became angry. He also was disturbed by persistent reports that Grant's army was "as demoralized by the victory of Fort Donelson as was that of the Potomac by the defeat of Bull Run." Halleck worried that Grant had become complacent after the victory at Donelson and "sits down and enjoys it without any regard to the future." He received authority to arrest Grant and replace him with Charles F. Smith, but Halleck merely put Smith in charge of the contemplated move up the Tennessee River, even though it was rumored that Grant was drinking to excess. When Grant learned of all this, he assumed some personal enemies had tried to cause ill feelings between him and his superior. In fact, neither commander heard from the other for two weeks. Grant took the accusations personally and offered to resign, but Halleck wisely ignored him. In the middle of his fight with Grant, Halleck was given authority over most of Buell's department in the wake of a reshuffling of commanders in Washington. McClellan no longer would serve as general in chief, but he would continue to command the Army of the Potomac as it prepared to move against Richmond.[23]

The Tennessee River seemed a wide-open avenue for further penetration of the South. Grant believed that no sizable Confederate force could interfere with Union boat traffic up that stream, and that the Federals had "such an inside track of the enemy that by following up our success we can go anywhere." Halleck's plan to send an expedition upriver to cut rail lines quickly evolved into an effort to permanently control territory. Grant began to shift troops to Pittsburg Landing, upstream from Savannah, Tennessee. He left nearly 6,000 men at Fort Henry and 1,200 at Fort Donelson, but transported more than 25,000 on overcrowded steamers to the landing during March. Some of the men were hit by sniper fire from the river bank, or were taken prisoner when details went ashore to chop wood, or drowned when they fell off heaving decks into the choppy water.[24]

But the Federals also witnessed periodic expressions of joy by local residents at the sight of the Union flag. Grant was impressed by the signs of loyalism in Savannah, noting that five hundred area residents volunteered to join the Union army and many more than that number came into town seeking protection for their property. "With one more great success I do not see how the rebellion is to be sustained," he wrote. When other residents complained that their slaves were taken away by soldiers in his division, John McClernand grumbled that the army seemed caught by uncertain policies emanating from Washington. He was not supposed to help slaveowners retrieve their property if the owners were not loyal, and yet the army had little opportunity to gauge their allegiance. At the same time, Grant became irritated that his officers often arrested civilians on suspicion of disloyalty without filing charges against them. This not only embarrassed the army but also brought potential spies into camp. Grant also worked to counter Tennessee governor Harris's order to enforce Rebel conscription by sending details to various towns to break up enrollment efforts. To secure the river-based logistical system as it more deeply penetrated Confederate territory, Halleck revoked the licenses of pilots and engineers and forced them to reapply for new ones, affording officials the opportunity to reexamine their allegiance to the U.S. government.[25]

The Federals concentrated at Pittsburg Landing because it allowed them close access to Corinth, little more than twenty miles to the southwest. Corinth was, as Grant put it, "the great strategic position at the West" because of its rail connections. The Confederates were concentrating to defend the town, spurred by a pressure group centered at Memphis and in the Mississippi River Delta. While Albert Johnston led his Bowling Green force from Nashville via Huntsville, Decatur, and Tuscumbia, Braxton Bragg brought troops up from Mobile and Daniel Ruggles advanced his men from Grenada, Mississippi. Polk evacuated Columbus and moved its garrison to Corinth as well. The Confederates stripped their military manpower from all of middle Tennessee and from the Gulf coast of Florida, Alabama, Mississippi, Louisiana, and Texas. "Our entire forces must be thrown towards the Mississippi, for the defense of that river and of the Memphis and Charleston

Railroad," Secretary of War Benjamin told an officer in the field. With Buell beginning a ponderous march from Nashville to join Grant at Pittsburg Landing, Confederate hopes centered on striking before that union took place. If the two Federal armies did link up, then Davis could only hope that the people of the Southwest would "rally *en masse* with their private arms" and help Johnston "oppose the vast army which will threaten the destruction of our country."[26]

Along the Mississippi River, the only Confederate defenses left were at Island No. 10, New Madrid, and Fort Pillow, the latter located fifty miles upstream from Memphis. Convinced that the Federals would continue to push south on the river system, engineer Jeremy F. Gilmer tried frantically to plan more defenses at key points lower than Fort Pillow. Governor John Pettus of Mississippi was worried that Federal domination of the river would allow the enemy to be "in contact with the slaves" and allow them "great facilities for plunder." He advised the organization of mounted companies to harass Federal landing parties and suppress slave unrest, a plan approved by military authorities but not implemented due to lack of time and opportunity.[27]

Shiloh

Albert Johnston was barely able to concentrate his manpower at Corinth and strike at Grant before Buell arrived, precipitating the first major battle of the Civil War near Pittsburg Landing. Popularly known as Shiloh, after a Methodist meetinghouse nearby, the battle engulfed some thirty thousand Federals and an equal number of Confederates in a daylong match on Sunday, April 6, 1862. Shiloh seemed to make every previous battle in the war pale by comparison, with its ferocity of fighting, its long casualty list, and the seeming lack of tactical decisiveness. It foretold the nature of Civil War combat.

But the Federals had no indication of what was to come before gray-clad troops emerged from the tangled landscape around Pittsburg Landing. On April 3 Grant wrote with supreme confidence to his wife that he was anxious to move against Corinth. "I do not feel that there is the slightest doubt about the result," he exuded. On the same day, Johnston called on his green but eager troops to "remember the precious stake involved, remember the fair, broad, abounding land, the happy homes, and ties that will be desolated by your defeat. The eyes and hopes of 8,000,000 of people rest upon you." His ill-disciplined men made so much noise on their short march toward battle that General Beauregard, Johnston's second in command, suggested the attack be called off. "I would fight them if they were a million," Johnston retorted.[28]

Shiloh cyclorama. A section of the cyclorama that depicts the fighting on April 6, 1862, showing a brigade of Arkansas and Louisiana troops commanded by Colonel Randall L. Gibson. (Johnson and Buel, *Battles and Leaders*, 1:505)

When the Confederates fired the opening shots at 5:00 A.M., on April 6, the Federals were largely taken by surprise. Long lines of Rebel troops moved across the cluttered landscape, calling out "Bull Run" while moving through acres of Union camps, but the Federals hastily organized proper defensive lines. The initial surprise gave way to organized resistance, and many terrain features grew to almost legendary stature when people remembered Shiloh in years to come. The lexicon of battle in the Civil War was enlivened by the addition of place names like the Sunken Road, the Hornet's Nest, the Peach Orchard, and the Bloody Pond, even though the battle was decided by fighting that took place elsewhere. Union divisions under Brigadier General William T. Sherman and Major General John A. McClernand provided the most stubborn resistance to Johnston's plan on the Federal right, delaying the Confederates long enough for Grant to assemble a last line of defense near the landing.[29]

As the armies grappled, they became engaged in relatively static combat along an irregular line. The Confederates were hampered by their comparative inexperience and a faulty organizational plan that placed each corps in a separate line, one behind the other, which soon broke down. For the attacker, Shiloh became a series of local actions by individual brigades only loosely controlled by division and corps leaders. Johnston often busied himself with the duties of an inspirational leader rather than a coordinator of his army's movements. On the Union side, Grant could do little more than encourage, shift a few units about, and hope that the van of Buell's army showed up as soon as possible. On both sides, the battle weighed heavily on the shoulders of the rank and file. Although several thousand Federals broke and ran, huddling around the landing all day, most men in both armies strove to fulfill their duty.[30]

By midafternoon, the Confederates began to lever the stubborn Yankees out of their defensive positions, although in the process General Johnston was mortally wounded. The army commander was hit by a stray round, possibly fired by his own men. Their flanks uncovered, the Federals in the Hornet's Nest fought on as long as possible before trying to escape encircling Rebels, but some two thousand of them failed to make it back to the rear, becoming the first major haul of Union prisoners taken by Confederate forces in the West.[31]

It was 6:00 P.M. by the time the Federals pulled back toward the landing, and by then the Confederates had precious little time to consolidate tactical gains and prepare for an attack on Grant's last line. In the end, due to many circumstances, Beauregard decided not to launch that last attack of the day. After some thirteen hours of vicious combat, the Federals had lost 7,000 killed and wounded and some 3,000 captured, while about 10,000 stragglers had absented themselves from the fight altogether. The Confederates lost about 8,000 men that day but failed in their primary purpose of crushing Grant before Buell arrived. Even before the fighting stopped that evening, two divisions of the Army of the Ohio arrived in the vicinity and the rest of Buell's army was just behind them. There is every reason to believe that a final Confederate attack on Grant's last line would have failed. Though severely battered, the Union Army of the Tennessee managed to save itself and its forward position within striking distance of Corinth. Despite the valor of its soldiers, the Confederate Army of the Mississippi had struck too late to prevent a joining of the two major Union armies in the West.[32]

A heavy rain fell that night as Buell moved his men across the Tennessee River to the crowded landing, and the gunboats *Tyler* and *Lexington* fired at intervals to annoy the enemy. The next day, Beauregard was forced on the defensive as Buell bore the brunt of counterattacking during the morning and early afternoon. It was the blooding of the Army of the Ohio, which managed to press the Confederates slowly back. Beauregard finally admitted the obvious and disengaged, making his way back to Corinth without serious trouble. The Federals were content to claim the tortured battlefield and declare a victory at Shiloh.[33]

Among the casualties was the putative governor of Kentucky. George W. Johnson had accompanied Albert S. Johnston's headquarters ever since the retreat from Bowling Green and served as a volunteer aide for John C. Breckinridge during the battle. His horse was shot out from under him on April 6, and he joined Company E, 4th Kentucky, that evening. Johnson was mortally wounded the next day and died in Union hands on April 8.[34]

Shiloh stunned the governments and the population of both belligerents because of its huge casualty lists. About thirteen thousand Federals were lost and ten thousand Confederates fell during the two days of fighting. Twice as many Americans were lost on April 6–7, 1862, as during the previous major battles of the war combined, and more men fell on the battlefield of Shiloh than in all previous wars of American history. Such losses made it difficult for many Yankees to understand that Shiloh had been a great strategic victory for the North and a serious setback for the Confederates. It initially shocked Grant and his men to be suddenly thrown on the defensive, but the end result of the battle was to instill a supreme sense of confidence in their ability to handle battlefield crises. Long after the war ended, Grant characterized Shiloh as "the severest battle fought at the West during the war, and but few in the East equaled it for hard, determined fighting." Even though he wrote his wife only a week after the engagement to express assurance in whipping the Confederates in one more battle, Grant had a different view of the matter when he penned his memoirs twenty years later. The former general and U.S. president then saw Shiloh as proof that the Confederates meant to fight to the death to achieve independence and nothing but "complete conquest" could stop them; that included confiscating their property and destroying slavery.[35]

William T. Sherman, who gained his first battle experience as one of Grant's division commanders on April 6, was later persuaded that the bloodbath at Shiloh was a necessary foundation of later Union success. "It was not then a question of military skill and strategy," he wrote, "but of courage and pluck, and I am convinced that every life lost to us that day was necessary" to prove to Southerners that Northern men "could fight as well as they." Sherman consistently identified fighting spirit as the basis of Union victory in the Civil War; he believed the Federals in the West established a dominance in that region over their enemy beginning at Shiloh. He also noted that a certain amount of tension developed between the Army of the Tennessee and the Army of the Ohio in their first joint operation. Sherman had been relieved to see the van of Buell's army arrive, but he resented the fact that Buell wrote so much about the stragglers who cowered at Pittsburg Landing and undervalued the hard fighting done by Grant's men before his arrival.

For their part, members of Grant's army "indulged in severe criticism at the slow approach" of Buell during the days preceding the Confederate attack.[36]

Corinth

The Confederates were thrown on the defensive after their defeat at Shiloh, but a passive stance frustrated many Southern partisans. Further loss of territory would depress civilian morale, already reeling from the heavy casualties at Shiloh. If, on the other hand, Beauregard could crush the Federal concentration preparing to advance on Corinth, Confederate sympathizers in Tennessee would rally and join the ranks by the thousands. An invasion of Kentucky to rouse its latent pro-Confederate sympathies would be the next step. At least that was the thinking of an ardent Southerner in Jackson, Tennessee, who shared his views with the harried commander at Corinth.[37]

But Beauregard's Army of the Mississippi was in no condition to take the offensive. It had been hastily thrown together only the month before with woefully inadequate time to organize and establish the corporate culture that underwrote the character and performance of every field army. Braxton Bragg, who commanded one of its corps, was astounded by the lack of discipline so painfully evident in the army. It had manifested itself since March, and it seemed as if officers high and low failed to do anything to correct the widespread plundering of civilian property. Some Confederates "would do less harm by serving in the ranks of the enemy," Bragg thought. Thousands of Confederates straggled at the start of the fighting on April 6, and the army's loss of equipment on the battlefield was difficult to replace. "Universal sufferage, furloughs & whiskey have ruined us," Bragg complained to his wife. "If we fall it is our own fault."[38]

Bragg had true cause for concern, because the near catastrophe at Shiloh sparked a massive Union reaction. Halleck directed every available unit in the West to Pittsburg Landing, even drawing from the small force that was moving down the Mississippi against Confederate defenses on the river and from meager forces traversing the Trans-Mississippi. Within a month of the battle, he accumulated a massive army of one hundred thousand men in rural southwestern Tennessee. Halleck came to Pittsburg Landing to take personal command of this host, demoting Grant to a meaningless position as his second in command.[39]

In early May Halleck began a ponderous advance toward Corinth, ordering his units to construct fieldworks every night to prevent another surprise attack like the one that almost ruined Grant at Shiloh. The dirt roads could not support such a large number of troops and wheeled vehicles; after a few days of spring rain, they became ribbons of mud, requiring corduroying in low-lying areas and through swampy marshes. Fifty horses were needed to pull one Parrott rifle out of the mud. The slow, methodical advance wore on men and officers alike. Soon many Federals were referring to their commander as "Granny Halleck."[40]

The harried general warned Secretary of War Edwin M. Stanton in Washington not to expect quick results. He noted that Memphis was vulnerable to a river-borne strike by Federal troops who had captured New Orleans; if they did not take the city, he would need much time and tedious siege operations to capture it after seizing Corinth. Even after taking these important places, Halleck believed that he would need much additional time to repair the railroad system in the area to support further advances.[41]

Regardless of the frustration felt by many Federals, Halleck's slow advance on Corinth worried the Confederates into evacuating the town. They were outnumbered at least two to one, and Corinth had no easily defensible terrain. Halleck's use of field fortifications negated the possibility of a major Confederate attack on his command. Corps commander William J. Hardee advised Beauregard that the best course was to pull out and lure the Federals into the interior of Mississippi, away from their rail- and river-based supply systems. The Deep South was less well endowed with both railroads and highways and offered a much broader expanse of deep territory, where Yankee "mechanical superiority will not avail him." Settled and developed only since the 1820s, the Deep South's infrastructure paled in comparison to that of the Upper South, which had evolved since the 1770s. The Deep South population was more loyal to the Confederate cause; most of the cotton in the South was grown there and most of the slaves lived there. The lower tier of slave states was the first to secede from the Union; this is where the heart of the Confederacy lay. Hardee wanted to take advantage of these assets and force the Federal host to penetrate that heart.[42]

Beauregard admitted the necessity of giving up Corinth without a battle and anticipated retiring southward along the Mobile and Ohio Railroad toward Meridian, Mississippi. Tupelo, fifty-two miles south of Corinth, seemed the next best place to make a stand where his men could expect to find ample supplies of water. The pullout was well planned, taking place on the night of May 29–30, with few Federals aware of what was happening. The retreat to Tupelo was disorderly, and Bragg tried to discipline his wayward men on the march. They tried to stop at civilian houses for water or to take whatever food could be found. Bragg ordered one man shot for firing at a chicken in the yard of a civilian home and hitting a slave instead, killing him on the spot. This summary punishment seemed to frighten the other men into better behavior.[43]

The Federal reaction to Beauregard's retreat was mixed. Celebration over the capture of Corinth at such little cost intermingled with disgust that the Rebel army managed to escape undamaged. "Halleck captured many pieces of wooden artillery and a dirty, filthy town," commented Richard W. Johnson. "This was considered a great victory, and throughout the North there was great rejoicing." Grant wondered if Confederate morale had not been improved by Beauregard's success in slipping away, unnoticed, carrying with him most of the usable equipment and supplies at Corinth.[44]

But many Federals saw signs of impending collapse in Beauregard's army, and in the Confederacy at large, following the fall of Corinth. Major General John Pope, who led his troops forward to follow up the Rebel retreat, reported that the "enemy drive away and carry off everything for miles around," leaving civilian families hurting for lack of food. Residents told him that Beauregard's men were desperate for something to eat and seemed but a rabble. Deserters assured the Federals that the "Rebel army is getting out of heart. They have been driven so much that they are now beginning to believe the Union army Is invincible." Coupled with Union victories elsewhere—the capture of New Orleans and Yorktown—it seemed to many that the Rebel attempt to create a nation already was crumbling. Sherman hoped that the Confederate leaders would "admit now that they have been defeated."[45]

The war in the West reached a plateau in June 1862. Following a remarkable string of successes, ranging from the relatively easy capture of Fort Henry to the bloodbath at Shiloh and the crunching advance on Corinth, the Federals had completely changed the course of the war by collapsing the Confederate posture in Kentucky and western Tennessee. They captured fifty thousand square miles of Confederate territory, plus Nashville and other major cities of the South. Northerners had established an operational pattern; drawing on their superiority in river and rail transportation, they deeply penetrated Southern territory and achieved an advantage in morale over their opponent, all of which were essential elements in long-range hopes for Union victory. The Northern belief that the South would quickly collapse proved unrealistic, so the pattern would have to be pushed time after time in recurring series of campaigns until the Rebel edifice crumbled. But Confederate partisans were determined not to let that happen without a fight.[46]

4 } Occupation

It became an item of received wisdom after the war to criticize Henry Halleck for not advancing deep into Mississippi following the fall of Corinth. His large army of some one hundred thousand veterans "could have gone to Mobile, or Vicksburg, or anywhere in that region," asserted William T. Sherman, "which would by one move have solved the whole Mississippi problem." Sherman considered it "a fatal mistake" that Halleck dispersed his grand army to consolidate control of territory recently captured by Union troops. Grant felt the same way after the war, and John Pope dramatically claimed that there was "scarce a ripple of opposition" to Halleck after Beauregard evacuated Corinth. "What, then, prevented an active campaign toward the Gulf and why was not the Confederacy cut in two and the Mississippi opened in 1862[?]," Pope asked in his memoirs.[1]

The passage of time and events gave Sherman, Grant, and Pope every opportunity to analyze the past in any way that suited them. In truth, there was every reason for Halleck to stop after the fall of Corinth and consolidate Union control over the vast territory that had fallen into Federal hands after Grant captured Fort Donelson. Halleck knew that a column of Union troops and seagoing vessels were on their way north upriver from New Orleans to attempt the capture of Vicksburg. If it failed, he had every intention of sending troops downriver to succeed. He also knew that guerrilla activity already was beginning to crop up behind Union lines in occupied Tennessee, which posed a direct threat to his supply lines with the North. Vast stretches of the state were under the control of no organized military force at all, the civilians existing in no-man's-land, unable to rely on protection from either the Union or Confederate armies. Nashville and Clarksville were about the only cities in middle Tennessee that had a Union presence, and Memphis had not yet been secured. Moreover, it was absurd to believe that no opposition existed south of Corinth; Beauregard's ragged army had nearly crushed Grant's troops on April 6, and it was ready for another try at the Federals.[2]

Distance and logistics rendered Union military operations in the

Upper South quite different from what they would be in the Deep South. Kentucky and Tennessee were older states; both had well-developed turnpikes and rail systems in the heart of their territory that helped the Federals to deliver their military strength on key targets. Nothing could prove that point better than to recall Grant's and Buell's movements from early February through late May 1862. The river system of western Kentucky and western Tennessee also played an important role in this delivery.[3]

The Deep South was another matter. Settled only after the War of 1812, its road system was primitive compared to that of the Upper South. While rail lines penetrated the expansive country, distance prevented a complete network of steam-powered land transportation similar to that of its older sister states to the north. Except along the Mississippi, the river system of the Deep South did not favor Federal use of steamboats to supply large concentrations of troops. In short, the Deep South was a far more difficult sphere of operations for invading armies. To sustain a force of one hundred thousand men overland into Mississippi from Corinth by a single track would have required enormous preparation. In the light of later operations, Grant could not do it in December 1862 when he had only thirty thousand men to feed. Sherman managed to support his one hundred thousand men during the Atlanta campaign in May–September 1864, but only after two years of experience in building up the rail system of the Upper South to make this possible.[4]

In June 1862 Halleck did not have the logistical capacity to penetrate the interior of the Deep South. Most of his available manpower was concentrated at Corinth, and too few troops were north of that point to protect his lines of communication. In truth, he had too few men to hold the necessary points in the Upper South and wrest new territory from the enemy in the Deep South at the same time. Not until Lincoln issued a call for three hundred thousand additional volunteers in July 1862, nearly doubling the size of the Union army, were efforts made to correct this deficiency. Despite suffering a string of defeats, the Confederacy was not collapsing and the war was evolving into a far bigger, more demanding endeavor than Northerners had anticipated. Northerners had reached a plateau by June 1862 and needed to consolidate, resupply, and mobilize more manpower before tackling the tough objective of reclaiming the underdeveloped land that constituted the Deep South. Governor Joseph E. Brown of Georgia recognized the strategic advantage of his region to the Confederate cause. "We can confine ourselves within the limits of the cotton and tobacco states," he proposed, "and defy the combined Federal forces for years to come."[5]

Halleck began to disperse his large concentration of troops at Corinth to occupy key points along the rail system through Tennessee and Kentucky. He also sent Buell's Army of the Ohio eastward to secure control of Chattanooga, one of the most strategically important rail centers in the West. Chattanooga was a linchpin of east-west and north-south rail lines across the Confederacy, in addition to serving as a gateway to the Deep South. By dispatching Buell to take this objective, Halleck separated the two major Union armies in the West and set them off toward divergent but equally significant objectives, restoring a two-pronged movement into the Western Confederacy after temporarily concentrating for the drive on Corinth.

But Buell's advance eastward was hampered by logistical difficulties. He had to rebuild several rail lines to support his move into the Appalachian terrain that surrounded the Chattanooga area. Buell advanced his divisions with due speed into that mountainous area but then dispersed them to occupy key points along his lines of communication. He concentrated on building the network necessary to support a final push to Chattanooga itself. As a result, delay and frustration set in as the summer unfolded.[6]

An initial Union thrust toward the city resulted in Chattanooga's first brush with the Yankees. On June 7 a Federal column approached from the north and shelled the place. In retiring, the Federals took along eighty prisoners and a considerable number of cattle and horses, having been feted by hundreds of loyal mountaineers along the way. Meanwhile, Buell's other troops, who settled in towns across the region, began to steal food and fence rails from local civilians, prompted by a growing awareness that short rations would be the order of the day for some time to come.[7]

Buell was not the first Federal commander to experience the difficulties of occupying or moving through the mountains. Ormsby M. Mitchell's division of seventy-four hundred men had earlier entered this region to show the flag after the fall of Fort Donelson. Mitchell reached Huntsville, Alabama, on April 11, securing two hundred prisoners, fifteen locomotives, and lots of railroad cars. As he dispersed his units into occupation duties in the northern part of the state, trouble soon developed between these isolated detachments and rebellious civilians, made worse by the tendency of some troops to pillage property. Confederate cavalrymen, aided by civilians, attacked some Federal troops at Athens, Alabama, on May 1, and brigade leader John Basil Turchin led reinforcements to the town, tearing it apart for several days. His men mostly stole property and wrecked buildings, but they refrained from burning the town or committing widespread personal attacks on residents. Turchin was later court-martialed and found guilty of improperly disciplining his command, but he was able to return to duty and turn in a strong record of field service.[8]

Though distressed by the incident at Athens, Mitchell refused to reimburse the citizens for the more than $54,000 worth of property Turchin's men destroyed. He had worked for weeks trying to reconcile the civilians to Union occupation but could not reach the most recalcitrant members of the community. Ironically, the people living in the rural areas of northern Alabama tended to be loyal to the U.S. government, whereas the residents of the railroad towns, which had important commercial links with the cotton-based economy of the South, tended to be pro-Confederate. "There is a most bitter feeling of disappointment," Mitchell informed Buell, "that we have not been driven out long since, and scarcely a day passes without some attack upon our bridge guards, our trains, or telegraph wires."[9]

Mitchell's presence in northern Alabama spurred a unique attempt to raid and disable the Confederates' major rail line in the region, the track that linked Chattanooga with Atlanta. J. J. Andrews, a Kentucky loyalist, concocted a scheme to lead a group of volunteers and infiltrate Confederate territory to tear up stretches of that track. Mitchell authorized it and allowed volunteers from his regiments to participate, dressed in civilian clothes. Altogether, twenty-two men managed to rendezvous at Marietta, north of Atlanta. They hijacked a locomotive, the *General*, along with three cars at Big Shanty on April 12. Racing northward, their plan to stop and tear up track was foiled by the crew of the locomotive *Texas*, which gave chase. After nearly one hundred miles, the *General*'s fuel and water gave out, forcing the raiders to flee through the countryside. All of them were eventually captured. Andrews was executed on June 7 and his men endured brutal treatment in various jails; seven of them were also executed on June 18. Six more escaped in October 1862. The Confederates easily repaired the little damage done to the rail line.[10]

Mitchell hoped to pacify the area by opening free trade in cotton. He prevailed on his son-in-law to recruit cotton brokers from New York to go to northern Alabama, where he estimated that 5,000 to 10,000 bales could be found. Before mid-May, Mitchell had captured 270 bales and sold them to private buyers for government benefit, providing rail transportation at a reasonable rate for them as well. Huge profits were possible for the few who had connections with the army, and inevitably the cause became a bit tainted by commercialism, with little apparent softening of attitudes toward the Yankee occupiers.[11]

The Mountains

The Confederates continued to hold eastern Tennessee following the fall of Fort Donelson. When Edmund Kirby Smith took command of some seven thousand troops in that mountainous region in early March 1862, he was shocked by the mood of its inhabitants: "I find East Tennessee an enemy's country, and the people, where removed from the immediate presence and fear of the Confederate troops, in open rebellion." Of thirty-two counties, Kirby Smith estimated that only six were mostly pro-Confederate. He was convinced the loyalists would take up arms "whenever an enemy's column makes its appearance." A thousand loyalists trekked to Union-held Kentucky in only one week about the time Kirby Smith took over in Knoxville. He wanted to hold on to eastern Tennessee to threaten the flank of Union forces operating in middle Tennessee and along the Mississippi River, but needed at least ten thousand troops to adequately guard the region from a Federal incursion.[12]

When state elections put mostly Unionists in local offices that spring, Kirby Smith reacted by arresting the most prominent loyalists. With his encouragement, the Confederate government suspended the writ of habeas corpus in the Department of East Tennessee and imposed martial law on April 8. Within a week upward of six thousand men of military age fled the region, an exodus that increased when the Confederate Congress passed a harsh conscription law on April 16. To ameliorate the situation, Kirby Smith asked the government to suspend the draft in eastern Tennessee, and that was done on May 13. Kirby Smith also tried to administer an oath of loyalty to the Confederate government to weed out loyalists from county offices. It did not work, as many took the oath but did nothing to aid the Confederate cause.[13]

At times, Confederate officers were able to intercept Unionists before they made it to Kentucky. A Rebel column stopped one group of loyalists a few miles from the border near Big Creek Gap, killed and wounded about 60 of them, and captured 423. These prisoners were shipped to Georgia, their fate to be decided at a later time. Kirby Smith was willing to release another group of nearly 600 loyalists, who had been caught on their way to Kentucky, when they took the oath of allegiance to the Confederate government. He continued to hold 76 of them because he could not trust their fealty.[14]

The command of the Confederate Department of East Tennessee changed hands many times in 1862, but no officer could devise a workable solution to the problems involved in administering a hostile population. John P. McCown succeeded Kirby Smith in August and received orders to resume conscripting in the mountains. This initiated another surge of refugees, but, because the Confederates were in the process of invading Kentucky, they simply fled their homes and hid in the hollows. Samuel Jones replaced McCown on September 19 and continued enforcing the draft, but he tried to be conciliatory at the same time. Jones convinced a handful of Unionist leaders to issue public statements encouraging the people to accept Confederate authority, but it did little good. When Kirby Smith resumed command of the department in October, he continued to push conscription but garnered few reliable troops for the Rebel army. Future commanders (Daniel Donelson in January 1863 and Simon Buckner in May 1863) also failed to fatten Confederate muster rolls with mountain riflemen through the draft. Conscription was probably the most hated aspect of Confederate rule in eastern Tennessee; it made many enemies for the Southern cause. No matter how hard commanders tried to mollify sentiment, they could not uproot the residents' deep-seated loyalty to the U.S. government. Moreover, with Union forces tantalizingly close by in Kentucky, there always was hope of seeing a blue-clad column wending its way across the next ridge.[15]

The Federal success in securing eastern Kentucky in January 1862 led to great hopes of sending troops into eastern Tennessee as well, but those hopes failed to materialize in any substantial way. An expedition organized by Buell under George W. Morgan maneuvered the small Confederate garrison out of Cumberland Gap in June. This bloodless victory represented the first Federal incursion on eastern Tennessee soil, but it was a tentative presence on the fringe of the state and at the end of a line of communications dependent on unreliable mountain roads. Nevertheless, Morgan reported that hundreds of loyalists from Tennessee, Kentucky, and Virginia came to Cumberland Gap to greet their liberators. One group cried when Morgan officially "welcomed them back to the old flag." The Federals fortified the gap and stockpiled supplies for the division that Morgan commanded, but he was too weak to push deep into the Tennessee Valley and approach the Confederates at Knoxville.[16]

Island No. 10

Federal forces cleared the stretch of the Mississippi River from Columbus to Memphis by June 1862. They reduced the first Rebel stronghold at Island No. 10 after weeks of tedious operations that resulted in little fighting but a major haul of Confederate prisoners. So named because it was the tenth island south of the Ohio River, Island No. 10 had been occupied since the previous August. By March 1862, the mile-long, narrow island sported nineteen heavy guns dispersed in five batteries. With the addition of a floating battery and emplacements on the Tennessee shore, a total of fifty-two artillery pieces offered a choke point for Union shipping at a sharp bend in the river. The Confederates also fortified New Madrid, Missouri, a few miles downstream at another sharp bend.[17]

John Pope was put in charge of dealing with Island No. 10. He gathered ten thousand infantrymen and two thousand cavalrymen at Commerce, Missouri, and set out on February 28, positioning his troops close to the enemy works at New Madrid. Soon after opening with heavy guns on March 13, the Confederates evacuated the town without a struggle. Additional reinforcements brought Pope's total force to eighteen thousand men, designated the Army of the Mississippi, whereas the Confederates could spare no more than five thousand troops to hold Island No. 10 and the Tennessee shore. Pope's numerical superiority would mean nothing, however, if he could not find a way to place his troops on the east bank of the Mississippi. The boats needed to accomplish this passage were stymied by the island's artillery, and Andrew H. Foote was reluctant to risk them by running past the guns. A fleet of ten mortar boats opened fire on the island, pumping shells daily during the last two weeks of March. On two different days a German aeronaut ascended in a balloon, the *Eagle*, to spy on the Confederate position, the only use of aerial reconnaissance in the Western theater of operations.[18]

The impasse broke when the idea of bypassing the island instead of running past it was born. Who initially thought of the idea became a point of contention later, but engineer troops scouted a route across the wide bottomland on the west bank of the Mississippi, temporarily flooded by spring rains, and began to cut trees below the waterline to open a canal of sorts. Up to eight hundred men worked for nineteen days to make a passage fifty feet wide and at least four and a half feet deep. The New Madrid Channel stretched for twelve miles, part of the way through flooded bayous.[19]

Enough boats made it through, before the waters began to subside, to transport Pope's troops across the river miles downstream from Island No. 10. But before preparations were completed, Foote finally allowed two ironclad gunboats to run past the batteries so they could lend fire support to the crossing. The *Carondelet* successfully steamed past on the night of April 4, while the *Pittsburg* ran past two nights later. On the morning of April 7, Pope crossed the river and Confederate resistance collapsed. Some forty-five hundred Rebel troops surrendered the next day.[20]

"I do not think it can be claimed by the Confederates that they made a vigorous defense of the Mississippi," Pope later concluded. The river was "their strongest line of defense," yet they seemed to have invested comparatively few resources on its protection. Even so, every Rebel stronghold on the stream had "to be reduced by long and hazardous operations." Pope rightly praised the Island No. 10 campaign as a model of efficient and cost-saving methods.[21]

New Madrid Channel. This sketch illustrates the inventive and industrious spirit that drove much of the Union war effort in the West. (Johnson and Buel, *Battles and Leaders,* 1:505)

Fort Pillow and Memphis

The fall of Island No. 10 cleared the way for a fleet of thirty transports to convey Pope's Army of the Mississippi to the next Rebel strongpoint, Fort Pillow, about fifty miles north of Memphis. The fleet arrived near the fort on April 14 and Foote's gunboats opened fire, but there seemed to be no easy way to outflank this objective. Soon, an order arrived from Halleck to shift most of the men to Pittsburg Landing. Pope left two regiments behind to support the gunboats and steamed upriver with the rest, eventually joining the concentration of force gathering for the advance on Corinth. Captain Charles Henry Davis relieved Foote in command of the fleet on May 9, and the next day he was greeted with a surprise attack by the Confederate fleet defending Memphis. The battle took place near the mouth of Plum Run Creek six miles north of Fort Pillow. Eight Confederate gunboats, comprising the River Defense Fleet under Captain James E. Montgomery, sallied against Captain Davis's ironclads. These boats, converted from wooden civilian craft with only light armor, sank two Pook ironclads by ramming before breaking off the attack. The ironclads were later raised because they had settled in shallow water, but the battle of Plum Run Bend embarrassed the Federals.[22]

The Confederates evacuated Fort Pillow without a fight on June 3, but Captain Davis had to contend with the Rebel fleet to secure Memphis. When he was ready to move, he had an additional advantage: a fleet of swift rams recently created by Charles Ellet Jr. A civil engineer, Ellet had selected seven civilian steamers for their speed and transformed them into effective rams. Commissioned a colonel and put in charge of the fleet, Ellet brought in several close family members as trusted subordinates, making the Ellet ram fleet something of a private domain. He nevertheless proved its worth in the naval battle near Memphis on June 6. As crowds of civilians watched from the river bluff, the Federal ironclads slowly steamed downriver as Montgomery's rams approached; then Ellet's rams dashed through the ironclad formation to surprise the Confederates. In swift-flowing action both fleets damaged the other, but the Federals won a decisive edge. The ironclads followed up Ellet's advantage to clear the river. Only one of the seven Confederate boats escaped capture or destruction, and the Yankees landed troops to secure Memphis. The Rebels managed to evacuate several incomplete boats, including the ironclad *Arkansas*, before they gave up the city. Ellet died of a leg wound suffered during the battle, but his relatives continued to command the fleet he had created.[23]

East and West

The Union sweep from Columbus to Memphis completed one leg of Halleck's effort to consolidate Federal control over Southern territory left open by the fall of Fort Donelson. But efforts were made to deny him the use of a substantial number of troops. George McClellan had driven to within nine miles of Richmond with one hundred thousand men in the Peninsula campaign of April-June 1862, but that advantage was threatened by a surprising counterattack conducted by Robert E. Lee beginning on June 26. The resulting Seven Days' campaign created a crisis in Washington as Lincoln sought to reinforce McClellan, who erroneously believed Lee outnumbered him with two hundred thousand men. Reports indicated that the Confederates were shifting Beauregard's command from Mississippi to Virginia as well, and Washington called loudly for Halleck to send help. Lincoln wanted this to be done, however, without endangering any territorial gains in the West.[24]

On June 28 Secretary of War Stanton instructed Halleck to send twenty-five thousand men east. Halleck protested that such a diversion of strength would force him to stop Buell's advance toward Chattanooga and impair his ability to hold western Tennessee. This stalled Washington's efforts to strip the West of its available manpower, as Lincoln wanted very much to seize eastern Tennessee as well as to keep all Federal gains of the past few months. As a show of good faith, Halleck began to prepare McClernand's division for shipment east, but he warned Stanton: "To surrender any territory we have acquired is certain death to all Union men in that territory." Plans hung fire until the Seven Days' campaign ended with the battle of Malvern Hill on July 1. McClellan was driven away from Richmond and the Confederates won a spectacular victory. Lincoln continued to ask for more troops, this time ten thousand infantrymen. Halleck consulted his subordinates, and they all agreed that it was impossible. As he told the president, "I must earnestly protest against surrendering what has cost us so much blood and treasure, and which, in a military point of view, is worth three Richmonds."[25]

Fortunately for the Union cause in the West, no troop transfers took place that summer. Halleck knew there was no reason to believe that Confederate troops had been transferred east, and he was convinced Washington had no idea how long Federal lines of communication were in the West. The defeat of the Seven Days had "worked them up to boiling heat," and he could resist pressure to denude Union positions in the West only through the greatest difficulty. But Lincoln, desperate to find someone to fill the vacant post of general in chief, persuaded Halleck to move east.[26]

Halleck was preceded by John Pope in a miniwave of successful Western commanders transferred east that summer. Pope later recalled how astonished he was to find the atmosphere so different in Washington than it had been in the Western theater. When he first visited Stanton in late June, he noted an "air of mystery worn by everyone, accompanied by the knowing look." It was obvious, he felt, that people looked out for their personal or partisan interests rather than the general good, "so different from my experience in the West." Pope went so far as to describe it as "a sort of moral odor of sewer gas in the air, which left a bad taste in the mouth," Pope initially resisted the plan to place him in charge of a new field army in Virginia. "Being a Western man by birth and infused with the Western feeling and sentiment," he preferred to remain with "the Western armies and their environment." Whether these sentiments were the result of hindsight or not, the truth is that Pope accepted the offer to command the Army of Virginia.[27]

Henry Halleck tried to avoid a transfer to the East as long as possible. "I have studied out and can finish the campaign in the West," he informed Sherman. "Don't understand and cannot manage affairs in the East. Moreover, do not want to have anything to do with the quarrels of Stanton and McClellan. The change does not please me, but I must obey orders." Sherman felt the same way about the two theaters of operation. "I attach more importance to the West than the East," he told Halleck. "The one has a magnificent future. . . . The other is comparatively an old country. The man who at the end of this war holds the military control of the Valley of the Mississippi will be the man." During the first few weeks of his tenure as general in chief, Halleck was absorbed in Eastern problems and had no time to think of the West. He could only urge Sherman and other Western commanders to wait until Lincoln's July 7 call for troops produced new regiments; then they could resume the offensive throughout the vast territory west of the Appalachians.[28]

Occupation Troubles

Now that the Federals were in control of the full breadth of Kentucky, and of west and middle Tennessee, they began to experience the full weight of problems associated with occupying a territory where most of the residents were inimical to their politics. Moreover, occupation exposed many other problems, such as armed resistance, economic issues, and humanitarian aid to residents made destitute by the passage of armies. The Union military was the only authority in this area for months to come; officers had to spend more time dealing with the land and its people than with enemy troops, as their desire to reclaim the seceded South was put to the test.

The civilian population reacted in diverse ways to the Yankee occupiers. Many of them fled rather than endure subjugation, yet most remained in their homes. A variety of opinions about the war existed everywhere; the only difference lay in which way the majority of residents leaned in any given area. The near presence of Union troops tended to influence civilian opinion and action. Because Federal commanders could not occupy every town and village, they tended to garrison the more significant communities on or near lines of communication. Instead of a well-defined front that stretched across the landscape, the zone separating Union occupation from both Confederate territory and neutral ground was a patchwork. Around every community that boasted a Union garrison, there developed an area patrolled by the Federals but not constantly occupied by them. Beyond that zone lay a no-man's-land until one neared the presence of a Confederate force.[29]

The Federals learned to pay close attention to the civilians among whom they worked. Commander Stephen A. Hurlbut advised a subordinate to watch the most disloyal residents of Bolivar, Tennessee; if they left town in a hurry, it probably foretold an attack by guerrillas. When Grant led the first occupation troops into Memphis, he was surprised at how much time he spent listening to residents who brought him all sorts of problems, stories, and requests. As the occupation lengthened, army commanders came to understand that dealing with the myriad challenges of the civilian population was one of their chief concerns. Sorting out the loyal, the disloyal, and the neutral residents became their worst headache.[30]

Political regeneration was an early concern in the Union occupation of western and middle Tennessee, a matter that military governor Andrew Johnson pushed strongly. Johnson hoped to inspire and direct the readmission of Tennessee into the Union through state-level action as soon as the Rebels were entirely driven out, and he encouraged local action as a prelude to that happy event. In fact, even army commanders saw grassroots political action as an early goal of their occupation, but it was stymied by a number of factors. The most consequential was the lack of consistent direction from Nashville. Johnson wanted not only to reconstruct loyal politics but also to punish the traitors of the state. "We have all come to the conclusion here that treason must be made odious and traitors punished and impoverished," he informed Lincoln in July 1862. "I am doing the best I can." This harsh policy made enemies more readily than friends among those Tennesseeans who might have been cajoled back into the fold. As time went on Johnson became more cynical in his hopes for rejuvenating the mass of Tennesseeans, and he therefore enacted harsher policies. This led to a split among the state's Unionists, and more and more Johnson relied on his eastern Tennessee cronies to support his increasingly controversial military governership.[31]

There was more success in resurrecting local government, at least in the important commercial port of Memphis. When Sherman took charge of the city, he encouraged the municipal government to continue to function and shared with it responsibility for maintaining law and order. Military needs, however, would take precedence in any clash between the city and the army. "I prefer that the city authorities should execute their powers vigorously, not timidly; suppress crimes, keep your streets guarded, lighted, and cleaned," Sherman informed Mayor John Park. The city could impose its own taxes, but state and county taxes could not be collected until the state and county governments became fully functioning. Meanwhile, if the Memphis authority needed additional funds, Sherman offered to use the military to raise money by assessing the wealth of pro-Confederates. Sherman created a tight alliance between the preexisting city government and the Union occupiers, even using his provost marshal to supervise the 100-man Memphis police force. He insisted on a strict separation of authority between the civil and military in Memphis. Sherman also required civil authorities to maintain a curfew during the night and to treat runaway slaves in town according to preexisting city laws that applied only to free blacks.[32]

Federal commanders all across the newly occupied territory faced similar problems and dealt with them in similar ways. Initially, they endeavored to discipline their own troops to prevent plundering of civilian property, hoping this would demonstrate to the local residents that they had everything to gain from cooperating with their new masters. John A. Logan urged a subordinate to "cultivate a conservative, friendly feeling with the people where you may be." Logan directed that his officers either pay for property taken from civilians or offer them receipts that could be redeemed from the Federal government after the war. When soldiers pillaged civilian houses anyway, commanders often issued general orders deprecating the occurrence and threatening to punish officers if the rank-and-file perpetrators could not be identified.[33]

No one deplored soldier plundering more than Sherman. When it became necessary for his division to feed off the surrounding countryside, he sought to reduce the size of foraging parties in order to lessen the possibility of pillaging while his men performed what he called "a delicate right" to subsist off the occupied land. As he moved his command to Memphis in July 1862, Sherman noted that it seemed to have many more horses and mules than allowed by army regulations. He ordered his officers to count the animals and send the excess to his quartermaster. After arriving at Memphis, Sherman clamped down on soldier misconduct so as not to arouse the antagonism of its residents. One of Sherman's regimental commanders, Thomas Kilby Smith of the 54th Ohio, commented: "Soldiers are great thieves on principle; when they can't steal from the enemy, they circumvent each other to keep in practice." Kilby Smith came to this conclusion when his clothes and books began to disappear from his tent one at a time.[34]

The next stage in commanders' efforts to deal with the civilian population was to use the oath of allegiance to the Union as a litmus test of loyalty. Andrew Johnson began doing this in May 1862, sorting out the mayor and city administrators in Nashville, in addition to clergymen and newspaper editors. When Sherman began to require loyalty oaths in Memphis, more than seventeen hundred residents reportedly left the city in three days rather than swear them. At Trenton, Tennessee, Major General Grenville M. Dodge arrested any civilian who refused to take the oath. According to Union authorities stationed at Columbus, Kentucky, ex-Confederate soldiers who were living as civilians behind Union lines not only had to take the oath of allegiance but also surrender their weapons. The provost marshals assigned to individual commands were responsible for dealing with political prisoners.[35]

Whether taking the oath helped the cause of the Union occupiers or not is an open question. There is plenty of evidence that Johnson's oath policy in Nashville made more enemies than friends. But General James S. Negley at Columbia thought the policy worked to tame formerly outspoken pro-Confederates by branding anyone who refused to take the oath as an enemy of the occupiers. Many Union soldiers themselves thought it was a farce.

Richard W. Johnson recalled that his men often joked about oath taking. "'I have got a rattlesnake,'" one would say. "'What shall be done with him?'" The answer was, "Administer the oath and let him go home."[36]

If oath taking did not make good Union citizens of the inhabitants, harsher measures soon followed. Negley came to advocate the arrest of "a few of the active secessionists" of Columbia to prevent them from intimidating Unionists. In fact, Federal commanders across the occupied South were ready to arrest civilians who harbored sympathy for the Rebel cause. They did so too often in the eyes of many commanders. Grant cautioned against the promiscuous arrest of civilians on the word of a supposedly loyal citizen who refused to testify in court. Arresting people was especially attractive to Union occupiers as a stern measure to counteract guerrilla activity. Since it was difficult to find and catch guerrillas, it was easier to put pressure on the civilians who were known to aid and support them. Andrew Johnson threatened to arrest five or more Confederate sympathizers for every Unionist who was attacked. When a group of civilians killed one Federal and wounded three others who were part of a foraging party near Moscow, Tennessee, Sherman rounded up twenty-five civilians and planned to hold them until they revealed the culprits. "I am satisfied we have no other remedy for this ambush firing than to hold the neighborhood fully responsible, though the punishment may fall on the wrong parties."[37]

Arrests often went hand in hand with seizure of property as a way to punish rebellious citizens. Commanders made up property lists of those individuals who were known to sympathize with the rebellion. When Grant sent an expedition to Pocahontas, Tennessee, he authorized subordinates to seize all useful property from pro-Confederate families along the way. After Congress passed the Second Confiscation Act in July 1862, commanders in the field usually made a distinction between their normal seizure of property and the provisions of the act. "We have nothing to do with confiscation," Sherman informed a quartermaster. "We only deal with possession, and therefore the necessity of a strict accountability, because the United States assumes the place of trustee." In fact, Lincoln required that the attorney general assume responsibility for implementing the Confiscation Act, taking it out of the hands of the military. It was obvious, however, that soldiers were in a position to play a large role in seizing the property of anyone who supported the rebellion, so the line between enforcing the Confiscation Act and the routine seizure of property that the military authorities had long practiced before the passage of the act was blurred. In truth, military commanders rarely considered what they were doing as implementing the letter of the act, even if they considered the congressional law to morally support what they intended to do anyway. The military occupiers had their own reasons for taking the property of civilians who sympathized with the rebellion: they took it when they thought it necessary; they also took needed supplies to feed their commands, regardless of congressional action.[38]

Most Union soldiers believed that seizure of property hurt Rebel sympathizers far more than requiring them to take the oath. By August, after two months of occupation, Sherman believed that Memphis residents were more resigned to Yankee rule. He attributed this to his and Grant's policies regarding seizure of their material possessions. The residents were "about as sensitive about their property as Yankees."[39]

Only a small percentage of the civilians in occupied areas resorted to violence as a means of showing their hatred of the Federals; nevertheless, they caused enormous problems for the occupiers. In late May 1862, Federal boats transporting troops to Pittsburg Landing found the body of a Union soldier floating in the Tennessee River. He had been shot through the heart. The perpetrator was never found, but this small instance was indicative of what was to come. Southern guerrillas, though small in number, tended to come from families with deep roots in their local communities—networks of support they could rely on to sustain their lonely endeavors. The guerrillas fought private, or communal, wars; their actions were not directly supported by the Confederate military, and they recognized no higher authority than their own self-appointed mission. In truth, while many guerrillas may have been motivated by devotion to the "cause," as time went on they seem to have fought for themselves more than for the Confederacy.[40]

To the Union occupiers, any small accretion of guerrillas spelled trouble. Halleck urged Grant "to clean out West Tennessee and North Mississippi" by arresting civilians who supported them. "Handle that class without gloves, and take their property for public use." In late July Dodge warned of "a general uprising among the guerrillas along the Obion and Hatchie Rivers." He received immediate word of it through friendly civilians and dispatched companies to pursue three bands that took off in different directions. Dodge urged his subordinates to move fast and strike quickly as the best way to break up the bands. James B. McPherson complained of "almost constant interruption" on the Memphis and Charleston Railroad by August. Guerrillas burned bridges and water tanks and fired into passing trains. In one month crews had to rebuild seven bridges between Tuscumbia and Decatur, Alabama, hampering Buell's lumbering effort to advance toward Chattanooga. In one incident, guerrillas fired 150 bullets into the cars and engine of a train near Courtland, mortally wounding the conductor and injuring other crewmen. In another instance, guerrillas took up a rail and forced an engine off the track. The 25-man train guard fought them off, but the guerrillas managed to burn the engine before they left. Colonel Rodney Mason surrendered the town of Clarksville, Tennessee, when about 800 Confederates (probably roving cavalrymen rather than guerrillas) attacked his 150-man garrison. They were joined by a "large number" of disgruntled civilians who helped the Confederates. Other Federal troops were sent to restore control, but Mason was cashiered from the army.[41]

It is possible that the eight hundred Rebels who intimidated Mason were members of a partisan unit. The Confederate government authorized the creation of partisan bands in April 1862 and tried to exert some degree of control over them. It was an effort to regulate a developing irregular war over which the government authorities had little control. Some partisan commanders listened to Richmond and others did not. When the Union commander of the post at Bolivar arrested two men of Colonel R. V. Richardson's 1st Tennessee Partisan Rangers and threatened to try them for murder and arson, Richardson protested that they were prisoners of war, not civilian criminals. Federal troops had plundered Richardson's own house and threatened his wife and children with bodily harm. Richardson declared he would kill twice as many Yankee soldiers if the Union officer hanged his men at Bolivar. Further, he would kill on sight any Federals caught harassing civilians and burn twice as much property belonging to pro-Unionists. By March 1863, Richardson commanded more than a thousand men. While he attacked Union transportation systems, he also plundered civilians who allied with the occupiers and did not always obey orders from Confederate authorities. Richmond eventually revoked his commission as a partisan.[42]

The next stage in treating rebellious citizens in the occupied West was deportation from Union lines. By mid-July Grant asked Halleck's permission to do so in Memphis, citing the "great many families of officers in the rebel army here who are very violent." Halleck supported the idea, and many of the most vocal Southern sympathizers were forced to move south into unoccupied territory or areas controlled by the Confederates. The same was done at Shelbyville, Tennessee. Commanders justified this somewhat drastic measure by noting that Confederate sympathizers had disowned allegiance to the U.S. government and deserved to be "amongst *their friends*." Their continued presence within Union lines opened the possibility of spying on Federal forces as well. However, as Sherman remarked in Memphis, if everyone who was not friendly was compelled to leave, "but few will be left." So he determined to be patient and deport only when necessary.[43]

For Sherman, at least, the dangers of guerrilla warfare were highlighted when shipping on the Mississippi and its tributaries became a target. In

August, guerrillas boarded and burned two steamers as they lay at the bank of the Tennessee River near the mouth of Duck River, loading and unloading cargo. About the same time, guerrillas fired on the steamer *Champion* as it made its way down the Mississippi near Columbus. A local Union officer captured twenty-two guerrillas who were thought to be the culprits and wanted to try them before a military commission. "The River is far from being a safe place for boats," Sherman commented to his wife in late August, when he reported two more attacks on steamers. In early October, after guerrillas fired on the *Forest Queen* and *J.J. Roe* near Randolph, Tennessee, with women and children on board both vessels, Sherman burned the entire village in retribution. He announced that if the attacks continued, captured guerrillas would be put on boats or families of Rebel soldiers would be deported from within Union lines.[44]

Sherman's threats did not work. A short time later, the Confederates fired on two steamers with a twelve-pound howitzer; both received minor damage. Sherman again publicized his policy, declaring that "this practice of firing on boats must be punished with terrible severity." The two boats had no guns or soldiers on board, only civilian passengers and food for Memphis citizens. But not until the *Gladiator* and three other vessels were attacked did Sherman implement his plan. In the case of the *Gladiator*, two civilians were killed, several were wounded, and the boat was set on fire. Sherman chose by lot forty names from a list his provost marshal had prepared and required that the entire families move at least twenty-five miles from Memphis. This measure caused a temporary lull in boat attacks. Sherman defended his action against all who protested: "The absolute destruction of Memphis New Orleans & every city town and hamlet of the South would not be too severe a punishment to a people for attempting to interfere with the navigation of the Mississippi." Sherman's attitude toward dealing with a hostile civilian populace was hardening with the passage of time. "We cannot change the hearts of those people of the South," he wrote Grant, "but we can make war so terrible that they" would not resort to it again. Southerners "cannot be made to love us," he continued, "but may be made to fear us."[45]

For military and geopolitical reasons, Sherman was unshaken in his belief that the Mississippi River was the most important element in the Union war effort. The Confederates needed to realize that the people of the Northwest meant "to fight till the death for the Mississippi River. This is my hobby," he admitted to Grant. He believed that firm control of the stream was the key to Union success. Although the Federals could send expeditions into the vast interior of the Deep South to cut rail lines and disrupt Confederate operations, they should generally leave the heart of the Confederacy alone, for it was too inhospitable a place for major action. In Sherman's view, the Mississippi was "the great artery of America, and whatever power holds it, holds the continent." To him, the idea of invading the Deep South was daunting. "To attempt to hold all the South would demand an army too large even to think of," he observed in a letter to his brother John.[46]

In every occupied community, opinions about the war were divided. To a greater or lesser extent, some residents continued to favor the Confederacy, others were pro-Union but often afraid to speak openly, while the rest seemed indifferent or feared both sides. Federal occupiers tried exacting oaths of allegiance, arresting people, and deporting them as methods of suppressing one class and encouraging another to come forward, but these methods never fully worked. Grant believed that using the army to exert calm, as well as restoring normal activities like commerce and mail delivery, would help a great deal. If the Union army could create "the assurance that we can hold" the territory, the people would eventually reconcile themselves to it. It was important, however, that the Federals not lose any significant battles, for much depended on appearances of strength. To Grant's way of thinking, most Southerners living in occupied territories were disloyal to the U.S. government because they feared the consequences to themselves if the Yankees were driven away and the Confederates reoccupied their area. Many other commanders agreed and tried to steer a moderate course in treating civilians.[47]

But, as time went on, the military occupiers tended to harden their attitudes and their treatment without any apparent softening of the civilian mood. Thomas Kilby Smith was amazed at the depth of the hatred toward Yankees he encountered near Memphis; he was ready to conclude that Southerners could never be reconciled to Northern rule. "Children are reared to curse us," he reported, while adults were fed such "strange and absurd" stories about the Northerners that many looked at him "as if I were a wild beast in a menagerie." Even the slaves believed the Yankees had black skin.[48]

Sherman also came more and more to assume the worst of Southern civilians and to believe they could not be won over except through force. As the Federal armies passed through Southern territory, "the war closes in behind and leaves the Same enmity behind," he wrote. If it was impossible to reclaim their loyalty to the old flag, then the only recourse — in Sherman's opinion — was to depopulate the South and encourage good Northern patriots to replace the recalcitrants. By August 1862 Sherman was convinced that the Federals could not count on finding a large proportion of Southerners who were quietly loyal to the United States and waiting for an opportunity to come forth and reclaim their own land. Instead, the level of Southern commitment to independence was deep. The only recourse was to eliminate slavery, dispossess the worst among the Southerners of their land, and ship them out of the country. He expected it would take half a century to finish the job of reconstructing the Union.[49]

Many other Federal commanders tended to agree with Sherman's pessimistic view. To a subordinate at Tuscumbia, Alabama, William S. Rosecrans relayed these instructions: "Notify the inhabitants within reach of your lines that any words or actions hostile to the Government will oblige you to treat the parties as enemies, who can receive only the rights of belligerents, whose property belongs to the United States. The women and children will be ordered beyond our lines, their property seized for the benefit of the United States, and their houses burned."[50]

Commerce

The network of prewar commerce was decisively broken by military operations, but there was every reason to restore it after the shooting stopped and Union garrisons were established in key towns. How to do this was somewhat baffling at the outset. When Grant took possession of Memphis in June 1862, he reported that a board of trade had been set up "to regulate what goods are authorized to be received and who [are] authorized to sell." This worked well enough in a large, commercial center like Memphis but was impractical in smaller towns. Grant asked Halleck for instructions. In his response of early July, Halleck informed Grant that the U.S. Treasury Department would be in charge of issuing permits to trade on the Mississippi River, and the army must regulate traffic to see that no material useful to the Confederates was shipped. Grant also sought to reduce the use of hard currency in transactions south of Cairo to keep gold out of Confederate reach. He directed subordinates to inspect the baggage of traders moving south to keep specie out of the area, alerting them to pay special attention to Jewish merchants.[51]

With steamboat traffic to Memphis in full swing, Sherman nevertheless wondered if the concept of "'letting trade follow the flag'" was counterproductive. He thought it mostly benefited greedy speculators from the North. The worst problem associated with trade was that it promoted the flow of contraband goods into areas where they were accessible to the enemy. To curb this flow, Sherman began restricting access to Memphis by land, posting guards on five roads to search the baggage of all travelers. Guards continually found salt, percussion caps, and clothing in the possession of people trying to leave town, only to have them confiscated. Sherman also clamped down on the circulation of gold specie, certain it would find its way into Confederate hands and be used to purchase weapons and other matériel. Though he encouraged area farmers to bring their produce into Memphis, he believed that a complete stoppage of commerce was the best policy to follow if the government meant to conduct a vigorous war policy.[52]

But a complete cessation of commerce was not possible, if nothing else because residents had to eat. Thus Union occupiers were forced to deal with all the headaches that accompanied trade. The opening of the Mississippi down to Memphis led to a flood of Northern vendors looking for ways to make a quick profit; Sherman was convinced they had few scruples about what they sold and who they sold it to. Memphis became a port of entry for a variety of goods sought by the Confederates, many of them also needed by the civilian population. While it was easy enough to identify guns and ammunition as contraband of war, seemingly innocuous items such as salt and clothing could be used by anyone in or out of uniform in the South. Sherman might have worried less if he had known that many Confederates felt the same way about trade. They felt that the flow of goods between Memphis and the Confederate-held interior of Mississippi weakened the Rebel cause. It made the civilian population dependent on Northern commerce for their survival and created an opening for Yankee spying.[53]

Of all items associated with trade, however, cotton was the most prominent. It was America's most valuable agricultural product, at least in terms of ready cash to be made in the Northern market and overseas, and the war had virtually stopped its export from the South. The temptation to turn a fast profit by buying and selling a few bales created enormous problems for the military occupiers. As Lincoln put it, "The question of profit controls all, regardless of whether the cotton seller is loyal or rebel, or whether he is paid in corn-meal or gun-powder." Cotton buyers worked in occupied areas and no-man's-land alike, and, lacking other means of transportation, relied on the army to help them move their bales to shipping points. Traders offered large sums of money to officers at Bolivar, Tennessee, and officer Leonard F. Ross thought the army should participate and make money for the government. Initially, military policy favored the shipment of privately owned cotton for a fee. U.S. Treasury Department regulations also mandated that the army should not restrict the cotton trade in any way except where violations of the permit policy occurred. The army was not to seize cotton directly, either, except to get it away from Confederate hands. If the cotton was owned by a Rebel, it could be sold at public auction and the proceeds pocketed by the government. If owned by a loyal citizen, the money was given to him, minus transportation costs incurred by the government.[54]

By late summer 1862, however, government policy changed. It became advantageous for the North to facilitate the flow of Southern cotton into Northern and foreign markets, so all restrictions on the use of gold to buy it were dropped. The army was encouraged to offer every help it could to anyone who found and purchased cotton, and to seize the white gold outright whenever possible. It was a controversial move that made the army an agent of commerce, with consequent demoralization of the troops and widespread dealing by greedy army officers. Fortunately, the policy was temporary, and after a few months the worst effects of it lessened, but it greatly increased the problems associated with administering a captured population.[55]

Fully aware of the Northern desire for cotton, the Confederates sought to deny it as much as possible. In the wake of Fort Donelson, the Confederate Congress passed an act requiring authorities to destroy cotton and tobacco rather than allow it to remain in abandoned areas. After the evacuation of Corinth, the Yankees had access to wide swaths of territory in northern Mississippi that were filled with cotton. Some Confederate commanders in the area were ready to implement the congressional law. Mansfield Lovell thought such a measure would "bring the people of the North and of Europe to an exact appreciation of the determination of our people to be free." Orders went out to burn cotton in danger of Union seizure both on land and along the river. Four boats ranged the Mississippi between Memphis and Vicksburg so troops could burn all they could find up to ten miles inland, while a company of partisans reportedly destroyed thirty thousand bales in Tennessee and Mississippi. It was but a partial implementation of the congressional plan, which did little more than put a small dent in the available supply.[56]

One need only look at what happened at Helena, Arkansas, to understand that most of the cotton in the valley was intact. This river town, located about sixty miles south of Memphis, was occupied by Brigadier General Samuel Ryan Curtis's Army of the Southwest in July, after a long campaign through southwestern Missouri and across northern Arkansas. Since Halleck could not scrounge up troops to continue the advance to Vicksburg, Helena was the southernmost Union outpost on the Mississippi for months to come. Curtis scoured the banks for miles south of Helena to seize craft capable of transporting Confederate troops, but a shortage of Union shipping prevented him from operating against Little Rock or Vicksburg. Instead, Helena became the focal point of intense cotton trading and the target of hundreds of runaway slaves attempting to flee their plantations. Curtis treated the blacks leniently, offering free papers to two thousand of them and helping them to sell a bale or two of cotton for their subsistence. He also put the blacks to work on fortifications or gave them cash outright.[57]

The trade in cotton at Helena became almost scandalous, and Curtis tried to regulate it as much as possible. Initially, he allowed anyone to trade "but soon found my camp infested with Jews, secessionists, and spies." Then he began to issue permits only to a select few. Curtis sometimes confiscated loads if they were purchased from civilians of suspected disloyalty. He allowed boats under government contract to haul privately owned cotton at three to four dollars per bale—normally at night, when the army's demand for hauling capacity was less pressing. Controversy swirled when disaffected merchants, who were refused permits, spread rumors that the general himself was profiting from cotton trade. Curtis's liberal treatment of blacks also rubbed some of his more conservative officers the wrong way. Worse still, many subordinate officers became fascinated by the opportunity to make a profit in cotton, investing their private funds with those of the traders to acquire some bales. They often used their men in blatant ways to secure and transport the white gold. "We are willing to take cotton by force of arms for the Government but will not do so for an officer's private benefit," Wisconsin soldier Thomas Priestly wrote home. When Curtis was transferred to a higher command in St. Louis, his successor, Frederick Steele, reversed most of his liberal policies regarding blacks at Helena but continued to allow the trade in cotton.[58]

Curtis had established an enlightened policy toward runaway slaves. While Grant never duplicated it, he did feel compassion for the people often called "contraband," because their legal status was as yet undefined. Grant used them as laborers around army camps. "I don't know what is to become of these poor people in the end," he wrote his sister, "but its weakning [sic] the enemy to take them from them." By early November, the problem became so acute that Grant improvised a policy to deal with the thousands of blacks seeking aid. He appointed Chaplain John Eaton Jr. of the 27th Ohio to take charge of the contraband and establish a camp at Grand Junction, Tennessee. Eaton was to organize the able-bodied in work details to pick cotton on abandoned plantations. It was a landmark effort to systematize the use of contraband as organized laborers, and the first camp was followed by several more across the occupied South. Secretary of the Treasury Salmon P. Chase had been concerned that Union officials were not taking advantage of the only class of Southerners who were genuinely loyal. Now, Grant was beginning to do that in an organized way. Moreover, the Confederates were quite sensitive to the possibility of their enemy making use of slaves, either as laborers or potentially as soldiers. In July 1862 Simeon

Tidwell was tried by a Confederate military commission at Tupelo, Mississippi, on charges of stealing slaves to give them to the Federal troops. He was found guilty and sentenced to be executed. Whether the sentence was carried out is unknown, but the trial and its conclusion is a powerful indication of how harshly the Confederates were willing to deal with anyone threatening the security of their slave labor force.[59]

5 } The Gulf

Federal authorities had enough resources to operate large numbers of troops supported by naval power along selected areas of the Confederate coast. In addition to incursions along the North Carolina and South Carolina shores, they also planned to strike at New Orleans and open the lower Mississippi Valley to Union control. Ship Island, which lay sixty miles southeast of the river's mouth, could serve as a staging area. Vessels transporting an invading force from ports in the Northeast were able to stop at the island, which had been used as a supply depot for Union blockaders, before mounting an attempt to steam up the great river. Two masonry strongholds, Fort Jackson and Fort St. Philip, were located at a bend in the river sixty miles south of New Orleans. Engineer officer John G. Barnard proposed a plan to capture the city with a land force of twenty thousand troops and naval support, then proceed northward to take Natchez, Vicksburg, and Memphis. Barnard believed this "would bring us almost to the close of the war." He envisioned occupying the entire Gulf Coast. Barnard knew that Federal control of the coastal shipping lanes offered enormous advantages. If nothing else, the capture of New Orleans would close down the major commercial port of the Confederacy.[1]

By early December 1861 significant numbers of Union troops began to occupy Ship Island. It was "a long, narrow strip of land," according to John W. Phelps, barely a few feet above water level. Five miles long and up to twelve hundred feet wide, Ship Island had a masonry coastal fort but no civilian houses. Fine white sand blew around with every gust of wind, "causing great irritation to eyes, skin and stomach." By March 23, 1862, approximately fifteen thousand Northeastern troops gathered in this place under Major General Benjamin F. Butler to strike at New Orleans. Captain David G. Farragut was named commander of the Western Gulf Blockading Squadron and charged with supporting Butler's mission. George McClellan, in giving Butler command of the Department of the Gulf in February, urged him to continue upriver after taking the Crescent

David Glasgow Farragut. (Library of Congress, LC-DIG-cwpb-05210)

City and cooperate with the forces moving down the Mississippi Valley from the north. Butler was then to strike at Mobile and Pensacola.[2]

The Confederates were keenly aware of the significance of New Orleans and of its vulnerability to a seaborne attack. Future secretary of war James A. Seddon called the city "the commercial emporium of the South" posted on "the great artery of trade in the West." But Confederate resources were limited, and there were many equally significant places in the new nation that demanded protection. The Confederate commander at New Orleans, Major General Mansfield Lovell, who had assumed his post in October 1861, did all he could to arrange for the defense of the city. Lovell dug fortifications, acquired guns and boats, and mobilized local troops. But Grant's drive up the Tennessee and Cumberland Rivers compelled the Confederates to strip Lovell of many of his gunboats and rams, as well as several of his best regiments. The current Confederate secretary of war, Judah P. Benjamin, told Lovell that "New Orleans is to be defended from above by defeating the enemy at Columbus; the forces now withdrawn from you are for the defense of your own command." It was an argument that did not convince Lovell, who pointed out that a fleet of oceangoing vessels was beginning to enter the mouth of the Mississippi that appeared more formidable than the river fleet descending from the north. "This city has been already too much weakened by the detachments of all kinds," the general complained as he refused to give up the last six warships under his control. The fall of Donelson prompted Lovell to move available supplies from Baton Rouge to New Orleans, because the state capital "could be taken and all the public property there destroyed by half a dozen gunboats at a dash."[3]

With President Davis's approval, Lovell declared martial law in the parishes around New Orleans in mid-March 1862. He justified the action based on the city's large, heterogeneous population. The people of New Orleans, who numbered 170,000, were "excitable" and "easily led into excesses." There were so many competing interest groups among the citizens, "each jealous of the other," that it was "difficult to govern" the city. Lovell required all white men over sixteen years of age to register with one of his provost marshals and to take an oath of allegiance to the Confederate government. Persons who arrived in New Orleans from a Northern state after May 21, 1861, were liable to be arrested unless a provost marshal issued them a permit to stay.[4]

The Federal attack on New Orleans occurred at an opportune time, when Lovell's resources were thin and Confederate attention was focused on affairs in Tennessee. On April 18 a fleet of mortar boats opened fire on Forts Jackson and St. Philip, pumping fourteen hundred rounds into their works and setting the barracks in Fort Jackson on fire. The Union's nineteen schooners, each with a thirteen-inch mortar, continued to fire for several days. Farragut judged that the mortar fire would not silence the forts so he ran his fleet past the works on the night of April 23, crossing the broken barricade of hulks that Confederate engineers had erected across the Mississippi. It was an exciting encounter as Union ships engaged Rebel gunboats and the ironclad *Louisiana*. A fire raft set adrift came alongside Farragut's flagship, the *Hartford*, but on the whole Union losses were light. Only one vessel was sunk and one was seriously damaged. Farragut lost 36 men killed and 135 wounded in passing the two forts. Now there were seventeen Yankee vessels, mounting 192 guns, between the coastal forts and New Orleans.[5]

Lovell had only three volunteer regiments, plus three thousand militia troops, to defend the city against Farragut's guns and Butler's army. He evacuated New Orleans, retiring by rail to Camp Moore nearly eighty miles to the north. When Farragut's ships neared the docks on April 25, they discovered many fires started by the retreating Confederates by torching cotton, warehouses, and other resources. Another ironclad, the *Mississippi*, came floating down the river in a mass of flames. In the rain that afternoon, Farragut sent two officers into the city to demand that Mayor John T. Monroe surrender New Orleans. Because Monroe needed time to think, the two officers returned to the flagship through an angry mob that evening.[6]

The next day, April 26, a contingent of Federals landed and raised the national flag over the U.S. Mint building, but a citizen named William Munford tore it down in defiance. Another round of negotiations with Monroe resulted in his declaration that New Orleans was an open city, and he formally invited the Federals to enter and take possession. On the night of April 27, the garrison of Fort Jackson mutinied and both forts gave up the next day. The fall of New Orleans led to the Confederate evacuation of Pensacola, Florida, in May, but Mobile, the other major port on the Gulf Coast, remained in Confederate hands for the rest of the war.[7]

Mansfield Lovell was grieved that he had to relinquish the Crescent City and tried to work out a fallback position for the meager Confederate resources under his command. He viewed Vicksburg as the ultimate last stand of the Rebels in the Mississippi Valley and wanted to fortify the city, but he had no heavy guns or engineers to spare. By early May, with the Federals largely confining themselves to New Orleans for the time being, Lovell was willing to remain closer to that important city and leave the defense of Vicksburg to other commanders. Fearing the effect on Confederate morale if he retired too far north, he instead sought to keep the Yankees hemmed in around their prize for as long as possible. Lovell counted on the deleterious climate of the Gulf to harass the Federals. He also defended himself at every turn, reminding Beauregard that the troops he had accumulated to defend New Orleans had been taken away from him in March and had fought well at Shiloh. But, Lovell admitted, even with twenty thousand troops he could not have stopped Farragut's ships from steaming up the river to demand the surrender of New Orleans.[8]

If the Confederates could not hold the city, at least they could try to burn the most important crop of the South within reach of the occupiers. A resident of Tuscaloosa, Alabama, told the new secretary of war, George W. Randolph, that the loss of New Orleans "has produced fear and alarm amongst the people," yet authorities could contain the ill effects of that loss by systematically burning cotton in the lower Mississippi Valley. The "South is essential to the civilized world," he believed, because of its production of the staple, so why not "let them suffer while we are a ruined people." It was a notion that resonated with many Confederates; Secretary Randolph had already issued orders to Lovell to do just that. Soon after evacuating the city, the general called on all patriotic Southerners to burn their crop. Citing Northern claims that "the remotest commercial interest of the civilized world will have cause to side with them," now that Lincoln's men controlled the lower valley and could protect cotton exports, Lovell reminded Louisianans that their land would be worthless anyway if slavery were destroyed during the process of fighting the war.[9]

Louisiana governor Thomas O. Moore admitted that the fall of New Orleans had a disheartening effect on the residents of his state; many were "demoralized" by the news. They feared Federal raids now that the river was open to Union ships. Moore also worried that communication between the west and east banks of the Mississippi would be cut off, a considerable problem given that Louisiana was split by the great stream. The state's adjutant general issued an order ending all trade with the city, but some devoted Southerners were afraid that Union control of the port might lead to a movement within the state to have Louisiana secede from the Confederacy and form an alliance with the North to protect its commercial interests.[10]

Vicksburg

Reeling from the loss of the upper Mississippi River and its mouth, Confederate authorities became desperate to hold on to what was left. Vicksburg was the most important strongpoint between Helena and New Orleans. Located about 225 miles north of New Orleans and about the same distance south of Helena, it commanded the river from atop high bluffs on the east side of the stream and just below a very sharp bend in the channel. In late April Beauregard sent his trusted engineer, David B. Harris, to begin the enormous task of fortifying Vicksburg. He also mobilized a large force of black laborers to help Harris. Beauregard warned the engineer to evacuate Vicksburg if the Federals got there before him and retire fifty miles east to Jackson, the state capital, destroying the railroad between the two cities.[11]

Harris reached Vicksburg in time to lay out the origins of its river battery system as Brigadier General Martin Luther Smith took command of thirty-six hundred men and eighteen heavy guns in the town on May 12. Six days later, on May 18, Farragut's ships arrived with about fifteen hundred soldiers on board, under the command of Brigadier General Thomas W. Williams. When the Federals issued a demand that Vicksburg surrender, Smith refused. Many of its residents fled, but those who remained strongly supported the Confederates against the first Union attempt to take their city. The Federals opened fire on May 26 and continued the bombardment sporadically until mid-June, when reinforcements doubled Williams's strength and the mortar boats were brought up from New Orleans to add their weight to the bombardment.[12]

The Confederates also increased their strength at Vicksburg by mid-June, with the addition of fifteen thousand men. Major General Earl Van Dorn arrived to assume overall command of the Confederate forces on June 28, the very day that Farragut took two sloops and six gunboats past the Harris batteries, fighting their way upstream, and taking post just above the town. Here they met Lieutenant Colonel Alfred W. Ellet's four rams, which had steamed downriver to this point four days earlier. Charles H. Davis's gunboat fleet also came down from the north by July 1, effecting the first union of the northern and southern naval columns on the Mississippi River. Meanwhile, Williams did not feel strong enough to attack Vicksburg directly with his meager force. Instead, he used the troops to dig a canal across De Soto Point, the peninsula formed by the giant bend of the river opposite Vicksburg, hoping to enable Union boats to bypass the Confederate batteries. From the vantage point of Washington, it was assumed that Butler's overall plan to clear out the Mississippi River would bear fruit any day. As late as mid-June, Beauregard himself believed that Vicksburg would fall.[13]

With the exception of land-based artillery, the Confederates had virtually nothing with which to oppose the Union ships until the css *Arkansas* was finished at Yazoo City. Van Dorn urged its commander, Lieutenant Isaac N. Brown, to strike immediately, and Brown started out on July 14. The next day, he attacked three Federal boats ten miles from the mouth of the Yazoo River, scattering them downstream, and entered the Mississippi. Brown then steamed through the combined Union fleet as it mostly lay at anchor, firing away. The Confederate ship was somewhat damaged by return fire but

css Arkansas *running through the Federal fleet. This Confederate ironclad took the Unionists by surprise when it steamed out of the Yazoo into the Mississippi River on July 14, 1862.* (Johnson and Buel, *Battles and Leaders,* 3:556)

managed to reach the docks at Vicksburg. It was a humiliating experience for the Federals, and Farragut was forced to steam south past the Vicksburg batteries on the night of July 15 to protect the mortar schooners below the city. He did so without loss. Davis conducted a strike against the Rebel ironclad at dawn on July 22, sending three of his boats to ram and fire at the *Arkansas* as it still lay at the Vicksburg docks. Though damaged during the assault, the Confederate vessel survived all Federal attempts to neutralize its potential threat.[14]

By the time the *Arkansas* was operational, a decided note of frustration became evident in Union reports on the operations against Vicksburg. While the Federals dominated the river, despite the presence of the Rebel ironclad, they had far too few infantrymen to take the bluff city. Moreover, neither Halleck nor Butler could spare additional troops for Williams. "The finest strategical point on the river is neglected by" the army, complained David Dixon Porter to Farragut, even though Vicksburg was "of more importance than any point on the Mississippi." The Federals could not afford to risk their river fleets at such a distance from effective land support too long. Farragut sailed downstream, taking on Williams's troops and depositing them at Baton Rouge before proceeding to New Orleans. Charles Davis steamed northward, leaving some of his boats at Helena. Forty percent of Van Dorn's infantry force was now ill, greatly reducing his effective strength; Williams's men also suffered a high rate of sickness. It was obvious that the Federals needed to mount a much larger effort to take Vicksburg, and the Confederates would have to match it as best they could to retain control of the city.[15]

The Confederates justifiably celebrated their victory by pointing out that the Federals were within range of Vicksburg for sixty-seven days yet failed to dismount a single Rebel gun. Southern losses amounted to only seven killed and fifteen wounded, though two civilians were killed by the Union bombardment. One of them, a Mrs. Gamble, had endeared herself to the Rebel soldiers by tending the sick and injured in army hospitals. She was "a martyr to the cause she loved," observed Martin L. Smith.[16]

Baton Rouge

Van Dorn followed up the Union retreat from Vicksburg by dispatching Breckinridge's division of four thousand men to Camp Moore by railroad. This Confederate camp of instruction was located only 60 miles northeast of Baton Rouge, the Federally occupied capital of Louisiana. General Thomas Williams established a garrison of twenty-five hundred men to hold the city, which lay 150 miles south of Vicksburg. Van Dorn wanted possession of Baton Rouge to serve as the southern shoulder of a Confederate corridor across the Mississippi River, with Vicksburg as the northern shoulder. The Red River Valley on the other side of the Mississippi was a fruitful source of supplies that could be shipped east of the river if these two points were firmly in Southern hands. Van Dorn's strategy was sound, but Baton Rouge was poorly situated for defense. Lying on low ground along a stretch of the river that was wide and deep, it was vulnerable to Union gunboats. The Confederates had little in the way of naval power on the Mississippi to challenge their enemy. Moreover, as Breckinridge prepared at Camp Moore, sickness withered his division from four thousand to twenty-five hundred men, bringing his available manpower down to par with that of Williams.[17]

Nevertheless, Breckinridge advanced toward Baton Rouge and attacked on the foggy morning of August 5. Initially, the Confederates pushed the Federals back, and Williams was shot in the chest while leading a regiment early in the action. By midmorning, however, Union resistance stiffened. Breckinridge had counted on the *Arkansas* to support his assault, having coordinated plans with Captain Brown, but the ironclad failed to make an appearance. With only about one thousand men left for immediate action, Breckinridge broke off contact and destroyed supplies captured in the Union camps for want of transportation to haul them away. Breckinridge hovered in the vicinity of Baton Rouge until word arrived late in the afternoon that engine trouble had delayed the *Arkansas*; then he retired to Camp Moore. The battle of Baton Rouge had cost him 453 casualties, while the Federals lost 383 men.[18]

On August 6, the short career of the *Arkansas* came to an end when the Federal ironclad *Essex* approached the vessel while it was anchored a short distance upstream from Baton Rouge. The Confederate crew members abandoned their boat and set it on fire. Yet, in the aftermath of the fight at Baton Rouge, both sides sought a reason for pride. Breckinridge reported that civilians in the area assisted his command by providing wagons with which to carry away the wounded. In fact, "a few, armed with shot-guns and other weapons, had been able to reach the field in time to join in the attack." Noting that a handful of Western regiments helped the New England units defend the capital of Louisiana, Butler proclaimed: "The Northeast and Northwest mingled their blood on the field" of Baton Rouge.[19]

Although a Union victory, the engagement unsettled Butler's fragile military mind. He sent his chief engineer, Godfrey Weitzel, to inspect the post and received a recommendation that Baton Rouge should be evacuated. Butler understood the political significance of holding on to the state capital and ordered Weitzel to lay out defenses and start digging in. Van Dorn, on the other hand, gave up all hope of reclaiming the city; instead, he sent what was left of Breckinridge's division to Port Hudson, located about 130 miles south of Vicksburg, which he planned to make the southern shoulder of his corridor. Planted on high bluffs, it was a far stronger position than Baton Rouge. Defenses already were in progress when Breckinridge arrived on August 16, but no guns were yet in place. Ironically, on the very day that Breckinridge reached Port Hudson, Butler ordered the evacuation of Baton Rouge based on false reports that the Confederates intended to attack New Orleans. He meant to concentrate his limited manpower for the defense of the Crescent City. When they left Baton Rouge on August 21, the Federals took the books of the Louisiana State Library and shipped the city's statue of George Washington to New York for safekeeping. Baton Rouge remained in a sort of limbo for months to come. The Federals reoccupied it in late December without a fight and held it for the rest of the war.[20]

Occupying New Orleans

Butler made no further attempt to expand his holdings up the Mississippi Valley, while the Confederates solidified their control of the middle stretch of the river, shipping heavy guns to be planted at Vicksburg and Port Hudson. Just as Halleck had to call a halt to further advances south of Corinth, so did Butler have to recognize that his available manpower was inadequate for the complete conquest of the Mississippi Valley. Lincoln's call for three hundred thousand additional troops in July would dramatically change this situation within a few months, but for the time being, Federal operations in the West ground to a halt.

Butler busied himself with the task of governing New Orleans, the base of his operations in the lower Mississippi Valley. As he put it, "The city was untamed." When Federal ships steamed up to the wharves on April 25, some fifteen thousand citizens lined the riverbank. "The City along the Levee appeared to be in the Hands of a mob," reported a sailor; they were "setting on fire cotton [and] tobacco. . . . Many women were waving secession flags & men cheering for Jeff Davis." In retaliation, musicians on board the vessels played "Hail Columbia" and "The Star Spangled Banner." This set the tone for the early phase of Butler's occupation of New Orleans. It was early in the conflict, and the city had fallen after little resistance. The pro-Confederates in New Orleans acted out their frustration and humiliation, undaunted because they had not yet suffered from the dire effects of war.[21]

One of the earliest, most prominent issues Butler dealt with was to try William Munford for tearing down the U.S. flag that Farragut's men had raised over the U.S. Mint. Munford, locally known as a playboy, had been feted for his action. Butler decided to make an example of Munford and tried him before a military commission in late May 1862. The commission found him guilty and sentenced him to death, a decision that Butler approved. He was hanged a week later amid howls of protest from many local residents. A great number of people across the Confederacy were also shocked, calling the execution "a brutal murder, not justified by any act committed by" the accused. It was a major factor in the growing Confederate view that Butler was nothing less than a "Beast."[22]

During those first few months of the Union occupation, Butler carefully considered his every action in New Orleans. With a large, diverse populace, the city was a powder keg ready to explode if the situation at issue was not handled properly. Butler wanted to exhibit strength in his tenure as the de facto government of the city. "The line is to be distinctly and broadly drawn," he told one civilian. "Every citizen must find himself on the one side or the other of that line, and can claim no other position than that of friend or enemy of the United States." He declared martial law in New Orleans on May 1, 1862, very soon after stepping foot on its streets. Butler required that all civilians surrender their arms, banned any displays of flags or emblems other than those of the United States, required the swearing of loyalty oaths, banned the use of Confederate currency and bonds, and required that news-

Benjamin F. Butler. (Library of Congress, LC-DIG-cwpb-04894)

papers print nothing derogatory of U.S. authority. Butler also prohibited all public assemblies. He meant to rule with a stern hand and tried to demonstrate that hand with the execution of Munford.[23]

At the same time, however, Butler saw his role as that of a benevolent tyrant. Early on he announced that the Federals were in New Orleans "not to destroy but to make good, to restore order out of chaos, and the government of laws in place of the passions of men." The city had many classes of people, he explained, and each one had a different attitude toward the war and suffered from various problems. It was his job to craft a different approach to every group; he was quite ready to reach out and help those in need while treating rebellious elements with an iron hand. Butler, in short, regarded himself not only as a stern, unbending authority, but as a responsible steward of the public welfare. He was also a master of show and public spectacle. Years of experience currying favor with the working class of Lowell, Massachusetts, before the war had taught Butler many tricks he used to good effect in New Orleans. He understood how to take advantage of class tensions and how to sway the public mood with band music on the streets, displaying the U.S. flag, and demonstrating a show of force to intimidate angry mobs on the street. He sought in every way to subdue Confederate sympathizers and encourage loyalists to come out of the woodwork—in the words of a modern historian, to make it appear that the U.S. government was "the champion of the poor." There is plenty of evidence that the mutiny inside Fort Jackson was motivated by a sincere disaffection felt by the garrison toward the Confederate cause, worsened by simmering class tensions within the city's population from which the garrison was recruited.[24]

Because the city's most rebellious elements were riding high during the spring, summer, and fall of 1862, every move Butler made created controversy. His attempt to use the loyalty oath as a litmus test of sentiment did not have the desired effect. A Federal officer reported that fewer than 20,000 of the city's 170,000 residents took the oath. By October, Butler required that anyone who had not yet sworn the oath should register with a Federal provost marshal, reporting the names of all members of their household and listing all the family's property. It is likely that the citizens responded to this order with even less faith than that with which they took the oath. In November, Butler reinforced efforts to confiscate weapons held by disloyal people, accumulating about six thousand guns. He had more success in appropriating the property of pro-Confederates after the U.S. Congress passed the Second Confiscation Act in July 1862, when he created a military commission to administer the process. The commission first determined who was loyal and who was not, allowing those who merely voiced disloyal sentiments but did not act against the government to retain their property. Even so, the commission took more than $1 million in personal property within the Department of the Gulf and sold it for government use before the end of 1862. This was probably the most extensive, systematic application of the Second Confiscation Act within a single military department in the country, and it likely had more to do with quieting anti-Federal activities than any of Butler's other policies.[25]

High-profile actions against individuals had some effect as well, although they often resulted in virulent protests. When Mrs. Eugenia Levy Phillips laughed from the balcony of her house as the funeral procession of a Union officer passed by, Butler had her arrested and confined on Ship Island. Phillips had also been accused of teaching children to spit on Union officers on the street. In another incident, bookstore owner Fidel Keller displayed a skeleton he acquired from the Mexican consul on which he attached a label with the word "Chickahominy." Because Federal officers thought Keller meant to imply that it was the skeleton of a Union soldier who had died during the Peninsula campaign, he was arrested and sent to Ship Island for two years of hard labor. Following Keller, John W. Andrews was apprehended for exhibiting a cross he claimed was made of the bones of a Union soldier. By September, at least sixty political prisoners were held on Ship Island, demonstrating Butler's determination to make secessionists pay for their continued defiance of U.S. authority.[26]

Butler's controversial attempts to teach the women of New Orleans to refrain from insulting Federal officers drew more adverse public response than any other action. Frustrated that the ladies verbally abused and spat on his men, Butler, on May 15, issued General Orders No. 28 declaring that any woman who persisted in this behavior would be "treated as a woman of the town, plying her avocation." A shocked Mayor Monroe protested that this directive would lead to civil unrest, but the opposite seems to have happened. Butler proudly reported that, even though no one was arrested under the order, women in New Orleans stopped offending his men. Respectable ladies did not want to be branded as common women, and common women wanted to be seen as respectable ladies. Butler wisely understood that to have arrested women for spitting on his soldiers would have caused unnecessary trouble; to his mind, his "woman's order" solved a thorny problem with minimal effort. But anti-Union sentiment was muted, not eradicated, by such measures. As Butler was preparing to leave New Orleans at the end of the year, he received a letter from "One of Your She Adders," who wrote: "Ever since you came among us, we have felt for you *hatred* so violent that no words can express it. We have always regarded you as a monster in whose composition the lowest of traits were concentrated."[27]

The fury aroused by such actions as the "woman's order" overshadowed important things that Butler did for New Orleans. As the only authority in town, the Union army felt the full weight of dealing with the city's municipal and human problems. Butler stepped forward and attacked these challenges with commendable energy, investing a good many Federal resources in taking care of the Crescent City and its occupants, most of whom barely understood or appreciated his work. Perhaps in no other occupied city of the Confederacy did the residents need the Federal government so much, yet acknowledged its help so little, as in New Orleans.

The city was the South's premier commercial emporium, but its seaborne commerce had been largely curtailed since the onset of the U.S. naval blockade. Now, when the sea-lanes were open to its wharves, the city was cut off from the interior of the South. The Lincoln administration was keen to use the resumption of commerce "as a most effective means of bringing this unhappy civil strife to an end, and restoring the authority of the Federal Government," as Secretary of State William H. Seward put it. Butler suggested that New Orleans be declared an open port in early May, and he encouraged the shipment of cotton and sugar from the interior to be sold in the open market. Slowly, the city began to take on its old appearance as a major point of buying and selling.[28]

Maintaining law and order in this turbulent place was difficult at best, especially when Butler fired its civilian police force for refusing to take the oath of allegiance. While hiring a new police force, he temporarily relied on his own soldiers to keep the peace, though they had little experience or training as policemen. Benjamin F. Morse of the 8th Vermont admitted that when assigned the task he had no idea how to do it, but he actually "got along very well" and "made a good many arrests." Eventually, Morse reported, the populace calmed down and stopped hurling insults at every blue uniform that passed their door. Now that martial law had been imposed, Butler created a military commission consisting of five officers to try capital cases.[29]

The Federals did their best to relieve the suffering of poor people and to clean up the city. Butler blamed destitution among the working class on Confederate authorities, who had taken away supplies when they evacuated New Orleans. The Federals had no idea they would have to deal with this problem and were unprepared for it. Food shortages led to sky-high prices, out of reach of working-class families. "The question of how to feed the people of this city and the surrounding country becomes of the utmost magnitude," Butler informed Secretary Edwin Stanton. The general made arrangements to encourage the shipment of flour, beef, and other food items from Confederate-controlled areas into the city. In addition, he arranged to tax the most prominent Confederate sympathizers for the purpose of raising at least $75,000 to feed their neighbors. Butler sold small amounts of army rations to those who could afford to pay for them and gave food to those who could not. By the end of May, the Federals were feeding an estimated 32,400 people in and around the city. The problem grew worse during the summer, with Butler reporting that many people "literally come down to starvation." He was disbursing $50,000 worth of food every month to white residents and issuing to indigent blacks double the amount of army rations consumed by his own troops. These measures strained Butler's limited logistical system, dependent as it was on seacoast shipping coming from New York, some 2,100 miles away.[30]

Butler also addressed the problem of pollution in New Orleans, chiding its residents for the filth he found on city streets. Mayor Monroe did nothing about it, so Butler took charge. He hired three thousand unemployed workers to clean up the streets and sewers, paying them fifty cents per day plus rations, and required that homeowners clean up their grounds. Those who did not comply went to jail. Butler's motive in this case was largely to stave off the onset of yellow fever, a perennial problem in New Orleans. Such measures would help the residents, but mostly he sought to prevent his own Northeastern troops from succumbing to this Southern disease. Because New Orleans lay literally below the level of the Mississippi River, due to the extensive system of levees in the area, Butler assembled work crews of black refugees managed by white foremen to repair the levees. He fed the blacks but did not pay them a wage, financing the work by taxing local landowners near the levees. Butler hired a former tax collector of Orleans Parish to go door-to-door to collect the money. Though shot at several times, the tax man survived the ordeal and brought in most of what he was supposed to collect. An additional two thousand local men were hired to clean up the drainage canals in the city.[31]

Another of Butler's concerns related to the refugee blacks who sought deliverance with the Union army. Many of those streaming toward New Orleans had run away from their masters; others were forced off the plantation by their owners, who refused to feed and care for them. By mid-June, 60 refugees were working for officers in the 12th Connecticut and 150 more hovered around its camp, seeking work or handouts. Captain John W. DeForest observed "women and children squatting in the wet grass under pouring rain, all waiting for liberty."[32] The same was true in most other regiments. There was what one officer called "a great floating population of blacks" in

Union-occupied areas in and around New Orleans. Five hundred blacks flocked to Baton Rouge when the Federals still occupied it in August.

The Federals at New Orleans put the black refugees to work when possible, fed the women and children when necessary, and tried to discourage more from entering the city, but these expedients were not a permanent solution to the problem. The black refugees further strained an already-burdened logistical system. Butler started with a modest number of troops, lost a great many of them to disease, and had to rely on a long, tenuous supply line with the Northeast. Secretary of the Treasury Salmon P. Chase thought Butler should enlist the black refugees in the army to supplement his white regiments.[33]

This idea was enthusiastically endorsed by Butler's subordinate, John W. Phelps, one of the most vigorous prosecutors of the Union war effort to be found in the Federal army. Phelps understood that the act of running away from their masters was a decisive intellectual and emotional break for slaves, which made them "ripe for manumission." He also felt that re-creating the civil court system, as well as arresting and executing a handful of prominent secessionists, would do more to restore the Union than any number of military victories. An abolitionist, Phelps thought it shameful that his nation had not "made our declaration good" even now, some eighty years after proclaiming that all men were born free. When complaints about Phelps reached Washington, D.C., Lincoln argued that Southerners had only themselves to blame for his presence among them. He noted that they could easily get rid of Phelps by bringing themselves back to a firm allegiance to the U.S. government. Butler himself grew frustrated with Phelps when his subordinate began to organize black men into Union regiments, anticipating that this would be Federal policy within six months. Phelps resigned when Butler refused to support this unauthorized procedure. Instead, Butler did what Grant was doing in Tennessee: organizing able-bodied blacks as work gangs to harvest cotton on abandoned plantations in Louisiana.[34]

Time worked in favor of the Federals. Benjamin Morse reported that, as early as mid-June, the citizens of New Orleans were feeling more comfortable with their Yankee guests and the Federals felt more at ease with their hosts as well. Butler was proud of his accomplishments, noting that his aggressive policy of taxing the well-to-do populace had lessened the suffering of the poor. It also had generated funds to help compensate the U.S. government for the cost of his expedition to New Orleans. In the end, Butler's regime had imposed law and order on the city, cleaned up its streets and sewers, maintained its protective levee system, fed thousands of its starving people, and slowly brought back its people into the Union fold. Though obscured by sensational actions such as the hanging of William Munford and the "woman's order," these quiet achievements were more fundamentally significant to the story of the war in the lower Mississippi Valley. New Orleans not only was the South's most important foreign port; it also contained 40 percent of all white residents of Louisiana. Butler denied the Confederacy access to that population and to the city's wharves for most of the Civil War.[35]

But the story did not end there. Butler also engaged in deep, widespread profiteering, banking on his all-powerful position in New Orleans to invest private funds in schemes that he could manipulate to his benefit. His brother Andrew moved to the city and participated in these activities. The Butler brothers quietly amassed personal fortunes during their brief stay in New Orleans. Whereas Benjamin had been worth $150,000 before he arrived, and Andrew apparently had very little wealth, the former commander at New Orleans claimed to be worth $3 million in 1868. Most likely the huge increase resulted from his private dealings in the occupied city, as Butler managed to balance his public duties with war profiteering during America's internecine conflict.[36]

6 } Kentucky and Corinth

Don Carlos Buell had a big job to do in the summer of 1862. Pushing the Army of the Ohio eastward across territory recently abandoned by the Confederates and restoring his line of railroad communications to support the objective to occupy Chattanooga took more time and effort than anyone had anticipated. Buell moved his headquarters from Corinth in mid-June and established it at Huntsville by the end of the month. His forty thousand men, divided into six divisions, occupied positions across Tennessee and northern Alabama. Two divisions were at Battle Creek, only thirty miles west of Chattanooga, while one division each took post at Decherd and McMinnville, Tennessee, and Huntsville, Alabama. The last division, George W. Morgan's, occupied Cumberland Gap. The Army of the Ohio was arrayed on a discontinuous line sixty miles long from McMinnville to Huntsville, with Morgan detached from the rest. Here they stayed for the time being as work crews tried to get rail lines from both Nashville and Memphis working again.[1]

Buell pinned his hopes on the longest rail line of communications any Federal commander had relied on since the war began. At least three hundred miles of iron stretched southward from Louisville toward his most advanced position, crossing dozens of large bridges and using three major tunnels. Because he was about to penetrate the Appalachian Highlands to reach Chattanooga, he could not count on foraging off the countryside to feed his men. The mountains were the home of small-scale, subsistence-level farms, and large concentrations of troops and draft animals would eat out an area in a matter of days. The railroad system provided the only means of deeply penetrating the southeast portion of the Confederacy.[2]

Yet that railroad system was vulnerable to mounted raids and small bands of guerrillas. On July 13, 1862, Nathan Bedford Forrest and his men struck at Murfreesboro, capturing most of the Federal garrison and destroying an immense amount of property. They also burned several bridges in the area. Even worse, John Hunt Morgan's cavalry took Gallatin, Tennessee, on August 12 and wrecked the nearby Big South Tunnel; three months of hard work would be required to repair the tunnel before supply trains could roll southward from Louisville. Meanwhile, Guerrillas had hit the Memphis and Charleston Railroad east of Corinth and cut it in late July. Moreover, Buell could not rely on steamer traffic to make up for the interruptions in his rail system. Unlike the Mississippi, the Tennessee and Cumberland Rivers often were too low for boats to go upstream farther than Pittsburg Landing or Nashville.[3]

"My advance has not been rapid," Buell admitted to Halleck, "but it could not be more rapid under the circumstances." To protect the rail system, he had to distribute troops along the 300-mile line and construct fortifications to defend key locations. Guards were placed on every train. He also worked to build fortifications at Nashville to defend his forward supply depot and the headquarters of Tennessee's military governor. The Federals occupying Huntsville went on half rations, "and even this supply is not altogether certain," according to James B. Fry, Buell's chief of staff. Yet, at the same time, when his hungry troops foraged off the countryside without authorization, Buell tried to maintain discipline by clamping down on what Fry called "wholesale marauding."[4]

To anyone unaware of Buell's logistical difficulties, it would seem as if he was inexcusably slow in completing his mission. Eastern Tennessee loyalists, in particular, wrote blistering criticism of his performance. Frustration over Buell's apparent tardiness grew so strong in Washington that Halleck worked hard to forestall his replacement with another commander. "The advance on Chattanooga must be made with the means of acting in force," Buell lectured Halleck; "otherwise it will either fail or prove a profitless and transient prize." Until the railroad was fully working, he could barely supply his divisions with wagon trains, "living from day to day."[5]

Buell was right to argue that his large army needed adequate supply lines to penetrate and hold the mountainous region of eastern Tennessee, northern Alabama, and northwestern Georgia, but Grant later offered an alternative to Buell's approach to that problem. Rather than position his entire force in a wide arch just within the mountains, yet some distance from the prize, and then sending work details to the rear to repair the railroad, Grant thought Buell should have detached two or three divisions to press the work more quickly and guard the lines while taking the rest of his army on a quick strike to secure Chattanooga. Such a strategy probably would have worked because, for the time being, no sizable force of Confederates held Chattanooga. During June and July most Rebel troops were concentrated at Knoxville, and they would have been outnumbered by even half of Buell's army.[6]

Bragg's Offensive

As the Confederate Army of the Mississippi retreated from Corinth in early June, some desperate effort to quickly restore the strategic momentum by taking the offensive against the Yankees filled the minds of many officers. Albert S. Johnston's deadly battle at Shiloh had failed to reverse the string of misfortunes starting with the fall of Fort Henry, and Beauregard found it impossible to hold the rail center of Corinth. Some counteroffensive now seemed the only way to win the war in the West. Many plans were discussed: for example, flanking Halleck's huge army as it advanced south of Corinth toward Tupelo or moving quickly to Chattanooga by rail to block Buell's offensive, then invading middle Tennessee. That would enable the Confederates to "carry the war into Yankee-dom and thus force Halleck to take the back track," as engineer officer Samuel H. Lockett put it.[7]

When Beauregard took sick leave on June 20, Braxton Bragg assumed command of the Army of the Mississippi with a determination to take offensive action. A West Pointer who had seen distinguished service in the Mexican-American War, Bragg had been a planter in Louisiana before the outbreak of the Civil War. He helped to organize the Army of the Mississippi and had commanded one of its corps at Shiloh. Because Halleck demonstrated no desire to invade Mississippi and Chattanooga was threatened, Bragg sought to defend that endangered city by cooperating with the Confederate forces under Edmund Kirby Smith at Knoxville to seize the strategic initiative. He hoped to at least reclaim middle Tennessee and possibly to invade Kentucky. Bragg initially sent one division by rail starting on June 26. The troops traveled by way of Mobile and Atlanta, reaching Chattanooga by July 3. Bragg spent another month accumulating much-needed wagons since he could not count on a rail or river supply system to support his strike northward. His men would travel light, depending on wagons to haul ordnance and whatever food possible but relying mostly on foraging off the countryside for subsistence and fodder. Bragg moved the remainder of his thirty thousand men on July 23, consuming six days to advance eight hundred miles—from Tupelo to Chattanooga—in the first rapid movement of a Confederate field army by rail in the war.[8]

Bragg left sixteen thousand men at Tupelo under Sterling Price to watch the Federals and another sixteen thousand under Van Dorn around Vicksburg. He expected that both commanders would join him when their presence in Mississippi was no longer required. On reaching Chattanooga, Bragg consulted with Kirby Smith to hammer out a complex plan. He already was thinking in terms of reaching for the ultimate goal—seizing Kentucky and

Braxton Bragg.
(Library of Congress,
LC-USZC4-7984)

planting the Confederate flag on the south bank of the Ohio River—rather than the more limited aim of recapturing Nashville and middle Tennessee. It was decided that Bragg and Kirby Smith would operate in two separate columns to cover more ground, with Kirby Smith advancing from Knoxville directly into southeastern Kentucky and heading for the Bluegrass. Bragg would strike out from Chattanooga and threaten Nashville but bypass Buell's positions and enter central Kentucky. "You will see the tide seems to have taken a turn in our favor," Bragg wrote his wife, "and I think the prospect is of a long and strong flood."9

In fact, the prospect of reclaiming lost ground and seizing slave territory that never had been part of the Confederacy electrified many observers. Governor Harris pleaded with the War Department to allow the quick transfer of Tennessee regiments serving with Robert E. Lee's army in Virginia to

Bragg, so they could help liberate their homeland. Jefferson Davis, Bragg, and many other officials received support to invade Kentucky, and the presence of all prominent Kentucky officers with Bragg's army seemed necessary to encourage sympathizers in that state to rally to the Southern cause. No one was more optimistic about an invasion of Kentucky than P. G. T. Beauregard, who wanted the Confederates to construct fortifications along the Ohio River from which to fire on steamer traffic. "There could be no difference of opinion as to the advantage of invading over being invaded," Davis wrote as he contemplated the redemption of his native state. "My early declared purpose and continued hope was to feed upon the enemy and teach them the blessings of peace by making them feel in its most tangible form the evils of war." Initially, Bragg's rapid movement by rail confused the Federals. When they realized he had departed from Tupelo, they assumed he was on his way to Virginia to reinforce Lee's army.[10]

Kirby Smith Takes the Bluegrass

For the first time in the West, the Confederates had gotten the strategic jump on their opponents and they made the most of it. Kirby Smith was eager to strike into Kentucky, arguing that there was a "golden opportunity" to take advantage of what many Southerners thought was dissatisfaction with Federal rule in that border state. He left Knoxville in mid-August and crossed Cumberland Mountain, bypassing Morgan's division at Cumberland Gap, and rested several days at Barbourville. His men "carried their own subsistence in their haversacks," as Kirby Smith cut himself off from a secure line of communications. He compared his expedition to that of Hernan Cortes, the Spanish conquistador who burned his ships before setting out to penetrate the Aztec Empire. While Kirby Smith realized the residents of the mountainous region of Kentucky were anti-Confederate, he expected to find friends as soon as his men debouched from the mountains and entered the Bluegrass. As he later wrote, "Before [us] there was plenty, behind certain starvation."[11]

Kirby Smith met a hastily assembled force of Union troops in battle near Richmond, Kentucky, located just inside the Bluegrass, on August 30. The Confederate veterans took the tactical offensive against the bluecoats, most of whom were newly raised troops under Lincoln's July call. The 71st Indiana, for example, had conducted its first battalion drill the day before the engagement. Despite offering as much resistance as they could, the Federals were outmaneuvered and outfought. In the words of the 69th Indiana's David Shockley, "We got whipped Bad." Both sides had about 6,500 men engaged; the Federals lost 5,353 (4,303 of them captured or missing), whereas the Confederates lost only 451. The battle of Richmond led to Confederate seizure of the entire Bluegrass and the fall of Lexington and Frankfort. "I never witnessed such enthusiasm as was exhibited by the citizens," exuded a Confederate staff officer as he entered Lexington. The town was one of the oldest and wealthiest in the West and strongly pro-Confederate in its sympathies. Rebel flags flew by the dozen as Kirby Smith's column entered town, and "the whole country seems to be aroused."[12]

Kirby Smith settled in at Lexington, making it his primary base of operations, while sending a large force to the south bank of the Ohio River opposite Cincinnati. This column took post for a while in front of the extensive Union earthworks protecting Covington, Kentucky, but in the end made no attempt to take them or to cross the river. Lew Wallace was in charge at Cincinnati, a major commercial port on the Ohio with a population of two hundred thousand. Wallace had only twelve thousand newly raised troops, plus sixty thousand minutemen hastily organized from the citizenry of Ohio. The Confederates concentrated on gathering supplies and recruiting troops for their cause. In the former endeavor, they succeeded admirably, but no more than about four thousand Kentuckians were willing to don gray uniforms.[13]

While Kirby Smith's men achieved dramatic success in capturing the heart of Kentucky, Carter L. Stevenson's division kept a close eye on Morgan at Cumberland Gap. The Union position was far too strong for a frontal attack; not only the terrain, but also extensive Federal earthworks prevented the Rebels from ever taking it by storm. But Kirby Smith had cut Morgan's line of communication with the North, and the Federals could not hope to stay at the gap without food. They thus destroyed whatever ordnance stores they could not load onto wagons and evacuated the gap on the night of September 17. Morgan then led his men on an exodus through the mountains of eastern Kentucky, taking the difficult back roads to avoid Confederate troops, fighting skirmishes along the way, and literally making roads for themselves when the Rebels felled trees before the column. In sixteen days, Morgan pushed his men 219 miles through some of the most inhospitable country imaginable until they reached the Ohio River at Greenup, Kentucky. He had lost the gap but had saved his command.[14]

Bragg and Kentucky

It was now Bragg's turn to duplicate Kirby Smith's spectacular success, but, unlike Kirby Smith, he had to deal with Buell's army. Just before he left Chattanooga, subordinates found Bragg optimistic, enthusiastic, and confident. The Army of the Mississippi was in good condition, except for limited wagon transportation, and the men fully expected to fight a major battle near Nashville or Louisville. On August 28 Bragg took twenty-seven thousand men from Chattanooga and began to cross the Cumberland Plateau, heading northwest to threaten Nashville.[15]

Buell had known since August 22 that Bragg was concentrating his army at Chattanooga, and he expected some sort of strike into Union-controlled territory. He reasoned that only a small force could advance into Kentucky from Knoxville and was aware that Bragg's route would take him through middle Tennessee. While sending division commander William Nelson to take charge of affairs in Kentucky, Buell planned to fall back to protect Murfreesboro and Nashville rather than try to meet Bragg atop the Cumberland Plateau. His ultimate goal was to protect his logistical network, including Louisville. By the time it became apparent that Bragg would bypass Nashville and the battle of Richmond took place, Buell realized he could not depend on the scattered Union troops in Kentucky to secure the rear areas. He then had no choice but to give chase to Bragg and hope to intervene between the Confederate Army of the Mississippi and the vital logistical center at Louisville.[16]

On September 5 Bragg crossed the state line, entering Glasgow, Kentucky, a week later. His men were proud of their marching achievement thus far; they expected to take Louisville as well as all of the state. Bragg reported that, "Without firing a gun," he had forced the Federals to largely give up northern Alabama and middle Tennessee south of Nashville. He took time to issue a proclamation assuring the people of Kentucky that "we come not as conquerors or as despoilers, but to restore to you the liberties of which you have been deprived by a cruel and relentless foe." Bragg promised to respect their property and even vowed to leave "if we find you wedded in your choice to your present lot."[17]

But Bragg delayed his further advance to capture a small Union garrison at Munfordville. He had sent James Chalmers's Mississippi brigade to cut the railroad at that town, where a major bridge took the track across Green River. Chalmers unwisely attacked the small, fortified garrison at the bridge on September 14 and was repulsed. The Confederates lost 288 men, whereas the garrison counted only 37 casualties. Angry at this humiliating setback, Bragg decided to take the entire army to Munfordville to secure the place. Even after receiving reinforcements since Chalmers's attack, the Federals were greatly outnumbered and Buell was not yet within supporting distance. Colonel John T. Wilder, the garrison commander, delayed negotiations as long as possible but on September 18 had no choice but to surrender his 3,546 men. The following day Buell arrived at Cave City, only fifteen miles south of Munfordville. For the next several hours the two armies merely

glared at each other, neither commander willing to assume the tactical offensive, until Bragg lost patience and left on September 20. He did not have
enough supplies to tarry longer at Munfordville and was anxious to join
Kirby Smith. With Buell so close by, Bragg gave up hope of entering and
securing Louisville, which already was being ringed with a line of heavy
earthworks. Instead, he headed to Bardstown, Kentucky, only thirty miles
southeast of the city. The Federals marched into Louisville on September
24, securing the base of their operational system in central Kentucky and
middle Tennessee.[18]

Ironically, though Buell had reacted to Bragg's strategic advance in
time to save Louisville, confidence in the Yankee commander's judgment
quickly eroded as the campaign progressed. His officers were very impressed
with the speed and celerity of Bragg's move. Gordon Granger testified that
Bragg's campaign was "almost without a parallel, cutting loose from his base
of supplies and skedaddling all over the country is something to which history scarcely affords a parallel." The rank and file troops blamed Buell for
wasting their efforts to take Chattanooga and refusing to attack Bragg at
Munfordville. As they exhausted themselves in rapid marches northward,
the Federals began to feel that Buell was a traitor, or at least incompetent.
They began to plunder the countryside, desperate for food and fence rails
because their own supply system was held in abeyance due to the rapidity
with which they moved. Buell's chief of staff, James Fry, heard many men
say they stole goods from civilians because they were frustrated in not being
allowed "to strike a blow at some point upon the enemy" and had to take it
out on anyone available.[19]

Bragg was jubilant with his progress, even though he had failed to secure
Louisville. "My Army is in high spirits and ready to go any where the 'old
general' says," he wrote his wife. "With but one suit of clothes, no tents,
Nothing to eat but meat and *bread*, or when we can't get that *roasting ears*
from the corn fields along the road, we have made the most extraordinary
campaign in military history." Bragg thought that "the title of *Slow* would at
last be removed from this Army." The morale of his men was high, despite
the tough marching, and Bardstown had welcomed them with open arms.
If the situation looked good from the ground, it seemed even more hopeful
from afar. In Richmond, chief engineer Jeremy F. Gilmer hoped that Bragg's
success, together with Robert E. Lee's nearly simultaneous and equally bold
invasion of the border state of Maryland, would "induce the Yankees to think
about stopping the war: it is getting to be a serious matter for them as well
as for us."[20]

But now Bragg was lodged deep in Kentucky, only miles away from the base of a larger Union army, with no secure lines of communication to his homeland. Whether the Confederates could stay in Kentucky depended entirely on whether the people would support them, and whether Bragg and Kirby Smith could concentrate their forces and fight in a united way.

The Confederate Senate had passed a resolution on September 12 that required all military forces entering Union territory bordering the Mississippi and its tributaries to assure the residents that the Richmond government would guarantee free navigation of the Western waters. On September 26 Bragg issued a proclamation to that effect, addressing it "To the People of the Northwest." He also blamed New England for starting the war over economic issues. The Mississippi was "a grand artery" that connected the Northwestern states with the South, and an independent Confederacy would naturally cooperate with those states in keeping the river open to trade. Simon B. Buckner, who accompanied Bragg's army, issued a proclamation of his own "To the Freemen of Kentucky" from Bardstown, trying to use Lincoln's issuance of the preliminary Emancipation Proclamation two days before as a weapon against the North. Buckner declared: "If the will of this abolition autocrat can be fulfilled, he will make his people a nation of bandits, and will light the incendiary torch around every Kentucky fireside." He implied that Kentuckians could expect a race war and the loss of their slave property because of Lincoln's new policy. Bragg himself called on the young men of the state to rally to the Confederate standard.[21]

At the same time that Bragg and Buckner issued these clarion calls to the inhabitants, Bragg, for one, was fast becoming disappointed at their lackluster response. "I regret to say we are sadly disappointed at the want of action by our friends in Kentucky," he informed Richmond. While Kirby Smith had barely signed up enough men to make up for Confederate casualties thus far in the campaign, Bragg received no recruits. He had hauled fifteen thousand small arms from Chattanooga and had "no one to use them. Unless a change occurs soon we must abandon the garden spot of Kentucky to its cupidity. The love of ease and fear of pecuniary loss are the fruitful sources of this evil." Bragg estimated he needed fifty thousand additional troops to hold the state, but the government had no reinforcements to send him. "Enthusiasm runs high," Bragg reported to President Davis, "but exhausts itself in words."[22]

Buell on the Offensive

Buell spent several days refitting his army at Louisville and plotting his advance toward Bragg's position. In hindsight, it is apparent that he had already turned the tide in the fast-flowing campaign by beating Bragg to

Louisville and securing the city. From this point on the Federals had all the advantages of resources and secure supply lines, yet Washington was tired of Buell's tardiness. The general tried to explain why the situation had developed as it had thus far — Bragg had seized the strategic initiative and had the inside track in the march northward from Chattanooga, and the troops in Kentucky had failed to stop him or to safeguard Buell's supply line, necessitating a late decision by him to march northward.[23]

Explanations availed little; Federal authorities wanted quick action, not words. Lincoln authorized Buell's relief from command of the Army of the Ohio and his replacement by George H. Thomas. Halleck's instructions to Thomas, to be delivered after Buell relinquished his post, was to "operate against the enemy; find him and give him battle." Halleck wanted Thomas to strip the army of excess transportation and live off the land, either paying for food or giving receipts for future settlement to the citizenry. Everyone had been so impressed by Bragg's rapid march that they thought the Federals ought to practice the same art. After a few days, Washington officials decided to give Buell another chance. Lincoln postponed his firing to enable him to fulfill Union objectives in Kentucky.[24]

After incorporating new troops and resting a bit, Buell led the Army of the Ohio out of Louisville to execute a smartly planned approach to the Confederates, sending one small column toward Frankfort and the rest of the troops directly toward Bardstown. Yet Bragg had failed to prepare for this offensive. He had been unable to convince Kirby Smith to join the two Confederate columns. Bragg unwisely busied himself with arrangements to install the Confederate governor of Kentucky, Richard Hawes, who had been selected to replace George W. Johnson. Hawes and his cabinet had accompanied Bragg on the northward march into Kentucky. An inauguration ceremony took place in Frankfort on October 4 amid much hoopla, but the sound of Union artillery booming to the west forced everyone to cancel the celebration that evening and leave town. Hawes never returned to the state capital.[25]

Just two months before, Beriah Magoffin, the only legitimate governor of Kentucky, had resigned because he had become isolated by the legislature and by Union generals who commanded the occupation troops in his state. Speaker of the Kentucky Senate James F. Robinson, a supporter of the Union cause but not of Lincoln's emancipation policy, replaced Magoffin. Kentucky was exempted, at any rate, by the terms of that policy.[26]

Bragg's army pulled away from Bardstown in an attempt to move east and join Kirby Smith, but the Federals approached the rear of his column so closely that the Rebels turned and offered battle near Perryville on October 8. The engagement developed largely because of actions by subordinate commanders, rather than by Bragg or Buell, and it involved most of the Confederate army but only a portion of the Union force. Nevertheless, when the Rebels struck at the First Corps under Alexander McDowell McCook, surprising the Federals on the open, rolling countryside, one of the more vicious battles of the war took place. Due to a peculiar atmospheric condition that dampened the sound of battle, Third Corps troops hardly knew that a fight was in progress and the Second Corps was not engaged at all, even though nothing but a thin line of Confederate cavalry lay opposite its position. While Buell had done very well to bring Bragg to battle before he could unite with Kirby Smith, the Federal general exercised little command and control once the fight began. As a result, the Confederates crushed nearly one-third of the Army of the Ohio while the rest of that large force failed to take advantage of its numerical superiority.[27]

Pushed by energetic division and brigade commanders, the Confederates slammed into McCook's corps and slowly pushed it back in heavy, costly fighting. The Rebels "attacked us with the desperation of Demons," reported a member of the 33rd Ohio. The Federals responded with a devastating fire that "swallowed them up in death." Repeated advances succeeded initial repulses, until McCook's men were worn down, pressured from different directions, and retired in stages. Yielding ground, McCook called repeatedly for help that arrived only near the end of the day. The First Corps saved itself by dusk, but Buell's left wing was mangled. Union losses amounted to 4,276 out of 55,261 men available on the field, while Confederate casualties totaled 3,401 out of 16,800 engaged.[28]

Having stopped the Union pursuit for the time being, Bragg pulled away from Perryville and joined Kirby Smith a few days later. He now had roughly equal numbers with Buell, but the lack of civilian support continued to haunt him. Bragg recognized that the Federals continued to hold the strategic advantage despite the drubbing administered to McCook. When Bragg and Kirby Smith moved to the east side of Dick's River to assume a strong defensive position, a shortage of wagons forced them to abandon most of the supplies laboriously accumulated at Lexington. There seemed little to gain from a continued presence in Kentucky, so Bragg began a long retreat toward Cumberland Gap on October 13. The Confederates moved through the mountains as rapidly as possible, dangerously short of food and fodder. Many men lived on nothing but corn taken from fields and parched over a campfire. Bragg's commissaries issued no food for they had none to give, and the men scrounged what they could from the barren countryside during halts in the rapid march. During one part of the journey, the horses of Semple's Alabama Battery pulled their loads for forty hours without any food. When Kirby Smith's column reached Cumberland Gap, to the rear of Bragg's column, he reported that his men had "suffered on this march everything excepting actual starvation. There must be not less than 10,000 of them scattered through the country trying to find something upon which to live."[29]

Buell followed up Bragg's retreat until he began to enter the mountains, then called a halt, sparking the last round of controversy regarding his tenure as commander of the Army of the Ohio. The Washington authorities pushed him to chase Bragg closely but the general refused. The mountains were "almost a desert," he asserted, accurately predicting that Bragg would have to pass through them quickly or starve. Buell said he could not catch up with the Confederates, nor could he feed his own army in that country. Bragg marched along one road, "and that a bad one," where the mountain passes offered him ample opportunities to delay Buell's advance at minimal cost. Rather than undertake a fruitless pursuit, Buell wanted to transport his army to Nashville, certain that city would be Bragg's next target. If his superiors insisted on an advance into eastern Tennessee, Buell estimated he would need thirty thousand men to protect Kentucky, twenty thousand to hold middle Tennessee, and eighty thousand to enter the eastern part of the state.[30]

Although the Federals did not have troops available in such numbers, Lincoln insisted that rescuing eastern Tennessee should be Buell's main objective. Halleck explained the president's feelings: "He does not understand why we cannot march as the enemy marches, live as he lives, and fight as he fights, unless we admit the inferiority of our troops and of our generals."[31]

Buell offered a cogent explanation for his reluctance to accede to the president's desire. He estimated that eastern Tennessee might supply some forage and perhaps half his men's bread ration, but everything else had to be hauled over rutted roads. While Buell admitted that Bragg had moved his army remarkably well during the campaign, in part because he had no fully functioning line of communications, he also noted that Bragg had been forced to evacuate Kentucky largely for the same reason. The only sure way to enter and secure eastern Tennessee was by enormous logistical preparation, and Buell clearly did not believe the prize was worth it.[32]

While fighting his battle with Washington, Buell was forced to appease Governor Robinson, of Kentucky, who complained that the Federals were stealing too much food from innocent civilians. Buell regretted these depredations but explained that many of his troops were new, ill-trained volunteers. He also pointed out that poorly disciplined soldiers of all armies tended to steal "without reference to the cause for which they fight or the people among whom they are. It would be the same if they were in Indiana or Ohio." He laid plans, contrary to the wishes of his superiors, to move his troops out of Kentucky to middle Tennessee.[33]

This move broke the patience of everyone in Washington. Orders were sent to William S. Rosecrans, recently victorious in a hard-fought defense of Corinth against a major Confederate attack, to relieve Buell as commander of the army. According to Halleck's written instructions, Rosecrans was to secure middle Tennessee, as well as invade the eastern part of the state before winter set in. Rosecrans could follow up Bragg's march or select a better route directly east from Nashville. Either way, he must travel light and live off the land. "The time has now come when we must apply the sterner rules of war, whenever such application becomes necessary, to enable us to support our armies and to move them rapidly upon the enemy," Halleck wrote. "Neither the country nor the Government will much longer put up with the inactivity of some of our armies and generals." Rosecrans assumed command of the Army of the Ohio on October 30.[34]

By the time Bragg reached Cumberland Gap, his superiors in Richmond wanted to know what he intended to do next. They asked him to devise a plan that would involve cooperation with Confederate forces holding Mississippi and the Trans-Mississippi. President Davis's preference was to reoccupy middle Tennessee because no move seemed more apt to compensate for "the depression produced by the failure in Ky." Bragg laid plans to establish his worn army between the Tennessee and Cumberland Rivers where he hoped to secure ample provisions from farms in the area.[35]

Richmond authorities still hoped that, after resting and refitting, Bragg would take the offensive and reenter Kentucky, but the army commander had no intention of trying that hazardous experiment again. Privately, nearly every commentator recognized that Bragg's failed effort demonstrated the futility of Confederate attempts to conquer new territory. As Jeremy Gilmer put it, "Bragg's campaign in Kentucky is pronounced here a magnificent failure—big show and no result—a march up the hill and down again, and his troops, like the army in Flanders, I have no doubt 'swore terribly.'" President Davis was "sadly disappointed" that the residents of his native state did not rise up to support the Southern forces and vowed to keep that fact in mind whenever anyone urged him to invade Kentucky again. If Bragg had been able to remain in Kentucky long enough, Beauregard had intended to hold a conference between Confederate officials and the governors of the Northwestern states to see if a separate peace with them could be hammered out.[36]

The verdict on Bragg's Kentucky campaign was predicated on what the

Confederates could have achieved if he had remained in control of the state. But Bragg offered a different way of interpreting the result of his first and only offensive as commander of the main Confederate army in the West. He argued that his campaign, while not securing Kentucky, had led to a reassertion of Confederate control of the southern portion of middle Tennessee, Cumberland Gap, and northern Alabama. He had lived for two months on "supplies wrested from the enemy's possession" and had only given up territory that the Confederacy had never before possessed. His campaign had taken Confederate forces farther north than any other offensive in the West.[37]

Confederate governor Richard Hawes trouped on, even though he had no opportunity to govern anything, expressing grievous disappointment that Kentuckians had not opted for the Confederacy in greater numbers while they had the chance. He continued to press Davis with requests for future support that fell on deaf ears. Commanders in eastern Tennessee established recruiting camps as near the Kentucky border as possible to entice young men to the Confederate flag, but the effort resulted in little gain.[38]

Within Union-occupied Kentucky, Federal officers clamped down on anyone who had shown favor to the Rebels while they had controlled the state. A number of people were arrested and sent south to be delivered within Confederate lines at Vicksburg. Later, Federal authorities decided to send them to Camp Chase "as political prisoners." The private property of these people also was confiscated. Jeremiah T. Boyle superintended the undertaking so vigorously—in some cases, without proper evidence—that it produced "bad feeling" in the state. Stanton ordered Boyle to stop the arrests, but a number of political prisoners wound up at Camp Chase before the order went into effect. Any attempt to control or punish the civilian population was complicated. As Horatio G. Wright, commander of the Department of the Ohio, told a subordinate, "Much is left to your own judgment necessarily." But Wright urged him to remember, "Old feuds, more recent dislikes, have an influence in controlling the judgments of the most loyal" citizens. To avoid allowing innocent people to become victims of personal grudges, the subordinate had to sift through solid evidence of disloyalty rather than rely too heavily on testimony by the neighbors of the accused.[39]

When the fate of these political prisoners became known to Bragg, he sent a protest to Wright, pointing out that many Southerners had urged him to arrest Unionists within Confederate lines and hold them as hostages for the release of these Kentuckians. Bragg so far refused to do so, believing it dishonorable, but he warned Wright that his patience was wearing thin. There were never easy solutions to the problem of population control in wartime.[40]

Iuka and Corinth

While Bragg and Buell were fighting for control of Kentucky, Confederate forces left behind in Mississippi took the offensive to support the bold strike to the Bluegrass. The issue was whether those Mississippi forces should join Bragg or attack Federal positions in northern Mississippi and southwestern Tennessee. The desperate need to divert forces for the defense of Vicksburg complicated this question for weeks, and it did not help that Confederate troops in Mississippi were divided into two separate commands, one led by Earl Van Dorn and the other by Sterling Price.

Bragg wanted the Mississippi troops to take action in some form, and Price initially opted for combining with Van Dorn and striking at Corinth. If successful in recapturing that place, they could sweep northward toward Paducah "and thence wherever circumstances may dictate." Price hoped to recruit troops in Tennessee and Kentucky from among "those . . . who have seen and felt the wretchedness of northern domination." Van Dorn was of a similar mind: "We should try and shake them loose from all points in West Tennessee; then march to join Bragg, if necessary." This plan was seconded by Beauregard as well.[41]

But not until after the battle of Baton Rouge on August 5 could Van Dorn devote serious attention to the planned offensive, and he needed more time to refit and ready his army while stationing adequate garrisons in the key Mississippi towns he still held. Meanwhile, Bragg's campaign heated up and prompted urgent requests for aid. Price felt compelled to do something even before Van Dorn was ready and began to move his command into a position where it could either head directly for Bragg's fast-moving army or return to combine with Van Dorn's men. The best place to do so was the region of Iuka, a railroad town in northeastern Mississippi. It was only twenty-three miles east of Corinth and therefore vulnerable to a Union strike from that rail junction. In fact, a small Federal garrison was just in the process of evacuating Iuka when Price approached the place on September 14. Price waited several days to determine whether he should go to Bragg or Van Dorn. A message from Van Dorn on the eighteenth decided the matter, and he prepared to return south. Van Dorn wrote that Davis had placed him in charge of operations in the entire state, and he wanted Price to join him.[42]

Price would have to fight his way south because by this time Grant had readied his force to strike him at Iuka. Two Federal columns moved east, one of them from Rosecrans's Army of the Mississippi and the other under Edward O. C. Ord, consisting of Grant's men from the Army of the Tennessee. Both columns departed Corinth on September 16. Rosecrans approached Iuka a few hours before Ord. When Price learned of this approach, he mounted an attack on the head of Rosecrans's column a short distance southwest of town on September 19. Taken by surprise, the Federals retired several hundred yards while putting up stiff resistance. After they stabilized their position, the fighting came to a halt. It had been a small but hard battle, with the Federals losing 790 men out of 2,800 actually engaged and Price losing 525 out of 3,179 in action. The Confederates were heavily outnumbered in the area, but Price managed to slip away that night.[43]

The two Rebel commanders joined their forces at Ripley to form the Army of West Tennessee, some fifteen thousand strong. Van Dorn set out on September 30 for Corinth, now held by Rosecrans's twenty thousand men. The Confederates attacked the outer defenses of the town in sweltering heat on October 3. They pressed forward against the northwestern sector of Corinth's perimeter, where Rosecrans had only two-thirds of his available manpower, and forced the defenders to fall back in heavy fighting. Guns became so hot that "several cartridges exploded when pushed into the piece," reported the colonel of the 52nd Illinois. Rosecrans failed to strike Van Dorn's exposed left flank because of a miscommunication with his subordinate. The Federals ended the day's fighting by taking position in the inner ring of detached earthworks they had previously constructed around Corinth.[44]

Van Dorn opened the fight at 4:00 A.M. on October 4 with an artillery barrage, then sent his divisions in to attack. North of town, the Confederates pushed back defending Union forces and captured Battery Powell but stalled, and the lines stabilized once again. Farther west, the Rebels mounted a strong attack against Battery Robinett and held the work briefly before falling back in the face of a fierce counterattack. Other Confederate troops managed to advance between the earthworks and entered downtown Corinth, only to be driven out by Union reserve troops. It was a close call for the Federals, who convinced Van Dorn to break off that afternoon and retreat southward. Confederate casualties amounted to 4,838, while Rosecrans lost 2,520.[45]

Grant's garrison troops in southwestern Tennessee responded to Van Dorn's offensive by attempting to cut him off before he could find refuge deep in Mississippi. On October 4 Major General Stephen A. Hurlbut led eight thousand men from Bolivar and nearly blocked Van Dorn at the Davis Bridge crossing of the Hatchie River the next day. After the Federals won a seesaw fight for possession of the bridge, Van Dorn crossed at a different location and slipped away. His men were starving, for the Confederate commander had mounted his offensive with little logistical support. Most

*Confederate dead near Battery Robinett, Corinth. Among the few
photographs of battlefield dead exposed on a Western field, this remains
one of the most haunting images of the effect of combat on its participants.*
(Library of Congress, LC-DIG-cwpb-01438)

Confederates survived on some flour cooked on a stick in the morning. The
Federals marveled that Rebel prisoners at Corinth had little more than a few
ears of corn in their haversacks, plundered from nearby fields.[46]

The effect of Van Dorn's campaign was decisive. Though he used all of
the available Confederate manpower in Mississippi, Van Dorn found the
Union's system of fortified posts, amply garrisoned, too strong for capture.
Obviously, there was no hope of taking fifteen thousand men, subsisted by a
few ears of corn, through that system and on to the Ohio River. Bragg was on
his own, and Van Dorn had to worry about a renewal of the Union offensive
into Mississippi.

Van Dorn's defeat inspired the Northern troops in Mississippi and western Tennessee. Though impressive, according to Grant, Bragg's invasion and
Van Dorn's operations were "spasmodic effort[s] without anything behind
to fall back on." He believed the Federals had also gained "a moral advantage" over their opponents after both offensives were defeated in Kentucky

and Mississippi. Sherman was convinced that Van Dorn's sound defeat, in particular, had "shaken the confidence of their adherents" in Memphis. The victory at Corinth "changed the whole aspect of affairs in West Tennessee," for it offered the Federals an opportunity to take the offensive once again. Southerners agreed. C. C. Clay Jr., of Huntsville, Alabama, was dismayed by the reports of Bragg's defeat in Kentucky. Many of his fellow citizens were "preparing to abandon their homes and to seek security in the mountains of Middle Alabama as soon as the army of Buell reaches the southern boundary of Kentucky."[47]

7 } Winter Campaigns

The hiatus in Union offensives along the Mississippi River came to an end by the late fall of 1862 as the new regiments Lincoln had called for in July became available, swelling the size of Federal field armies. The gunboat fleet was reinforced and reorganized as well. David D. Porter replaced Charles Davis as commander of the Western Flotilla on October 15, and the gunboats were transferred to the control of the Navy Department and designated the Mississippi Squadron. Porter began to construct fifteen additional mortar boats and six more ironclad gunboats. The *Eastport, Lafayette, Choctaw, Indianola, Chillicothe,* and *Tuscumbia* added strength to the Pook Turtles. In addition, the Federals started building tinclads (light draft vessels with lighter armor) to patrol stretches of river and protect against guerrilla attacks. By the end of the war, sixty tinclads were in operation. Porter also altered the *Blackhawk* to make it more like a tinclad and claimed it as his flagship.[1]

Porter proposed the creation of an infantry, cavalry, and artillery force light enough to be transported on steamers and mobile enough to land when necessary and deal with Confederate forces along the river. On his recommendation, Alfred Ellet was appointed to organize it, and the War Department authorized the Mississippi Marine Brigade in November. Ellet's command was an army unit but cooperated with Porter's squadron.[2]

The period between Van Dorn's defense of Vicksburg and the resumption of Union advances down the Mississippi had not dimmed Confederate views of the river's significance. Jefferson Davis understood that the Federals could use the Mississippi as a base from which to extend east and west into Confederate territory. He pinned his strategy to defend the valley on his commanders' ability to hold fast to Vicksburg and Port Hudson. "Nothing will so certainly conduce to peace as the conclusive exhibition of our power to hold the Mississippi river," he informed Theophilus Holmes, his Trans-Mississippi commander. In a speech to the Mississippi legislature, Davis expressed the hope that continued control of "that great artery of the Confederacy" would compel the Northwestern states to

David Dixon Porter. (Library of Congress, LC-USZ62-113173)

trade exclusively with the Northeastern ones, paying so much in transportation rates that they would make peace overtures to the Confederacy.[3]

Many citizens agreed with their president. W. P. Harris suggested giving up all points along the seacoast and in eastern Tennessee in order to garner enough troops to hold the Mississippi. Losing that great valley was "equivalent to giving up the cause," he argued. C. G. Dahlgren noted that the Yankees could buy a bale of cotton in the occupied portions of the valley for $250 and sell it for as much as $750. He strongly suggested that Confederate authorities make a greater effort to remove or destroy all cotton within reach of the occupiers.[4]

Joseph E. Johnston echoed these sentiments when he took command of the western Confederate troops in the late fall. "Our great object is to hold the Mississippi," he proclaimed, while seeking ways to increase troop strength in the region. The new Confederate commander in Mississippi, John C. Pemberton, had only 22,000 men in the northern part of the state, while Vicksburg had a garrison of 6,000 and Port Hudson was held by 5,500. According to Johnston, the Federals outnumbered Pemberton in that region, whereas the Confederates seemed to outnumber their opponent in the Trans-Mississippi. Everyone was loath to give up middle Tennessee and transfer Braxton Bragg's renamed Army of Tennessee (formerly the Army of the Mississippi) to Mississippi. Moreover, even if the move were desirable, Bragg estimated it would take a month to march his 42,000 men to join Pemberton. Yet Johnston recognized that if Vicksburg fell, he would never be able to drive the Federals out again and the river would be lost forever.[5]

Grant's North Mississippi Campaign

Grant had every intention of moving toward Pemberton as soon as possible, for new regiments were dribbling in from the North. He had about 17,500 men at Corinth, 7,000 at Memphis, and close to 24,000 dispersed at various points in Kentucky, Tennessee, and even Illinois. All of this manpower was deployed in a defensive posture, and even then the Federals were barely able to keep open the extended rail lines that Grant relied on to feed his troops. He reasoned that consolidating positions and freeing up a mobile column of thirty thousand men would put the Rebels on the defensive and indirectly protect the occupied region just as effectively as stationing troops all over the place.[6]

Van Dorn's defeat at Corinth early in October served as a prelude to the Federal move on Vicksburg. Grant began to place the newly raised regiments on garrison duty to free up veterans for the push south. He planned to move in stages, aiming first at Holly Springs, Mississippi, and then Grenada. All the while, Grant intended to repair and maintain the single track of railroad that stretched southward from Grand Junction, Tennessee, as his supply line. In the first few days of November, he moved three divisions from Corinth and two from Bolivar toward Grand Junction, where the Mississippi Central Railroad joined the Memphis and Charleston Railroad. The Federals reached the junction by November 8 without fighting, moving into a region not completely controlled by either side. As he made necessary repairs on the track, Grant authorized foraging off the countryside, giving receipts for food taken if the owner was available. More supplies arrived by rail from Columbus, Kentucky, and Memphis as work crews improved the road's condition.[7]

Grant made arrangements for running the rail line as he advanced south. He needed six additional locomotives and two hundred cars. The equipment might be found in Indiana and Michigan, he believed, although Halleck noted that more of it was available in the Eastern states. The additional rolling stock was necessary. "Our army cannot move without" it, Grant's chief engineer reported.[8]

Pemberton had no desire to risk his troops in a confrontation so far north; thus by November 13 he evacuated Holly Springs without a battle and concentrated his strength at the railroad crossing of the Tallahatchie River just north of Abbeville. Grant dealt with this roadblock by advancing Sherman and three divisions from Memphis, heading southeast toward Pemberton's flank, and arranging with Samuel Curtis to send a column from Helena eastward to threaten the railroad in Pemberton's rear. He added his own move, using cavalry to secure a crossing of the Tallahatchie downstream from the Confederate position. These multiple threats had their effect, as Pemberton evacuated his fortifications without a fight in mid-November. The Confederates fell back to Grenada and dug in on the south side of the Yalobusha River. The Federals moved as far as Oxford but dispatched troops a few miles farther south to repair the railroad as other detachments reconstructed the track north of that town. At Oxford Grant hesitated in order to receive more troops, noting that Pemberton could consolidate his strength while retreating. Grant, on the other hand, was forced to disperse more men to repair and guard the rail line.[9]

During the first week in December, Grant asked Halleck: "How far south would you like me to go?" He worried that he did not have enough manpower to guard the railroad all the way to Jackson, which was about forty miles east of Vicksburg. Now the commander of the Department of the Tennessee began to think it best to pin Pemberton at Grenada and count on a river-borne force to strike at Vicksburg, using the Federal advantage in steamers and gunboats to penetrate the Deep South. Grant's first strike at Vicksburg had reached a turning point.[10]

Occupation Problems

Grant's men were plunging into territory that had not yet seen a Federal soldier. This move south brought with it all the difficulties experienced when they drove into western and middle Tennessee and northern Mississippi the previous spring. Each newly invaded swath of the Confederacy opened up rich possibilities for soldiers and civilians alike, and often led to excesses. The commander's job, in addition to managing troop movements, worrying about the enemy, and planning strategy, was to deal with these myriad problems as they arose.

Grant tried to live off the land as much as possible to supplement his rail-based logistical system as he advanced south. Quartermasters and commissaries were supposed to offer receipts to owners for their provisions, stating which side of the political contest the owner favored. At the end of the war the citizen could present these receipts to an authorized government agent for reimbursement or rejection, depending on his or her circumstances. But Grant insisted that "in no case should wanton destruction of property be tolerated."[11]

Nevertheless, the rank and file often took the foraging policy as a license to help themselves. "We were ordered to subsist upon the country," reported the commander of the 12th Iowa, "and as the people seemed to have an abundant supply we helped ourselves without much reluctance, the men faring rather sumptuously." Plundering of private property began as soon as the troops initiated their move south, and by November 5 it rose to such a level that officers worried about discipline in the ranks. Grant issued a special field order deploring "gross acts of vandalism" on the march from Corinth and Bolivar to Grand Junction. Orders regulating the proper mode for foraging were widely ignored, and officers were largely to blame. They had to impose control, root out offenders, and withhold the pay of everyone in the unit if the perpetrator could not be found. "Confiscation acts were never intended to be executed by soldiers, and if they were the General Government should have full benefit of all property," Grant reminded his men. Putting teeth in his warning, he authorized the assessment of $124.66 from the 20th Illinois after members of that regiment pillaged three stores in Jackson, Tennessee, and the discharge of two captains who failed to stop it or to investigate the incident.[12]

While the 20th Illinois was an old regiment, Sherman thought the newly raised units had even harsher attitudes toward civilian property in the South. "The new troops come full of the idea of a more vigorous prosecution of the war," he wrote Halleck, "meaning destruction and plunder." Responding to complaints of vandalism, Sherman reasoned that "all our Volunteer soldiers have for years been taught that the people . . . are 'king' & can do no wrong. They . . . come to us filled with the popular idea that they must enact war, that they must clean out the Secesh, must waste & not protect their property, must burn waste & destroy." Sherman tried to discipline his troops, calling on them to adopt an "honorable tone which characterizes the army of a great nation." He reminded them that the government was the chief source of food for the army, and "officers and soldiers have no right to look to any other quarter for compensation and subsistence."[13]

Soldiers in all wars, in every army, have a natural tendency to take property from civilians living in the country they pass through. This happens both because army logistics tend to supply them with only basic, often minimal provisions, and because they have an advantage over civilians in terms of the power they can exert. Anytime Civil War officers or the civilian government encouraged living off the land, the men took full advantage of it, spurring this basic tendency to extremes. Many men in blue genuinely regarded pillaging as an act of war against the enemy, as Sherman suggested, but probably the majority of them looked on it as fulfilling basic needs that had little to do with the politics of the conflict.

What Grant's men were beginning to do as soon as the northern Mississippi campaign began had little relevance to the official, government policy of confiscation. Authorized most fully by the congressional act of July 17, 1862, Lincoln entrusted its execution to Attorney General Edward Bates. He had the power to authorize attorneys and Federal marshals to seize property belonging to Rebels and, if necessary, could call on the military for aid. Bates, a conservative Democratic from Missouri, was unenthusiastic about the policy, as was Lincoln himself, and consequently little was done through official channels. The Confiscation Act had a much greater impact unofficially, as it inspired soldiers in the field to justify the natural tendency to take property for their own purposes rather than for the benefit of the government. Commanders were never able to curb this tendency, and the level of destruction increased as the war progressed and Federal troops entered new territory richly endowed with resources.[14]

Grant tried to impose some control over the inclination to regard property as an integral part of waging war on the Confederacy. As his army penetrated northern Mississippi, he ordered subordinates to seize cotton belonging to civilians widely known to have supported the rebellion and sell it for the benefit of the government. He wanted his provost marshals to keep careful records of all property formally taken. If it was of a kind that normally fell into the domain of ordnance or commissary officers, it could be used immediately; otherwise, it should be delivered to the quartermaster at the nearest army post for storage or shipment north. There are no records of how much material was thus formally processed, nor a comparison with how much property was informally seized by the rank and file during the campaign.[15]

Grant did encounter the property of a well-known Rebel at Oxford. Jacob Thompson, who had been accused of preparing for war while serving as secretary of the interior in the Buchanan administration, was currently a colonel in the Confederate army. While using his house as a hospital, the Federals found documents that demonstrated what Grant called "the treasonable character of at least a portion of the Cabinet" that served Buchanan. As a Federal officer put it, Thompson "did not think the war would ever be at his own door." A quartermaster sold five hundred bales of cotton believed to have been owned by Thompson, bringing fifteen hundred dollars into the Federal treasury.[16]

By early December 1862, Grant authorized the resumption of trade in western Tennessee and encouraged the collection of cotton in northern Mississippi — all subject to Treasury Department regulations. Pressured by authorities in Washington to do so, Grant gave permits to traders to operate as far south as the Tallahatchie River, a few miles behind the forward lines.[17]

The resumption of trade opened the floodgates to a variety of Northerners eager to cash in on supplying the starved market for cotton. Immediately, problems developed that affected army discipline, as cotton traders began to bribe officers to help them transport bales to Memphis. Grant and others, including Charles A. Dana, an emissary of Edwin Stanton, identified Jewish traders as particularly obnoxious in their shady dealings in cotton. Soon after opening trade, Grant sought to restrict it by not offering permits south of Jackson, Tennessee, especially to "Israelites." A few days later, he ordered all railroads to stop Jewish merchants from traveling south "from any point," calling them "an intolerable nuisance"; still later he issued general orders to expel them from the Department of the Tennessee altogether. The order was enforced sporadically until Halleck told Grant to revoke it, due to widespread protests in the North, which the general did in early January.[18]

It was nearly as impossible to avoid guerrilla attacks as it was to resume trade without suffering the ill effects of greed and corruption. Attacks seemed to pick up when Grant marshaled his strength from the garrisoned towns in western Tennessee to drive south into Mississippi. Near Troy, Tennessee, "a hot-bed of traitors," three Unionists were captured by guerrillas operating from a base in the Obion River Valley. The local Federal commander wanted to give the town three days to release the men or he would burn it to the ground and then sweep the Obion River for the culprits. "This will be a pleasure to me," the Federal officer admitted. When Jeremiah C. Sullivan learned that guerrillas were preparing to strike at the railroad near Jackson, he admonished his subordinates to remember that "guarding railroads and keeping communication open to the army is now the vitally important duty of troops in this district." He urged them to let everyone know that the Federals would destroy their property if they assisted the guerrillas. In contrast, the civilians around Bolivar seemed more reconciled to Federal authority. Most had taken the oath of allegiance, "a great portion observing its obligations in good faith," reported Mason Brayman, while "a few require wholesome surveillance, and have it."[19]

The Union army continued to offer welfare for destitute civilians within their lines as Grant drove deeper into the Confederacy. He observed that "distress and almost famine" had resulted from the movements of his own and Pemberton's armies along the railroad. He authorized sutlers to sell items to needy families under strict regulations by post commanders and wanted to raise funds to help the poor by taxing the wealthy civilians who were disloyal.[20]

Of all the classes of Southerners, blacks were both the most needy and the most supportive of Union objectives in the war. Grant was entering a part of the Deep South with a heavy concentration of slaves (nearly half of the residents of Mississippi were black), and they swarmed to his army the deeper he penetrated the state. Grant selected Chaplain John Eaton of the 27th Ohio to take charge of the refugees, authorizing him to establish contraband camps where the army could house and feed the men, women, and children. Eaton created the first camp at Grand Junction, with more to follow at Memphis and Corinth. He recalled that the rush of refugees "was like the oncoming of cities," and the individuals were often poorly clothed and sick. "Sometimes they were intelligent and eager to help themselves; often they were bewildered or stupid or possessed by the wildest notions of what liberty might mean," expecting it to be a paradise of "idleness and freedom from restraint."[21]

Eaton organized work details from among the able-bodied males to harvest the cotton on abandoned plantations and hired them out to loyal or neutral planters. They received twelve and one-half cents per pound for their labor, and the abandoned cotton was shipped north to be sold for the benefit of the U.S. government. Eaton encountered much resistance from some army officers. "We were making a difficult experiment in the interests of humanity," he wrote. His assistants had to "obey all military regulations, and at the same time to stand as mediators between the townspeople or planter . . . and also between the contrabands and the army." But a flow of donations and volunteers from the North helped his cause. By early December, Grant ordered all his subordinate commanders to send refugee women and children, plus unemployed men, to the contraband camp at Grand Junction.[22]

Interestingly, white refugees became a problem as well. They came mostly from the poor white class, and their meager chances for subsisting within a war zone led them to move toward the invading Federal army and seek security in the North. Grant sent them to Cairo, which became a port of entry for white as well as some black refugees. Many army officers arranged jobs for these refugees with their friends and relatives in the North.[23]

Now that the fighting front had moved south, military governor Andrew Johnson tried to reconstruct local and state government in Tennessee. From his headquarters in Oxford, Mississippi, Grant cooperated by calling on the people of western Tennessee to hold elections for the U.S. House of Representatives and various county and state positions on December 24, 1862. Local judges were to oversee the process, and Federal officers could appoint judges if none were currently sitting in their area of control. Though many people in western Tennessee supported holding these elections, as did President Lincoln, the effort proved ineffective. Voting was heavy in some areas; for example, eight hundred people cast ballots in McNairy County to elect an area man who was serving as an officer in the Union army, but he never claimed his seat because of the time consumed by his military duties. In other counties, Confederate activities and confusion regarding the date of the election prevented balloting.[24]

Sherman, McClernand, and Vicksburg

With Federal troops once again moving south, Sherman eagerly supported Grant's idea to mount a second column against Vicksburg by way of the Mississippi River. "Time now is the great object," he wrote Porter. "We must not give time for new combinations." Sherman wanted to transport a large force downriver by steamer, cut the rail connections west of Vicksburg to Monroe, Louisiana, and east from the river city to Jackson, Mississippi. Then he hoped to steam up the Yazoo River and ascend the high bluffs on which Vicksburg was situated. On December 8, Grant issued orders for

Sherman to return to take charge of this expedition; for the time being Grant intended to keep his own force in northern Mississippi in order to hold Pemberton at Grenada. If the Confederates moved south, Grant could follow, possibly using the Yazoo River as his line of supply until he joined Sherman. Grant hoped that the forces at Helena, now under the command of Frederick Steele, would cooperate by adding more strength to Sherman's column. He directed his engineers to gather materials and tools to rebuild the railroad east of Vicksburg once the Federals gained control of it. During the past several months, Sherman had converted Memphis into an effective base of river operations. He secured a variety of building materials as well as provisions from the local area, giving receipts for the property to be settled after the war. His quartermaster had taken possession of more than six hundred buildings in the city, using many of them for army purposes and renting the rest to garner over $12,000 income for the government every month. Memphis thus would serve as the all-important depot for the Vicksburg campaign.[25]

Grant's decision to send Sherman down the river was prompted, in part, by a desire to forestall the appointment of another general to lead the Vicksburg expedition. He had gotten wind that John A. McClernand had been negotiating with Washington for the command. Grant sensed, he admitted after the war, that his superiors in Washington would support any move to push Sherman ahead of McClernand.[26]

McClernand had indeed gained the ear of administration officials about leading a special expedition down the river for the capture of Vicksburg. Everyone recognized that this Confederate stronghold was the key to control of the Mississippi, and Lincoln had discussed the need to find troops for its reduction as early as the previous July. Buell could not spare any of his divisions, and Curtis had barely enough troops to protect Missouri and hold Helena. Assistant Secretary of the Interior John P. Usher suggested raising a special force of volunteers to do the job, but Halleck preferred that the new volunteers replace veterans in garrison duty so commanders could send the hardened troops downriver. Lincoln already, in August 1862, was thinking of recruiting blacks as soldiers and using them to garrison key points along the Mississippi to maintain its free navigation.[27]

In September 1862, McClernand visited Washington for an extended stay to energetically lobby for an expedition to Vicksburg, with himself in command. Born in Kentucky but raised in Illinois, McClernand was a prewar politician with a background similar to Lincoln's. He made a "very favorable impression" on the politicians. McClernand seemed, in Salmon P. Chase's words, "brave and capable, but too desirous to be independent of every body else." But the Illinois politician moved the Washington authorities by assuring the president, "I would carry the war into their heart, . . . as the quickest and surest way to reopen the Mississippi River." Citizens in the Northwest were "deeply interested" in restoring navigation, and control of the river would allow the government to send supplies to Butler's troops at New Orleans at cheaper rates than by coastal shipping. Warning that the Northwesterners might lose their patience and their allegiance to the Federal government if their commercial needs continued to be frustrated, McClernand asked for as many as sixty thousand men to take Vicksburg. By October McClernand was willing to try it with twenty thousand—a leavening of veterans and new troops.[28]

On October 21 the War Department ordered McClernand to Springfield, Illinois, where he could speed up the organization of new regiments. After Grant received all the new units he needed for his overland operations in Mississippi, McClernand was to take the rest for his downriver expedition. Lincoln authorized Halleck to superintend these arrangements. "The importance of the expedition on the Mississippi is every day becoming more manifest," Stanton wrote McClernand a few days later. "I long to see you in the field striking vigorous blows against the rebellion in its most vital point."[29]

It was already apparent to Grant's staff by late October that McClernand was likely to lead a downriver expedition, although no official word was issued to those in the field until Halleck wired Grant on November 10 that Memphis would serve as the base of operations for a strike against Vicksburg. Yet Halleck did not mention McClernand. When Grant asked for clarification, Halleck gave him a blank check by assuring him that he had "command of all troops sent to your department, and have permission to fight the enemy where you please." This was enough to bolster Grant's selection of Sherman to take charge of the regiments McClernand was sending south.[30]

By mid-December McClernand sensed what was going on and telegraphed Stanton. The War Department, Stanton explained, planned to organize the troops in Grant's Department of the Tennessee into three corps, with McClernand to command one of them on the river expedition, while Grant would exercise "general supervision." Whether the Washington politicians ever intended to allow McClernand an independent command is an open question, but the irate general had no intention of letting Sherman take charge of the expedition he had worked so hard to generate. He solicited orders to leave Springfield on December 28, several days after Sherman's men left Memphis and just before they became engaged in battle a few miles north of Vicksburg.[31]

With help from Washington, Grant managed to prevent McClernand from acquiring an independent command he did not deserve. At about the same time, Confederate cavalrymen attacked Grant's line of communication in northern Mississippi, where the Union general was acutely conscious of his vulnerability: "I am extended now like a Peninsula into an enemies country with a large Army depending for their daily bread upon keeping open a line of rail-road running one hundred & ninety miles through an enemy's country, or at least through territory occupied by a people terribly embittered and hostile to us." In the end, it was not guerrillas but a brigade of Confederate cavalry under Earl Van Dorn that took advantage of the opportunity. The Confederate horsemen rode around Grant's left flank and attacked Holly Springs on December 20. Many members of the small Union garrison offered little resistance; the Confederates easily captured the town and fifteen hundred prisoners. For several hours they helped themselves to food and weapons before destroying huge amounts of goods. A complimentary raid by Nathan Bedford Forrest with twenty-five hundred cavalrymen, sent to wreck railroads in western Tennessee, had occurred during the first two weeks of December.[32]

Given the fact that he was only fifty miles deep into Mississippi, and had about two hundred more miles to go before reaching Vicksburg, Grant felt he could not afford to rely on the railroad to support a further advance. James B. McPherson, who was Grant's chief subordinate now that Sherman was off on his own expedition, advised that the Federals fall back to the north side of the Tallahatchie and send more troops to reinforce Sherman. McPherson also urged Grant to personally take charge of the Mississippi River drive. "It is the great feature of the campaign, and its execution rightfully belongs to you," he wrote.[33]

Grant readily agreed with the suggestion to fall back, but he hesitated about superseding Sherman on the river. As the Federals retired northward, they scoured the countryside for fifteen miles east and west of the railroad to find supplies, leaving only two months' worth of food for the civilians. They justified it to the citizenry by blaming Van Dorn. Living on half rations as they trudged through Holly Springs, the Federals were amazed at the amount of destruction in the small town. They took it as a blank check to seize everything they needed from the residents, not just food but furniture, books, and "bric-a-brac—in fact all kinds of household articles." The rank and file needed only the slightest encouragement to live off the land, and they did it with gusto, easily shading their actions into the realm of plundering.[34]

Chickasaw Bayou

Sherman prepared vigorously for his downriver expedition. He assembled twenty thousand men at Memphis and requested that an additional ten thousand men join him as he passed by Helena. "Such a force operating at Vicksburg in concert with the gunboats will make something yield and prepare your way," he wrote to Grant's chief of staff. But it took some time to assemble enough steamers to transport such a force. On December 11, Quartermaster Lewis B. Parsons received Grant's order to have sixty boats ready, but there were no more than ten available at St. Louis. Parsons had to scramble to find more and load them with all the available coal. The steamboat captains received instructions to use whatever wood they could locate at wood yards along the way when the coal ran out, and Sherman gathered axes so his troops could cut fresh timber if the wood yards were empty. It took Parsons several days to accumulate sixty-seven boats to haul Sherman's three divisions, plus ordnance and ammunition. Then he went along with the boats to superintend this large enterprise. "General Sherman is a trump," he told Halleck, "and makes things move. I like his business mode of doing things, his promptness and decision."[35]

The fleet left Memphis at almost the same time and maintained a relatively compact formation as it steamed down the Mississippi. The boats shook a great deal as the pilots carefully negotiated the falling water level. Fifty miles south of Helena, after Sherman picked up the promised reinforcements, guerrillas fired at some of his boats. He ordered a halt to burn the buildings and cotton gin at Abercrombie's Landing, where the guerrillas had taken position for the attack.[36]

Sherman planned to ascend the Yazoo River, which emptied into the Mississippi a few miles above Vicksburg. From there he would disembark and operate in the bottomland as he tried to find a way to ascend the river bluff, some 250 feet higher, where the Confederates had admirable defensive positions. Gaining a secure lodgment on the bluffs was the key to his expedition. Sherman later commented that the Mississippi River steamers were superbly designed for transporting and disembarking troops and guns almost any place they could tie up to the bank. The real problem lay with the six thousand Confederate soldiers who were available to defend the bluffs north of Vicksburg.[37]

Landing on December 26–28, the Federals advanced a short distance across the Yazoo bottomland toward their objective. The Confederates, under Stephen Dill Lee, waited behind light fieldworks on the bluffs. "We were soon in trenches flat of our you know what[,] snug as fleas in a sheep skin," wrote Henry C. Lee to a lady friend. The Federals were hampered as much by the terrain as by Confederate resistance, for the Yazoo bottomland was flat and wet. Chickasaw Bayou drained into the river from origins near the foot of Walnut Hills, the local name of the bluff.[38]

The Federals attacked on December 29. Sherman sent six brigades forward in loose coordination across the bayou and through natural obstructions as well as man-made slashings of timber. The combination of enemy fire and the cluttered nature of the battlefield prevented most units from reaching the foot of the bluffs, but a few, such as the 6th Missouri, lodged close to Confederate positions. The attack ended when nothing could be done to further this meager success. Sherman wanted to load his men back onto the boats and steam farther up the Yazoo to attack Hayne's Bluff, which was located much closer to the river bank and seemed to be not as well fortified. But a heavy fog prevented this move on December 30, followed by a drenching rain on January 1. In fact, so much rain fell that everyone assumed the Yazoo would suddenly rise, endangering the Union positions on the bottomland. Sherman ordered a pullout after suffering 1,776 casualties — most of them on December 29. The Confederates lost only 187 men.[39]

Sherman retreated a short distance up the Mississippi to Milliken's Bend, unwilling to make his repulse seem worse by retiring all the way to Memphis. Due to a breakdown in communications, he had not received a single dispatch from Grant since he returned to Memphis to organize the expedition in early December, and he waited before deciding what to do next.

Meanwhile, the Confederates celebrated their deliverance at such a slight cost in casualties. Stephen Lee kept his troops in the trenches for several days in case the Yankee boats reappeared, the men enduring their waterlogged works as best they could. Jefferson Davis viewed Sherman's repulse as vindication of his grand strategy—retain control of the great river, cause dissatisfaction among residents of the Northwest, and then enjoy the consequences as a rift developed between those states and the East that would "paralyze the power of both" and lead to Confederate independence.[40]

Arkansas Post

McClernand made his way downriver to claim command of the Vicksburg expedition but reached the troops too late to influence the operations at Chickasaw Bayou. A War Department order dated December 18, dividing Grant's troops into four corps with McClernand to command one of them, forced Grant to accept the troublesome politician as a subordinate. McClernand took command from Sherman at Milliken's Bend on January 4 and, to his credit, sought ways to further Union goals. If the bluffs were unassailable, McClernand considered trying to find a route to bypass Vicksburg on the west side of the river. However, he changed his mind on learning the Confederates had captured a boat called the *Blue Wing*, which was hauling coal barges to Sherman's fleet. The Rebels had taken it to Fort Hindman at Arkansas Post, some twenty-five miles up the Arkansas River. Rather than look for a new route south, he would move up the Arkansas River and capture the fort in order to secure the Federal line of communications with Memphis. McClernand banked on a quick victory and a speedy return to the main target at Vicksburg.[41]

Fort Hindman was a bastioned fort located at a sharp bend of the Arkansas, with some of its guns protected by iron-plated casemates. McClernand set out on January 5 and landed three miles downstream of the fort four days later. The Federals maneuvered to close on the fort and its outnumbered garrison on January 10, as the Confederates quickly dug a line of earthworks extending from the fort to expand their defensive position. Porter's gunboats steamed close and fired heavily on Fort Hindman that evening, but it was too late in the day for McClernand to launch a supportive attack on land.[42]

The navy resumed firing the next day, effectively silencing most guns in the fort as the army continued to maneuver and press close to the Confederates. The Federals failed to locate the Rebel left wing, which was unprotected, but they managed to get several regiments close enough to the Rebel front to be in position to launch a general attack by the afternoon. Confederate commander Thomas J. Churchill, however, decided to surrender at 4:30 P.M., largely due to the gunboats silencing his river batteries, which would have allowed Porter to enfilade the infantry line. Bickering between the navy and the army as to which service deserved the lion's share of credit for the victory obscured the fact that McClernand had won a sizable triumph at little cost. The Federals suffered 1,092 casualties while taking nearly 5,000 prisoners and seventeen guns.[43]

When Grant heard about McClernand's expedition up the Arkansas, he initially considered it "a wild goose chase" because it diverted Federal attention from the real target. He became more supportive of the diversion after learning how successfully it had been conducted. McClernand considered moving farther up the Arkansas to seize Little Rock, but falling water and Grant's peremptory order to return to the Mississippi compelled him to shelve that idea. McClernand issued an order prohibiting his men from taking Confederate property from Fort Hindman for their personal use, giving a twenty-four-hour grace period for anyone to give up their booty before disciplinary action would be taken. He ordered the demolition of the Confederate defenses, as much as was possible in a short time, and then boarded his boats for the return to Milliken's Bend. The Federals mercilessly sacked Napoleon, a small town located at the mouth of the Arkansas River, as they passed by. Although Sherman tried to limit the damage, the town was too far gone before he had a chance to stop it.[44]

Grant Takes Charge

Grant remained in northern Mississippi for some time following the Holly Springs raid, overseeing the retirement of his units north of the Tallahatchie River and repairs on the railroad system north of that stream. He located his headquarters at Holly Springs from December 23 until January 10, then moved to Memphis. Grant planned to send two divisions down the Mississippi to join McClernand's force; he felt compelled to accompany them and take overall command. Most of the Union's river steamers available on the Western waters were tied up in transporting and supplying the large concentration of troops already with McClernand, and the additional two divisions would increase the logistical burden. Nevertheless, everyone agreed that the river was the true line of advance for Grant and the quartermasters had to find more boats to sustain the operation. Grant instructed McClernand to discharge any steamers he could spare as soon as he returned to Milliken's Bend so they could be used to haul supplies and McPherson's two divisions from Memphis.[45]

One of those two divisions left the city on January 20 on a string of steamers. Cyrus F. Boyd of the 15th Iowa marveled at the sight as eleven boats followed the leading steamer, each one about two hundred to four hundred yards apart from each other. By this time Memphis had been "rehabilitated" enough to permit many residents and visitors to stand on the bluffs, waving flags and cheering the Federals "as the long winding fleet turned to the South," Boyd noted in his diary. "We move to capture the stronghold of the rebels in the Valley of the Mississippi," McPherson told his men when the other division was ready to leave in February. "We go to plant our flag upon the ramparts of Vicksburg."[46]

The Confederates were well aware of the danger if Grant combined his forces with McClernand's. Johnston warned Davis that the Federals could move large numbers of troops on the river faster than he could learn of it and react by moving men on land. If Grant were able to lay siege to Vicksburg, Johnston would have only eleven thousand men near Jackson, Mississippi, and would be unable to break the investment. If, on the other hand, Grant bypassed Vicksburg and laid siege to Port Hudson, Johnston would be unable to save that point as well. Despite their impressive victory at Chickasaw Bayou, the Confederates seemed to be suffering many disadvantages while trying to hold the corridor between Vicksburg and Port Hudson.[47]

Stones River

Unlike in the previous fall and winter, Federal authorities pushed forward with simultaneous offensives in the West in late 1862. As Grant began to manage the complex operations in Mississippi, William S. Rosecrans took command of the Army of the Ohio from Buell on October 27. Most of his troops were in the process of moving in easy stages to Nashville following their campaign in Kentucky. Rosecrans advanced one corps quickly to Nashville, based on reports that Rebel troops were already appearing at Murfreesboro, thirty miles southeast of the fortified capital of Tennessee. He continued to hold the other two corps along the railroad north of Nashville to make repairs. The first cars rolled into the city by November 26, but more repairs and refurbishment continued for another month before Rosecrans finished his link with Louisville.[48]

During November and December Bragg also took his Army of Tennessee to Murfreesboro in stages, intending to secure at least a portion of middle Tennessee for Confederate use and to block further Union advance toward Chattanooga. When President Davis visited the army in December, he reported hearing Bragg tell his troops "that he hoped again to lead them into Kentucky, and to the banks of the Ohio river." That was a rhetorical flourish meant to bolster flagging spirits, for Bragg had learned a hard lesson in Kentucky. His army could not count on a secure line of communication with the South if it extended itself so deeply into Union-controlled territory. The dream of adding Kentucky to the constellation of Southern stars and threatening an invasion of Illinois, Indiana, and Ohio would remain just a dream for the remainder of the war. For the rest of his tenure as commander of the Army of Tennessee, Bragg set himself firmly on a defensive course of action.[49]

Moreover, Bragg had to contend with soldiers who could not resist the temptation to steal food and other articles from the local inhabitants, even if they were Southerners. Based on civilian reports that his men were "visiting, loitering, and marauding," and some were even forcing civilians to provide sleeping quarters, Bragg issued a general order forbidding such unmilitary acts. His men had no right to insist "that they should be entertained" by the people they enlisted to protect.[50]

The Washington authorities expected great things of Rosecrans. Most of all, they wanted an early offensive against Bragg to complement Grant's enormous activity in Mississippi and Ambrose Burnside's offensive against Robert E. Lee at Fredericksburg, Virginia. Rosecrans resisted all pressure as he prepared his worn-out troops and assembled his army at Nashville in December. The War Department renamed his command the Department of the Cumberland and temporarily designated the old Army of the Ohio as the Fourteenth Corps. Rosecrans renamed the three corps in Buell's old organizational plan as the Right Wing (led by Alexander McDowell McCook), the Center (led by George H. Thomas), and the Left Wing (led by Thomas L. Crittenden). He also insisted that his men be properly equipped and supplied before taking the field. Lincoln was extremely anxious that the army drive the Rebels from middle Tennessee by December 10 so news of that victory could cross the Atlantic and influence the January session of the British Parliament. Washington feared that the British government might succumb to pressure from English textile concerns and recognize the Confederacy in order to ensure their supply of raw cotton. Rosecrans's campaign "may be, and perhaps is, the very turning point in our foreign relations," Henry Halleck told the general.[51]

Rosecrans could not deliver on Lincoln's timetable due to the absolute need to secure his rail line, which had been damaged at the outset of Buell's previous campaign and neglected as that general tried to save Kentucky from Bragg's invasion. Through hard work, the Federals managed to rebuild forty-five miles of track in three weeks. Even then, Rosecrans spent another three weeks stockpiling supplies at Nashville so his army would have a month's worth of food before starting the next campaign. He could not supply the men by living off the countryside because of a shortage of cavalry to protect foraging parties from roving Confederate horsemen. Horatio G. Wright, commander of the Department of the Ohio, was responsible for guarding Kentucky. He assured Washington that Rosecrans's men depended for their "very existence" on the railroad; "without it, his army would be forced to retreat or starve."[52]

While preparing his army in Nashville, Rosecrans dealt with civil-military relations in his departmental command. He issued a general order spelling out the duties and privileges of loyal citizens and what disloyal residents could expect from the Union army. Those who exhibited hostile behavior toward the U.S. government "have no rights," and could appeal only to the "laws of war and the dictates of humanity." Guerrillas were little more than "pirates and robbers." In addition, Rosecrans tried to clamp down on depredations by his own soldiers to prevent ill-feeling toward Federal authority.[53]

Rosecrans attempted to scale down the arrests of civilians by his provost marshals, ordering them to consider the character of informants and file

William Starke Rosecrans. (Library of Congress, LC-DIG-cwpb-06052)

proper paperwork so he could keep tabs on how many were arrested for disloyal actions and speech. He forbade the issuance of passes to women to travel by rail to Nashville and allowed only a few to men, since his quartermaster was having difficulty shipping adequate supplies for the army. Moreover, George H. Thomas thought women were "more insinuating and far more dangerous than men." Rosecrans was sympathetic to those Confederate soldiers from Kentucky who now wished to desert and go home, permitting them to take the "non-combatant's parole and give proper security that they will keep it." He prohibited military sutlers from selling goods to area residents, because many items thus sold wound up in the hands of the Confederate army.[54]

The Fourteenth Corps left Nashville on December 26, traversing the countryside south and southeast of the capital in three columns to deal with Bragg's dispersed formation. As the Federals approached the Confederates, Bragg consolidated his army near Stones River, a short distance northwest of Murfreesboro. Rosecrans brought his army opposite this position by the evening of December 30 and prepared to strike with his left wing the next day, hoping it could cross the river and enter the town. Ironically, Bragg also prepared to strike the next morning with his left wing; his objectives were to drive away the Federals, capture the Nashville Pike, and isolate Rosecrans from the state capital. He sent a brigade of cavalry to screen his left flank and damage the retreating Federals as much as possible.[55]

As it happened, Bragg began his offensive before Rosecrans on the morning of December 31. The Confederates attempted a difficult maneuver, swinging several divisions like a giant gate across a countryside cluttered with cedar brakes and limestone outcroppings, with a few cleared farms and roadways. The outer end of the Confederate line had to advance about three miles in a great arc. The battle of Stones River—or Murfreesboro, as the Confederates called it—devolved into a series of loosely coordinated brigade actions, but the veteran troops of Bragg's army performed magnificently, forcing the Federals to conduct a fighting retreat across the battlefield as they repeatedly outflanked their opponents' formations. Union general Philip Sheridan's division managed to hold on longer than many others, gaining valuable time. More importantly, William B. Hazen's brigade secured a wooded area, called the "Round Forest," along the Nashville Pike against spirited Confederate attacks. Hazen's brigade became the pivot upon which the Federal right wing bent back, saving Rosecrans's position from complete collapse. By the end of this long day of bloodshed, the Federals were firmly planted along the Nashville Pike and the Nashville and Chattanooga Railroad that ran parallel to it.[56]

Battle of Stones River. This view depicts a brigade of Indiana, Kentucky, and Ohio troops under Colonel Samuel Beatty in action on December 31, 1862. (Johnson and Buel, *Battles and Leaders*, 3:622)

The two armies remained largely idle only a few hundred yards from each other all day on January 1. Bragg resumed the offensive on January 2 by sending John C. Breckinridge's division against a Union force that had crossed Stones River on the Federal left flank. Breckinridge was able to drive away the blue-coated infantry, but his men marched into the teeth of a Union artillery concentration that assembled on the high ground west of the river. Forty-five Union guns pummeled the division, inflicting many of the seventeen hundred casualties suffered among Breckinridge's five thousand men, as the battle of Stones River came to an end.[57]

Believing reports that Rosecrans was receiving reinforcements, Bragg pulled away on the night of January 3. He established a new defensive position at Shelbyville, about thirty miles to the southeast along the line of railroad. Both sides had lost about 13,000 men in this fierce encounter, close to one-third of the troops engaged. Rosecrans had lost 433 men for each mile his drive from Nashville secured for the Union; at that rate, he could expect to lose an additional 38,104 troops before getting to Chattanooga and nearly 44,000 to go from there to Atlanta. Even though he had lost the battle, Bragg

The woods at Stones River. Taken in the Stones River National Battlefield Park, this photograph demonstrates the rugged terrain on which much of the fighting took place on December 31, 1862. (Earl J. Hess)

had exacted a price in blood that the Federals could barely afford if they hoped to have any strength left to finish the war.[58]

Rosecrans put a facade of bravado on his victory by proclaiming his desire "to push them to the wall" following his occupation of Murfreesboro, but in reality he settled down to once again refit his army. There was no doubt that the army needed rest and additional supplies and equipment. Rosecrans loudly called for reinforcements, more artillery, more cavalry, horses, and revolving rifles to mount some infantry units, all of which the harried War Department officials gave him. But Rosecrans extended the preparatory phase of the next push toward Chattanooga into a six-month-long stay at Murfreesboro, adding much to the frustration of war planners in Washington.[59]

The Union victory at Stones River inspired loyalists in Tennessee. Although Andrew Johnson was pleased that Bragg had been pushed thirty miles farther away, he continued to pressure Lincoln for the liberation of eastern Tennessee. He correctly argued that the entire state had to be secured "before confidence can be inspired with the mass of the people that the Govt. has the power to assert & maintain its authority."[60]

Monument to Hazen's Brigade, Stones River Battlefield. Constructed by survivors of the brigade commanded by Colonel William B. Hazen within months after the battle, this monument was one of the first to honor those who fell in the Civil War. (Ray D. Smith Oversize Photograph Collection, Special Collections and Archives, Knox College Library, Galesburg, Illinois)

The fighting at Stones River took place during a historic time in American history. Lincoln's preliminary Emancipation Proclamation became effective on January 1, 1863, setting free every slave living within territory controlled by the Confederate government. The final draft of the proclamation excluded all of Tennessee, however, at the insistence of Andrew Johnson and other state loyalists. Johnson thought emancipation would be too controversial for the state's wavering element. Lincoln justified exempting Tennessee and other areas under Federal control because, he argued, the proclamation had "no constitutional or legal justification, except as a military measure." In areas under Federal dominance, such "military necessity did not apply." Nevertheless, the Confederates made the most of the proclamation in their propaganda. Gideon J. Pillow, newly appointed head of the Conscript Bureau in the West, viewed it as an incitement to race war and urged able-bodied Southerners to enlist in the Confederate army.[61]

The Washington authorities were pleased with Rosecrans's victory, although won at great cost and resulting in limited strategic gain. "God bless you, and all with you!" Lincoln telegraphed Rosecrans. Six months later, when the general complained that his further accomplishments in the Tullahoma campaign went unrecognized, Lincoln consoled him by writing: "I can never forget, whilst I remember anything, that about the end of last year, and beginning of this, you gave us a hard earned victory, which, had there been a defeat instead, the nation could scarcely have lived over." The sense of crisis that suffused the period of December-January had resulted from the fear of British recognition of the Confederacy, the horrible defeat of Burnside at Fredericksburg, and the frustration of Grant's first strike at Vicksburg. Tension also filled the air as the North implemented its controversial emancipation policy. Moreover, as the president reminded Rosecrans, Democratic opposition to Lincoln's war policies in the fall of 1862 contributed to the sense of anxiety that winter. Costly and limited it may have been, but the Union victory at Stones River was badly needed.[62]

8 } The Vicksburg Campaign and Siege

The Vicksburg campaign evolved more from circumstances than from a coherent plan. When Grant sent Sherman down the Mississippi, it was with the intention of executing a strong, fast strike that could capture the Rebel stronghold, with no thought as to what would be done if the strike failed. Sherman's refusal to fall back to Memphis after he faltered pinned the Federals to a forward position, close to Vicksburg, where there was little dry land to camp troops. Moreover, the army was at the end of a supply line nearly two hundred miles long in a straight line south of Memphis, dependent on dozens of river steamers. Vested with a stubborn character, Grant continued to operate in that narrow river setting after he joined the expedition, unwilling to give the impression of a strategic defeat by retiring to Memphis. He was determined to win or lose by operating at the extreme end of his logistical support system, trying to find a way to either bypass the stronghold or reach the bluffs from which it impeded Northern navigation of the great river.

Grant claimed that the main reason he decided to go down and take personal charge of the campaign lay in his distrust of McClernand's ability to handle the situation. If Sherman had remained in command, Grant may have remained at Memphis to administer his department. After visiting McClernand at Napoleon on January 17, Grant came away with the impression that most of his subordinates shared his view. He instructed McClernand to take the troops down to Young's Point and Milliken's Bend, then returned to Memphis to arrange for security in his rear.[1]

After returning to the scene of operations at Young's Point on January 29, Grant felt that the "real work of the campaign and siege of Vicksburg now began." It would be a "work . . . of time, and will require a large force at the final struggle." The enormity of the task was beginning to be felt in Washington as well. Newspaperman Charles A. Dana, sent by Secretary of War Stanton to serve as an observer in Grant's camp, recalled the opening of the Mississippi River as "that toughest of tough jobs."[2]

More troops arrived soon after Grant reached the expedition.

Twelve to fourteen boats left Memphis on January 21 and deposited their human cargo only fourteen miles from Vicksburg on the low-lying bottomland of the stream where steamers lined the bank as "far as the eyes can reach," according to Cyrus F. Boyd. The troops were "in a most filthy and sickly condition from being on the boats so long. No hog-pen will compare." Boyd found the area "knee deep in black mud." The levee—ten feet tall and twenty feet wide at the base—was the only high ground. Boyd came across many small hospitals filled with sick soldiers surrounded by newly dug graves along the levee. Still, there was an air of industry packed into this small space, with dozens of boats unloading supplies as well as men, everyone making maximum use of each square foot of available ground.[3]

Grant began searching for a way to get his command out of the bottomlands and moving toward the enemy as soon as possible. He pinned his initial hope on enlarging the canal across De Soto Point that Thomas Williams's small force had begun the previous summer during the first Federal effort against Vicksburg. Early on, despite the enormous number of troops involved and the use of steam dredges, it became clear that the canal had problems. The angles at which it joined the river at both ends were too sharp to allow enough water to flow through, and the Confederates began to construct artillery emplacements at Warrenton on the east bank of the river, directly opposite the southern end of the canal. Yet Grant continued for weeks to work on the artificial waterway, in part to give employment to his troops. The Mississippi itself impeded work on the canal when the waters rose in March due to spring rains and broke a retaining dam at the northern end. By then, Confederate artillery commanded the southern half of the canal, making it less likely that Grant would use it even if his men managed to finish the channel.[4]

What Grant really wanted was an avenue out of the bottomlands and up onto the high ground east of the Mississippi. "Foot once upon dry land on the other side of the river I think the balance would be of short duration," he wrote his wife. Grant explored at least three routes across the expansive bottomlands of the Mississippi to find a way to attain his goal. Lake Providence, which lay on the west side of the river seventy-five miles north of Vicksburg, offered access to a series of waterways that eventually connected to the Red River, which in turn drained into the Mississippi many miles south of Vicksburg. Grant could use this route to take all or part of his force south and join troops under Major General Nathaniel P. Banks, who had replaced Benjamin Butler as commander of the Department of the Gulf, in attacking Port Hudson. The Lake Providence route would also "open a vast foraging district" for the Federals and allow them to interrupt the shipment of supplies from the Trans-Mississippi to the east side of the river. Grant assigned James McPherson the task of managing the Lake Providence expedition with a full division of his Seventeenth Corps. He instructed the Federals to collect able-bodied blacks in the lake area and send them to work on the canal near Vicksburg.[5]

Grant explored other routes, too. The Mississippi Delta country stretching northward from Vicksburg represented an expanse of bottomland fifty miles wide between the river and the high ground. A possible route through this region lay in the Yazoo Pass, a short waterway that formerly connected the Mississippi with the Coldwater River about ten miles south of Helena. Since a levee had been constructed along the east side of the Mississippi ten years before, the pass had not been used. Its sharp bends would barely be manageable by the kind of steamers at Grant's disposal, but the Federals were determined to try it. On February 3, they cut the levee and pushed a division of troops aboard thirteen transports, headed by ironclad gunboats, into the tortuous channel. During the first four days the fleet traveled only fourteen miles until it reached the Coldwater and then made thirty miles in six days. Entering the Tallahatchie, the Federals were stymied near its junction with the Yalobusha at Greenwood by Confederate Fort Pemberton, hastily made of cotton bales on the lowland south of the river. The ironclads bombarded the fort twice in mid-March but could not silence the few guns in the work or run past it due to the narrow confines of the stream. The expedition was stuck some eighty miles north of Vicksburg.[6]

The Yazoo Pass expedition demonstrated how much Grant's campaign relied on the support of the navy gunboats and the large fleet of civilian craft contracted to carry troops and supplies. The Federals literally could not have survived without these resources. "The army depends on us to take entire charge of them on the water," boasted David Dixon Porter, "and it employs every vessel I have." Everyone keenly felt the dependency. "To be caught without . . . stores . . . at so remote a point as the vicinity of Vicksburgh, with the river infested by guerillas in the rear, would indeed be a dilemma," wrote McClernand. But it is wrong to assume that Northern resources could easily meet the army's needs. When Grant added McPherson's troops to the concentration of men near Vicksburg, it strained Federal logistical capacity to the utmost. Fifty steamers suddenly were called for and sent, but quartermasters had to meet the supply needs of the expedition by using towboats with barges because there were not enough steamers left. Since the army kept most of the boats employed downriver, the strain of shipping needed supplies everywhere else along the Mississippi and its tributaries increased with each passing week.[7]

When Grant requested thirty steamers of a special type (smaller and powered by side wheels to better navigate the Yazoo Pass and the Lake Providence route), Federal authorities protested. Though these steamers were common on the Ohio River, they were currently "very scarce," as Henry Halleck told Grant. Quartermaster Lewis B. Parsons, based at St. Louis, informed Grant that he could find no such boats along the Mississippi and warned the general that the majority of all civilian steamers normally available to him were already in use, and he was having difficulty meeting logistical needs in Tennessee and Kentucky. Grant explained that the boats had been retained because, with rising spring waters, they were needed to save troops from flooded campsites. Resourceful quartermasters found a few small boats on the Ohio for Grant, but the experience was a lesson to the general that Northern logistical resources were not unlimited. Meanwhile, Quartermaster General Montgomery C. Meigs agreed that any civilian steamers damaged by the tortuous passage of the Yazoo Pass route should be repaired with U.S. government money.[8]

While Grant struggled to find a way out of the bottomlands, Confederate guerrillas began to make trouble for the string of boats that kept his army alive. "Men lurk in the woods without a flag or distinguishing mark," wrote Porter, "and fire at any human being they may see on a deck of a steamer without caring or knowing whether it is friend or foe they are about to murder." A Federal hospital boat was thus fired upon even though it held many wounded Confederates from the Arkansas Post battle. Samuel R. Curtis suggested arming civilian steamers with small cannon, but Halleck informed him that there were only a few old pieces of ordnance available and the suggestion was never implemented.[9]

The Yazoo Pass expedition proved to be a failure, too. Grant sent reinforcements under Isaac Quinby with instructions to push past Greenwood and into the Yazoo River. If Quinby was able to clear the bluffs down to the Confederate guns planted at Haynes' Bluff, the Federals could meet the expedition by steaming up the Yazoo. However, the problem lay not in scarce infantry but in the logjam at Greenwood, and Quinby could not find a way to bypass the Confederate guns. Rising waters made the situation even worse. Meanwhile, the Federal troops idling their time on cramped steamboats became restless. When allowed to roam over the soggy bottoms, they plundered whatever farms and plantations they could find. The Federals gave up in early April and made their way back to Grant's army.[10]

Before the abandonment of the Yazoo Pass expedition, Grant launched another push through the bottomland via Steele's Bayou, which emptied into the Yazoo River near the old Chickasaw Bayou battlefield. He hoped this force could cooperate with Quinby in clearing the Yazoo. Before it reached Steele's Bayou, the boats had to make their way forty miles along Black Bayou, which was cluttered with felled trees, then into Deer Creek, and then into Rolling Fork and the Big Sunflower. Porter himself led five of his ironclads and only two steamers filled with troops. Sherman kept more infantrymen at Black Bayou as Porter's gunboats penetrated the fertile land along Deer Creek. He made only half a mile per day due to the winding stream and the trees felled by retreating Confederates. Eventually, the route became too much for him, and Porter sent a message that he needed help or else his ironclads, stuck in the stream, would be overpowered by the enemy. Sherman raced troops ahead to save the boats, and then the Federals retreated.[11]

Grant was disappointed at the failure of both the Yazoo Pass expedition and the Steele's Bayou approach. With no faith in the canal, he had pinned all his hopes on reducing the Confederate position at Haynes' Bluff by maneuver. Now he feared he might have to attack it directly to gain the high ground east of the Mississippi, a prospect he knew would lead to heavy casualties. "But I think it can be done," he wrote. Meanwhile, he assured Halleck that Porter and Sherman had recovered "several thousand bales" of cotton and harvested huge amounts of provisions and "several hundred negroes" during the Steele's Bayou expedition.[12]

Naval Action

The Confederates continued to shift large amounts of supplies from the Trans-Mississippi through the corridor between Vicksburg and Port Hudson. In an attempt to interrupt that flow, Charles Ellet (Alfred Ellet's brother) ran the *Queen of the West* past the Vicksburg batteries on February 2; the *Queen* received many shots but suffered only light damage. Ellet's job was to patrol the river south of the city. During the next three days he sank three vessels and captured a boat to serve as a tender to the *Queen*. In order to close down the Red River as a major conduit of supplies, Ellet steamed upstream sixty miles to Gordon's Landing on February 14. There he tried to capture three boats tied up near a fort but grounded the *Queen* in the attempt. Ellet had to abandon the vessel and escape on the tender, pursued by the Confederate ram *William H. Webb*. Ellet found help when he rendezvoused with the *Indianola*, which had run past Vicksburg with coal barges, on February 16.[13]

The Rebels now took the offensive in this developing river war. On February 27 several Confederate boats attacked the *Indianola*, and a fierce engagement ensued. Outnumbered, the Union vessel was rammed seven times and captured with most of its crew; it later sank in shallow water. The next day the Confederates abandoned the sunken craft on reports that a Union ironclad had run the Vicksburg batteries and was on its way. This vessel later proved to be a dummy ironclad, a raft made of logs with simulated wheelhouses, casemates, and Quaker guns, but it had a dramatic psychological effect on the Southerners.[14]

With forces from the Department of the Gulf now gearing up to operate against Port Hudson, David Farragut decided to take some of his oceangoing vessels upstream to intercept Confederate supply arrangements at the Red River. He ran several ships past Port Hudson on March 14 and sailed nearly to Vicksburg, where he established communications with Grant. Porter was off on the Steele's Bayou expedition, but his subordinate, Henry Walke, refused to risk his ironclads by running them past Vicksburg. But Alfred Ellet was willing to do so. He sent two speedy rams past the Confederate guns, but one of them was sunk and the other severely damaged. Farragut was on his own.[15]

Naval activities on the river demonstrated that it was possible to pass the Confederate guns at both strongholds, although very risky. Yet river navigation could never be fully restored until the land positions at Vicksburg and Port Hudson were taken by infantry forces. Still, it was obvious that even more naval power could help the Union effort. The Navy Department contemplated shifting all but two coastal ironclads currently outside the harbor of Charleston, South Carolina, to the Mississippi River, though in the end it never followed through with the plan.[16]

Life on the River

While the boats tried to spearhead paths through the bottomlands, or attempted to curtail Confederate supply lines, Grant's infantrymen lived precariously along the Mississippi. When the river was low, they could camp on the bottomland west of the levees as well as on the artificial embankment. Many of them became sick after being "pent up so long a time on steamers," as Grant put it, and camping in winter weather on low, soggy ground. When the Mississippi began to rise with the coming of spring, the situation grew worse. The lowland west of the levee slowly became inundated, forcing the Federals to move their camps to the embankment. Grant was compelled to keep a large number of steamers available to evacuate the men if it became necessary, as everyone depended on the strength of these man-made strings of earth. "Kilby Smith's Brigade is roosting on the Levee with bare standing room," Sherman reported in mid-March. His Fifteenth Corps was "strung along the Levee for four miles." There were not enough steamboats "to float us and if we had there is no dry land to go to." The Army of the Tennessee barely survived within the severe limitations of its water-bound environment.[17]

In addition to the problems of supporting a large accumulation of manpower and finding a way to approach Vicksburg, Grant also had to contend with difficulties associated with trade. The Federal move to Milliken's Bend had opened up two hundred miles of the Mississippi Valley to Northern interests. Commerce already was lively between Memphis and Helena even before the start of Grant's Vicksburg campaign, and many of the goods bought and sold eventually wound up in Confederate hands. Worst of all were the cotton traders, who aggressively penetrated uncontrolled areas along the riverbank to buy the white gold at almost any price and often bribed army officers for their assistance. It became clear to Porter and Grant that stopping all trade south of Helena would be in the Union's best interests. Porter argued that he had not boats enough to take care of Grant's army and protect civilian steamers from guerrilla attacks at the same time. Ironically, the Confederate government had also tried to stop the sale of cotton to Northern buyers at the start of the war, willing to confiscate the cargo, levy fines and prison sentences, and share the proceeds with informants, but it seemed to have no effect on the traffic.[18]

Grant acted, without consulting Washington, to stop all trade south of Memphis on January 20. Protests forced him to resume commerce between Memphis and Helena, but the military intended to strictly enforce restrictions south of Helena. Porter instructed his subordinates to stop and search all civilian steamers for contraband of war and to seize all cotton on board. Further, he wanted his officers to send parties ashore, where it was safe to do so, and seize all the cotton they could because "it is all rebel property," he reasoned.[19]

While vigilance enforced the trade restrictions south of Helena during the course of the Vicksburg campaign, greed ran riot at Memphis. "Honesty is the exception and peculation the rule wherever the army is brought into contact with trade," moaned Stephen A. Hurlbut, the commander at Memphis. Cotton traders bribed army personnel "beyond all calculation" in and around the city. In addition to cotton, Memphis was a major port for a wide range of supplies used by both civilians and the army. A flourishing trade in a wide variety of goods took place between the city and interior Mississippi, and Confederate military personnel wound up in possession of many useful items. Many people smuggled contraband out of Memphis that, if found by Union authorities, would have been confiscated. Captured Confederates boasted that the fall of Memphis "has been of great service to them, as they now obtain abundant supplies," as Lorenzo Thomas reported to Stanton.[20]

Union officers assigned to inspect boats on the river often found contraband articles, such as Confederate dispatches secured in a lady's satchel and hidden in a cabin. One inspector discovered a trunk on board the *John D. Perry* that held quinine and guns in a false top; the trunk's owner carried more than two thousand dollars in gold. In early April Grant sent a trusted staff officer to Memphis with instructions to more fully set up a system of inspecting boats coming upstream with cotton and those going downstream with items potentially useful to the Confederates, but he was never able to completely stop the illicit trade.[21]

Grant relented a bit on the cotton trade for what he believed were humanitarian reasons. A few families living along the river, seemingly loyal or at least neutral in the sectional contest, were given permits by corps commanders to take cotton to Memphis in order to raise money for their subsistence. Many of these families lived near McPherson's troops at Lake Providence. "I have never done one act against the union," declared Thomas L. Van Fossen when he asked for a permit to sell up to four hundred bales of cotton. Federal soldiers had taken nearly all of his eighty-five slaves, forty cattle, thirty-three mules, and even his family's clothes—"in short we have been nearly ruined." McPherson gave him the permit. J. J. Shermard, who claimed that "I have never aided nor abetted the Confederates Except in sofar . . . I was obliged to countenance there doings to save my neck," received permission to sell more than three hundred bales. Grant personally issued permits for several others.[22]

Although Lincoln had vested the implementation of the Confiscation Act with the attorney general, Porter vigorously attempted to execute the act himself by seizing cotton belonging to anyone guilty of aiding the rebellion. In late February 1863 his subordinates confiscated at least 120 bales from three people. The army also flirted with implementing the confiscation policy. When William Sutton's property near Lake Providence was burned by Federal troops, division commander John A. Logan decided to assess the value from the pay of regiments involved in the destruction because, as "a disloyal man," Sutton's property was subject to confiscation and its destruction was a loss to the government.[23]

Grant admitted that his mode of giving permits to seemingly deserving applicants had been abused by conniving men. By April 1863 he ended the practice altogether, convinced that nothing less than total stoppage of trade, or complete governmental control over it, would suffice. Any system that allowed private cotton trades to operate at all was a corrupting influence on military operations. Grant told his father that he would like to see cotton speculators "drafted at once and put in the first forlorn hope" rather than allow them any freedom within his zone of authority.[24]

Enlisting Black Soldiers

"The colored population is the great *available*, and yet *unavailed* of, force, for restoring the Union," Lincoln wrote Andrew Johnson as Washington geared up to recruit black troops. "The bare sight of fifty thousand armed, and drilled black soldiers upon the banks of the Mississippi, would end the rebellion at once." In urging the new policy on Grant, Halleck argued that the "character of the war has very much changed within the last year. There is now no possible hope of reconciliation with the rebels. The Union party in the South is virtually destroyed. There can be no peace but that which is forced by the sword. We must conquer the rebels or be conquered by them."[25]

The justification for arming African Americans went deeper than merely adding much-needed troops to Union ranks. It denied the Confederates an opportunity to use those men as laborers, thus weakening the Rebel war effort even more. In late March 1863, Federal authorities sent Adjutant General Lorenzo Thomas to initiate the organization of black regiments in the Mississippi Valley. Thomas was also tasked to report on the condition of all contraband and on any officers who dealt in the cotton trade, though raising black regiments was his major assignment. He found Commander Stephen A. Hurlbut at Memphis ready to cooperate and eager to use black soldiers as garrison troops.[26]

But when Thomas launched an informational campaign, talking to large assemblies of Grant's men from Helena southward, he often encountered a mixed response. Thomas enlisted popular officers to give talks; Benjamin M. Prentiss, C. C. Washburn, and Alvin P. Hovey spoke to seven thousand troops at Helena in early April. Another eleven thousand men heard the message at Lake Providence. By the time Thomas reached Milliken's Bend, he reported that the "prejudice in this army respecting arming the negroes is fast dying out." His message was more hopeful than accurate, for many soldiers did not find the thought of fighting side by side with freed slaves appealing. Sherman and Frank P. Blair accompanied Thomas in a presentation to Blair's division and two Missouri regiments at Young's Point on April 21. Standing on boards stretched across two wagons, Thomas stressed that only white men dedicated to the project would be allowed to serve as officers in the black regiments, and that he had the authority to discharge anyone from the army who opposed the policy of enlisting blacks. Sherman told the men that, despite their individual opinions, he expected everyone to obey orders, a message essentially repeated by the other speakers. A German colonel translated everything in a language the two Missouri regiments could understand. It would take time for the rank and file to more fully appreciate the advantages of arming blacks; in the spring of 1863, it was still a new and controversial idea.[27]

As Thomas toured northern Mississippi in May, his message often received a lukewarm reception. While everyone was willing to give three cheers for the president, many greeted the concept of arming slaves with muted protest, unwilling to risk censure or discharge while waiting to see if the idea would work.[28]

While every slave south of Helena was, by the terms of the Emancipation Proclamation, free in 1863, and therefore a fit candidate for a blue uniform, Tennessee had specifically been excluded from the proclamation. Hurlbut wondered what was to be done in "the present anomolus situation" of the state, which was "neither exactly loyal or altogether disloyal, but yet wholly deprived of all the machinery by which civil government operates." State laws that protected slavery before the war were now held in abeyance in favor of a military government. The army acted mostly as if slavery were already dead, even if it was not legally so. Five thousand black refugees lived in Hurlbut's district besides many others who worked for the government. He estimated that three-fourths of them were women and children, and the rest were men too infirm to work. Hurlbut continued to feed the entire group. At least two thousand additional blacks lived precariously in Memphis without government support, occupying abandoned houses and sheds. Hurlbut did not know what to do about this human problem, and Grant, his superior, was too busy operating against Vicksburg to offer advice.[29]

Indeed, Grant had his own black refugee problem south of Memphis. African Americans flocked by the thousands to the various army camps along the Mississippi. "They fly for their freedom to the union army and we are not able to do much for them as it is all we can do to take care of ourselves," wrote Cyrus F. Boyd. Many of Boyd's comrades greeted the refugees with "cries of 'Kill him' 'drown him,'" expressing their deep-seated racism. "The prejudice against the race seems stronger than ever." In mid-February 1863 Grant felt compelled to issue a general order restricting the flood of refugees. Those who had already entered Union camps could remain, but the Federals were not to encourage any more to come in.[30]

Deeper exposure to the human dimension of slavery made many converts to Lorenzo Thomas's policy. When his regiment moved to Lake Providence, Boyd encountered a woman of light features with a girl who had an even lighter appearance. The woman admitted that she had three children, all fathered by her master. One of Boyd's comrades became angry at this news and vowed to fight on to destroy slavery at any cost. Yet, when Boyd's colonel tried to test his men on the new policy the next month, he encountered much resistance. Colonel Hugh T. Reid called for a vote on a resolution supporting the arming of blacks that had been adopted by Marcellus M. Crocker's brigade. He was surprised when only half of his men voted yes, one-fourth voted no, and the rest abstained. His adjutant noted the names of those who voted no and Reid began to question them. The men countered with questions that the colonel could not answer, creating an embarrassing situation. Lieutenant Colonel William W. Belknap saved the colonel by calling for three cheers for the Union. Everyone heartily complied and ended the standoff.[31]

There was considerable resistance in the Army of the Tennessee, at least initially, to the idea of arming blacks. This could be attributed to the fact that the string of victories achieved by Grant's men made that course seem unnecessary to win the war. When Thomas reported this resistance to Washington, the authorities put pressure on Grant to do something about it. Grant then issued a general order requiring everyone in his department to fully support the organization of black units. All officers, in particular, were to do everything they could to help "in removing prejudice against" the policy.[32]

Thomas pushed ahead with his work, establishing a system to examine white officer candidates. He officially designated the new regiments U.S. Colored Troops (USCT) and provided regulations to formalize their mobilization by late May. Thomas suggested a distinctive uniform for the African Americans, one that would be "of less cost . . . something a little more gay" than the regulation dress, but fortunately that suggestion was ignored.[33]

The Confederates were mindful of this Yankee policy. Gideon J. Pillow, who had been appointed to head a new Conscript Bureau in Bragg's department, called on planters to hire out their slaves to the Confederate government as teamsters to free up white soldiers for fighting and to prevent the slaves from being taken by the Federals and used for their own purposes. From being a nuisance in army camps, refugee blacks had now become an asset that both sides coveted. The competition between Union and Confederate authorities to make full use of African American men heated up as the war continued its bloody course.[34]

John Clifford Pemberton.
(Library of Congress,
LC-USZ62-90939)

Spring Operations

Confederate general John C. Pemberton felt, at least until mid-April 1863, that his subordinates in the Department of Mississippi and East Louisiana had been "entirely successful" in defending their portion of the Confederacy. Pemberton was partly right, although one could hardly consider that allowing thirty thousand Federals to lodge permanently a few miles north of Vicksburg was anything to be proud of. Richmond officials continued to view control of the Mississippi between Vicksburg and Port Hudson as of prime importance to the Confederate strategy, although they had scant resources to do so. Pemberton had about 42,000 men in his department, and Joseph E. Johnston believed he needed at least 24,000 of them to hold the two strongholds on the Mississippi. The Federals had advanced a large number of troops against the northernmost stronghold, and they could move a sizable force against Port Hudson from New Orleans. Johnston was of the opinion that he did not have enough men to relieve a siege of either place. Only adroit handling of manpower could compensate for the Confederate shortage of resources in Mississippi, but Johnston seemed reluctant to concentrate them, given the large geographic district under his control.[35]

As early as January 1863, Grant realized that he might have to approach Vicksburg by moving past it and operating south of the fortifications, but he spent many weeks that winter attempting to gain the bluffs north of the city. With the failure of both the Yazoo Pass and Steele's Bayou expeditions, and the discovery that the Lake Providence route was impractical, Grant scouted the possibility of attacking Haynes' Bluff by steaming up the Yazoo River on April 1. He concluded that such an undertaking would be too costly. He now gave up all hope of approaching Vicksburg from the north and prepared to move his army southward from Milliken's Bend. Needful of river support, Grant began to ready steamers to run the Vicksburg batteries with tugs and barges ordered from St. Louis to help in transporting food and coal. He planned to move one corps southward along the western edge of the river, protected from attack by Confederate troops in the Trans-Mississippi because the expansive bottomland was flooded. That corps could cross the river and capture Grand Gulf, whose high bluffs stood thirty miles south of Vicksburg, using the point as a base of operations to advance eastward from the Mississippi.[36]

The Federals prepared four steamers to run past the batteries by protecting their machinery with hay bales and sandbags. When most of the civilian crew members and two of the four captains of the boats refused to run the batteries, Grant called for volunteers from infantry regiments. The passage, which took place on the night of April 16, was less costly than expected. During the two-and-a-half-hour ordeal, only twelve Federals were wounded and none were killed, though all four steamers were hit and one of them, the *Henry Clay*, was sunk. Several gunboats and rams made it through safely as well. The boats then joined two divisions of McClernand's Thirteenth Corps at New Carthage, on the west side of the river.[37]

Grant was so encouraged by this success that he organized a second passage on the night of April 22. The six steamers and twelve barges involved suffered heavier losses, with one boat and half the barges sunk. Grant insisted that the civilian craft lost or damaged during the two passages be repaired or compensated at government expense.[38]

Grant was open to the idea of bypassing Vicksburg altogether for the time being and moving south to help Banks capture Port Hudson. Washington favored this move. Lincoln and Assistant Secretary of the Navy Gustavus Fox had little faith in Banks's ability to take that stronghold on his own, and they considered Port Hudson the lesser of the two Confederate bulwarks on the Mississippi. The combined forces of Grant and Banks could then operate more successfully against Vicksburg from the south. Grant believed he could, at least, spare McClernand's corps to assist Banks but sensed a golden opportunity east of Vicksburg. Despite his successful passage of the batteries, there was no sign that the Confederates were concentrating troops to prevent him from taking Grand Gulf or any other point on the east side of the Mississippi. With quick action, he could operate in the vicinity of Vicksburg with all the advantages of movement and surprise on his side. In this scenario, Grant envisioned Banks as being helpful by holding the Port Hudson garrison in place, and even moving north to help him operate against Vicksburg if the port fell quickly. Although he had promised to send troops to Banks, Grant reneged on that agreement in favor of moving against Vicksburg as soon as he had gained a foothold on the east side of the river.[39]

The Confederates indeed offered Grant an opportunity to implement his plan. After the first passage, Pemberton conceded "the navigation of Mississippi River as shut out from us now. No more supplies can be gotten from trans-Mississippi department." Yet neither he nor Johnston concentrated strength to locate and meet Grant on the bank of the river. Pemberton seemed fixated on holding Vicksburg, while Johnston appeared reluctant to compel a concentration of force before it was too late.[40]

Grant keenly understood that once he gained possession of a good spot on the east bank, the tide would turn in the Vicksburg campaign. He tried to take Grand Gulf on April 29, but the defenses there were too strong. Seven ironclads bombarded the Confederate batteries while ten thousand of McClernand's troops waited on transports, ready to land. Yet five hours of intense firing failed to silence those batteries. At least two hundred Confederate rounds landed on the ironclads, all of which suffered damage. Porter, who called it the "hardest stand up fight of the war," admitted defeat, but Grant would not let the rebuff stand in his way. The troops disembarked and the transports ran past the batteries that night, protected by gunfire from the ironclads.[41]

The hard fight at Grand Gulf further cemented Grant's determination to operate east of the river rather than go south to join Banks, for the lines of communication connecting him with the North were too uncertain. Boat traffic was dangerous, at best, because of the dozens of Confederate batteries lining the east bank at Vicksburg, Warrenton, and Grand Gulf. The single wagon road snaking along the levees and high ground—only twenty inches above the waterline on the west side of the river—was an equally frail line of supply. Grant had to move east and somehow regain contact with his river-borne supply line from the North, and that as quickly as possible. He selected Bruinsburg, located ten miles south of Grand Gulf, as the crossing place. Safe from interference, the Federals shuttled McClernand's men

Federal attack on Grand Gulf. This sketch depicts the failed attempt by David Dixon Porter's fleet to reduce the Confederate batteries at Grand Gulf and pave the way for Ulysses S. Grant to land troops on the east side of the Mississippi River on April 29, 1863. (Johnson and Buel, *Battles and Leaders*, 3:568)

across with the transports. An accident occurred when the *Horizon* rammed into the *Moderator* at 3:00 A.M. on May 1, sinking it with the loss of Battery G, 2nd Illinois Light Artillery.[42]

Once McClernand's command was safely lodged at Bruinsburg, Grant "felt a degree of relief scarcely ever equaled since," he wrote in his memoirs. "I was now in the enemy's country, with a vast river and the stronghold of Vicksburg between me and my base of supplies. But I was on dry ground on the same side of the river with the enemy." His first objective was to secure Port Gibson, a hub for roads that led to Grand Gulf, Vicksburg, and Jackson. On May 1 Grant met a detachment of Pemberton's army near Port Gibson. It was a hard-fought battle, made worse for the Federals by the terrain that was deeply carved into sharply defined ridges, forcing them to advance on narrow fronts. Persistent shoving eventually forced the Confederates away, and the important road center fell into Union hands.[43]

Grant was greatly encouraged by the victory at Port Gibson, informing Sherman that the "road to Vicksburg is open; all we want now are men, ammunition and hard bread." He anticipated relying on the countryside to feed his animals and gather as much food for the men as possible. Sherman and McPherson hurried their corps along McClernand's path west of the river

Road near Port Gibson. Along rural roads like this one, Grant began to move east from his landing at Bruinsburg to begin the pivotal phase of the Vicksburg campaign. (Earl J. Hess)

as Grant was forced to delay while concentrating the rest of his army. There was time for one last thought about Banks and Port Hudson, but word arrived that Banks would not be in position to connect with Grant until May 10. This was because Banks had moved first to clear the Red River as far as Alexandria, Louisiana, before moving directly against Port Hudson. Grant could not afford to wait. He later urged Banks to forget Port Hudson and come north to join him in "the great struggle for opening the Mississippi River" at Vicksburg. He had decisively shifted the strategic flow of events in favor of retaining his independence. Banks outranked him and therefore would have had the chance to command the combined armies. Moreover, Grant's decision held the promise of more decisively opening the river by striking at the more important of the two objectives.[44]

Grant had to wait until May 6 to accumulate three days' rations and establish a shorter wagon road west of the river now that the water levels in the Mississippi had fallen. He had no intention of completely cutting himself off from his line of communications. The busy transports hauled the wagons across the river, and the trains took supplies to the troops as they moved inland, returning empty to the river for more material. The Federals relied on their line of communications for supplies they could not expect to find in the countryside, such as ammunition, hard bread, coffee, and salt, but the rest they foraged from civilians along the way. Cornmeal and meat were plentiful enough to keep Grant's men fed, but this insecure mode of supply could not last. "We must fight the enemy before our rations fail," Grant informed McPherson, "and we are equally bound to make our rations last as long as possible." The men of Ralph Buckland's brigade had to leave their baggage, tents, and most of their cooking utensils on the other side of the Mississippi; they received no army rations at all during their march east of the river. They suffered from hunger, getting some food here and there on the march, but they soldiered on. The 4th Minnesota fared better. It drew its last rations on May 4, but the quartermaster scoured the countryside along its line of march and found "sugar, molasses, salt, corn meal, and bacon," which lasted until the regiment received army rations again on May 17. Grant estimated that, overall, not more than five days' rations were issued to his men in twenty days of campaigning, "yet there was neither suffering nor complaint."[45]

Because Grant was willing to move without a fully functioning supply line, he was able to seize the initiative and hold it during the key period of the campaign. As a result, the battles that followed were fights between fragments of the available Confederate manpower in the area around Vicksburg and Jackson, and the Federals won every engagement. They defeated a detachment of Johnston's force at Raymond on May 12, then compelled Johnston to evacuate Jackson itself on May 14. The Federals destroyed many buildings of public use in the capital before moving west toward Vicksburg. Pemberton managed to concentrate most of his available troops at Champion Hill, where Grant met him on May 16 in the largest battle of the campaign, a hard-fought engagement that teetered one way and then another until the Confederates were soundly defeated. The fight at Champion Hill was the decisive moment of Grant's movement eastward from the river, for he repelled Pemberton's first and only effort to confront his progress with the majority of the Confederate forces defending Vicksburg. The Federals lost more than 2,400 men, while the Confederates suffered over 3,800 casualties.[46]

Pemberton had conducted his part of the Vicksburg campaign with caution and indecision. He felt that protecting the river batteries at Vicksburg and the town itself was the core objective: "Nothing can be done which might jeopardize it." Moreover, Pemberton believed he had too few men to take the offensive against Grant and inadequate cavalry to cut the Federal supply line. He pulled his forces away from points south of Vicksburg to protect his base until Grant approached, then he set out to meet him and be defeated at Champion Hill. Pemberton manned a fortified bridgehead on the east side of the Big Black River, where the railroad linking Vicksburg with Jackson crossed the stream, to allow a division that had become separated from his army to cross. The Federals attacked the bridgehead on May 17 and captured 1,700 Confederates. After months of floundering in the miry bottomlands, Grant had decisively turned the tables on his adversary by separating their two forces and penning up Pemberton in his Vicksburg defenses.[47]

Siege

Grant hoped to capitalize on his success by attacking the Confederate works as soon as possible, believing Pemberton's troops were demoralized. On May 18 he began to deploy opposite the northern and eastern rim of Vicksburg's defenses, making contact with Porter's fleet north of the city to restore his supply line. Then, on May 19, the Federals sallied forth against the earthworks. They were repulsed with losses of nearly one thousand men, compared to only two hundred Confederate casualties.[48]

The Federals prepared longer for their next attack, a much larger affair with heavy assaults planned by each corps. Grant ordered his subordinates to synchronize their watches, so they could launch their attacks at exactly the same time, and urged his men to their best. "If prosecuted with vigor, it is confidently believed this course will carry Vicksburg in a very short time," he reassured them in a general order. "Every days delay enables the enemy to strengthen his defences and increases his chances for receiving aid from outside." But the massive Federal attack on May 22 failed to produce the desired result. Although conducted with spirit and determination, the terrain as much as searing Confederate fire and the earthen defenses proved too much for the Unionists. Pemberton's men, far from demoralized, bravely repelled each assault, ousting some of McClernand's men who had gained entry into a corner of one large redoubt. McClernand sent an overly optimistic report of his progress, which caused Grant to renew hopeless attacks on other corps fronts. The outcome only added to the casualty list. "[McClernand] is entirely unfit for the position of Corps Commander both on the march and on the battle field," Grant informed Halleck. "Looking after his Corps gives me more labor, and infinitely more uneasiness, than all the remainder of my Dept." In June, Grant relieved McClernand of command for publishing an order congratulating his men in the newspapers without departmental approval.[49]

The bloody fighting on May 22 resulted in 3,100 Federal casualties out of 40,000 engaged, while Pemberton suffered only 500 losses out of the 14,000 men holding the targeted lines. Grant was forced to conduct siege operations, while his optimistic spirit led him to assure Washington that the city's fall "can only be a question of time." His lightning campaign, following months of dreary stalemate in the Mississippi bottomlands, had captured the imagination of the North. In the words of Salmon P. Chase, "Every eye is turned towards Vicksburgh."[50]

Grant's biggest worry was that Johnston might attack from the east to relieve the besieged garrison. The Union general sent a trusted division commander, Peter J. Osterhaus, to establish a fortified outpost at the railroad crossing of the Big Black River to watch developments toward Jackson, which Johnston had reoccupied as soon as Grant evacuated the capital. Osterhaus had instructions to tear up the railroad as far east of the river as possible and strip the countryside of slaves, food, forage, teams, and wagons. He was to do "every thing . . . to prevent an Army supplying itself coming."[51]

Estimating that Johnston had up to twenty-five thousand men, Grant called for reinforcements. He directed Hurlbut to strip his district around Memphis "to the very lowest possible" number of garrison troops, evacuating less important posts. Hurlbut was to maintain adequate garrisons only at the places significant for supplying the troops at Vicksburg. Halleck, who had always understood the need to concentrate force at critical times and places, eagerly helped to find more troops for Grant from the Trans-Mississippi.[52]

Even the Army of the Potomac inadvertently provided reinforcements for Grant's siege of Vicksburg. Since the disastrous battle of Fredericksburg on December 13, 1862, that army's commander, Ambrose E. Burnside, had been under a cloud. He was relieved more than a month later with a decision to send him west with two divisions of his old command, the Ninth Corps. A Confederate spy who spoke with these troops just before their departure from Virginia reported that the men were unhappy about the move, "fearful of the climate [and] their health." The Easterners, however, adjusted well to their new assignment. While Burnside remained in Kentucky to assume command of the Department of the Ohio, the two divisions of Ninth Corps troops boarded steamers that were riddled with bullet marks and semifortified to protect their boilers for a trip down the Mississippi. Wherever they stopped along the way, Western troops flocked to the riverbank to see the new "boys" and playfully taunt them. To at least one Easterner, the Western troops seemed "very jealous of any interference," but Burnside's command performed well by fortifying the most vulnerable sector behind Grant's besieging force at Haynes' Bluff. They adapted to Western ways, taking available property for their own use and driving "the people off before us farther into Dixie."[53]

At the height of the siege, Grant had seventy-one thousand men at his

Ewing's approach at Vicksburg. Some remnants of the massive Union system of covered approaches to the Confederate defenses of Vicksburg. Ewing's approach was aimed at the Stockade Redan along the Graveyard Road. (Earl J. Hess)

disposal, more than enough to ensure that the investment was not broken. "Johnstone will have to come with a mighty host to drive me away," he wrote his father. Banks continued to ask Grant for troops even after he laid siege to Port Hudson. "Vicksburg is the vital point," Grant explained in his refusal to comply.[54]

As the siege of Vicksburg lengthened, the Federals crossed no-man's-land by regular approaches. Although the Army of the Tennessee had no experience in constructing such works and was inadequately supplied with engineer officers, it did surprisingly well at digging parallels, saps, and mines—all of which were designed to minimize losses. The Federals assembled able-bodied blacks from the area to help in the heavy work.[55]

On the other side of no-man's-land, the Confederates were "exposed without shelter to the broiling sun and drenching rain," wrote division commander Carter L. Stevenson. Their rations were inadequate, and they endured a nearly constant stream of artillery fire and sharpshooting. As time dragged on, the carcasses of mules and horses killed by Federal snipers littered the area behind the works. Many citizens evacuated their homes and

Explosion of mine at Vicksburg. Depicting the explosion of a Union mine under the Confederate Third Louisiana Redan along the Jackson Road on June 25, 1863. (Johnson and Buel, *Battles and Leaders*, 3:541)

lived in caves skillfully carved out of the compacted loess soil around Vicksburg, which made for easy digging. Dogged determination alone kept the city and the garrison going week after week as the enemy slowly pushed closer to the ring of earthworks that protected the Rebel position.[56]

Along the Jackson Road, troops of McPherson's corps advanced close enough to the 3rd Louisiana Redan to plant a mine under the work. The defenders prepared a rear line from which to seal the breach when the mine exploded on June 25. For the rest of that day the Federals shoved regiment after regiment into the crater, in rotating shifts, in a vain attempt to break through. In the process they lost 243 men, while the Confederates lost 94. Little daunted, the Federals planted another mine there and exploded it on July 1 but did not throw troops into a follow-up assault.[57]

The Confederacy relied on Joseph E. Johnston to save Pemberton's army as well as Vicksburg, but Johnston felt tied down by the lack of resources. At most, he considered distracting the Federals long enough to enable Pemberton to evacuate the doomed city. Governor John Pettus suggested that if Johnston did not have enough troops to accomplish the twin goals of saving both Pemberton and his position, then maybe Braxton Bragg ought to dispatch thirty thousand troops to Mississippi to assist him. President

Davis informed Pettus that to do so would be to abandon Tennessee to the Yankees, and there seemed little to be gained by trading one important region for another. P. G. T. Beauregard, now commanding the area around Charleston, South Carolina, came up with one of his patented schemes to achieve Confederate independence. He suggested the reverse: that Johnston abandon Mississippi, join forces with Bragg to defeat Rosecrans and invade Kentucky, where he was confident the Confederates could recruit an army big enough to conquer Missouri or reclaim all of Virginia. Neither of these suggestions was strategically feasible, especially Beauregard's fantasy.[58]

Even the more down-to-earth plan to save Pemberton's force by distracting the Federals seemed unworkable, for the garrison was unable to move as a unit. The men were exhausted from continuous duty in the trenches, food was running short, and the troops could not move fast enough to reach safety even if they broke through Grant's iron ring. The only hope lay in outside support, and Richmond had no troops to increase Johnston's strength. "Our resources are not ample enough to enable us to afford absolute security anywhere," Secretary of War Seddon explained to the mayor of Charleston. Vicksburg—currently the most important point in the Confederacy—was in imminent danger of falling, and all available strength had to be diverted to Mississippi. Ironically, the troops Johnston already possessed were plundering civilian homes in the area around Jackson because the Confederate government was not feeding them enough. Southerners placed a desperate hope in the belief that Mississippi's summer climate would incapacitate enough Yankees to make a difference in the campaign.[59]

Johnston hoped to draw support from Edmund Kirby Smith in the Trans-Mississippi. Kirby Smith could interrupt Grant's supply lines or "drive beef into Vicksburg," or even join the garrison by crossing the Mississippi, but he was reluctant to take any drastic steps. The Trans-Mississippi forces attempted to disrupt river traffic by attacking the Federals holding Milliken's Bend on June 7. Several hundred white troops and thirteen hundred black soldiers put up surprisingly stiff resistance, aided by two levees that served as convenient breastworks and by the fire of two gunboats. Members of the 49th USCT had as yet received little training, and most of them had never fired their guns before the Confederates attacked, yet they fought well. Even Confederate officers praised the performance of the Union's black troops. The garrison saved one of Grant's supply depots and provided one of the first significant uses of black men in combat during the Civil War. Many Northerners were impressed by their conduct on the field. "So let them fight," wrote William Taylor of the nearby Ninth Corps. "The army begins to like the idea."[60]

Joseph Eggleston Johnston. (Library of Congress, LC-DIG-cwpb-06280)

The coming torrid season in Mississippi concerned Grant. While he did not doubt the ultimate success of the Vicksburg siege, he had hoped to capture the city much earlier so as to operate more deeply in the state before the truly hot weather set in. Now, the fall of Vicksburg would open the river and demoralize the Confederates, but "I intended more from it"—meaning the subjugation of all Mississippi.[61]

The Vicksburg siege neared a climax by late June. Grant worried that Kirby Smith might concentrate troops on De Soto Point to help Pemberton escape, or to funnel supplies into Vicksburg. He also believed Johnston might strike any day, having stripped other sections of the Confederacy of troops to build up a powerful relief force. The siege neared a crisis point for the beleaguered garrison. The Confederates were down to a biscuit and a couple of mouthfuls of bacon each day. "If you can't feed us, you had better surrender us, horrible as the idea is," warned "Many Soldiers" in a plaintive request to Pemberton. Grant was confident he could repulse the expected attack by Johnston and then break into Vicksburg, planning a major attack on Pemberton's defenses for July 6.[62]

Before any attacks took place, Pemberton wrote a note to Grant requesting terms of surrender on July 3. Grant had none to offer. "Men who have shown so much endurance and courage as those now in Vicksburg, will always challenge the respect of an adversary," he replied, assuring Pemberton that he would treat his men "with all the respect due to prisoners of war." But the Confederate commander knew from intercepted signals that Grant's logistical capacity was stretched to the limit by supplying his large concentration of troops, and that insufficient steamers were available to haul Confederate prisoners north. He pressed for terms and got them; parole for his men instead of a trip to prisoner-of-war camps. It took several hours and a personal conference to work out the details, but the formal surrender of Vicksburg took place on July 4, 1863. More than 30,000 troops, 170 guns, and 50,000 small arms fell into Union hands, as well as the Gibraltar of the Mississippi. Federal casualties since May 23 totaled 642, while the Confederates lost 3,202 from May 18 to July 4. Although initially resistant to the idea of paroling the garrison, Grant later said it was for the best. "It leaves the transports and troops for immediate use," he explained.[63]

The impact of Vicksburg's fall was enormous. For William T. Sherman it represented "the first gleam of daylight in this war," while a Sixteenth Corps soldier on garrison duty near Memphis was so happy "I do not know what I am saying half of the time. We go around here yelling like a parcel of Indians." A Thirteenth Corps officer proclaimed it "the most brilliant campaign in modern times; the most important in its results," because it

Levee and steamers at Vicksburg. With the fall of the city, the river was opened to Union boat traffic. (Library of Congress, LC-DIG-cwpb-01012)

achieved a two-year dream of the Northwest, the reopening of the Mississippi. Naval officers shared the glory as the spearhead of Grant's army, "until the name of a gun-boat became a terror to the rebels." Abraham Lincoln frankly admitted to Grant that he had had no faith in his course during the winter, as the Yankees floundered through the bayous. He was certain the general had made a mistake when he chose to move east of the river instead of reinforcing Banks. "I now wish to make the personal acknowledgment that you were right and I was wrong," the president graciously told his general.[64]

The loss of the Mississippi River was like a weight on the Confederacy. An officer in Bragg's army called it "certainly the heaviest blow that we have yet received." He feared that Confederate independence would be set back one or two years, and the Federals would plunder the rich Mississippi Valley.

Secretary Seddon referred to the "shock of despondency and foreboding" as the news of Vicksburg's fall spread across the South. An Alabama officer succinctly asserted, "We cant afford to lose Vicksburg." In terms of territory, the Confederacy had been severed in half, and there was no possibility that the Northwestern states might break away from the Northeast and create an understanding with the South over trade issues. A major turning point in the war had arrived.[65]

9 } Occupation and Port Hudson

or a good part of Grant's forces the fall of Vicksburg was not the end of campaigning that summer. Sherman was ready to advance against Johnston's concentration near Jackson as soon as the Gibraltar fell. Grant instructed him to drive Johnston away, destroy his resources, "and do the enemy all the harm possible." He reasoned that Sherman's move against Jackson would prevent the Confederates from trying to relieve the siege of Port Hudson. Grant hoped to send help to Banks in his efforts to reduce the last Confederate stronghold on the Mississippi, and return the Ninth Corps troops to Burnside as soon as possible.[1]

Sherman moved out the Thirteenth Corps, now under the command of Major General Edward O. C. Ord, the two divisions of the Ninth Corps, plus troops from the Fifteenth, Sixteenth, and Seventeenth Corps. Johnston received him in the ring of fortifications that firmly protected Jackson, and Sherman was forced to begin "a miniature Vicksburg," as he put it. Besides an unauthorized attack by a single brigade, Union operations at Jackson consisted mostly of heavy skirmishing and attempts to outflank the Confederate works. Johnston had no intention of being trapped in the city, and he evacuated Jackson early on July 17 before Sherman could gain a position of advantage. For the second time in the war, the Federals were in possession of Mississippi's capital; unlike Pemberton, however, Johnston had saved his command.[2]

Now the Federals began the work of destruction. Thirteenth Corps troops tore up the Mississippi Central Railroad north of the capital, working "with a right good will, and . . . leaving nothing but the road-bed." Other soldiers destroyed twenty flat cars, fifty box cars and passenger cars, and four thousand bales of cotton they tore out of the revetment of Jackson's fortifications. The Yankees spread out to wreck the railroad forty miles north, sixty miles south, and ten miles east of the city. "Jackson ceases to be a place for the enemy to collect stores and men from which to threaten our great river," Sherman proclaimed. It "is now a ruined town." This marked the first time in the war that the Federals destroyed and left a major city they occupied, rather than garrison it permanently. The reason lay in the city's location. The Federals had no plans to conduct further operations along permanent supply lines in any direction from Jackson.[3]

Sherman's men lived off the land during the Jackson campaign. "Corn, beef, bread, flour, Sugar almost every thing is seized," Ord told his wife. "The land we pass over is a desert, families have to fly or be left almost to starve." Ninth Corps troops were astonished at how the Westerners plundered their way to and from Jackson. "The western armies burn and destroy everything they come across," remarked George Washington Whitman, an officer in the 51st New York. They did "three times the damage of the army of the Potomac," leaving "splendid bound books" strewn along their line of march and smashing expensive pianos as well as plundering farms of edible property. They did so with the approval of their superiors, for Grant had informed Sherman to "leave nothing of value for the enemy to carry on war with," and noncontraband property became adjunct targets. Ironically, Confederate troops also committed depredations during the Jackson campaign. Division commander John C. Breckinridge issued a circular warning his men that "the presence of the army will be regarded as a curse instead of a protection" if they did not stop stealing from local civilians. A Confederate soldier agreed with him, noting that his comrades took as much food as the enemy, despoiling a 200-acre crop in only one night. The only thing the Confederates did not do, compared to the Yankees, was wantonly burn civilian houses.[4]

After gorging themselves on the comparatively rich area around Jackson, the Federals suffered on their return march to Vicksburg. Traversing a region cut up by military operations for the past two months, this area had little food available. Ord's men ate green corn and drank from stagnant water holes near the road. As a result, the rate of sickness in the Thirteenth Corps dramatically increased by the time his men reached Vicksburg. Indeed, July was the start of the hottest part of the year in central Mississippi.[5]

Occupation

Occupation duties now concerned Grant. He planned to establish guards to control entry into and exit from Vicksburg and detailed one regiment to preserve law and order in the city. Other troops gathered "all captured property" and rounded up able-bodied blacks for work details. Furthermore, the Federals prepared to feed destitute citizens.[6]

Grant dispatched a force under Brigadier General Thomas E. G. Ransom to Natchez, seventy miles south of Vicksburg, after receiving a report that the Confederates were crossing cattle from the Trans-Mississippi. Reaching

Natchez on July 13, Ransom captured five thousand Texas beef cattle; he sent nearly half of them to Banks at Port Hudson and the rest to Vicksburg. Upon discovering that 150 wagons filled with ordnance were in the process of crossing to the west bank, he managed to seize three hundred muskets and two hundred thousand rounds of ammunition before the column moved out of reach. The civilians in Natchez were "completely surprised" by the intrusion of the Yankees. Their country abounded in horses, mules, and ample crops. Blacks soon began to flock to the city, and Ransom had to feed about five hundred refugees, sending many to Vicksburg to relieve the strain. "They are all anxious to go," he informed headquarters. "They do not know where or what for."[7]

The surrender of Vicksburg "produced . . . a general relaxation of effort," in Sherman's words. "I fear the Northern people are again settling back into one of their periodical states of apathy, on the supposition that the war is over." Hurlbut apparently believed the reopening of the Mississippi spelled the war's end, for he expressed a desire to return to civilian life only days after Vicksburg capitulated.[8]

But the war in the West was far from over, not even in the newly conquered territory. Confederate officials were determined to deny Northerners undisputed use of the Mississippi for commerce and logistical support. As Secretary of War Seddon wrote Johnston, this "would deprive the North of most of the fruits of their late successes." The use of cavalry armed with field artillery might persuade the Northwest that it could never enjoy the river "as an avenue of trade without peace and amity with the Confederate States." Some Rebel officials advocated turning the Mississippi Valley into a wasteland by removing all the civilians and blacks from Federal reach. In addition to regular forces, they recommended the use of sharpshooters to harass shipping and "render the navigation of the Mississippi cumbersome and expensive, dangerous and practically useless for gain or advantage to the enemy."[9]

Nathan Bedford Forrest, one of the South's most effective cavalry commanders, put forward a plan to raise troops from counties lining the Mississippi from Vicksburg to Cairo for the purpose of obstructing river shipping. In his proposal to the Confederate War Department, Forrest noted that he had lived on the river for more than twenty years and for much of that time was "engaged in buying and selling negroes." He therefore knew the land and the planters, and could find men who understood the river intimately. Forrest believed he could recruit up to ten thousand men in only two months. But he was too valuable as a cavalry officer, raiding Union supply lines, to assume the responsibility for implementing such a plan.[10]

But other officers began to put into effect the government's goal of disrupting river traffic. A Louisiana artillery officer cut embrasures in the twelve-foot-tall levee a dozen miles south of Donaldsonville, on the east bank of the Mississippi, and fired at a boat on July 7. He made more embrasures two days later and engaged several Union gunboats and transports, finding that the levee provided ample protection for his gun crews. Not until Federal forces landed upstream and approached his position did he evacuate.[11]

Even more effective than regular military forces were the secret agents hired by the Confederate government to burn civilian steamers. These boat burners were mysterious figures, yet their handiwork blazed across the newspapers of the North. The first documented instance occurred on August 4, 1863, when the *Ruth* burned at Columbus, Kentucky, destroying $2.5 million in cash bound to pay Grant's army. The *Champion* burned in late August at Memphis, reportedly the work of a man named William Murphy who received a $3,000 bounty from the Confederate government. A fire started on the *Imperial* while it was tied at the St. Louis levee on September 13 and spread to three other boats; all four vessels were destroyed. A witness believed the blaze was started by a man who disguised himself as a black worker. The *Imperial* was the first steamer to travel to New Orleans from Vicksburg on government business after the opening of the river. A few days after the St. Louis incident, another report of a black man setting fire to a steamer at Milliken's Bend surfaced. The perpetrators of these burnings were never caught.[12]

Despite these dangers to river navigation, Northern merchants eagerly sought to take advantage of Grant's military success and trade along the Mississippi. The Union general had made it difficult for them to do so during the course of his Vicksburg campaign, so the U.S. government shifted authority over commerce entirely to the Treasury Department. A "License of Commercial Intercourse," issued on March 31 and publicized through a War Department order on April 3, allowed Treasury agents to give licenses to civilian traders without military approval.[13]

Grant was not satisfied. He continued to prefer stopping all trade until he had a chance to subdue the region. In his view, trade so interfered with military operations that it weakened his force by one-third. Any amount of commerce made it impossible to prevent supplies from getting into enemy hands. Citizens of the Mississippi Valley were "nearly subjugated" following the fall of Vicksburg. A complete stoppage of trade would allow the army to finish the job; then trade could be reopened without restrictions of any kind. Secretary of the Treasury Salmon Chase could not accede to Grant's request, for public pressure was too great. He did send a special agent to work out a system with Grant to require bonds of those who received trade permits to guarantee their compliance with regulations. Moreover, Grant was able to convince the special agent not to allow cotton buyers to travel south of Memphis; sellers would have to ship the bales there for sale. Even this modified system did not entirely please Grant, but he was willing to work with it.[14]

The army cooperated with the Treasury agents by collecting cotton used in the fortifications of Vicksburg and sending it to Memphis to be taken up as government property. The new trade regulations failed to eliminate trouble, however. An Illinois man who claimed four hundred bales of cotton tried to bribe gunboat officers to haul it to Memphis for him when they detected irregularities in his business practices. Subordinates all along the great river echoed Grant's frustration that trade could not be shut down completely for even a few months, as the political and commercial realities of the day overruled purely military considerations.[15]

The Federals made full use of the available black population, for there was much work to be done at Vicksburg. In fact, Grant postponed enlisting able-bodied blacks in the army so they could be used as laborers. Soon black workers swarmed over the levee, loading and unloading steamers, and they worked on a new line of Union earthworks to protect Vicksburg from Confederate attack. The personal servants of Pemberton's officers were informed that they were free, but they were given the choice of remaining with their masters. Slavery was "already knocked out" in the South, Grant announced. "It would take a standing Army to maintain Slavery in the South if we were to make peace to-day."[16]

Grant was eager to organize as many African American regiments as possible as soon as black workers could be spared from the levee at Vicksburg. They would be very useful to garrison posts along the Mississippi and would free up veteran white units for further operations in the field. Lincoln was happy, sending Lorenzo Thomas back to the Mississippi Valley in early August to continue what he had started the previous spring. The president envisioned a force of one hundred thousand black troops that would deal a death blow to the Confederacy.[17]

The Federals now agressively enlisted blacks in the valley; troops had to be sent inland to find them, as Southerners drove off able-bodied slaves from a zone within twenty miles of the great river to keep them out of Yankee hands. Although the area around Vicksburg and Natchez fell under the provisions of the Emancipation Proclamation, Grant continued to respect the sentiments of Unionists in the region and ordered his subordinates not to take their slaves without consent. Supporters of the Confederacy received no such consideration.[18]

Even after the black regiments were organized, many of them were used primarily as labor battalions. Orders went out not to use white troops for heavy labor anymore in order to spare them exertion in the hot, humid summer. The 50th USCT was organized at Vicksburg, mostly from blacks transported from Natchez, in August 1863. The recruits were already "in a half-famished condition" when they arrived, but they were immediately assigned to move ordnance stores and other supplies, some of them working around the clock. The army failed to give then adequate food, clothing, tents, or blankets; thus rainy weather and unrelenting work caused a good deal of illness. Although thirteen men died on August 14 alone, conditions soon improved. When the men of the 50th USCT were relieved from "excessive fatigue duty" in early September, their health improved. On October 15 the regiment finally received guns and began to learn how to drill.[19]

Administering Captured Territory

"Mississippi is thoroughly broken-spirited," Hurlbut wrote Lincoln in mid-August 1863 with a good deal of pride. Grant echoed that sentiment. He believed the Southerners were "ready to accept anything" and he reassured them they would not be troubled by the Federal government as long as they lived in peace, accepted the destruction of slavery, and entered into labor contracts with their former slaves. Sherman agreed with Grant that an important change of feeling seemed to have taken place in the wake of the Union capture of Vicksburg, and he encouraged a fair, even-handed method of dealing with the civilian population. That included clamping down on plundering by Union soldiers and issuing cash or receipts whenever it was necessary to take food from the citizenry.[20]

Confederate authorities also felt the change of mood in the state. Governor John J. Pettus called the Vicksburg campaign an ordeal "of sore tribulation," while President Davis was shocked at its outcome. He believed, so he wrote to several people, that he had sent enough men to Mississippi "to accomplish the destruction of Grant's army." If Johnston had been able to combine the garrisons of Vicksburg and Port Hudson with his own force, then victory would have been inevitable. Some Southerners saw the fall of the Mississippi River as the doom of Confederate hopes for independence; they wondered why General Robert E. Lee had been allowed to conduct a fruitless invasion of Pennsylvania while Grant maintained his stranglehold on Vicksburg. Southerners blamed Pemberton for their misfortune and many began to talk about rejoining the Union. Johnston's reaction to such talk was to recommend that they be arrested. But it was impossible to threaten residents who lived throughout central and eastern Mississippi into giving up their feelings of vulnerability. Sherman's Jackson campaign demonstrated how easily the Federals could raid the area and destroy everything if they wanted to do so. As Oliver G. Eiland of Louisville, Mississippi, put it, "Vixberg is gone and as a consequence Mississippi is gone and in the opinion of almost every one here the Confederacy is gone."[21]

But the Federals had no intention of suppressing the entire state of Mississippi. The area north of the Yalobusha River was a zone of operations for those troops extending from Memphis, but south of that river there was nothing of military value to tempt Yankee incursions. The Mississippi Delta region was accessible because of its proximity to the Mississippi River, while Vicksburg and Natchez were important strongpoints on the river itself. The area ten miles south and forty miles north of the railroad that linked Vicksburg with Jackson and Brandon was "completely devastated" by the armies of both sides, causing much civilian suffering and the need to provide Union army rations for the most destitute. In fact, the majority of the state's territory was not under Union army occupation at all and only lightly held if occupied by the Confederates.[22]

The reopening of the Mississippi to Northern commerce meant as much to Sherman as it did to any merchant, and he experienced an intense feeling of pride and accomplishment when Vicksburg fell. The problems attendant on occupying newly acquired territory, however, held no charm for him. When Grant gave Sherman the choice of Natchez or the Big Black River railroad crossing as a camping place for the Fifteenth Corps, Sherman chose the Big Black River because it lay in a devastated area with few material goods to tempt greedy soldiers. Natchez, on the other hand, was yet untouched by the hand of war and holding that town would result in "one endless strife about run away Negros, plundering and pillaging soldiers and I am sick and tired of it," he wrote a family member. "Our men are now all Expert thieves, sparing nothing[,] not even the clothes of women, children & Negroes. Nothing is left between Vicksburg & Jackson so I can have peace here."[23]

But Sherman had to deal with other occupation woes in central Mississippi. He was willing to feed destitute civilians from army stores but asserted that it was an act of charity by the government, considering that civilians also fired on steamboats. While Sherman believed the North would have been justified in depopulating the area, its true goal was to politically rehabilitate the citizens, and he urged everyone to cooperate in that goal by remaining peaceful. The only way citizens could protect their property from thieving soldiers was to reconstruct local governments that were loyal to Washington, thus removing the need for military occupation altogether.

As always, Sherman considered all occupation issues within the context of ensuring control of the Mississippi River. After the fall of Vicksburg, he continued to maintain that every area near its tributaries was as deeply interested in the great river as was Louisiana. There could be no peace unless the central authority controlled the entire length of this backbone of American enterprise, even though Sherman recognized that railroads had somewhat redirected much of the commerce it formerly carried.[24]

Confederate authorities tried to make the best of their lot after losing Vicksburg. When the state legislature met at Columbus, Mississippi, Governor Pettus urged it to pass a law forcing slaveowners within reach of Yankee patrols to move their blacks farther into the interior. The affected counties ran along the Mississippi Delta and included the entire northern part of the state. The Confederates could do little about saving a large accumulation of railroad stock stranded north of Grenada by the Federal destruction of tracks near Jackson. Grant heard that sixty locomotives and four hundred cars were stuck in a pocket of territory without connecting rail lines either north or south. He planned to send a cavalry expedition to claim them and rebuild the line toward Memphis. Grant even thought of rebuilding the railroads in Mississippi at U.S. government expense to help in the resumption of commerce, which he was certain would aid in the process of encouraging the citizenry to be loyal to the Union. His men made it to the rolling stock but were forced to destroy it when threatened by a Confederate force.[25]

The fall of the Mississippi River exposed a great deal of cotton in the valley to Northern capture, and Confederate officials were eager to remove or destroy it. The Rebel government had purchased nearly two hundred thousand bales from area planters but had not yet had an opportunity to take possession of it. Many of the planters had abandoned their homes, and the cotton was vulnerable to Union confiscation.[26]

Private traders who obtained permits from U.S. Treasury agents and even the Union army worked to find and haul out this cotton. Federal officers found it difficult to restrain their men from plundering the countryside whenever they had an opportunity. The Confederates could do nothing to stop them in northern Mississippi as the level of depredations seemed to increase with the lengthening of the war. In fact, Sherman tried to convince a committee of concerned citizens from Hinds County that he fell back from Jackson after driving Johnston away to lessen the destruction of private property by his soldiers. "You have seen enough of armies to know that they are so intent on overcoming their opponents that the poor people receive very little consideration at their hands," he wrote.[27]

Department of the Gulf

Although overshadowed by the immense campaign against Vicksburg, the Federals who held the lower Mississippi engaged in a large campaign of their own to complete the opening of the great river by besieging Port Hudson. Lincoln made a significant change in the Department of the Gulf when he replaced Benjamin Butler with Nathaniel Banks late in 1862. Like Butler, Banks had been a Massachusetts lawyer and politician before the war, serving as Speaker of the House of Representatives in Washington and then as governor of his state when the war broke out. Butler's administration of the Department of the Gulf had created many enemies, especially among the foreign consuls in New Orleans, and Lincoln had little faith in the general's ability to conduct campaigns in the field. When issuing his orders, Halleck told Banks that his first priority was to reopen the Mississippi and that he would receive twenty thousand additional troops to do so. Halleck promised the cooperation of Grant's forces coming down the river as well. Banks was then to take the Gulf port city of Mobile, Alabama. Halleck also suggested operating inland from the Mississippi to strike at Jackson or to go up the Red River in Louisiana to access supplies of sugar and cotton, and possibly use that river as a base of operations in Texas. But the reopening of the Mississippi was the top priority, and Banks was not to "lose a moment in accomplishing it."[28]

When Banks arrived in December 1862, he found that conditions in the Department of the Gulf demanded his attention before he could launch a strike against Port Hudson. He was surprised to find "an immense military government, embracing every form of civil administration." Butler had created the most extensive military government of the war in what had become his own little fiefdom. It was done out of necessity, for the Federal occupation area in the lower Mississippi Valley was largely isolated from the outside world, dependent on a thin line of coastal steamers for communication with Northern ports. Butler had been forced to find expedients to take care of his own needs and those of the citizens who were forced to look to the Union army for many basic services. As Banks informed Halleck, his predecessor had been involved in "the assessment of taxes, fines, punishments, charities, trade, regulation of churches, confiscation of estates and the working of plantations." Learning the system and revising it created "a necessary diversion" in Banks's schedule, as he found himself spending more time on civil matters than on military affairs.[29]

Butler had been feeding nearly eleven thousand families by the time Banks took charge of the department. The new commander reduced that number to six thousand because of abuses found in the system, and because the War

Department ordered that all confiscated property be turned over to Treasury agents, which reduced his available funds. But that still meant twenty-four thousand people relied on the army for their subsistence. Banks suggested they become the responsibility of the Treasury Department, but that was never taken seriously by Washington. Still, Banks reduced the amount of money spent on public relief from $70,000 to $30,000 per month.[30]

The problems associated with the African American population were particularly acute. Banks spent $60,000 in one month to help blacks in need, and the problem was growing as more refugees streamed into the lines. Banks published the Emancipation Proclamation through a general order in late January, noting that many parts of the Gulf Department were exempt from it. But congressional law prohibited the army from returning refugees to their masters, so Banks intended to put them to work on abandoned plantations. He also received authorization from Halleck to begin large-scale recruiting of black units. Butler had initiated this process even before the Federal government made it a general policy, but Banks intended to create a Corps d'Afrique consisting of eighteen regiments. Initially, he thought it best to limit the size of each regiment to five hundred men to make it easier for white officers to properly train and discipline them.[31]

While Banks worked energetically to reform affairs in the Department of the Gulf to suit his particular notions, he became a controversial administrator. Partisans of Butler immediately began to criticize him for being too lenient on the citizenry, and, indeed, Banks deliberately held them up to a less stern measure of loyalty than had Butler. His efforts to conciliate earned him the displeasure of many, including Treasury Secretary Chase. "This is less a Union City now than when Gen. Banks came here," declared a Treasury agent working in New Orleans. Many observers believed the soldiers themselves preferred Butler over Banks, judging Banks to be a "complete failure" only a month after taking command. In addition, a wave of Northern speculators came in Banks's wake, all of them expecting "to be a millionaire in six months" and possessing "few scruples about the means of satisfying their cupidity."[32]

By February 1863 there were loud calls for Butler's return. "You are the man they all swear by in that village," reported a correspondent in New Orleans to Butler, "both sides, one swearing by you, the Loyalists, and the other side about you, the Rebels." Lincoln eventually caved in and devised a plan for Butler and Banks to share responsibility—the one for administration and the other for field service—in the Department of the Gulf, but Butler was not ready to accept such a situation and the Gulf was stuck with Banks, for better or worse.[33]

Though Banks had hoped to move against Port Hudson immediately, he postponed the campaign for three months. The reinforcements promised him proved to be mostly nine-month regiments, transported at enormous cost to the government. Their terms of enlistment imposed a tight schedule on Banks. He reoccupied Baton Rouge in late December 1862, but Banks's idea was to approach Port Hudson not directly from the south, but from the west. He wanted to first move up the valley of the Red River into northwestern Louisiana to cut off the flow of supplies from the Trans-Mississippi to the area east of the great river, then approach Port Hudson.[34]

Before setting out, Banks lent a hand to David Farragut in his attempt to take some oceangoing warships north of Port Hudson to seal off the flow of Confederate supplies across the river; if successful, his own plans to invade the Red River country might be unnecessary. Banks moved his infantry north of Baton Rouge to divert the Confederates as Farragut steamed past the guns on March 14 with seven vessels, losing one of them in the process, while four others failed to make it past. Two boats were not enough to cut off the flow of supplies, but Banks returned to Baton Rouge, his men pillaging civilians along the way. He wanted help from Grant before putting his Red River plans into operation, but it would take many weeks of tedious correspondence, delivered by brave couriers along the Confederate sector of the Mississippi, before the effort to get Grant's cooperation fizzled.[35]

In late March 1863 Banks moved west of the river with sixteen thousand men of the Nineteenth Corps. Two divisions marched up the west side of Bayou Teche, while another division under Brigadier General Cuvier Grover advanced by boat up Grand Lake to flank and approach the rear of a Confederate force at Fort Bisland under Richard Taylor. Banks skirmished with Taylor at the fort on April 12 and 13, but the Confederates discovered Grover's movement and evacuated the position before they were trapped. Still, the Federals lost 224 men and the Confederates 450 at Fort Bisland. Grover crossed Bayou Teche on April 13 and fought Taylor's rear guard the next day at Irish Bend, losing 353 men and failing to catch the Confederates. Banks skirmished with the Confederates at the crossing of Vermillion Bayou, after which Taylor abandoned the Bayou Teche country. Banks marched into Alexandria, the major city of northwestern Louisiana on the Red River.[36]

Banks continued to call on Grant for assistance, requesting a corps to help him descend on Port Hudson. He expected the stronghold to fall easily now that he believed he had cut off the flow of supplies from the Trans-Mississippi by occupying Alexandria. Although Grant was willing to cooperate, Banks dallied at Alexandria long enough to derail the tentative plan for McClernand to join him. By May 12 Banks realized it was likely that the

Confederate defenses at Port Hudson. Impressive remnants of the earthen defenses of Port Hudson, the Alabama-Arkansas Redoubt. (Earl J. Hess)

hoped-for junction would not take place, and that he would have to strike Port Hudson alone. His three divisions left Alexandria on May 14, when Grant was deeply involved in his movement to the east of Vicksburg, and reached Bayou Sara, located ten miles north of Port Hudson, on May 22. Meanwhile, two other divisions moved northward toward Port Hudson from Baton Rouge. Banks joined his two wings on May 23 and invested Port Hudson. By then it was abundantly clear that Grant "had been diverted from his original plan" and was laying siege to Vicksburg.[37]

Banks was able to bring close to 30,000 men against a garrison under Major General Franklin Gardner that numbered only 7,500, but the Confederates were protected by a ring of heavy earthworks that grew in strength as the siege progressed. The Federals launched an attack on May 27 with two regiments of mostly free blacks from New Orleans and another consisting chiefly of former slaves—all three of which had been organized by Butler. The attacks that day were poorly coordinated and launched with inadequate information about the enemy's defenses. The Federals were repulsed with heavy casualties.[38]

Banks again requested help from Grant, informing him that the Rebel position was too strong for the number of men he had available. He could not afford to send aid to Grant without lifting the siege of Port Hudson.

Banks urged concentration of force, otherwise "the enemy will beat us all in detail, and the campaign of the West will end like the campaign of the East, in utter and disgraceful defeat before an inferior enemy." The view from Washington was different; while Halleck fully supported the idea of concentrating force on key points, he believed Vicksburg was far more important than Port Hudson. The authorities in Washington were surprised that Banks did not march directly to Grant's army from Alexandria, since the map indicated that the city was as far from Grand Gulf as from Port Hudson. In fact, Halleck hoped Banks would lift his siege and send all the men he could spare to Grant. "The moment Vicksburg falls there will be no serious difficulty in taking Port Hudson," he assured Banks. Also, joining the two forces at Vicksburg would lessen a logistical problem, for both could be supplied by river steamers from the North.[39]

Halleck's last point was significant, for the entire Department of the Gulf suffered from a shortage of adequate river transportation, and it was very expensive for the government to send supplies and reinforcements along the coast to New Orleans. Although Banks received nine additional regiments by June 1, that increased the strain on his logistical system. Fortunately for him, the Confederates did not have a relief force in the immediate area. On June 14 Banks launched another attack, which was poorly coordinated as well. The Federals again failed to break through the Confederate line, and the siege dragged on.[40]

The participation of black units in the May 27 attack drew quite a bit of attention in the North. It was seen by advocates of black enlistment to prove the worth of the policy. "This freedmen's charge has settled forever the question whether negroes will fight," asserted Salmon Chase. As the siege progressed, Banks formalized the creation of the Corps d'Afrique on June 6.[41]

Joseph Johnston commanded the only Confederate force in Mississippi that could have attempted to relieve Gardner at Port Hudson, but he had no intention of doing so. In fact, just as he had done with John Pemberton, Johnston urged Gardner to evacuate the post when it became apparent Banks might invest it. Gardner was unable to do so before the Federals arrived, and Johnston was faced with the problem of dealing with two sieges — with a force inadequate for the relief of even one, as he thought. "Vicksburg fully occupies me," he told Gardner in dispatches smuggled into Port Hudson. "Hold the place as long as you can, and then, if possible, withdraw in any direction, or cut your way out." In the Trans-Mississippi, Edmund Kirby Smith was just as reluctant to try to save Port Hudson as Vicksburg. He told Richard Taylor to give up tentative plans to recapture New Orleans because the fall of Vicksburg "entails the loss of Port Hudson and the Mississippi."

Retaking New Orleans would merely place Confederate troops "in a *cul-de-sac*, from which there could be no extrication."[42]

Halleck accepted the fact that Banks would remain at Port Hudson and tried to find help for him. He contemplated shifting troops from Quincy Gillmore's command, which was preparing to operate against the Confederate forts on Morris Island, at the entrance to Charleston Harbor, South Carolina. He reasoned that Gillmore's men could be returned as soon as Grant secured Vicksburg and was then able to send aid to Banks. In the end, Banks did not receive any help at all. The small Confederate garrison held out until word of Vicksburg's fall was confirmed, then Gardner surrendered on July 9. Casualties due to combat amounted to more than 5,000 for the Federals and about 500 for the Confederates, but Banks had up to 4,000 men too sick for duty by the end of the siege. Gardner's garrison suffered proportionately by illness as well, with only about 3,000 troops fit to man the trenches by July 9. The Confederates thus had no real hope of saving themselves at Port Hudson; the fall of Vicksburg hastened an almost inevitable conclusion.[43]

The fall of Vicksburg and Port Hudson, coupled with the great Union victory at Gettysburg and Rosecrans's conquest of the rest of middle Tennessee in the Tullahoma campaign, created an impressive string of Union triumphs in July 1863. It seemed to many that the tide had turned in the war and that "the rebellion is going up." The men in the Department of the Gulf enjoyed their share of the glory in reopening the waters of the Mississippi. In a general order, Banks told his subordinates that it was a feat "of equal import with [the] discovery and settlement" of the valley "and makes the Union a nation." No other part of the war offered a "nobler theater for intelligent enterprise than the Valley of the Mississippi." Banks proclaimed: "Never was a country better worth fighting for, better worth defending." Before going to New Orleans, he had encouraged the recruitment of three cavalry regiments in Massachusetts for the Department of the Gulf, believing that "the East should at least assist in the opening of the Mississippi." Although those regiments had been diverted to service in Virginia, Banks was one of the few prominent Easterners who pointed to "the necessity of a participation in the western military movements" by the Northeastern states.[44]

To many Federals, Banks's conduct of the siege had left much to be desired. Rather than skill, "pertinacious pummeling and out-digging the Rebels" had won the place for the Union, while the "fall of Vicksburg expedited the matter." When Gardner's men surrendered, many of them were defiant because of their stout defense against overwhelming odds. "Well, you have cut the Confederacy in two. But we shall not give up the contest, and I think we shall tire you out at last," a Rebel captain told John W. DeForest of the 12th Connecticut.[45]

Banks called loudly for a variety of help as soon as the siege ended, feeling his resources were inadequate to secure the enlarged territory his troops had won. He wanted all the spare troops from the upper Mississippi Valley that could be sent, a number of 100-pound Parrotts to arm the forts guarding New Orleans, and gunboats to keep open the line of communications along the Mississippi against "marauding bands and detachments." Light draft gunboats capable of patrolling the smaller tributaries and bayous were needed as well. To bolster his logistical capacity, Banks asked Grant for twenty-two civilian steamers and a great deal of coal and forage. When they arrived, his men were impressed and a bit afraid of the boats. They seemed much more frail than the oceangoing transports Banks had previously relied on, yet these vessels proved to be very durable for river travel. Moreover, they could load and unload almost anywhere along the riverbank, whereas the oceangoing transports needed docks. Banks was most grateful for their services.[46]

Grant finally fulfilled his promise to send troops by dispatching the Thirteenth Corps to Banks in late July. He expected that, with these additional four thousand men, Banks could secure the river south of Port Hudson. Since Grant had already occupied the Mississippi north of Natchez, Mobile seemed to be the next objective.[47]

In the fall of 1863 Banks conducted a joint operation with the Thirteenth Corps and his own Nineteenth Corps—but not against Mobile. Attempting a goal set for him when he took command of the Department of the Gulf, he sent a heavy column across Louisiana toward Texas while leading a smaller column by coastal shipping toward the mouth of the Sabine River, in the eastern part of that Rebel state. William B. Franklin, who commanded the overland column, reported a great deal of tension between the Westerners and the Easterners. They did "not know each other, and are consequently jealous of each other." Most of the friction originated with the Westerners. Edward O. C. Ord himself frankly admitted to his wife that the Thirteenth Corps boys were "a motley set of don't care a d–n fellows." The Westerners plundered freely across Louisiana during the Texas Overland Expedition in October and November 1863, taking "a special delight in destroying every species of rebel property that came within their reach," reported the surgeon of a New York regiment. The Eastern troops also foraged fully off the countryside, but they contended that the "Western men plunder worse than our fellows."[48]

The friction between men of the same uniform was nearly as threatening to army discipline as the indiscriminate plunder. Jealousy between the

Thirteenth and Nineteenth Corps troops became so great that "they almost became riotous," according to a man in the 30th Massachusetts. Surgeon Harris Beecher of the 114th New York called the Western men "arrant braggarts, continually dilating upon their wonderful achievements and forever depreciating the laudable efforts of others." They told the New England men that they came down the Mississippi to show "these paper collar and white glove gents how to fight." In the end, neither Western nor Eastern troops did much fighting during the Texas Overland Expedition. Banks's coastal column was stopped cold at Fort Sabine, and Franklin moved as far as Vermillionville before turning back after only a few small fights.[49]

Banks made so many requests for men and supplies that Grant came close to draining his own resources in the late summer of 1863. Halleck, too, assigned him a long list of tasks: send help to Banks, send the two divisions of the Ninth Corps back to Burnside so he could invade eastern Tennessee, drive Johnston out of Mississippi, prepare to use the river as a base of operations to project power inland, send ten thousand men to Helena in response to a Confederate assault on that post on July 4, and prepare to attack Mobile. Grant had the resources to answer many of these requirements, but taking the offensive to capture a strongly fortified post like Mobile was the most difficult one. Halleck agreed to postpone that move to the last.[50]

Grant tried faithfully to send Banks all that he could. He shared what coal was available at Vicksburg with the Gulf Department and forwarded tons of forage, ordnance stores, provisions, and two thousand mules. This created logistical problems for Grant; boats were in short supply upriver and the water level dropped, necessitating lighter loads for those who could make runs to Vicksburg. David Porter's requirement that they run in convoys protected by gunboats also worsened the supply problem because it delayed shipments. When the Federal defeat at Chickamauga forced Grant to dispatch large numbers of available troops to Chattanooga in late September, he was forced to cancel any further cooperation with Banks. Grant had only sixteen thousand men left to guard the Mississippi from Helena down to Natchez. Throughout the fall his subordinates continued to shift large amounts of material downriver to the Department of the Gulf, holding back only what they needed to maintain the river garrisons in the Department of the Tennessee. But even that limited cutoff of Banks's supplies caused tension between officers in the two departments, as Grant's people came to realize just how tenuously Banks had been supported before the reopening of the Mississippi.[51]

The campaign and siege of Port Hudson failed to win Banks any laurels among his own troops. Partisans of Butler continued to believe that most of the soldiers in the Department of the Gulf were more politically progressive than their commander. Treasury agent George Denison called them "thoroughly abolitionized." Whether that was true is doubtful, but Banks certainly did not satisfy those under him who believed civilians in the occupied South should be treated with an iron hand. When Edward Ord reached New Orleans with his Thirteenth Corps, he noticed the political cleavage. A conservative himself, Ord found the city "very quiet though clean and healthy, the citizens not much in love with Genl Butlers rule which has left its mark." In his view, Banks was "trying to efface by amiability the bad impression left by Genl Butler."[52]

Nathaniel Banks was by no means as conservative as many believed him to be. He raised an enormous number of black troops, reporting that twenty regiments had been created by August 1863. That amounted to twelve thousand men, including three other regiments already organized before he arrived at New Orleans. His expedition into the Bayou Teche country and his operations around Port Hudson had opened up new territory from which to secure able-bodied black males. Because most of the regiments in the Corps d'Afrique had been limited—as a preliminary measure—to no more than five hundred men each, there was an opportunity to double the number of black soldiers in the department if Banks could invade more new territory.[53]

The willingness of white soldiers to accept the concept of blacks in uniform continued to increase, although there was still some resistance in the summer of 1863. During his travels along the Mississippi from Memphis to New Orleans, George Denison found that many of Grant's men disliked the idea. "I don't mean to say it is general, but it is noticeable," he informed Secretary Chase, even as those white soldiers praised the performance of blacks at the battle of Milliken's Bend. There appeared to be far greater acceptance of the idea among white soldiers in the Department of the Gulf, although tension surfaced at Port Hudson, which was now garrisoned mostly by black troops. The post commander discovered that whites often verbally abused black sentinels and ignored their authority. He issued an order to have such behavior stopped, insisting that "any course of conduct tending to create ill-feeling between the colored troops and other troops of this command, are [sic] most strictly prohibited." Confederates lurking near Port Hudson did not take kindly to black soldiers, either. They captured several of them and killed some under uncertain circumstances. Though reports reached Port Hudson that two were hanged and others were beaten, the Rebel commander maintained that they were shot while trying to escape.[54]

As the Federals expanded their area of control in the Gulf Department, their humanitarian responsibilities increased. Banks was feeding 1,600 orphans and indigent people at twelve locations, plus an additional 20,000 to 25,000 at other places across the department, by late October. In New Orleans, up to 5,000 families were relying on the Union army for food. Banks's chief of commissary and subsistence, Colonel E. G. Beckwith, noted that this amounted to the same expenditure incurred by the entire U.S. Army to feed its enlistees before the war broke out. "These are unequaled and unheard-of charities in any age or country," Beckwith continued, "and completely reverse the very general rule of subsisting armies upon the countries in which they operate." He could have mentioned that the problem was exacerbated by Confederate efforts to stop trading between the Union zone of occupation and contiguous areas still under Rebel control. At least up to the end of 1863, that blockade was effective.[55]

With Port Hudson secure and the Mississippi reopened, President Lincoln had grander hopes for exploiting the Union enclave in the Department of the Gulf. He hoped Banks could encourage the loyal citizenry to create a state government that would acknowledge the end of slavery and develop a system whereby "the two races could gradually live themselves out of their old relation to each other." Banks did move forward along those lines as trade was reopened, "free from any military restriction whatever," between New Orleans and the upper Mississippi Valley. The Federals would have to fight to maintain that free trade, however; a report that nine hundred Confederates established four batteries at Morganza Bend, about forty miles up from Baton Rouge, led Banks to dispatch a division to deal with the problem in early September. The rear areas, especially along lines of communication, never seemed to be entirely secure.[56]

10 } From Tullahoma to Knoxville

O fficials in Washington had a difficult time juggling the needs of different military departments for more troops early in 1863. Following his bitter victory at Stones River, William Rosecrans cried loudly for more help, but Henry Halleck informed him that Grant's need for additional resources against Vicksburg was more pressing. He had hoped that Ambrose Burnside might move against Robert E. Lee's army and drive it beyond the Rappahannock River to enable him to detach troops from the East, but Burnside's second offensive resulted ingloriously in what observers derided as the "Mud March." Halleck feared that Braxton Bragg might detach strength to Mississippi while holding Rosecrans at bay in what was left of Confederate middle Tennessee. Rumors also floated that Lieutenant General James Longstreet, one of Lee's most important corps commanders, was bringing fifty-five regiments from the East to reinforce Bragg.[1]

The only sources of added manpower for Rosecrans's renamed Army of the Cumberland were the garrisons of Kentucky. Reasoning that the "certain defeat of Bragg's army" was the best way to secure the Kentucky posts, Halleck ordered Horatio G. Wright, commander of the Department of the Ohio, to strip his Kentucky garrisons to the bone. Wright was to abandon expendable posts but keep vital lines of supply open to Murfreesboro, which now was "the most important point . . . for both Kentucky and Tennessee." Rosecrans tried to improve his line of communications, a railroad that now stretched 212 miles from Louisville, by using steamers on the Cumberland River as far as Nashville. It was an uncertain adjunct to his railroad supply line because of tricky water levels at certain times of the year. The harried commander, still reacting to his near-disaster at Stones River, bombarded Washington with requests for everything imaginable. Halleck grew tired of it and reminded Rosecrans that limited resources had to be divided among several field armies; nevertheless, the War Department strained every nerve to ship as much as possible to the Army of the Cumberland. Stones River had its effect on Rosecrans's subordinates as well. Division commander Thomas J. Wood, when asked his opinion, thought the

Men repairing railroad near Murfreesboro. Maintaining the rail-based system of supply was a constant chore. (Library of Congress, LC-DIG-cwpb-02135)

army should not move until every possible man and all available resources were accumulated. If Bragg had equal strength, then a battle would result in "simply a prize fight, yielding the victor little than the ground he stands on, and by no means compensating for the expenditure of human life necessary to obtain the result."[2]

Rosecrans spent six months preparing for the next confrontation with Bragg's army, frustrating strategists in Washington and depleting the storehouse of goodwill he had accumulated with his hard-won victory at Stones River. He rebuilt the Army of the Cumberland, gaining additional troops from Kentucky, modern weapons to arm a few regiments, more cavalry, and more training for his men. In a sense, however, the long period of preparation placed even greater expectation for the result once he did move out against Bragg in late June 1863.[3]

Although the loss of territory was relatively slight following Bragg's withdrawal from Murfreesboro, civilians living near the theater of operations were apprehensive about the future. Confederate supporters in northern Alabama had suffered a great deal due to Ormsby M. Mitchell's occupation in the spring of 1862, and now they feared that if Bragg abandoned all of middle Tennessee it would happen again. There were no spare troops to satisfy their desire for six thousand men to guard the state line. Those Confederate sympathizers living near Bragg's army at Shelbyville and Tullahoma already felt the hard realities of military life as Rebel soldiers committed such "wanton destruction" that division commanders issued circulars to deal with the problem. The looting and devastation was bad enough against an enemy population, thought Jones M. Withers, but "among our friends and fellow-citizens it is an unpardonable outrage." The army's cavalry seemed to outdo the infantry, because they needed replacement mounts and could roam more freely across the countryside. Bragg declared that any cavalryman caught pillaging would be dismounted and sent to an infantry regiment as punishment. Bragg also issued orders to stop civilians from crossing through the lines unless they had a permit issued by his headquarters, for he believed that many people unsympathetic to the Confederate cause passed information to the enemy in this way.[4]

If the Federals had difficulty deciding how to allocate their available manpower, the Confederates had an even tougher time. Bragg needed an additional twenty thousand men, thought Joseph E. Johnston, to maintain his position in middle Tennessee. Such a force could hardly be spared from any other place, so Bragg tried to implement Confederate conscription by assigning brigade commander Gideon Pillow to take charge of the process in his Department of Tennessee. Three officers and three men of each regiment that had been organized in territory still under Confederate control were sent home to round up more men as well.[5]

With Rosecrans giving him six months to prepare, Bragg conducted numerous drills to train his troops and built extensive fortifications at Shelbyville and Tullahoma. The latter was ringed with five miles of earthworks and more than a dozen artillery emplacements. The trees were slashed for up to eight hundred yards in front of the works to create clear fields of fire. Like Rosecrans, who constructed the largest enclosed fieldwork of the war (big enough to hold thirty thousand men) just outside Murfreesboro, the opposing armies in middle Tennessee expended their energies on preparations instead of fighting for the first half of 1863. At the end of this waiting period, when the area's wheat crop ripened, Bragg used his own troops to harvest it, hoping to assemble an ample supply of flour for the Army of Tennessee.[6]

Federal Occupation

The six-month waiting period provided Rosecrans many occupation problems as well as work associated with preparing his army for further action. Civilians in the area now under Federal control tended to be wary and divided in their opinions. When Major General Joseph J. Reynolds of the Fourteenth Corps conducted an expedition from Murfreesboro to Auburn, Liberty, and Alexandria in early February, he found loyal families stripped of their property by the Confederate army, leaving Rebel sympathizers comparatively well off. The loyalists welcomed Reynolds's troops and begged them to treat Confederate sympathizers as harshly as they had been treated by Bragg's army. Nearly all the available young men had been conscripted into the Rebel service, from loyalist and Rebel families alike. Reynolds believed that most of the wealthy families supported the Confederacy and gave aid to guerrillas. Only Federal raids that destroyed their property and took their slaves seemed to change their attitude to one of neutrality; as soon as guerrillas reappeared, however, they again became rebellious. The middle-income families were generally, in Reynolds's view, inoffensive and capable of being turned into good Union citizens, while the poor were "all loyal." They suffered a great deal for their loyalty as well. "Will the Federal Army remain in Middle Tennessee?" they asked Reynolds's troops, displaying a "feeling of insecurity" that could only be erased by decisive forward movement.[7]

Reynolds concluded that there was little chance of turning the upper classes into good Union citizens for the foreseeable future, and he tended to advocate stripping them of their property and denying them their dominant position in local politics. Even if the Confederate armies were crushed, the rebellion would still live in the hearts of these local elites, and Reynolds anticipated what Sherman had often flirted with—deporting them from the land altogether. Rosecrans forwarded Reynolds's long report and recommendations to Halleck, who firmly approved of taking whatever property the Federals needed from the wealthy classes. He even approved of banishing them from Union lines. Halleck assured Rosecrans that, as department commander, he had the authority to execute any policies or laws on the books. "We have suffered very severely from this class, and it is time that the laws of war should be more rigorously enforced against them. A broad line of distinction must be drawn between friends and enemies, between the loyal and the disloyal."[8]

In an effort to administer his department more effectively, Rosecrans clamped down on civilians. Nashville was the focus of much of his attention. "The city being at once a camp, a garrison, and a great depot I found it absolutely necessary to put and keep it under a species of martial law," he informed Secretary of War Stanton. Rosecrans also created a surveillance system to keep an eye on trade as a way to stop smuggling, confiscating goods belonging to violators. He prohibited the use of Confederate money within the Department of the Cumberland and required cotton traders to prove their loyalty and comply with Treasury Department regulations. They also had to register with local provost marshals and ship their purchases only through Nashville. No one associated with the army was allowed to engage in the cotton trade, and Rosecrans vowed to seize all bales involved in transactions that disregarded his rules.[9]

Irregular activity picked up following Stones River and targeted the Union transportation system. A guerrilla leader named Peddicord and forty of his men wearing Union overcoats tried to burn a cattle guard on the railroad and tore up five miles of track about fourteen miles from Gallatin, Tennessee. Federal soldiers chased them away, but when the local Union commander learned that fifty citizens had gathered at the place and helped the guerrillas, he vowed "to make an example of some of them." A force of about seventy-five guerrillas placed an object on the track near Franklin, Kentucky, that caused an engine and two cars to derail on a sharp curve. They then fired into the disabled train, which carried about two hundred "women, civilians, and officers." When the passengers abandoned the cars, the guerrillas plundered the train, taking cash and mail, before elements of the 129th Illinois arrived and recovered most of the loot. The 26th Kentucky battled a force of approximately one hundred guerrillas that was cutting telegraph wires and burning the depot at Rocky Hill, Kentucky, north of Bowling Green. Steamers were not safe from "these predatory bands," either. The *Mary Crane* was captured while taking on wood at a landing on the Cumberland River; the guerrillas killed and wounded some of the unarmed crew, then set fire to the boat. Two other steamers were taken on the Cumberland River by twelve hundred guerrillas, who killed eight black crew members and one of the captains when he protested the murders.[10]

Guerrillas also attacked loyalists in an act of political terrorism. On the night of April 23, 1863, they abducted Unionist Thomas Norvill from his home near Richland, Tennessee, and took him fifteen miles away where they murdered the unfortunate man, "literally hewing him to pieces." Irregulars committed numerous robberies to obtain supplies for themselves. A different band took another loyalist in Union County, Kentucky, and mercilessly beat him with "large green hickory withes" because they thought he had given information about their location to Federal authorities. There seemed to be a seasonal aspect to these predations. The areas south of the Green River in Kentucky and north of the Cumberland River in Tennessee were comparatively quiet during the winter months, but as soon as spring leafed out the trees and provided moderate weather, local Union commanders expected an upsurge in guerrilla activity.[11]

The Yankees reinforced their garrisons with more mounted troops and tried, often futilely, to hunt down the guerrillas. They had an easier time finding and confronting recalcitrant citizens. By March, Rosecrans decided to deport civilian families who were destitute because their men were serving in the Confederate army, as well as those who were unwilling to support the Union. He granted them ten days to prepare for their departure and allowed them to take their personal property (except for contraband of war), promising to treat them as spies if they returned to the limits of his department. Rosecrans allowed them to remain only if they took the oath of allegiance and promised to "behave themselves as peaceable citizens." This led to a great surge of people flooding into the offices of provost marshals to take the oath; ten thousand did so by the end of May, and another thousand in June and July. The army arrested and deported only about one hundred people under Rosecrans's order. Bragg offered them food and transportation south.[12]

One of those apprehended and sent beyond Union lines was Fannie Battle, of Nashville, the daughter of a high-ranking Confederate officer. The chief of the special police force that Rosecrans formed from among his officers arrested her for spying, smuggling, and forging passes. "The prisoner is affable and attractive and well qualified by manners and mind to be influential for evil to the loyal cause," her jailer wrote before Battle was deported. Confederate commanders had few opportunities to counteract Union measures to control the civilian population. They relied on about ninety-six companies of Partisan Rangers (organized by mid-1863 to maintain some degree of order in areas not patrolled by Confederate troops), but partisan officers could only threaten the Federals in an attempt to curb Union actions against civilians. Colonel Robert V. Richardson threatened to shoot two captured Union soldiers for every citizen the Federals arrested and to destroy twice as much property belonging to Unionists as the Yankees confiscated from pro-Confederates. In a proclamation issued to all Federal soldiers, he urged them to escape "a war waged to free negroes and enslave white men" by deserting to Richardson's unit, where he promised to treat them "as friends and brothers."[13]

Whether Richardson enticed any Yankees to abandon their posts is doubtful, but the number of Confederate deserters in Union hands in the West became so large that officials sought ways to minimize the expense of holding them in prison. Colonel William Hoffman, the commissary-general of prisoners, suggested they be induced to take the oath of allegiance and then released. Stanton approved, but complications ensued as 250 men who claimed they deserted from John H. Morgan's Kentucky command wanted to be set free. Yet they were considered too dangerous to be returned to the civilian population. More complicated were the instances where Confederate officers were captured while trying to recruit men behind Union lines. When Federal authorities in Kentucky arrested two of these officers and sentenced them to be shot as spies, a sentence that Lincoln approved, the Confederates threatened retaliation. The Federals reminded them that Confederate authorities had executed some of the Andrews Raiders, and the Yankees had demonstrated extraordinary restraint by not retaliating in that case.[14]

In many ways, Kentucky remained an unusual occupied region because it was far to the rear of the major zone of military operations, yet not entirely secure or loyal to the Union. Horatio Wright fretted that he had only nine thousand men to hold the state and support the operations of both Rosecrans and Grant much farther south. His role was defensive in nature, fearing Confederate cavalry raids from eastern Tennessee, yet he barely had enough men to deal with the threat and guerrilla activity was on the increase. But Rosecrans refused to send him any additional troops. The situation was worsened by the fact that the civil government in Kentucky was only marginally pro-Union. Governor James F. Robinson complained about the effect of Lincoln's Emancipation Proclamation on public attitudes, even though the entire state had been exempted from its provisions. The army was prohibited from either helping owners recover their refugee slaves or helping slaves escape their masters. Nevertheless, the emancipationist policy had a "wilting and withering" effect on his people, Robinson believed, which made them ripe for a Confederate invasion.[15]

Military Action

During the first half of 1863 the Federals in middle Tennessee engaged in only limited action. Both sides moved significant numbers of troops to the area west of Murfreesboro to protect or to take advantage of approaches to Nashville from the south. On March 5 Colonel John Coburn's brigade clashed with a brigade of Confederate cavalry commanded by Brigadier General William H. Jackson near Thompson's Station, some four miles north of Spring Hill. Though it pushed the Rebels back, considerable reinforcements under Major General Earl Van Dorn arrived and counterattacked, surrounding and crushing the Federal unit. Van Dorn inflicted 1,600 casualties, capturing many of Coburn's men, while suffering only 357 losses. Federal prisoners reported ill treatment at the hands of the Southerners. Their blankets and other personal items necessary for comfort were taken away before they traveled across the South in poorly heated railroad cars with inadequate food.[16]

If Rosecrans was not ready to move his army against Bragg, Lincoln suggested he use small forces to raid Confederate transportation lines, much as John Morgan and Nathan Bedford Forrest had repeatedly done against Federal lines of communication in Tennessee and Kentucky. Rosecrans tried the experiment with a brigade of infantry commanded by Colonel Abel D. Streight, which he mounted on mules. Streight had orders to destroy railroads, cotton mills, and tanneries, and to take up all the provisions he could as he made his way across northern Alabama and northwestern Georgia, aiming at Bragg's rail link with Atlanta. He rendezvoused with eight thousand infantrymen commanded by one of Grant's subordinates, Major General Grenville M. Dodge, near Tuscumbia, Alabama. While Dodge moved toward Courtland to keep Forrest in check, Streight headed east on the night of April 26 with fifteen hundred men. Forrest disengaged from Dodge and gave chase to the Yankee raiders, harassing their rear and fighting several sharp engagements along the way. He cut off Streight near Rome, Georgia, preventing the Federals from doing much damage and convincing them to surrender on May 3. Streight had to leave many wounded men behind along the way, and Forrest's men stripped them of their blankets, leaving them to fend for themselves. Local loyalists saved a large number of them. About 150 blacks had managed to accompany Streight during the raid, and they too fell into Confederate hands. Streight and a handful of other officers managed to escape from Libby Prison in Richmond the next February.[17]

Tullahoma

Rosecrans had no intention of advancing directly on Bragg's fortifications at Shelbyville and Tullahoma when he was finally ready to move in late June 1863. He carefully planned a turning movement that involved gaining control of some gaps in a range of hills between Murfreesboro and those towns. Skirmishing took place at several locations. On June 24, in a sharp fight at Hoover's Gap, a newly mounted brigade of infantry armed with Spencer repeaters, under the command of Colonel John T. Wilder, demonstrated what could be done by good soldiers with this modern weapon. The Union's

Tullahoma campaign was well planned and finely executed; it forced Bragg to abandon both of his fortified posts without a major battle. Jubilation at Union army headquarters led to overstatements of the campaign's effect; Rosecrans's chief of staff and future president, James A. Garfield, reported that the "rebels are retreating in great confusion."[18]

There was far less confusion than frustration at Bragg's headquarters as he pulled back across the mountains to Chattanooga, giving up all of middle Tennessee. "Rosecrans refused to give me battle, except on his own terms," he complained to Beauregard, "and those I would not accept." Bragg criticized Johnston for not acting aggressively as Vicksburg and Port Hudson starved and Rosecrans moved forward. Bragg kept his focus on Atlanta, "the great point of most importance dependent on this army for protection." The Army of Tennessee conducted the retreat to Chattanooga with little loss and was ready to do battle at any time.[19]

After his Pyrrhic victory at Stones River, Rosecrans was bursting with pride that the Army of the Cumberland was able to drive eighty miles into Rebel territory in eleven days with fewer than six hundred casualties. But, from the larger perspective afforded the authorities in Washington, Tullahoma paled in comparison to the Union victory at Gettysburg and Grant's capture of Vicksburg. "You and your noble army now have the chance to give the finishing blow to the rebellion," Stanton telegraphed Rosecrans. "Will you neglect the chance?" Irate, Rosecrans reminded Stanton that the reclamation of all middle Tennessee at such slight cost should not be overlooked simply "because it is not written in letters of blood."[20]

Heavy rains set in to delay Rosecrans's follow-up to the Tullahoma campaign, but he already had unrealistic estimates of its effect on Bragg's army. Rosecrans believed reports that five thousand Confederates had deserted and that the retreat was "disastrous and demoralizing" to his enemy. He had visions of "overtaking and destroying their entire army." His extreme optimism was fed by the testimony of captured Confederates. Out of 1,634 prisoners taken during the Tullahoma campaign, 616 claimed to be draftees "tired of the war." The Federals paroled 195 of those self-reported draftees and administered the oath of allegiance on the understanding that all of them would "remain north of the Ohio during the war." Another 96 joined the Union army, and 325 "were released and permitted to return to their homes, within our lines." It was easy enough to assume that this was a sign of deteriorating morale in Bragg's army. Coupled with the immense victories at Gettysburg, Vicksburg, and Port Hudson, it seemed to many soldiers in Rosecrans's army "that the tide of the rebellion is turned."[21]

While preparing for the push against Chattanooga, Rosecrans ordered his cavalry to range across the newly acquired territory to impress civilians that the Federal government had taken firm control of all middle Tennessee. He also wanted the troopers to gather able-bodied blacks for labor and tried to clamp down on depredations by his own soldiers.[22]

Burnside and Eastern Tennessee

The Federals tried to coordinate a double approach to Confederate holdings in Tennessee that summer of 1863. The long-awaited Union invasion of the eastern part of the state was finally possible because Ambrose Burnside, who replaced Wright as head of the Department of the Ohio, had additional troops with which to conduct operations. On his arrival, Burnside brought two divisions of the Ninth Corps. Though instructions from Halleck directed him to protect Kentucky from Confederate raids and to secure Rosecrans's supply lines through the state, his major task was to reclaim eastern Tennessee and save its predominately loyalist population. The fear of raids was real, for Confederate authorities were keen to take advantage of political unrest in Kentucky stemming mostly from the emancipationist policy of Lincoln's government.[23]

In attempting to conquer eastern Tennessee, the biggest problem Burnside faced had to do with logistics. The mountain roads were a trial for wagon trains, and the distance was too long for comfort. Colonel Samuel A. Gilbert, who knew the region well, reported that Burnside could not expect to feed a sizable force from the countryside; he advised Lincoln's old idea of building a railroad between Nicholasville and Cumberland Gap at government expense.[24]

The Confederates, however, were vulnerable because most of the inhabitants of eastern Tennessee had become even more hardened in their resistance to the Richmond government. Moreover, manpower shortages meant that only about five thousand men were available to the commander of the Department of East Tennessee to defend an important line of railroad some two hundred miles long.[25]

Still, Burnside needed to feed his troops if he hoped to take and hold the region, and his efforts to mount an invasion were delayed by a number of factors. Taking command of the Department of the Ohio in late March 1863, he dealt with expressions of treason among the Copperheads of the Midwest (part of his military department), engaging in high-profile arrests of civilians such as Clement L. Vallandigham, a candidate for governor of Ohio. Then Burnside had to send most of his Ninth Corps troops to Grant to help in the siege of Vicksburg. That summer Brigadier General John Hunt Morgan mounted a major raid through Kentucky, across the Ohio River and into Indiana and Ohio, further delaying the planned offensive into eastern Tennessee. All of this added to the long frustration felt in Washington with Kentucky commanders.[26]

Finally, on August 16, Burnside was ready to move with sixteen thousand men from Camp Nelson, 220 miles from Knoxville. He planned to bypass Cumberland Gap and move swiftly to the south and then east. Relying on whatever food and supplies they could carry along, Burnside's column climbed the rugged sides of the Cumberland Plateau and made its way through a region almost barren of provisions. His troops were helped tremendously by a Confederate decision to concentrate available manpower against Rosecrans, who had now begun his push against Chattanooga. The Department of East Tennessee was stripped of its troops when Simon B. Buckner moved south to join Bragg. The van of Burnside's column entered Knoxville on September 1, 1863, without firing a shot, and the commander arrived two days later to a boisterous reception. Burnside then moved sixty miles north and compelled the surrender of a small garrison at Cumberland Gap on September 9.[27]

Because many of his men were recruits from eastern Tennessee, Burnside felt it necessary to issue a general order warning them not to seek personal revenge now that they were in the ascendant. Parson William G. Brownlow, the fiery newspaper editor who was one of the most prominent eastern Tennessee loyalists, returned to his home in Knoxville and resumed publishing his newspaper, calling it *Brownlow's Knoxville Whig and Rebel Ventilator*. The Federal government provided transportation and equipment, as well as a hefty cash subsidy, for Brownlow's return and the resumption of his newspaper editorials.[28]

No one was more jubilant at the redemption of this region than Andrew Johnson. He had long seen Federal occupation of eastern Tennessee as a necessary condition for the reconstruction of a loyal, civilian government in the state. A week after Burnside reached Knoxville, Lincoln urged Johnson to move forward toward that goal, but he cautioned him to make sure reconstruction in Tennessee brought with it a repudiation of slavery and the opportunity for loyalists to dominate the new state government.[29]

The late summer marked a major new push to find more troops for the Union army in Tennessee. Earlier Johnson had been authorized to raise twenty regiments and ten batteries from among the white population for Federal service, and Lincoln had urged him to raise black units too, even though Tennessee had been exempted from the provisions of the Emancipation Proclamation. Some of Rosecrans's subordinates also encouraged the recruitment of blacks in Tennessee. While Johnson seemed little interested in African American regiments, the Federal government decided to move forward with the plan anyway. Stanton appointed George L. Stearns to oversee the process in Tennessee, while Lorenzo Thomas continued to work primarily in the Mississippi Valley.[30]

Stearns received instructions, worked out by Lincoln himself, to guide the ticklish process of creating black regiments in a state where slavery was still legally intact. Slaves belonging to Confederate sympathizers were, of course, free to join under the Confiscation Act, but slaves belonging to loyalists presented a different problem. Lincoln judged that they be allowed to enlist with the consent of their owners, but they would become free at the end of their service. Department commanders had the option of recruiting slaves of loyalists without the master's consent if they deemed it necessary, but the U.S. government would have to compensate the owners for the loss of their property. Stearns met with Rosecrans to discuss the details and received enthusiastic cooperation. The recruiter believed the Department of the Cumberland was a good field to work, as there were many blacks in it, the officers seemed very efficient, and the civilian population was "in a much better state of preparation for the change than I had expected."[31]

Chickamauga

Officials in Washington were pleased with developments behind the lines in Rosecrans's department but uneasy with the slow pace of forward movement. "The patience of the authorities here has been completely exhausted," Halleck alerted Rosecrans in late July 1863 when the pause after Tullahoma lengthened. "It has been said that you are as inactive as was General Buell." The president and his advisers not only wanted to rescue the loyalists of eastern Tennessee, but also sought to penetrate Georgia to acquire more able-bodied blacks for the army. Rosecrans defended himself by describing the natural obstacles to his advance. In order to bypass Chattanooga to the south and threaten Bragg's line of communications, he had to cross the Cumberland Plateau and then the Tennessee River, a major stream. After that, two huge ridges—Sand Mountain and Lookout Mountain—stood in the way, with narrow valleys between them. The Army of the Cumberland faced a mountainous, sixty-mile trek into Confederate territory. Rosecrans's railroad link with Louisville, already more than three hundred miles long, had barely enough rolling stock to supply the day-to-day needs of his army, and he required fifty more cars to have a hope of supporting a forward move. Rosecrans warned of the danger to his army's morale, as well as to Northern public opinion, if he failed and was forced to fall back. Better to go slow but sure, he told Washington.[32]

On August 16 the Federals started on what Rosecrans called "a stupendous undertaking" against Chattanooga, which he recognized as a point of secondary importance to the Confederates, compared to Atlanta, which was a point of "vital" importance. Despite his logistical difficulties, Rosecrans sought to curb plundering by his soldiers. Struggling across the mountains, he tried to shore up his reputation with Washington by explaining to Lincoln that "few armies have been called upon to attempt a more arduous campaign."[33]

The Confederates fully recognized the significance of Rosecrans's approach with an army that by now outnumbered Bragg's. Lieutenant General Leonidas Polk suggested that most of Johnston's force move to Chattanooga from Mississippi, and that Buckner evacuate eastern Tennessee and do the same. The combined forces could crush Rosecrans, Polk reasoned, reclaim all of Tennessee and strongpoints on the Mississippi that were lost in 1862, and attack Grant from the north. One of many problems associated with a scheme like this was that Bragg was thoroughly reluctant to take the offensive, even with an enlarged army. He viewed the mountains that separated him from Rosecrans as a barrier, just as did his opponent. It was "destitute even of vegetation," and Bragg had more limited means of moving his available force across rivers than did Rosecrans. Pursuing a defensive policy, Bragg had his engineers work on the fortifications of Chattanooga and attempted to suppress pillaging of the local families by his troops. The Confederate cavalry received orders to evacuate all able-bodied blacks and destroy cotton as they fell back in the face of the Federal advance.[34]

Rosecrans was in for a rude shock as the Confederates managed the most effective concentration of their strength in the Western campaigns. While Johnston remained cold to moving his troops to Chattanooga, Buckner brought his men to Bragg. Two divisions of veteran troops from Lee's Army of Northern Virginia, under Lieutenant General James Longstreet, were on their way as well. Bragg evacuated Chattanooga, which elements of Rosecrans's army occupied without a fight on September 9, and then maneuvered in the country south of the city for an advantage over the enemy. His effort to catch a portion of the Union army in detail at McLemore's Cove, in the valley of the west branch of Chickamauga Creek, failed. Rosecrans was able to concentrate his marching columns in that valley as the Confederates groped toward a decisive showdown.[35]

The landscape along Chickamauga Creek was mostly level land but cluttered, as were many Civil War battlefields, with thickets interspersed with cleared fields. The greatest battle of the Western theater occurred there on September 19–20, 1863. The fighting on the first day consisted of a series of comparatively isolated engagements by divisions and brigades—seesaw combat that decided little except the fate of thousands of individual soldiers. A combination of factors contributed to the nature of the fighting on September 19; neither army was fully concentrated yet, leaders on both sides had difficulty exercising command and control, and the vegetation curtailed larger perspectives on the ebb and flow of action.[36]

John Bell Hood's division of Longstreet's corps reached Bragg in time to participate in the fighting on September 19, but he was not impressed by the Army of Tennessee. Meeting its major commanders for the first time that evening, Hood was surprised that "not one spoke in a sanguine tone regarding the result of the battle." Longstreet and his other division arrived later that evening, after a long rail journey from Virginia that had begun on September 9. Hood was overjoyed to make contact with his commander, "as he was the first general I had met since my arrival who talked of victory." One of Hood's men, J. B. Polley of the 4th Texas, also found it strange that the Army of Tennessee engaged in standing firefights with the Yankees instead of charging "the enemy at sight," as did Lee's veterans in Virginia.[37]

Alarmed at the course of events, the Federals secured their position in the valley of Chickamauga Creek by constructing breastworks, especially along their left wing held by George H. Thomas, which curved around to protect their hold on the road to Chattanooga. The sound of chopping could be clearly heard by the Confederate army. The next morning the Southerners were astonished at the strength of these improvised works.[38]

Bragg's right wing launched a series of assaults against Thomas on the morning of Sunday, September 20, all of which foundered on heavy fire delivered from behind the stout breastworks. Then about noon Longstreet directed a massive attack against the Federal center. He marshaled several divisions in a large formation, capable of pushing through a great deal of resistance, but it also happened that the apex of this formation hit a gap that Rosecrans temporarily created in his line as he shifted one division for another. The Confederates plowed through this opening and succeeded in collapsing the Union line, sending at least one-third of Rosecrans's army and two of his three corps commanders fleeing for Chattanooga. Rosecrans himself retired to the city, leaving Thomas to fight a rearguard action. The fighting on the afternoon of September 20 was some of the most stirring of the Western war, as remnants of McCook's and Crittenden's corps stopped on Snodgrass Hill, to Thomas's right, and made a stand. On this 200-foot-high wooded height, they repulsed attack after attack, with general supervision by Thomas, but mostly by the grit and fortitude of the rank and file. The spirited stand on Snodgrass Hill saved the Army of the Cumberland from a far worse disaster. Rosecrans's Reserve Corps, under Major General Gordon Granger, moved toward the fighting at a key point in time, without orders, and saved the position from being turned. The battered Federals retired to Chattanooga at dusk. Rosecrans lost 16,179 men out of 57,840 engaged. Bragg's casualties were the heaviest of his army's history at 18,454 men from among the 68,000 he employed.[39]

"It was the most obstinate fight we have ever had," Bragg wrote of Chickamauga. The heavy losses dampened his enthusiasm, but the Confederate commander solemnly hoped that "the tide is at last turned in our favor." The results of the sanguinary battle shocked the Federals, who had unbounded confidence in Rosecrans and fully expected Bragg to fall back all the way to Atlanta. As a soldier in the 10th Indiana put it, "A 'right Smart Chance' of the army were 'Demoralized as Hell'" after the Confederate breakthrough on September 20. After the Federals retreated to Chattanooga and dug extensive earthen defenses to protect themselves, they regained some of their confidence, "but there was Still a very ugly Bull looking us in the face." Rosecrans was hemmed in and dependent on a line of wagons for subsistence because Bragg positioned troops on Lookout Mountain to interdict the railroad into Chattanooga with artillery fire. The main portion of the Confederate army took post on Missionary Ridge. Only the approaches north of the city were open to the Federals.[40]

Immediately after the Army of Tennessee's greatest triumph, however, trouble intensified among its high-ranking officers. Longstreet met Bragg early on the morning of September 21 and suggested the army cross the Tennessee River above Chattanooga to threaten Rosecrans's slim line of communications and continue the offensive all the way to Nashville. If the army had insufficient transportation for this, Longstreet suggested that it advance toward Knoxville on the railroad to hit Burnside, then move into middle Tennessee. Bragg seemed to agree, but then he slowly brought the army close to Chattanooga and assumed positions on the high ground outside town. Bragg later explained that any offensive move was impossible due to the army's transportation difficulties. All of the troops that had reinforced him just before the battle had arrived without their own wagons or spare horses, and he had no bridging material to cross the Tennessee River. Longstreet's was a "visionary scheme," risky in the extreme, compelling the abandonment not only of Bragg's own line of communications with Atlanta but also thousands of wounded Confederate soldiers at Chickamauga. The "proposition was not even entertained," he wrote of Longstreet's idea, in his report to Richmond.[41]

The Federal reaction to Chickamauga could not have been more different.

Chattanooga as seen from Lookout Mountain. This view demonstrates the potential inherent in General Braxton Bragg's command of the high ground around Chattanooga. (Johnson and Buel, *Battles and Leaders*, 3:692)

As Rosecrans huddled in the city, the authorities in Washington scrambled to shift large numbers of troops to go to his rescue. Lincoln was determined to hold on to the city and to Knoxville at all costs, not just for political reasons but because he firmly believed that they were key positions of military value.[42]

The Federals now shifted the largest number of troops from one theater to another thus far in the war. The Eleventh and Twelfth Corps were placed under Major General Joseph Hooker and rapidly moved by rail twelve hundred miles in eight days. Some thirteen thousand men traveled from the Washington area to various stations along Rosecrans's railroad in a little more than a week. Unable to feed them at Chattanooga, the authorities retained the reinforcements for a time as a support to the Army of the Cumberland outside the city.[43]

These Eastern troops found the situation in the West very different from that in Virginia. Discipline among the Western troops appeared extremely lax, and the Westerners often resented the fact that these strangers were among them. "They seem to want to do all the fighting themselves," Twelfth

Corps division leader John Geary wrote home. The Westerners also were "regular robbers" who took whatever they wanted from local civilians. Bantering between the different units sometimes turned ugly, so much so that general orders were issued in an attempt to keep peace between soldiers of different regions.[44]

The Easterners also were amazed at the logistical difficulties faced by their comrades in the West. Twelfth Corps division commander Alpheus Williams called Rosecrans's 300-mile railroad "a monstrous line" for supplying the army. Major General Oliver Otis Howard, who commanded the Eleventh Corps, noted how impoverished the countryside appeared to be. The reinforcements divided their strength along the railroad and worked to repair bridges and other facilities for keeping the Federals in Chattanooga.[45]

In addition to the Eleventh and Twelfth Corps, Washington authorities began to move Grant's Fifteenth Corps and elements of the Seventeenth Corps from Mississippi. This was a far more difficult feat, shifting some twenty thousand men, eight thousand animals, and six hundred wagons up the Mississippi to Memphis during a period of low water. Then the columns under William T. Sherman's command had to march across country to Chattanooga.[46]

Washington also felt a new head was needed in the West. In mid-October, three and a half months after his victory at Vicksburg, Grant was named commander of the newly created Military Division of the Mississippi and given as his first assignment the securing of Rosecrans's position at Chattanooga. He traveled to Nashville, where he became fully aware that logistics were the prerequisite to success. In addition to a secure track, the railroad companies needed more engines and cars. One of Grant's first decisions was to replace Rosecrans with George H. Thomas. "Hold Chattanooga at all hazards," he telegraphed the new commander of the Army of the Cumberland. "I will be there as soon as possible." The trip was grueling. Grant had to ride the last fifty miles—from Bridgeport, Alabama, where the line crossed the Tennessee River, to Chattanooga—in a drenching rain. His experience so far convinced him that, even in good weather and without enemy interference, the rail line could barely supply an army in the mountains. The wagon link was no substitute, for the mule teams could carry only light loads across the rugged terrain into Chattanooga. Grant's "greatest apprehension" was that Bragg might move forces between Chattanooga and Knoxville; Thomas did not have the transportation capacity to shift and support large numbers of troops outside the city.[47]

In the Army of Tennessee, the Confederate high command remained deeply divided on how to follow up the victory at Chickamauga. Longstreet continued to urge an offensive move that Bragg was convinced could not be done. It was not until September 27 that the railroad bridges behind Confederate lines were repaired and the army received more than half rations. A frontal attack on the Federals was out of the question, so Bragg continued to wait on the heights near Chattanooga, imposing a quasi-siege on the Federals. Meanwhile, his men, especially the cavalry of Major General Joseph Wheeler, continued to scrounge around for food in the countryside to supplement their meager rations.[48]

The flow of events entirely favored the Federals, who moved to open a shorter, better supply line into Chattanooga. By deftly positioning troops on October 27–28, they were able to secure a wagon route from Bridgeport to the beleaguered city that lay mostly south of the Tennessee River. This "Cracker Line," as the soldiers called it, lifted spirits only days after Grant arrived to take charge of operations. Bragg gave Longstreet the task of closing it, but his attacks on the night of October 28–29 failed, in part due to confusion and mismanagement on the Rebel side.[49]

Longstreet's failure was the last straw for Bragg, who had Davis's support to continue as commander of the army even though many of his subordinates openly joined Longstreet in criticizing him. Southern officials had advised taking the offensive rather than passively waiting for Grant to complete his concentration at Chattanooga, and they often pointed to Burnside's isolated command at Knoxville as a viable target. From there, a Rebel force could invade middle Tennessee or Kentucky. When the Confederate president visited the Army of Tennessee in early October, he spoke to the rank and file as if Bragg would soon move north and plant the Confederate flag on the banks of the Ohio. The urge to take the offensive conflicted so deeply with Bragg's tempered reluctance to risk the move with inadequate resources that the only way to resolve the dilemma was to detach a part of his army to attempt the recapture of Knoxville. Choosing Longstreet and his two divisions would also rid Bragg of a harassing influence in his army. Davis agreed, and Longstreet was given his marching orders on November 3.[50]

Longstreet would come to understand the tremendous difficulties of moving a force of even twelve thousand men less than one hundred miles, along a rickety rail line, with inadequate logistical support. His men crossed the Tennessee River near Loudon, about twenty miles southwest of Knoxville, on November 14, as Burnside planned to pull his troops away from that area to draw Longstreet farther from Chattanooga. The only chance the Confederates had to win a decisive victory was to catch Burnside in the open before he found refuge in Knoxville. Longstreet came close to doing so at Campbell's Station on November 16, but Burnside fought a skillful delaying action and retired to the city, where his men dug a strong line of earthworks. Longstreet's situation at Knoxville was much like that of Bragg's at Chattanooga, and both commanders waited for events to develop.[51]

Grant also waited—for Sherman to reach him—before launching his well-developed plan to drive Bragg away from Chattanooga and help Burnside. In the meantime, he "never felt such restlessness" as when he contemplated the inability of Thomas to move troops outside the city. When Sherman rode ahead of his struggling column and met Grant on November 14, he was surprised to learn the true situation in Chattanooga. According to Sherman, Grant feared that the Army of the Cumberland could not be relied on to take the offensive after Chickamauga, and he looked to his old troops of the Army of the Tennessee to take the lead in attacking Bragg.[52]

The arrival of Sherman's veterans invited comparisons with the Eastern troops that guarded the Cracker Line. New York soldier Rice C. Bull noted that the Westerners wore large hats rather than caps and dressed and marched carelessly. He could see that they would fight well, even though they boasted of their prowess and criticized the Easterners for their comparatively neat appearance. Out of these encounters grew the story about how the Fifteenth Corps acquired its unit badge. The Eastern corps had long before adopted badges, but the idea had scarcely taken hold in the West. When a veteran of the Twelfth Corps asked a man of the Fifteenth about his badge, the grizzled Westerner blurted: "'Why, . . . forty rounds in the cartridge-box, and twenty in the pocket." When Major General John A. Logan, who later assumed command of the Fifteenth Corps, heard the story, he adopted the cartridge box as the corps badge.[53]

Once Sherman's troops became available and the Eleventh Corps was shifted to Chattanooga, Grant was able to put his offensive plans into operation. He began with a push by troops of Thomas's army against a knoll called Orchard Knob that lay between the lines occupied by advanced Confederate troops. It lay in the open, highly visible to both sides. Thomas's Fourth Corps (formed by consolidating Alexander McCook's and George Crittenden's Twentieth and Twenty-first Corps after Chickamauga) easily took Orchard Knob on November 23. Then Hooker moved three divisions—one from each of the field armies that had troops at Chattanooga—up the steep slopes of Lookout Mountain on November 24. Without Longstreet, Bragg could afford to defend this huge eminence with little more than a brigade. The terrain offered as much resistance to Hooker's operations as to the Confederates, but by late that night the mountain was cleared of Rebel troops.[54]

The bulk of Bragg's army remained on Missionary Ridge, a 400-foot-tall

Confederate prisoners at the railroad depot, Chattanooga. Captured in Grant's impressive triumph on November 23–25, 1863, these prisoners await transport north. (Library of Congress, LC-DIG-cwpb-02116)

feature that stretched across the southeastern approaches to Chattanooga. The Rebel troops had fieldworks on the ridge in what seemed like a daunting position that Grant hoped to approach from both flanks simultaneously. While Hooker was to attack the Confederate left from Lookout Mountain, Sherman would cross the Tennessee upstream from Chattanooga and assault the right. The plan quickly unraveled, as Hooker was delayed while crossing Lookout Creek and Sherman found stiff resistance while attempting to advance against Major General Patrick Cleburne's division, which secured Bragg's right flank, on November 25. To relieve pressure on Sherman, Grant ordered Thomas to strike at the Confederate center, intending it to be more of a demonstration than a serious attack. When Thomas sent four divisions, the officers and men took it upon themselves to convert this demonstration into a major assault. They scaled the daunting slope of Missionary Ridge and drove Bragg's army in confusion. A combination of faulty placement of troops on the ridge and superior Union planning, concentration, and logistical support led to one of the most spectacular Federal victories of the war.[55]

Bragg's army was badly defeated on November 25, although Cleburne blunted Federal pursuit with a firm stand at Ringgold two days later. The Army of Tennessee retired in safety to Dalton, Georgia, about twenty-five miles south of Chattanooga. Grant lost 5,335 men, while Bragg's losses amounted to 6,667. The inspiring charge up Missionary Ridge went a long way toward restoring confidence in Thomas's army. It also reclaimed the morale advantage the Western Federals had achieved over their opponents thus far in the war.[56]

Longstreet fared little better in his campaign against Burnside. The Federal defenses of Knoxville seemed too strong to be assaulted, and Longstreet spent several days seeking a weak point. He finally decided to strike at a reinforced angle in the line, where a redoubt named Fort Sanders seemed to offer an approach toward a bastion only partly covered by fire. Early on the morning of November 29, Longstreet threw some two thousand veterans against Fort Sanders. They became stuck in the deep ditch of the work, unable to climb out in sufficient numbers to enter the fort, which was defended by fewer than five hundred men. The Confederates lost more than eight hundred troops, one-fourth of them captured in the ditch, and failed to break into the city. Longstreet remained until Grant sent a relief force thirty thousand strong under Sherman to help Burnside; then he retired eastward on December 4.[57]

The major campaigns of 1863 went a long way toward reducing the ability of the Confederates to hold on to key territory in the West. The entire length of the Mississippi Valley, all of middle Tennessee, and most of eastern Tennessee fell under Federal domination. In fact, the entire Upper South, and a vital commercial corridor through the middle of the Deep South, had been reclaimed by the central government. It was a decisive turn of events that nevertheless presented tough problems for future Union military movements, for the remaining areas under Confederate control were not as accessible to Northern soldiers as the Upper South or the Mississippi River.

11 } Administering the Western Conquests

Quartermaster General Montgomery C. Meigs estimated that Federal forces in the West reclaimed 50,000 square miles of "revolted territory" in 1863. Added to the 150,000 square miles recovered in 1861–62, that amounted to "a territory as large as Austria or France or the Peninsula of Spain and Portugal." As the war progressed and the Union army continued to advance, problems associated with administering the conquered territory increased in importance and visibility. A different kind of war was fought behind the lines in the South than the one that captured the public imagination along the active battle lines.[1]

By 1863, the vast majority of Union officers and soldiers agreed that the only solution to the rebellion was military force rather than "compromise and offers of peace," as Halleck wrote Sherman. The general in chief had no faith in "civico-military government, under civilians," such as had been created by Andrew Johnson in Tennessee. "It merely embarrasses the military authorities without effecting any good." Until some process of political reconstruction could be found, the Union army had to govern the former Confederate territory as best it could.[2]

One of the chief problems for the military government was protecting supply lines to the front and keeping open the navigation of the Mississippi to civilian commerce. The Confederates denied Northerners complete freedom to use the river by mounting many small-scale attacks on steamers for the remainder of the war. Secretary of War James A. Seddon pushed for the detachment of units as large as a brigade to operate along the riverbank, and many guerrilla bands roamed independently of any government authority. In November 1863 a regularly organized battery under Captain T. A. Faries again placed guns behind the levee along the lower Mississippi and engaged steamers and ironclads for two days before retiring. Bands of up to fifty guerrillas ambushed boats when they landed to take on wood or make impromptu repairs. In December Confederate artillery fire riddled the steamer *Henry Von Phul* five miles north of Bayou Sara, killing its captain, two crew members,

U.S. gunboat Brown, *Mississippi River Fleet. One of many Federal gunboats that tried to suppress guerrilla attacks on Union steamers along the Western river system.* (Library of Congress, LC-USZ62-62362)

and three passengers before ironclads and other steamers came to its rescue. Two weeks later two women passengers were killed on the *Brazil* by musketry and artillery fire, reportedly from a brigade of Confederate cavalry.[3]

Perhaps more frustrating than the attacks conducted from the banks of the river were the mysterious agents who continued to set boats on fire. Federal authorities had no doubt that boat burnings were the work of "an organized band of incendiaries" financed by the Confederate government. By October 1863 fourteen "first-class boats" had been destroyed in this way, representing something like 10 percent "of the whole river transportation." Union officials identified some of the leaders of this movement. Among them was a man named Frazer; he and his fellow conspirators burned three steamers at the St. Louis levee on October 4. Halleck advised the quartermasters in charge of river transportation to place detectives on every boat operating for the government; the War Department offered a reward of ten thousand dollars for information leading to a conviction. Anyone arrested would be tried by a military commission rather than a civil court. Further precautions against boat burners included prohibiting all rowboats on the river near the levees at night and keeping tugs with steam up to tow a burning boat into the river. The latter tactic would prevent the flames from spreading to the line of steamers tied up along the levee.[4]

In addition to these efforts to deny Northerners unobstructed use of the river, the Confederates invested a great deal of energy to communicate across the Mississippi. "Chapters could be written on the expedients to which we were driven to get the mails back and forth across the Father of Waters," wrote Postmaster General John H. Reagan. Secretary Seddon worked with Joseph E. Johnston to set up a system for passing dispatches and money across the river at a point south of Memphis, cooperating with the troops under Kirby Smith in the Trans-Mississippi. Agents used rowboats to cross the stream on prearranged schedules. Kirby Smith had a line of signal stations crossing the Mississippi where an island in the stream was located in the lower stretches of the river. The Confederate army relied heavily on beef from the Trans-Mississippi, especially Texas, to feed troops east of the river; it had driven large herds across in the corridor between Port Hudson and Vicksburg before those points fell in July 1863. The Rebels tried to drive herds across even after July but found it increasingly difficult as the Federal navy tightened its grip on the river. Now and then they were able to send arms to Kirby Smith by moving the weapons in small shipments.[5]

The Federal presence along the entire length of the Mississippi River greatly weakened the Confederate position in Mississippi and Louisiana. Civilians within reach of Vicksburg, Natchez, Bayou Sara, Baton Rouge, and Ponchatoula began to trade with the Yankees, especially in selling them cotton, and Federal soldiers roamed around those areas to acquire supplies and sometimes to rob citizens. "A system of anarchy has reigned here since the fall of Port Hudson," reported a distraught Confederate officer. Northern Mississippi, which had been a no-man's-land since Grant's campaign stripped it of resources the previous winter, had also been visited by large Federal raiding parties three or four times during the remainder of 1863. The civilians were left with few resources to produce a crop and "the general destitution [was] very great." The Confederates stationed a garrison at Oxford that also lived off the countryside because it did not have a rail supply line until late in the year. Jacob Thompson, who had moved back to his Oxford home, reported that civilians were forced to sell cotton to the Yankees in order to survive. The destitution stretched into Alabama by the end of 1863. When Confederate commissaries organized droves of hogs for army use and moved them through the state, residents tried to steal the swine, requiring the Rebel army to escort the droves.[6]

Confederate officials worried that these conditions would wean the civilian population from their allegiance to Richmond. After Leonidas Polk took command of Johnston's troops in Mississippi, newly organized in the Department of Alabama, Mississippi, and East Louisiana, he tried to stop this process by issuing a general order reminding everyone that they could "expect nothing but universal confiscation of our property, abject social and personal degradation or death" if the Yankees conquered all. But Polk's message had little effect. Many residents refused to accept Confederate currency when selling supplies to the army; they feared that loyalists and blacks would inform on them to the next visiting Union patrol. Draconian measures were all that were left: pressing supplies by force, stripping vulnerable areas of able-bodied blacks to keep them out of Federal hands, confiscating wagons and mules of any one caught hauling cotton to Union lines, and burning cotton that could not be hauled out of reach of roving Yankee patrols. Such actions spurred protests from many Southerners. Slaveowners pointed out that if able-bodied blacks were taken away, their wives and children were more likely to leave the plantation. Other Southerners argued that the Confederate government could regulate and even participate in selling cotton to Northerners to raise money for war supplies and reduce civilian suffering at the same time. Jefferson Davis agreed to this plan and curtailed the removal of able-bodied blacks as well.[7]

Ironically, Federal authorities looked on the cotton trade as bothersome to their own cause. When Lincoln transferred control of this commerce to the Treasury Department, he relieved military officers of much trouble, but the move did not eliminate corruption or stop the flow of contraband goods to Confederate territory. Commanders up and down the Mississippi agreed with Grant that any trade, no matter who "controlled" the process, was injurious to strictly military concerns. Southerners violated the permit system regularly. A Federal patrol on a boat came across a steamer doing business at an isolated landing with about twenty Confederate soldiers and civilians. Even legitimate traders often tried to obtain special permission to use troops as escorts for wagons trying to haul bales from disputed territory; in one case, they spread rumors of a Confederate blockade of the river at a point where cotton could be obtained in order to follow the Federal troops when they entered that area and do business.[8]

The army continued to have a good deal of latitude in regulating trade in items other than cotton, but commercial activities of any kind tended to give the Confederates opportunities to acquire contraband goods. Sherman had come to the point of believing it best not to allow trade at all until the conquered territories were completely subservient to Federal authority. But for humanitarian reasons alone, Federal commanders had to allow some trade in noncontraband goods, though they tried to issue as few permits to traders as possible and to prevent large amounts of men's clothing, boots, and shoes to leave their lines. But James B. McPherson, who commanded at Vicksburg, was sure that a large amount of goods found their way into Rebel hands anyway.[9]

Memphis became the center of a smuggling epidemic. Federal government agents inspected every boat for contraband, but an anonymous Southerner who traveled from Memphis to St. Louis advised readers of his letter to the newspaper to oversee the examination of their luggage or risk losing something to a greedy inspector. Stephen A. Hurlbut became frustrated when the pickets he placed on the roads into Memphis were bribed by conniving traders. In November 1863 he decided to close his lines to trade altogether to prevent a "perpetual flood of fraud, false swearing, and contraband goods" that interfered "with all proper military control. . . . I am surrounded by hostile forces, regular and guerrilla, and they are fed and supplied from Memphis," he complained.[10]

Sherman never forgot the Mississippi Valley even though he was leading most of the available manpower of the Department of the Tennessee across country to Chattanooga that fall. The departmental boundaries included the east side of the Mississippi from its junction with the Ohio down to Natchez and along the Tennessee River up to Decatur and Bellefonte, Alabama. Sherman relied on McPherson at Vicksburg and Hurlbut at Memphis to manage affairs while he was away. Sherman's most vital concern about his department was maintaining navigation of the Mississippi River — "so delicate and important a matter." He disliked giving up the valley as his field of operations but kept in touch with developments by a stream of dispatches.[11]

Sherman was not overly concerned about guerrilla attacks on posts and patrols, for they were rare. He was highly sensitive about attacks on the river steamers, however, and wanted to teach guerrillas that firing on boats from "behind a big cotton-wood" tree could harm their friends and relatives, too. Sherman was willing to level whole towns in reprisal. "To secure the safety of the navigation of the Mississippi River I would slay millions," he assured a subordinate. "On that point I am not only insane, but mad." He asked David Porter to compile a comprehensive list of damages to steamboats and meant to assess compensation from civilians who lived along the Mississippi and its tributaries, allotting a force of eight thousand men to handle that immense chore. Porter suggested a more realistic approach, one that would require all steamers to stop only at the fifty Federal military posts along the Mississippi and guarding each woodpile with a detachment of soldiers to protect the boats as they refueled. The east bank between Memphis and Columbus was a hotbed of anti-Federal sentiment, and steamers were forbidden from touching that shore at all. Sherman again raised the idea of partially fortifying each civilian steamer, and Grant advised that neither the government nor private concerns be allowed to repair the levees along the Mississippi, because keeping some lowlands flooded impeded the ability of attackers to obtain positions from which they could fire at boats.[12]

The Federals were limited by money and manpower in their efforts to devise an effective strategy against boat attacks, and they never completely eliminated them. Post commanders sent large detachments to points threatened by a regular force of Confederates, often using steamers to transport them quickly. Word circulated that Nathan Bedford Forrest was organizing a special force from among engineers, mechanics, and boatmen to attack vessels south of Memphis. The Yankees had the resources to prevent their enemy from establishing a foothold on the banks, but they never were able to stop small bands of guerrillas. Ironically, accidents claimed many lives and boats as well, perhaps as many as guerrilla attacks. Forty people died and twelve hundred bales of cotton were lost when the *Sunnyside* burned at Island No. 16 in November 1863.[13]

Besides attempting to secure major lines of communication, Union occupation troops continued to confront a wide range of problems that they were ill-prepared to solve. Sherman tried to coach McPherson at Vicksburg to limit his range of responsibilities, to avoid trying to regulate relations between former slaves and their masters as "none of our business," and to concentrate on suppressing "all riots, disorders, and irregularities that disturb the peace." How to deal with the mass of civilians in occupied territories was "in truth the most difficult business of our army as it advances and occupies the Southern country," Sherman wrote. Like other commanders, he could offer only commonsense advice to ignore civilians who made no trouble and to treat harshly those who could not accept Federal rule. An important part of this strategy was to suppress depredations by Union soldiers, because they obviously had a tendency to inflame public opinion. Taking his cue from Grant, Sherman did not require that destitute citizens take the oath of allegiance before receiving army rations. This was done, in Sherman's words, "as a pure charity to prevent suffering."[14]

By the middle and latter part of 1863, another major component of Federal occupation policy was the aggressive harvesting of able-bodied blacks to serve as laborers or soldiers. Area commanders followed Lincoln's injunction to take advantage of this previously inaccessible resource, which now was readily available to the Federals, and make maximum use of the former slave population. Sherman also established regulations for handling Confederate deserters in the Military Division of the Mississippi. They were to be interrogated by the nearest division commander and, if deemed trustworthy, allowed to take the oath and given passes and army rations to get them to their homes, or offered employment by the army in behind-the-lines jobs. They also were exempt from the draft so they would not be in danger of being captured by the Confederates.[15]

Guerrilla attacks continued throughout the latter part of 1863, worsening in areas far to the rear of the front lines. In September, a group of men claiming to be Confederate soldiers, aided by civilians who sympathized with the Confederacy, robbed loyal citizens at Murray and Mayfield, Kentucky. The district commander was authorized to assess the amount stolen and add 50 percent extra from the property of "the most wealthy and notorious" disloyal elements in both towns to compensate the victims. The Federals did not recognize guerrillas as soldiers, treating them when caught as common robbers. Some irregular bands were nothing more than brutal murderers. Members of a gang led by a chief called Faulkner killed an officer of one of Andrew Johnson's regiments, stripped him of his clothing, and threw his body into the river. These bands remained highly elusive, hiding in the countryside and living mostly off stolen civilian property.[16]

Federal ideas about the depredations of their own soldiers, whom Sherman admitted were "pretty lawless," began to change by late 1863. There was now a stronger tendency among officers to blame guerrillas and recalcitrant civilians as the cause of their men's tendency to take what they wanted. "Our men are full of the idea that all the people are secesh," Sherman reasoned, "and would as leave plunder and kill all as not." Sherman was becoming impatient with efforts to reconcile the citizenry to Union occupation, and his subordinates tended to agree. McPherson told a delegation of residents of Tensas Parish, Louisiana, he would not give them permission to organize a local police force to protect themselves from "the excesses of the negroes," because they had previously refused to take the oath of allegiance. Hurlbut cut off all trade between Memphis and the interior not only to stop abuses in commerce but also to punish those civilians who abetted guerrilla operations.[17]

By the latter months of 1863, Sherman encouraged his regional commanders to patrol insecure areas to intimidate the residents and wean them from supporting guerrillas, taking all the supplies the army needed. He wanted these citizens to become agents of the central government, to organize and control local guerrillas, or they would be "overrun and plundered by both sides." He also threatened to banish people who refused to cooperate with this new direction in Union policy. McPherson put that new direction into effect by banishing the Kline family to the region east of the Big Black River for aiding guerrillas near Vicksburg. He allowed them to take furniture and clothing, but the government planned to confiscate everything the Klines left behind.[18]

After two years of dealing with Southern civilians, Sherman was more enthusiastic about repopulating the countryside with Northerners. "Some device must be made to deed houses and lands captured of the enemy," he wrote his brother John in the Senate. "The whole population of Iowa & Wisconsin should be transferred at once to West Kentucky, Tennessee & Mississippi, and a few hundred thousand settlers should be pushed into south Tennessee." Of course, this was an unrealistic dream, but it expressed Sherman's frustration with the minority of Southerners who persisted in attacking riverboats and Union troops. He felt that the Federals would be fully justified in repopulating the South, even if they could not practically do it.[19]

Some of Sherman's troops under Major General Grenville Dodge held the area around Pulaski, in south-central Tennessee, in order to rebuild the railroad lines to Chattanooga. Dodge was determined to subsist his men off the countryside because the region was a hotbed of pro-Confederate sentiment and the Union's logistical network was not yet fully functioning. He also was motivated by a desire to strip the region of food, over and above what was needed to feed the civilian population, so when his job was done a Confederate force could not itself subsist in the area. But Dodge wanted to gather provisions in an orderly manner and prevent unnecessary destruction of private property. Antiguerrilla patrols were authorized to give two kinds of receipts—one to loyalists that was not transferable to another person and payable after the war upon proof of loyalty. The other, which was not redeemable, would be given to Rebel sympathizers. Dodge had no faith in oath taking, for he knew many Southerners did not consider it seriously. "I . . . treat them as they act," he informed headquarters, insisting that they prove through their actions whether or not they supported the Union. Dodge held civilians living along the rail lines responsible for guerrilla disruption of the tracks and assessed their property to compensate the government for repairs. When Federal recruiters interfered with his attempt to round up able-bodied blacks to work on the railroad, he successfully appealed to Grant to receive priority in using this labor source. Having no resources to feed refugee black women and children, Dodge either returned them to their farms or placed them on abandoned lands to fend for themselves.[20]

Commanders in George H. Thomas's Department of the Cumberland faced their own problems with the civilian population. The Tennessee River Valley had been devastated by the recent campaign. Sparsely settled and with comparatively little arable land, the few farms in the area had already been stripped of resources by the winter of 1863–64, and many people were on the verge of starvation. Colonel Dan McCook, a brigade commander in the Fourteenth Corps, watched as a widow ate ravenously at his headquarters while begging for food to take home to her five children. The passage of both armies had reduced many civilians "to penury," and McCook felt that the government was obligated to do something about it. But Thomas still could barely provide for his own army at Chattanooga as the rail lines continued to be repaired.[21]

Guerrilla attacks also troubled Thomas. After capturing a wagon and three soldiers in Lincoln County, Tennessee, irregulars shot the men in cold blood at short range and threw their bodies into the river. Thomas proceeded to assess the property of Confederate sympathizers within ten miles of the incident to raise thirty thousand dollars as compensation for the families of the victims and vowed to shoot on sight anyone found guilty of the murders. Sherman had already instituted a policy of arresting Rebel sympathizers who would serve as hostages for the surrender of culprits, and Thomas adopted this plan in his department as well. Although such tactics gave the Federals an opportunity to feel they were not just passive victims, there is no evidence that they were effective in combating guerrillas.[22]

More successful were Federal moves to catch guerrilla forces in their own territory. Aggressive action generally cleared these bands out of the area west of Nashville and between the Cumberland and Duck Rivers south of the state capital, pushing them south of the Tennessee. In the process, at least two prominent guerrilla leaders were either killed or taken prisoner. A major drive from Gallatin, Tennessee, eastward to the Cumberland Plateau led to "numerous running skirmishes" with marauders, the taking of 102 prisoners, and the killing of 33 others. Federal troops "removed the women and children and burned" the village of Old Columbus, which, in the opinion of one Union officer, was "the veriest den of thieves and murderers." The commander of the expedition claimed to have "completely broke up for the time being the bands of Hughs, Hamilton, and Doherty." At least one of the men killed had a signed oath of allegiance in his pocket. The guerrillas in the region, estimated to have numbered up to six hundred, had "eaten out and plundered" the civilians "without regard to politics" until they were "bordering upon famine."[23]

In Kentucky, far behind the front lines, guerrilla activity continued with no letup, especially in the southern part of the state. On receiving a report that fifty marauders plundered stores at Gordonsville, Colonel Cicero Maxwell of the 26th Kentucky took forty men and gave chase. He tracked their path and dispersed them at the first volley, chasing the guerrillas thirty miles across the Tennessee state line as they dropped their booty along the road.[24]

Guerrilla operations did not slow down the recruitment of African Americans. By the end of 1863, Lorenzo Thomas proudly reported that he had raised more than twenty thousand black troops in the Mississippi Valley, within the boundaries of the Department of the Tennessee, in addition to those raised by Butler and Banks in the Department of the Gulf and those being organized in Tennessee. Grant continued to give priority to using blacks as laborers rather than as soldiers, although Brigadier General Daniel Ullmann complained that his black troops in the Gulf Department were too heavily employed in labor details. He feared that army officers intended to make black recruits little more than "diggers and drudges," even though, he was convinced, they could be turned into model soldiers if treated properly. Their morale suffered from bad weapons, less pay than white troops, and more labor assignments. On the few occasions they were given the opportunity to fight in skirmishes, such as repulsing Confederate cavalry at Moscow, Tennessee, on December 4, officers praised their performance in combat.[25]

Planning the Next Move

Intense discussions took place among both Union and Confederate officers as to the best strategy following Chattanooga and James Longstreet's siege of Knoxville. Grant continued to envision a long anticipated and often postponed strike against Mobile. He expected a winter campaign to take the port city, with a follow-up invasion of interior Alabama and Georgia, using Mobile as a base. Washington authorities liked the idea but could not approve it before Longstreet's presence in eastern Tennessee was resolved. The president, in particular, did not want to see the Confederates rebound in that region, or maintain a sizable presence among the loyalist population on an indefinite basis. Lincoln, Halleck, and Stanton were frustrated that Major General George G. Meade, commander of the Army of the Potomac, was doing nothing to compel the recall of Longstreet's divisions to Lee's army.[26]

By mid-December 1863, Grant began to focus his attention on driving Longstreet out of the state before initiating other moves. He traveled to Knoxville at the turn of the new year to investigate the situation, anticipating that the next great campaign might be in the mountains of eastern Tennessee. But Grant quickly realized that, with the railroad from Chattanooga to Knoxville not yet fully functioning and the concentration of troops at Chattanooga demanding the lion's share of whatever supplies could be shipped from Nashville, it was logistically impossible to conduct a major drive against Longstreet. The Confederates could retire many miles toward Virginia, shortening their line of communications while the Federals lengthened their own line. Washington allowed Grant to determine whether Longstreet was a serious threat, and he decided to maintain a defensive stance in eastern Tennessee while marshaling his troops for a major push elsewhere. Halleck agreed with Grant that it was important the Federals select their own "theater of operations" instead of "having [it] forced on us by the rebels." At any rate, once the Army of the Potomac began its spring campaign, Lee would be forced to recall Longstreet, they reasoned.[27]

Mobile, Atlanta, and Montgomery continued to top the list of objectives, but the large concentration of troops already assembled in the area around Chattanooga was a compelling reason to continue moving south along the rail line linking that city with Atlanta. Sherman preferred attacking Mobile and moving north and east from there into the interior of the Deep South, for the single track of railroad was a slender, vulnerable line of communication for the troops at Chattanooga. He even considered letting McPherson take command of the twenty-five thousand troops of the Department of the Tennessee that were at Chattanooga while he took charge of protecting navigation on the Mississippi River. That winter Sherman busied himself with arrangements to gain better control over wandering Confederate forces in the valley by sending expeditions into areas like the Yazoo River section of the Delta, where guerrillas were plentiful. Anyone who contemplated penetrating the interior of the Deep South did so only with the idea that highly mobile columns of Federal troops should live off the land and collect as many able-bodied black males as possible for Federal use. The rail line, which so far had barely supported Federal drives, could not be counted on to sustain an invasion of the Deep South.[28]

The railroad did not fully supply the Federal concentration at Chattanooga even weeks after Braxton Bragg had been driven away. In mid-December 1863 Quartermaster Meigs reported that the railroad between Nashville and Chattanooga was "in bad condition throughout," with many engines and cars off the tracks waiting to be recovered and put back into operation. Though guerrillas planted torpedoes on the track, they more effectively interfered with traffic by loosening rails, which caused engines and cars to slide off the roadbed. The line was shut down for several days at a time. More important still, the railroad companies simply did not have enough engines and cars to handle the heavy logistical needs of Grant's force at Chattanooga and had to scramble to find more among Northern railroad companies.[29]

Around Knoxville, where Federal troops had been on partial rations since Ambrose Burnside had entered the region in September 1863, the supply problem was worsening. It took months to rebuild the railroad bridge over the Tennessee River at Loudon, and the area's available provisions had already been stripped by two contending armies. Both Federals and Confederates were nearly destitute of all things, and their attempts to forage off the countryside caused untold suffering among the civilians—loyalists and Confederate sympathizers alike.[30]

Bragg was relieved of command of the Army of Tennessee on December 2 and temporarily replaced by corps commander William J. Hardee. The army tried to restore itself in winter quarters at Dalton, Georgia, but, as Hardee informed Richmond, it desperately needed more men and supplies following its drubbing at Chattanooga. Even Robert E. Lee feared that Grant would soon lead an advance into Georgia and threaten the logistical network that helped to feed his Army of Northern Virginia. Lee fended off overtures to lure him into assuming command of the Army of Tennessee by pointing to the fact that he was unacquainted with the officers and units that composed the hard-luck unit. Davis seemed unable to find anyone besides Joseph E. Johnston to permanently replace Bragg, yet Johnston's appointment raised confidence everywhere—in and out of the army.[31]

But if any Southern patriot hoped for a Confederate invasion of middle Tennessee or Kentucky before Grant launched his spring offensive, they would be disappointed by the Army of Tennessee's limited transportation capacity. Johnston recognized how much he had to do to ready that army for active campaigning, bombarding Richmond with dispatches relating to the need to gather forage for his animals, shoes and provisions for his men, and additional manpower to meet the Union host. Not until late January 1864 was the rail line from Atlanta able to supply the basic needs of his army, even though, as the Confederacy's quartermaster noted, it probably was in better shape than any other rail line in Rebel territory. Beauregard and others again urged a bold strategy of stripping unimportant regions of troops to mass one hundred thousand men at Dalton who could take the offensive before spring. Johnston thought such proposals were fantasies. The railroad would never be able to feed such a host, and the mountainous region he would have to traverse was destitute of food. The Army of Tennessee still did not have bridging material for crossing major rivers, and the cities along the way, such as Chattanooga and Knoxville, were heavily fortified. Longstreet's proposal to mount his twelve thousand men for a rapid raid into Kentucky was impossible as well, due to the Confederates' inability to find that many mounts. Johnston, it seemed, was forced to devise a defensive strategy.[32]

As it turned out, Grant did not personally conduct any more campaigns in the West, for Lincoln elevated him to Halleck's place on March, 9, 1864. When Grant became the new general in chief and moved his headquarters to accompany Meade's Army of the Potomac, Sherman assumed command of the Military Division of the Mississippi. Grant sought to exert a large degree of control over Union military movements, planning to advance them simultaneously with the intention of destroying Confederate field armies rather than merely acquiring territory. He also sought to feed Union armies off the Southern countryside as much as possible to lessen the growing logistical problems associated with penetrating the Deep South.[33]

By April 4, Grant finally decided that the best course of action in the West was for Sherman to move the heavy concentration of troops at Chattanooga toward Atlanta, once again relying on the rail line for primary logistical support. Though Grant left the details up to Sherman, he urged him to destroy as much of the South's war-making resources as possible, which included gathering supplies for consumption along the way. Grant hoped to move other forces toward Mobile too, but Atlanta became the main Union target in the West during the spring of 1864.[34]

If Sherman hoped to sustain a 100,000-troop drive into Georgia by relying on a single-track rail line, he had to prepare heavily—and with little time left before spring weather allowed him to move. In early April, he made a grand tour of his new command and consulted with the department leaders who would be expected to contribute troops to the campaign. McPherson would bring the Seventeenth Corps and personally lead the Army of the Tennessee, as well as the Department of the Tennessee, while the available troops of Thomas's Department of the Cumberland would take part as the Army of the Cumberland. Major General John M. Schofield, newly appointed commander of the Department of the Ohio, would bring a much smaller number of men from eastern Tennessee who were designated the Army of the Ohio.[35]

Sherman's most pressing problem was to organize a more vibrant and reliable supply of everything for his large field force—larger than any yet assembled in the West since Halleck's advance on Corinth. Halleck had relied on river transports along the Tennessee River and then a short, twenty-mile wagon link with his advancing army. Sherman had to use a vulnerable track stretching more than three hundred miles from Louisville. He depended on Thomas's engineers, railroad managers, and repair crews, for the line lay within the Department of the Cumberland. This caused some tension with McPherson's and Schofield's officers, who often felt they were slighted by the support personnel of the Army of the Cumberland. Sherman calculated that, by setting his target as low as possible, he would still need 130 carloads of supplies rolling into Chattanooga every day to support 100,000 men and 35,000 animals in the campaign toward Atlanta. But Thomas's quartermaster reported that he would need an additional 100 locomotives and 600 cars to meet that goal. Sherman aggressively gathered extra rolling stock from all the Northern railroad companies he could reach.[36]

Sherman issued strict orders prohibiting all civilian travel on the road to make more room for needed supplies, which raised "a new howl" from many people and agencies who felt they had a right or a need to visit the front. Sherman also ordered his subordinates to strip their field transportation to the bone, setting a personal example by planning to live simply in the field. He sought "to convert all parts of that army into a mobile machine, willing and able to start at a minute's notice, and to subsist on the scantiest food." To help him better anticipate how much he could depend on the Georgia countryside for provisions, Sherman obtained copies of the latest U.S. Census tables and tax compilations issued by the controller of the state of Georgia.[37]

Union military successes marked the year 1863 as a major turning point in the progress of the war. The Upper South had been completely cleared of organized Confederate forces and the Deep South penetrated down a narrow corridor along the Mississippi River. The all-important commercial-political goal of river navigation was secured, although navigation was still not completely safe. Federal strategy now called for another major penetration of the Deep South along the line of railroads that pushed into the southeastern part of the Confederacy. To anxious Southern partisans, the Union offensives of 1863 had appeared to be inexorable. Northerners seemed "as determined as ever to wage upon us a war of extermination," Beauregard warned a correspondent. "Our country is being gradually overrun." For their part, Unionists were greatly encouraged by the victories of 1863 at Vicksburg and Chattanooga. "The rebels are a gallant people," Montgomery C. Meigs asserted, "but it is exhaustion of men and of money that finally terminates all modern wars, and in their case that exhaustion rapidly approaches."[38]

12 } Atlanta

After a great deal of work to prepare his logistical support, Sherman was ready to set out against Johnston in the first week of May 1864. He faced sixty thousand Confederates in the Army of Tennessee, led by a careful commander in a rugged mountainous territory. Sherman moved the elements of his combined force, George Thomas's Army of the Cumberland (60,000), James McPherson's Army of the Tennessee (30,000), and Major General John M. Schofield's Army of the Ohio (10,000), to rendezvous near Dalton, Georgia. Johnston had planted his men there on Rocky Face Ridge, which towered some seven hundred feet high. "I do not want you to encounter field-works," Sherman warned Schofield as the latter approached Dalton from the north, setting the tone of his operational strategy throughout most of the campaign. He had no intention of wasting manpower on unwise attacks; maneuver so as to threaten Johnston's line of communications would be the modus operandi.[1]

While Thomas and Schofield pinned the Confederates in place, McPherson conducted a flanking march to turn Johnston's left by moving through Snake Creek Gap and seizing the railroad at Resaca, several miles south of Dalton. The holding actions resulted in several sharp, small-scale fights by Thomas's men, but those fights helped to divert attention away from the Army of the Tennessee. McPherson made it through the gap undetected but hesitated about moving on to Resaca, believing the place was more strongly held than expected. He knew that his own troops would be dangerously exposed to defeat in detail if Johnston managed to shift a large force his way before Sherman could react. McPherson opted for the safest course of action, retiring to the gap and digging in on May 10. "I regret beyond measure you did not break the railroad," Sherman wrote him, "but I suppose it was impossible." Nevertheless, the move persuaded Johnston to evacuate Dalton on the night of May 12.[2]

The Confederates fortified the high ground north and west of Resaca to protect Johnston's supply line, and here occurred the first major battle of the campaign. Sherman launched large-scale attacks on May 14 and 15 to divert attention from an attempt to cross the Oostanaula River downstream from town and turn the enemy's left flank once again. The Federal attacks were spirited and resulted in a couple of equally spirited Confederate attempts to find and turn Sherman's left flank north of Resaca. By the evening of May 15, Johnston evacuated his position, again because of a successful effort to threaten his flank. The Confederates lost about three thousand men at Resaca while the Federals suffered four thousand casualties.[3]

Johnston did not make another stand for some distance because the terrain immediately south of the Oostanaula did not seem to provide a good defensive position. Not until the Confederates reached Cassville, about twenty-five miles south of Resaca, did Johnston offer battle. "You will now turn and march to meet his advancing columns," he announced to his men on May 19. "Fully confiding in the conduct of the officers, the courage of the soldiers, I lead you to battle." But when he started to move forward to strike one of Sherman's advancing columns in detail, Federal cavalrymen appeared in an unexpected quarter and forced him to cancel his plans. Johnston instead retired to a 140-foot-tall ridge just south of town, but evacuated that strong post when Union artillery gained a crossfire on it and two of his three corps commanders said they could not hold their position. Whereas the rank and file had cheered when Johnston's order announcing an attack was read to them earlier in the day, their spirits plummeted as the army evacuated Cassville on the night of May 19.[4]

The evacuation brought Sherman to the Etowah River, one of the major watercourses along his line of advance. He intended to change his operational mode somewhat by moving away from the railroad and shoving columns of troops across the densely wooded country south of the river to conduct a wide flank maneuver well to Johnston's rear. He would take only limited rations along, hoping to find enough in the country to subsist his men for at least twenty days. As McPherson headed for the crossroads at Dallas, nearly twenty miles west of the railroad, Thomas advanced to his left and Schofield closer to the rail line. Sherman failed to fool Johnston, who shifted his troops in Sherman's path well in time to meet the Federals after they crossed the Etowah on May 23.[5]

The maneuvering resulted in three hard battles. On the evening of May 25 Thomas struck Hood's Corps at New Hope Church, with Hooker's Twentieth Corps pushing 16,000 men against one of Hood's divisions consisting of merely 4,000 troops. The thickly vegetated terrain limited the force of the attack; Hooker was repulsed with the loss of 665 men, compared to some 400 casualties among the Confederates. Two days later, the Fourth

Corps commander, Major General Oliver Otis Howard, led two divisions in an attempt to make a short turning movement to the east and ran against a brigade of Major General Patrick Cleburne's division near Pickett's Mill. The resulting attack was bloodily repelled with 1,600 Federal losses but only 448 Confederate casualties. On May 28 local Confederate commanders launched small attacks at Dallas, which McPherson's men handily repulsed at comparatively little cost to themselves. The armies then settled down into a tactical stalemate along the Dallas–New Hope Church–Pickett's Mill line.[6]

Johnston had protected his flank and checked Sherman, but he could not prevent the Federals from sliding to their left and regaining contact with the railroad by June 7. Union cavalry occupied Allatoona Pass, a deep railroad cut through the Allatoona Mountains just south of the Etowah River, which Sherman knew from prewar travels through Georgia was a potentially strong defensive position. As the Confederates evacuated Dallas as well as shifted their entire force back toward the railroad, Sherman once again vowed to Henry Halleck that he would "not run head on" to enemy fortifications. He began to transform Allatoona Pass into a strongly fortified forward depot for the mountain of supplies his army group consumed. Rain set in as the Federals worked hard to repair the railroad bridge over the Etowah. Sherman expected reinforcements in the form of Major General Frank P. Blair's Seventeenth Corps, of McPherson's Department of the Tennessee, which had been tied down in occupation duties in Mississippi since the fall of Vicksburg. Blair's men marched across country, for Sherman's railroad cars were too busy hauling food and ordnance to the front to accommodate them. As soon as his corps arrived (by June 8), Blair detached troops to serve as the garrison of Allatoona and other points essential to Sherman's logistical support. Also, Sherman created the District of the Etowah, with Major General James B. Steedman in command, to secure his rear areas as he drove deeper into Georgia.[7]

The terrain that now confronted the Federals was more open but dotted with huge mountains. Johnston took advantage of these high points by creating the Mountain Line. Anchored on the left by Lost Mountain, on the right by Brush Mountain, and in the center by Pine Mountain, the line stretched for ten miles. As Sherman moved troops to confront this position the campaign devolved into a siegelike confrontation, with heavy skirmishing, harassing artillery fire, and small fights along the line. Corps commander Leonidas Polk was killed by a Federal artillery round on June 14 while atop the 300-foot-high crest of Pine Mountain, and Johnston felt compelled to evacuate that part of his line the next day. Further retirements shortened the Rebel line and shifted it closer to Kennesaw Mountain, a twin-peaked eminence that dominated the landscape. As "hard and cold rains" continued to pound northwestern Georgia, Johnston made Kennesaw the centerpiece of his new position by June 19. A sharp fight occurred when Hood launched a poorly coordinated attack on Hooker's corps near Kolb's Farm, south of Kennesaw, on June 22. He lost one thousand troops while inflicting only three hundred losses on the Federals.[8]

Though the rain continued to fall, the Confederates could see nearly every move the Federals made from their perch on Big Kennesaw, seven hundred feet above the surrounding countryside. Even as he continued to assure Washington that attacking fortifications played no role in his campaign, Sherman began to think that an assault on Johnston's center might be necessary. "It may cost us dear," he wrote Halleck, "but in results would surpass an attempt to pass around." He determined to do just that on June 27, using three divisions at three points along the Confederate center. None of the troops could penetrate the Rebel defenses, stymied as much by terrain and the Rebel fortifications as by defensive fire. Sherman suffered three thousand casualties out of fifteen thousand men engaged, while Johnston reported losses of only about seven hundred men.[9]

Sherman spent much time and effort explaining away the failed assault of June 27 at Kennesaw. He argued that attacks were "necessary and inevitable," that his men should not fall into the notion "that flanking alone was my game." He discounted the scale of his losses when compared with the bloodbath that occurred under Grant in Virginia during May and June. Flanking, in fact, had become more difficult because of the long, well-fortified enemy line and the rains that turned dirt roads into quagmires. "The assault I made was no mistake," Sherman argued. "I had to do it."[10]

The Fourteenth Corps troops who conducted the attack on an angle in the Confederate line on June 27, unlike their compatriots on other parts of the line, did not fall back after their repulse. They clung to the earth only yards from the enemy trench and tenaciously dug in. For the next week they sniped at the Confederates and dug an underground mine under the angle, intending to blow it up as a further element of siege warfare was added to the Atlanta campaign. A truce was called on June 29 to allow the Federals to bury their dead between the lines. The Confederates tossed balls of cotton soaked with turpentine into no-man's-land to prevent the Yankees from conducting a night attack. The lines were close enough so that men could amuse themselves by tossing stones into the opposing trenches, and head logs placed on top of parapets were eaten away by the repeated striking of enemy bullets.[11]

Sherman finally broke the stalemate at Kennesaw when he decided to risk a major flanking move to the south, shifting much of McPherson's army from his left on the night of July 2. As soon as Johnston realized what was going on, he evacuated the Kennesaw Line that night. As the Federals entered the Rebel works early the next morning, Johnston took up another defensive position near Smyrna Station about half a dozen miles south. The Confederates held there only two days, evacuating the line on the night of July 4 and pulling back a short distance to Johnston's last line of defense north of the Chattahoochee River. This position covered the railroad crossing of the last major stream before Atlanta. Johnston had earlier called on the Georgia Militia to increase his troop strength and now used about one thousand black laborers to dig what came to be known as the "Chattahoochee River Line." Because his artillery chief, Brigadier General Francis Shoup, designed some new features in the earthworks, it deserved to be called the "Shoup Line." These innovative features—stockades constructed of logs and earth—became the object of ridicule on the part of some Confederate soldiers, while others thought they added a new element of strength to the basic trench.[12]

Sherman hoped to punish Johnston severely as he tried to move his trains across the river if the Federals could break through the position first. But, after the drubbing of June 27, he avoided attacking the Shoup Line after all. Instead, the Federals repaired the railroad and telegraph line up to the front and carefully planned their next move, with the buildings of Atlanta in sight from high ground within their lines. Federal cavalrymen seized paper, cotton, and woolen mills at Roswell, a few miles up the Chattahoochee River from Johnston's position, and deported four hundred women factory workers to northern states because the mills had been making material for Confederate use right up to the time of their capture. Two days later, on July 9, Federal troops crossed the Chattahoochee at two locations far removed from Johnston's defensive position. The Confederates evacuated the Shoup Line and crossed to the south side of the river that night, but Sherman continued to rest and prepare for operations south of the stream before crossing the bulk of his army group.[13]

Supply and Rear Areas

The struggle for Atlanta took place behind Union lines as well as in front of them, for supply was the key to Sherman's success. His support personnel had already transformed Allatoona into a major supply depot, and they now began to do the same to Marietta, a pleasant town located just south of

Fortified railroad bridge over the Cumberland River at Nashville—an example of the need to construct fortified positions for guards at key locations along the long rail system that allowed Union armies to invade the Western Confederacy. (Library of Congress, LC-DIG-cwpb-02092)

Johnston's Kennesaw Line. The garrison had orders to arrest all stragglers, to prevent Federal troops from staying in civilian homes in town, and to keep the flow of supplies going. Citizens known to be Rebel sympathizers were arrested, and all Confederate government property was confiscated. Any issues regarding privately owned cotton or other property were off limits for the duration of the campaign so as not to divert time and attention from the importance of the drive to Atlanta. A number of civilians who apparently caused trouble at Dallas right after the Federals evacuated that town were arrested for their misdeeds and for being Confederate sympathizers.[14]

Sherman was desperate to keep his supplies flowing. "Show no mercy to guerrillas or persons threatening our road or telegraph," he told the commanding officer at Allatoona. He explained to Lincoln why he could not ease up on orders preventing civilians from traveling on the railroad. Sherman ordered quartermasters not to feed blacks or other civilians who were not employed by the army. The problem was not food, but transportation; the single-track railroad stretching into Georgia was overworked. Ammunition received top priority as Fifteenth Corps ordnance officers maintained a supply of at least 140 rounds of small arms ammunition per man and 200 rounds of artillery ammunition per gun at all times. Schofield maintained 120 rounds of rifle ammunition per man, but on June 27 he informed Sherman that he had food for only two days. Sherman issued orders mandating that rations be reduced automatically whenever troops were out of direct touch with the railroad. Ironically, the most serious illness of Twentieth Corps troops during the campaign was scurvy. Fresh vegetables received the lowest priority in food shipments, and two-thirds of the men in Hooker's command experienced to some extent scorbutic symptoms. Only when blackberries and corn began to ripen were the men able to ease their discomfort somewhat, but cavalry horses often suffered immensely due to the lack of forage in the countryside or on the railroad cars. In early June they were "absolutely dying from starvation."[15]

Grant fully understood Sherman's logistical difficulties, but he also knew that as long as ordnance and basic foodstuffs could be transported, Sherman's men could hold out or, if necessary, cut loose from the railroad and establish a connection with shipping somewhere on the coast. The threat of a cutoff of supplies from Chattanooga was real, for small-scale attacks on the rail line occurred almost daily. Steedman reported from Chattanooga that the "whole country between this post and the front is infested with guerrilla bands." Local commanders along the line began to deport families from their homes near the railroad and patrol vigorously to find and kill the marauders before they could strike, but it was impossible to provide absolute security. Small groups cut telegraph lines, removed rails from isolated stretches of track, and burned culverts and small bridges. Johnston's cavalry commander, Major General Joseph Wheeler, sent squads of his men behind Union lines to conduct sabotage. Realizing that he would lose half a dozen trains every month as a result of such attacks, Sherman called loudly on the governors of several Northern states to raise militia troops to serve for one hundred days as rail guards. "The task of feeding this vast host is a more difficult one than to fight," Sherman told his wife. His men ate up whatever they could find in the countryside. "All the People retire before us, and desolation is behind."[16]

Area residents evacuated their animals and their slaves with them until northwestern Georgia seemed, to one Federal soldier, "a dese[r]tet count[r]y." A Twentieth Corps division commander, John W. Geary, reported that the men took whatever they could find until they left the region "as though all the locusts of Egypt had been upon it." Twenty-third Corps division leader Milo Hascall was appalled by the wanton destruction that visited the land. "I have no desire to serve with an army where the fundamental principles of civilized warfare are so shockingly violated at every step in our progress," he wrote one of Schofield's staff officers; nevertheless, Hascall soldiered on despite the fact that Schofield's attempts to clamp down on the destruction failed. George Thomas tried to limit the destruction by ordering that all foraging be conducted under the control of officers appointed by brigade commanders. Yet food shortages continued to plague Sherman's men as they drove deeper into Georgia.[17]

Sherman tried to alleviate his supply problem and combat guerrillas at the same time. He told Steedman to systematically collect all food for humans and animals to be found. "When ever the people are in the way ship them to a new country north and west." There is no evidence, however, that Steedman ever attempted to implement such a drastic policy. Among other problems, he had far too few men to do so while trying to guard the railroad.[18]

Sherman was sorry that the Georgians were driving their slaves south with them, for he badly needed laborers. Thus he refused Lorenzo Thomas's request that the army ship all able-bodied blacks acquired in Georgia to Tennessee for inclusion in black regiments. Sherman told Thomas he would prefer to have three hundred blacks armed with spades than a thousand blacks armed with muskets.[19]

Johnston also endured problems in supplying his large army by a single-track railroad from Atlanta, although guerrilla activity was not among them. Rather, his men suffered from short rations. Moreover, Wheeler's cavalry-men caused more hardships for surrounding civilians than any other Con-federates. They had the opportunity to affect far more families than infantry-men because of the nature of their service. Wheeler himself believed the real trouble lay in the fact that Confederates and civilians alike merely claimed to belong to his cavalry corps in order to justify their actions or to deflect blame. The infantrymen in Leonidas Polk's corps also imposed themselves on local civilians, although Polk—just before his death—asserted that the troublemakers were mostly members of the corps wagon train, since they had more opportunities to roam across the countryside than the soldiers. Hood, too, issued orders compelling his officers to clamp down on soldier depredations.[20]

Strategy and Tactics

One of the key considerations in Sherman's and Grant's thinking about the spring campaign was the need to prevent the enemy from shifting troops from one theater of operations to another. They were haunted by the transfer of Longstreet's two divisions from Robert E. Lee's army in Virginia, a shift that had spelled doom for Rosecrans at Chickamauga and required a drastic reorientation of Union strategy to respond to that calamity. A major reason that Grant insisted on continuous contact by Meade's Army of the Potomac and Sherman's army group in Georgia was to detect if such a shift took place and to react to it to prevent disaster. Before either campaign started, Grant and Sherman exchanged concerns about this point, and Sherman told his army and corps commanders that one of the chief objectives of the Atlanta campaign was to make sure that Johnston did not detach troops to help Lee. Throughout the progress of that campaign, Sherman and Grant reassured each other that they were alert to the danger and would do everything possible to prevent their opponent from duplicating Longstreet's success. "One of my chief objects being to give full employment to Johnston," Sherman wrote Halleck. "It makes but little difference where he is, so he is not on his way to Virginia."[21]

By late June, however, after driving the Army of Northern Virginia into the trenches protecting Petersburg and Richmond, Grant felt less concerned about Johnston sending troops to the East. Lee would have too much difficulty feeding the extra men; furthermore, the Rebel general could use fortifications to compensate for his low numbers. He informed Sherman that movements in Georgia no longer had to be tied to preventing Johnston from sending help to Lee. On the contrary, Grant worried about Lee sending help to Johnston. If that occurred, he advised, Sherman was to take up a strong defensive position until Federal reinforcements could reach Georgia. Sherman boasted that he had no fear of Johnston—even if the Army of Tennessee received twenty thousand additional men.[22]

Sherman had no intention of reverting to the defensive during the Atlanta campaign, and he urged Grant to continue offensive moves in Virginia as well. In Sherman's view, Grant's main task was to demonstrate to the Virginia Confederates that the Federals "can and will fight them fair and square" in order to create a "moral result" that had to "precede all mere advantages of strategic movements." That moral result had long since been established by the Federal forces in the West. "Out here the enemy know we can and will fight like the devil," Sherman told Secretary Stanton. "Therefore he maneuvers for advantage of ground."[23]

Ironically, the Confederates were concerned that Grant and Sherman might reinforce each other with troops. Lee hoped that Johnston would remain alert to the possibility and prevent Sherman from detaching to the East, and he vowed to be watchful. Johnston and his corps commanders also kept abreast of developments in Virginia and the Trans-Mississippi, trumpeting every sign of Confederate success to inspire their troops to greater endeavors. Hood urged his men to "think of their comrades in Virginia, battling against overwhelming odds," as he sought to create a bond between Confederates in both theaters.[24]

On the tactical level, the Atlanta campaign was noted for the extensive use of field fortifications by both sides. The Confederates dug in almost automatically whenever they halted, and their opponents did likewise. The rugged landscape of northwestern Georgia became scarred by mile upon mile of earthworks, adorned with head logs and fronted by extensive slashings of trees and other obstructions. The Federals emphasized skirmishing during the campaign, given that the armies were in almost constant contact with each other over the course of many weeks. Thomas's army of about sixty thousand men fired two hundred thousand rounds of small arms ammunition and twelve hundred rounds of artillery ammunition each day during May and June, most of it in skirmishing rather than pitched battles. Throughout the course of the campaign, Sherman's ability to drive deeper into Georgia was facilitated not only by his strategy of maneuver and the use of fortifications and heavy skirmishing, but also by the overwhelmingly positive morale of his troops. "Our soldiers think the world and all of Sherman," wrote Andrew J. Johnson of the 70th Indiana. "He believes in using the Spade and then flanking."[25]

General Joseph E. Johnston conducted what amounted to a fighting retreat from Dalton. Since the first week of May 1864, he had tried to justify his actions to an increasingly worried president in Richmond. "I have earnestly sought an opportunity to strike the enemy," he assured Davis, but Sherman covered his formations too well and usually advanced under cover of fieldworks. Johnston pushed forward work on the incomplete defenses of Atlanta and, according to Hood, told his corps commanders that he would retire to Macon if necessary. Whereas William J. Hardee, and sometimes Hood, expressed a strong desire to fight a major, deciding battle with the enemy before giving up Atlanta, Johnston sought to maintain the integrity of his army as long as possible while waiting for an opportunity to catch a cautious opponent at a disadvantage.[26]

Meanwhile, Johnston pinned his hopes on using cavalry to cut Sherman's tenuous supply line. Unable to spare the small force attached to the Army of Tennessee, he urged superiors in Richmond and colleagues in other districts to find enough mounted men to accomplish the task. With Union columns ranging across Mississippi, Nathan Bedford Forrest was distracted by defensive purposes so much that he could not launch a strike against the railroad in Tennessee, and no other sizable mounted forces were available. The authorities in Richmond could not spare additional infantry troops for Johnston, either. They reminded him that, even though outnumbered by Sherman, the disparity in manpower between opponents in Georgia was lower than in Virginia. There simply were no troops to spare from any other department to add strength to the Army of Tennessee.[27]

In contrast to the campaign in Georgia, Lee exacted a horrible price in blood for Union success in Virginia. Johnston failed to stop Sherman or decisively reduce his manpower. Understandably, Davis and other Richmond officials grew dissatisfied with his performance. Their patience ended with Johnston's retreat across the Chattahoochee River. Hood energetically criticized his commander to Braxton Bragg, who continued to serve as Davis's chief military adviser. Davis sent Bragg to consult with Johnston at Atlanta. Bragg reported that the commander had no "more plan for the future than he has had in the past." Davis then authorized his replacement with Hood. Johnston received the telegram on the night of July 17 and turned over the army the next day. The new commander was "a bold fighter," thought Lee, his former superior in the Army of Northern Virginia, but of doubtful metal as an army leader. "Be wary no less than bold," the secretary of war cautioned Hood.[28]

Hood's opponent had no intention of acting rashly. For several weeks before reaching the Chattahoochee, Sherman had matured plans to avoid the ring of heavy fortifications that protected Atlanta and swing around their circumference to cut all the railroads leading into the city. This would force the Confederates out or face starvation. There were numerous fords and ferries on the Chattahoochee, but Sherman chose to cross a bit upstream so as to fan out his army group in several columns, approaching the city from the north and the east in order to cut the Georgia railroad near Decatur. The bulk of his force crossed the river on July 17. Anticipating his approach from the north, Johnston selected a defensive position south of Peachtree Creek, intending to strike the Federals as they crossed the stream. Thomas approached this position head on, while McPherson moved to the railroad and Schofield tried to cover the ground between them.[29]

Although Hood implemented Johnston's plan, delays in positioning his troops caused him to strike on July 20 three hours later than anticipated. The poorly coordinated advance caught much of Hooker's corps and Major

General John Newton's division of the Fourth Corps by surprise. The Federals reacted boldly, however, and the combat at Peachtree Creek turned into a slugfest fought without the aid of heavy earthworks. The Federals held their own, inflicting 2,500 casualties on the 25,000 Confederates engaged in the battle. They lost 1,900 of the 19,000 men who fought that day.[30]

Hood demonstrated his own boldness by organizing another strike against McPherson's army. While a small Confederate force occupied McPherson's attention, he sent Hardee's corps on a long march to the south and east on the night of July 21 to turn the Federal left flank. The men were worn out and did not reach an advantageous position until almost noon the next day; fortunately for Sherman, units of Major General Grenville Dodge's Sixteenth Corps happened to stop on a high hill to the left rear of McPherson's position while on their way to extend the army's left flank. Dodge was thus able to save McPherson's army when the Confederates swept forward, handily repelling the attack. Other divisions of Hardee's corps, however, moved against McPherson's left flank, held by Blair's Seventeenth Corps, which was largely in the air. A mighty struggle took place as uncoordinated, brigade-level attacks pressed the vulnerable flank. Some of Blair's units had to repel assaults from three directions, jumping from one side of the earthwork to another. Men were shot down at incredibly close range. Colonel William W. Belknap of the 15th Iowa managed to capture Colonel Harris D. Langley of the 45th Alabama by grabbing his hair and pulling him into the Federal trench. An Iowa brigade lost heavily in prisoners when the extreme left of McPherson's line was engulfed, but the flank held as the Federals refused their line and fought on.[31]

On McPherson's front, troops from Benjamin F. Cheatham's corps sallied forth and broke the Union line, capturing the guns of one battery only to lose them in a counterattack by Fifteenth Corps troops. The battle sputtered to a halt by dusk, with the Army of the Tennessee intact and Sherman's flank secure. Hood lost 5,500 of the 35,000 men engaged, while the Federals suffered 3,722 casualties. The most prominent Union loss was James McPherson himself, who was killed by Confederate skirmishers early in the battle while riding from Dodge's position to Blair's corps. The loss shocked Sherman, who was a close friend.[32]

Hood bemoaned the "timid-defensive" attitude that seemed to infect his army because of Johnston's leadership as he sought blame for the failures of July 20 and 22. He issued general orders encouraging the rank and file to find safety by "getting into close quarters with your enemy." Hood argued that the Confederate cause was lost if the army continued to let Sherman get away with his flanking maneuvers.[33]

Sherman walked into a storm of controversy when he announced his decision to replace McPherson with Oliver Otis Howard. Major General John A. Logan, who had left his post with the Fifteenth Corps to take McPherson's job during the rest of the fighting on July 22, felt he deserved the honor to command the Army of the Tennessee permanently. But Thomas opposed Logan for the position because of some ill-feeling that had developed between the two. And while he admired Logan's fighting spirit, Sherman himself did not think the administrative skills of this political general were equal to the task of commanding a department. As he explained after the war, Sherman wanted "purely and technically soldiers, men who would obey orders and execute them promptly and on time." On Thomas's recommendation, Sherman chose Howard. Logan sulked for the rest of his life, never fully reconciling himself to Sherman's decision. Moreover, Hooker resigned in a huff because, as the senior corps commander in Sherman's army group, he felt that he deserved the honor. Sherman never wavered in his choice; he had developed a liking for Howard since the Chattanooga campaign had thrown them together.[34]

Howard justified Sherman's decision in his first engagement as army commander. He assumed the post on July 27, shortly after Logan pulled the troops away from the east side of Atlanta and started them around the north side to strike at the Macon and Western Railroad, which approached the city from the south. Hood sent his old corps, now under Lieutenant General Stephen D. Lee, to take a position on the Lickskillet Road and block Howard's progress south. He was under orders not to attack unless a favorable opportunity presented itself. Lee, however, got there too late to secure the road but decided to attack anyway, even though he had little information about the Federals' strength or position. The resulting battle of Ezra Church on July 28 proved to be a bloodbath. At 12:30 P.M. the Rebels assaulted Logan's Fifteenth Corps, which faced south as a refused right flank after Howard positioned the rest of the Army of the Tennessee facing east. Logan's men, though strained by the pounding, managed to hold their own, inflicting 3,000 casualties on the Confederates while losing only 632 men. Logan's troops had only a few rails hastily thrown together as protection, but it was enough to give them an advantage. Sherman was well pleased that Howard had managed the army to achieve this defensive victory, which he asserted "unusually encouraged" the rank and file.[35]

In the Confederate army, however, Ezra Church was the turning point in soldier morale during the Atlanta campaign. The men had attacked with spirit, but the apparent lack of coordination, the heavy losses, and the absence of anything like success broke the spirit of many men. Hood could do little more than order Stephen Lee to dig in and extend his line to block any Union attempt to continue moving south.[36]

President Davis supported Hood's shift from a slashing offensive to defensive measures as the best way to deal with Sherman, a move that reflected badly on the relief of Johnston. Davis urged Hood to avoid attacking earthworks and seek ways to throw Confederate cavalry on the Union supply line. This forced Sherman to feel his way farther south of Ezra Church with care. Schofield led the way with the Army of the Ohio, cautiously trying to cross the branches of Utoy Creek in early August. He was hampered by lack of cooperation from Major General John McAuley Palmer, commander of the Fourteenth Corps, who had orders to assist him even though he believed his commission predated Schofield's. The result was a two-day delay and partial moves instead of a decisive strike to reach the railroad. In the end, Palmer agreed to resign his command in favor of Major General Jefferson C. Davis. Sherman complained that the Fourteenth, the largest corps in his army group, was harder to move than a rock.[37]

The Confederates proved to be harder to move than a rock as well. On August 6 Schofield sent one of his brigades into an unwise attack against entrenched Rebels along Utoy Creek; he lost one-third of the troops engaged, while the defending Confederates lost a mere twenty men. Only by flanking the strong enemy position along the stream could Schofield continue the extension of Sherman's line southward, but even then he was at least two miles away from the railroad and moving south parallel with it. Hood managed to extend his own line to keep ahead of the creeping advance. By August 9, Sherman felt his manpower was extended as far as it could prudently go, yet he was far from touching the railroad southwest of Atlanta. He contemplated breaking off from his line of communications with the majority of his army group, leaving one corps behind to guard the railroad crossing of the Chattahoochee and taking the rest on a wide flanking movement to break up the rail lines south of Atlanta. It was a risky move, and Sherman waited for two weeks before deciding to implement it.[38]

Ironically, the Confederates also were feeling the strain of extending their meager manpower southward. Hardee confessed to his wife, "I have so long a line, and so few men to guard it, that I feel great uneasiness whenever I hear the enemy is advancing." Only by constructing a new line of works extending southwest from the city defenses, and manning all fortifications as thinly as possible, could the Confederates cover the front of their enemy's formation. "Let every man remember that he is individually responsible for his few feet of line," Hood reminded his troops, "and that the destiny of Atlanta hangs upon the issue."[39]

Confederate defenses of Atlanta. One of the most heavily fortified cities in Civil War America, Atlanta sported layered defenses such as can be seen in this image. (Library of Congress, LC-DIG-cwpb-02239)

For several weeks during August, the Atlanta campaign acquired more elements that were reminiscent of siege operations as Sherman prepared for what he felt was a risky but inevitable move. He shipped some heavy artillery from Chattanooga to pound the city of Atlanta and advised subordinates to push their troops as close as possible to the Confederate line. Sherman admitted he had no patience, or faith, in true siege operations but merely wanted to strain enemy resources and nerves while he considered taking the big step to reach Confederate supply lines south of the city. "Let us destroy Atlanta and make it a desolation," he told Howard. The Federals fired three thousand rounds of field artillery ordnance into the city on August 9 and added heavier metal when the bigger guns arrived a few days later. The bombardment killed a small number of civilians and damaged many buildings, but it failed to interrupt the delivery of Rebel supplies or do more than make life miserable in the city.[40]

On the firing lines, the "siege" of Atlanta intensified with constant skirmish firing by the Federals, who were lavish in their expenditure of ammunition. The 96th Illinois in Thomas's Army of the Cumberland kept one-third of its number on the skirmish line at all times and fired up to five thousand rounds daily. Federal skirmishers pushed their line forward at every opportunity to obtain positions as close as possible to the Rebel main line, delivering harassing fire all day. Both sides lived in trenches that soon became fetid with refuse, lice, and mud. Many men grew ill and some became demoralized due to the unrelenting pressure of staying in their cramped, dirty ditches.[41]

The Federals were perched at the end of a rail line that, according to Sherman, stretched for five hundred miles "within an hostile or semi hostile country." He counted it a triumph that his quartermasters could provide the men with basic food, ammunition, and other necessities, believing that merely supplying his army group in this campaign was a greater accomplishment than winning any battle. Yet the triumph presented severe limitations. Sherman had to make his plans with the understanding that the railroad could be broken one-third of the time during the campaign. He stockpiled supplies at Allatoona and Marietta to tide the men over during these interruptions. Even so, the cars brought barely enough for his large concentration of troops. Sherman set priorities for shipping: most important was ammunition, then clothing, then food for men, and last food for animals. Telegraph wires were cut so often that he set up a system of signals linking the army with Allatoona. Despite his best efforts, Sherman complained that too many civilians still managed to travel in the cars to the front; he tried to clamp down even further on that annoying problem by telling subordinates in Nashville to allow only the minimal number of passes to citizens as far as Chattanooga and absolutely none south of that city.[42]

There was little opportunity for the Federals to forage off the countryside, for duty in the trenches was too demanding. Moreover, the area had been stripped by civilians who mostly decided to "refugee" and took their movable provisions with them. In fact, Hood encouraged civilians to drive their pigs and cattle away from the reach of Sherman's men. Whenever Yankees did have an opportunity to roam about, they often plundered unmercifully, much to the distress of officers who feared the adverse effects of depredations on troop discipline. Hood also worried about the impact of plundering on the discipline of his own men, blaming most of it on stragglers. He issued orders claiming it had reached "intolerable" proportions. "It must come to an end." At least one of his cavalry commanders took this injunction seriously and tried to enforce it, warning his men that he could transfer them to infantry units for infractions of discipline.[43]

To curb his growing impatience, Sherman reminded his subordinates "that the siege of Troy lasted six years, and Atlanta is a more valuable town than Troy." With gloom in the North, due to the heavy casualties thus far in the year's campaigns, as well as the apparent stalemate in Virginia and Georgia, Lincoln's prospects for reelection the coming fall seemed limited. Sherman proposed to "give those southern fellows all the fighting they want," since "any signs of let up on our part is sure to be falsely construed" in the political arena. Grant planned more offensives at Petersburg, in part to bolster Northern morale as well as to prevent Robert E. Lee from detaching any troops to Georgia. Sherman also found it worrisome that a large proportion of his available manpower was due to be discharged at the expiration of their term of service in the late summer and early fall.[44]

Jonesboro

Sherman grew increasingly frustrated with Schofield's slow pace of incremental advances southward, which never reached the railroad south of Atlanta. He estimated Hood's line at fifteen miles long, yet it seemed to extend farther with each small step by his own forces. He considered bypassing Atlanta altogether, cutting loose from the railroad and raiding through Georgia toward the Gulf Coast. He had already tried, in late July, to use his available cavalry to cut the railroad linking Atlanta with Macon, but that raid had resulted in dismal failure because of aggressive Confederate cavalry moves to counter it.[45]

Sherman decided not to bypass Atlanta or rely anymore on his cavalry, but to stick with his original idea of swinging the majority of his troops southward to snip the railroad. Before he could implement that plan, Hood unleashed Wheeler's cavalry in a raid on the Union supply line with Chattanooga. The Confederate horsemen disrupted the railroad and telegraph line for a few days before riding north into eastern Tennessee. Sherman determined to attempt one more mounted raid of his own while the Confederate cavalry could not interfere. Brigadier General Hugh Judson Kilpatrick, who had previously shown some initiative, now was entrusted with the task of striking the railroad to Macon. He left on the night of August 18 and returned four days later after riding completely around the city. Though he gave a glowing report of the damage inflicted, Federal observers could clearly see trains pulling into Atlanta on August 23, once again proving that mounted raids could never cut an enemy's line of communications for more than short periods.[46]

Loading his wagons with fifteen days' rations, Sherman began shifting his troops on the night of August 25, continuing the bombardment of Atlanta up to the last minute. As the Twentieth Corps retired to positions guarding the Chattahoochee River crossings, the rest of Sherman's army group advanced south, well out of sight of Confederate observers. Initially assuming the movement meant a retreat north, Hood learned by August 27 that Sherman and his men were actually heading south. He did not know where or when they would strike his communications, so he prepared to react as quickly as possible when they made their appearance. Howard hit the Atlanta and West Point Railroad near Fairburn, nearly twenty miles southwest of Atlanta, and Thomas struck near Red Oak about five miles from Howard. "I want you to do the best job of railroad destruction on record," Sherman told his subordinates. He relayed detailed instructions to Thomas for accomplishing the task as quickly and as thoroughly as possible, which included burning ties, twisting rails, filling cuts with debris, and planting artillery shells rigged to explode if anyone tried to clear out the cuts. The Federals wrecked more than twelve miles of road. After weeks of frustration, Sherman finally had an opportunity to decisively cut his enemy's communications and force Hood out of his heavy earthworks.[47]

The Macon and Western Railroad was next, and Howard spearheaded Sherman's drive toward Jonesboro, fifteen miles south of Atlanta, to hit it. Howard moved within eight hundred yards of the rail line at Jonesboro by the evening of August 30, but dug in on the east side of Flint River because darkness prevented further progress. He was close enough to alarm Hood, who had shifted Hardee's corps to the small town to block Howard's advance. With orders to advance to Jonesboro quickly and attack at once, Hardee left at 4:00 P.M. on the thirtieth, and Stephen Lee began to move his corps to help him about midnight. Most of their commands confronted Howard by midafternoon of August 31, when twenty thousand Confederates attacked 12,000 Federals, who had an additional seventy-five hundred men in reserve. Despite the disparity in numbers, the attack was a dismal failure. Howard was ready for it, and many Confederates did not have their heart in the strike. Arthur M. Manigault recalled that long service in the trenches and loss of faith in Hood's generalship caused as much trouble for his brigade as Federal fire. A Georgia private reported that his comrades "just simply run in and out again, at a terrible sacrifice." His company lost eleven of nineteen men. Overall, the Confederates suffered 2,200 casualties to Howard's 772 losses on August 31.[48]

The Atlanta campaign came to a crashing end as Sherman managed to bring the rest of his large force onto the railroad. Even as Hardee attacked Howard, Schofield and elements of Thomas's army struck the line between Jonesboro and Atlanta on the afternoon of August 31, compelling Hood to recall Stephen Lee's corps while continuing to expect Hardee to save Jonesboro with only twelve thousand men. Hardee's line of earthworks had a weak spot at a ninety-degree angle that the Federals exploited. Fourteenth Corps units attacked the angle on September 1, capturing most of an Arkansas brigade and compromising the Rebel position, even though the rest of Hardee's command contained the rupture. Although the Federals had at least ten divisions on the field, as opposed to Hardee's three divisions, they used only four brigades in the attack. Still, it was clear that the Confederates had no hope of retaining Jonesboro; Hardee vacated his position that night after losing 1,272 men compared to Sherman's losses of 1,400 on September 1.[49]

Hood evacuated Atlanta on the night of September 1, directing all of his units to rendezvous at Lovejoy's Station, about five miles south of Jonesboro. They marched well east of the railroad to avoid the Federals. Elements of the Twentieth Corps advanced on the morning of September 2, after hearing the sound of exploding ordnance in Atlanta all night, to discover the city open to their entry. Mayor James M. Calhoun and a committee of citizens met the Yankees with a white flag and invited them in for self-protection. "So Atlanta is ours, and fairly won," Sherman proudly telegraphed to Halleck.[50]

Sherman moved south to Lovejoy's Station and skirmished with Hood for several days before deciding to break off contact and rest his men at Atlanta. He did not have confidence in his extended line of communications to continue the campaign, with the next major point being Macon some 103 miles away. Sherman bemoaned the fact that Hardee had not been demolished or captured at Jonesboro, ignoring the fact that he had so urged Schofield and Thomas to destroy track that they were too late to outflank Hardee's right on September 1. Still, he could console himself with a visible and politically charged prize: the seizure of Atlanta, which greatly improved Lincoln's chances of reelection two months later. His men could also take pride in having conducted one of the most grueling and successful campaigns of the war.[51]

On the Confederate side, Hood and his subordinates were surprised at Sherman's breaking off and retiring toward Atlanta, but grateful for the chance to rest their troops. They called loudly for reinforcements or else "Georgia and Alabama will be overrun," as Hardee told President Davis. Hood initially tried to convince Richmond that his men felt "every effort was made to hold Atlanta to the last. I do not think the army is discouraged." But he soon began to blame the rank and file for the failure of the campaign. Hood called Hardee's attack at Jonesboro on August 31 "a disgraceful effort," citing what he considered the low casualty rate as evidence. He blamed the "comparative spiritlessness of the Western Army" on Johnston's policy of retreating and of relying on earthworks. Hood pined for the decisive, aggressive style of generalship displayed by Robert E. Lee and Stonewall Jackson in Virginia, contrasting it with "the Joe Johnston mode of warfare. The one school elevates and inspirits, while the other depresses, paralyzes, and, in time, brings destruction." Having learned little from his bloody tenure as commander of the Army of Tennessee, Hood continued to view military operations as a matter primarily of morale and searched about for a way to retrieve the disastrous end of the Atlanta campaign.[52]

Neither Johnston nor Hood had been capable of dealing with Sherman's advance on Atlanta. Johnston had been too reluctant to assume the tactical offensive, relying instead on luring the Federals into bloody assaults that might drain their manpower, encouraging cavalry forces not under his control to raid Union supply lines, and giving up more territory in hope of engulfing the enemy within the recesses of the Deep South. Hood erred on the other side of the spectrum, relying on poorly executed attacks that achieved nothing but irredeemable casualties and blaming the rank and file for not fighting hard enough. The Atlanta campaign bred a bitter feud between these two men. Joseph E. Johnston, fifty-seven years old when he was replaced by thirty-three-year-old John Bell Hood, had one of the most distinguished careers in the prewar U.S. Army, serving as its quartermaster when he resigned to enter Confederate service. Johnston was the only officer to command both of the South's major field armies in the Civil War, having led the Army of Northern Virginia during nearly the first year of the conflict. Hood had little more than a reputation for aggressive tactical leadership as a brigade and division commander in Lee's army to recommend him for command of the Army of Tennessee. His performance as a corps commander during the Atlanta campaign had been lackluster at best.[53]

The men of the Army of Tennessee overwhelmingly loved and respected Johnston not because he won battles, but because he took care of them. As William Samuel Woods of the 20th Alabama put it, "Gen Johnson Does Evry thing in His Power for the Soldiers of His army. . . . Evry Soldier praises [and] Loves Gen Johnson & Will go With Him Any Where." Disgust with Hood was by no means universal; some members of the Army of Tennessee continued to place trust in his generalship even after the failed attacks against Sherman's troops. But many more survivors of the battles of Peachtree Creek, July 22, and Ezra Church grew sick of their new leader and his tactics. According to Stephen Cowley, a staff officer with Quarles's Alabama Brigade, the men could never get over the removal of Johnston and his replacement by Hood. It "has thrown a gloom over the veterans of this Army which will as long as the Army exists show on their war worn faces," Cowley wrote in August 1864."[54]

While Sherman battled his way toward Atlanta, the rear areas of Union occupation in the West were alive with activity. Strategic raids by mounted Confederate forces swept across western Tennessee and western Kentucky, hitting several Union garrisons and resulting in sharp battles at Paducah and a controversial slaughter at Fort Pillow, even before Sherman set out on his campaign for Atlanta. Sherman himself struck out from Vicksburg toward Meridian in an attempt to disrupt the Confederate position in Mississippi and tear up enemy lines of communication as preparation for major campaigning in the spring. After his massive host left Chattanooga, Sherman relied on subordinate commanders to continue applying pressure on Confederate forces in Mississippi to distract them from trying to interfere with his tenuous supply line through Tennessee. The rear areas were by no means calm, or inactive, throughout the year.

Meridian

During the winter months of 1864, before a firm directive to campaign toward Atlanta had been set, Sherman sought to improve the Union position in Mississippi by tearing up the network of railroads centering on Meridian. Such a move would disrupt Confederate shipment of provisions from the state to their major armies and hamper enemy efforts to move troops westward to threaten the Union occupation of Vicksburg and other Mississippi River towns. By leading a large force of infantry to the city, Sherman hoped to duplicate his success at Jackson the year before and make Meridian inactive as a transportation center for at least six months. If Nathaniel P. Banks could succeed in his drive up the Red River Valley at the same time, the Federals would significantly widen their "domain along the Mississippi River, and thereby set the troops hitherto necessary to guard the river free for other military purposes." Sherman hoped to free up twenty thousand occupation troops for the next campaign, as well as destroy Nathan Bedford Forrest's command in Mississippi.[1]

Sherman led four divisions of infantry from Vicksburg while William Sooy Smith brought seven thousand cavalrymen from Memphis. Both columns headed for Meridian, a march of 150 miles for the infantrymen. Sherman left on February 3, 1864, and reached Jackson two days later, occupying the state capital for the third time in the war. By February 9, the Federals were at Morton. Confederate general Leonidas Polk chose not to contest the Union advance. He evacuated Meridian and saved his command. When Sherman occupied the city on February 16, his men began to tear up 115 miles of track in all directions, including sixty-one bridges. They captured nineteen locomotives and twenty-eight cars. After five days of destruction, the Yankees returned to Vicksburg by March 6. Smith, however, never made contact with Sherman. Forrest stopped him near West Point by February 22, and Smith returned to Memphis with five thousand blacks, one thousand white refugees, and three thousand animals. As one Federal soldier put it, "We left every town that we passed through in ashes." Sherman later credited the Meridian raid with freeing up the Seventeenth Corps for the Atlanta campaign.[2]

Paducah and Fort Pillow

Soon after turning back Smith from his approach to Meridian, Forrest set out on a raid of his own deep into the Union occupation zone in the West. He led 3,000 mounted troops from Columbus, Mississippi, into western Kentucky to recruit men for the Confederate army. Forrest occupied the town of Paducah on March 25, driving the small Union garrison into a strong fort on the outskirts. Colonel Stephen G. Hicks held Fort Anderson with only 650 men, but he was aided by fire from two gunboats in the Ohio River. At one point, he laid down so much fire on Confederate sharpshooters hidden in buildings that Paducah was set ablaze. Forrest soon broke off the engagement and retreated. Federal commanders shed no tears over the burning of the town, for Paducah was a notorious refuge of Confederate sympathizers. In fact, many Unionists considered the majority of residents in western Tennessee and western Kentucky as "overwhelmingly disloyal." Stephen A. Hurlbut admitted, "I consider the damage done to Paducah as a proper lesson to that place and its vicinity."[3]

What Forrest and his troopers did at Fort Pillow, Tennessee, the next month, however, shocked every Federal soldier in the West. This large Confederate work had been occupied by the Unionists since June 1862; they had reworked its configuration to allow for a small garrison of black troops and Tennessee Unionists. Forrest struck the fort on April 12 with overwhelming force, capturing it in an assault that did not end with the garrison's surrender. For sometime afterward his men brutally killed unarmed prisoners, especially blacks. Survivors provided clear proof of the atrocity, and even Confederate soldiers confirmed it in their personal accounts of the attack. Forrest lost about one hundred men, whereas Federal casualties totaled nearly three hundred—close to half the garrison. Sixty-five percent of the blacks and up to one-third of the Unionists died in the battle. Forrest's men found about forty black women and children in the fort and returned them to their masters.[4]

Throughout the West, and even in the East, the news of Fort Pillow struck like a thunderbolt. It created intense anger and a desire for revenge among black troops, as well as among many whites who were sympathetic to their brothers in arms. "If this is to be the game of the enemy they will soon learn that it is one at which two can play," wrote General Augustus Chetlain at Memphis. The presence of Forrest in western Tennessee and western Kentucky that winter greatly encouraged the pro-Confederates of the region. Federal officers urged the few loyalists there to organize companies for home defense, but the Union occupation troops could not catch or drive Forrest out. Not until the spring campaigning season forced him to return to Mississippi did Forrest quit the area, which held so many friends of the Confederacy.[5]

Mississippi

Sherman initially relied on Brigadier General Samuel D. Sturgis to keep Forrest occupied in Mississippi in the spring of 1864, but Sturgis proved to be an unreliable support for the Atlanta campaign. He led an expedition out of Memphis in early May but failed to engage Forrest. Then in early June, just as Forrest was setting off to strike at the railroads in Tennessee, Sturgis mounted a second offensive from Memphis with eighty-one hundred troops. This move compelled Forrest to cancel his expedition and confront the Union column at Brice's Cross Roads, about seventeen miles north of Tupelo, Mississippi. Sturgis handled his command poorly, sending his cavalry out too far ahead to be supported by the infantry. Forrest took advantage of the mistake. He struck decisively, defeating the Federal troopers and then hitting the unprepared infantry column. The lightning victory overwhelmed Sturgis's command, creating a dismal Union defeat. The Federals lost 2,612 men, while Forrest suffered only 493 casualties and captured 250 wagons, 18 guns, and 5,000 small arms.[6]

Sherman was surprised at Sturgis's beating but was determined to hound

Forrest. He ordered another expedition under a different commander to "go out and follow Forrest to the death, if it cost 10,000 lives and breaks the Treasury. There never will be peace in Tennessee till Forrest is dead."[7]

Andrew Jackson Smith commanded the expedition. It consisted of fourteen thousand men, including a brigade of black troops. Smith slowly advanced from Memphis in early July as Stephen D. Lee, who had replaced Polk as commander of the Department of Mississippi, Alabama, and East Louisiana, assembled Forrest and 9,460 Confederates near Tupelo. Smith took up a defensive position at Harrisburg, west of Tupelo, and Lee attacked him on July 14. Although the Federals repulsed the poorly coordinated assaults, Smith retired the next day due to logistical difficulties. He suffered only 670 casualties while inflicting 1,326 losses on Lee. Smith failed to deliver a smashing victory, but his limited success at least kept the Confederates busy in Mississippi and prevented Forrest from striking Sherman's supply line.[8]

Smith again advanced in early August to tear up the Mississippi Central Railroad. By now, Stephen Lee had gone to Georgia to replace Hood as corps commander and Forrest bypassed Smith to raid toward Memphis. Taking the Federal garrison by surprise, Forrest rode into town with almost three thousand men on August 21. They had no opportunity to do more than steal eighty horses before the Federals drove them out, though Forrest nearly captured Hurlbut and another Union general. The Confederates lost almost sixty men in this dash on Memphis, but it embarrassed the Yankees and demonstrated how poorly the fortifications of the city had been planned. The roads leading into Memphis were not properly protected; Fort Pickering, constructed at great cost and labor, was an isolated, overly large work that failed to defend the place from sudden strikes.[9]

The Federals had every reason to be concerned about the protection of important posts on the Mississippi such as Memphis. Sherman warned his subordinates to maintain their grip on Vicksburg, for "we don't want the task of taking it again." Some Confederates suggested that only a thousand men were needed to recapture Vicksburg by a sudden strike, for it was held by a small garrison of black troops after Sherman shifted the Seventeenth Corps to Georgia. Other significant towns in Mississippi lay in the no-man's-land that separated firm Union control from Confederate territory. All of central Mississippi constituted such a zone, with Jackson already having changed hands three times. Its mayor complained that "a great deal of private property has been destroyed, a large part of the town has been burnt, and many of the citizens have been compelled to remove." He urged the commander of an advancing Union force to send reliable guards ahead of his column to establish order, as most destruction occurred during the first few hours of occupation.[10]

Federal commanders sought to conduct raids into the zone that separated the contending forces, often with black troops, to create a "wholesome fear on the part of the enemy, . . . that we have sufficient force . . . to move into the interior when desired." On one such raid, conducted late in 1864, the Federals traversed 450 miles of territory, tore up 80 miles of railroad, destroyed 35 bridges, and garnered 500 prisoners, 1,000 blacks, and 800 animals.[11]

Protecting the Mississippi River continued to be the primary concern of Federal forces in the valley, a mission that Sherman never forgot. Even while "thundering away at Atlanta" in late July 1864, he worried about the safety of river transportation. "The river Mississippi must be held sacred," he told James McPherson. The Federals contemplated running a telegraph line directly linking Cairo with New Orleans to facilitate river protection. They considered crossing the wire over the river at several points to save distance. Such an expensive undertaking was never attempted.[12]

With Sherman busy in Georgia, Major General Edward R. S. Canby acquired greater control over the garrison troops along the Mississippi in the summer of 1864. His Department of the Gulf extended up close to Natchez, where McPherson's Department of the Tennessee jurisdiction began. It was too cumbersome to divide authority over the length of the river, especially when the commander of one department was in Georgia, so Sherman authorized Canby to call the shots. "As long as we can pull together it makes little difference who commands," Sherman told Halleck. Canby became the master of Union forces on both sides of the river for some distance, to the annoyance of many officers in the Department of the Tennessee, but the arrangement made sense.[13]

The Confederates worked hard to maintain some degree of communication between the divided parts of their country. Scouts were recruited to carry messages across the Mississippi in small boats. The Confederate postmaster general contracted with other men to transport weekly express mail across the river. Weapons could be shipped in small amounts, but it was virtually impossible to cross large numbers of troops. If they were divided into small squads, officers could not prevent the men from deserting. In the words of a Rebel cavalry commander, "A bird, if dressed in Confederate gray, would find it difficult to fly across the river."[14]

But Southern partisans could make Northern travel on the Mississippi difficult and dangerous. Efforts to raise companies of partisan rangers under existing Confederate recruitment policies, specifically to interrupt river traffic, never panned out. But small guerrilla bands often took potshots at passing steamboats and small, regularly organized Confederate units frequently attacked vessels, too. "It is supposed we hold the Mississippi River," Union general Napoleon B. Buford sarcastically said to Chase, "but it is also true that the banks are lined with hostile people." Up to seventy-five guerrillas fired at the *Sir William Wallace* as it passed Islands No. 70 and 71 in February 1864. Protected by an improvised breastwork, they killed and wounded seven passengers. The officers of the *C. E. Hillman* had become so used to firing that they were not excited when bullets smashed through the glass windows of the pilot house. In October 1864 a large band of guerrillas struck the *Belle of Saint Louis* as it tried to land at Randolph, Tennessee. A number of them boarded the vessel just as it backed away from the riverbank. Some began to rob the passengers as two others entered the pilot house to force the pilot to return to shore. But two paymasters on board stormed the pilot house and had a shoot-out with the guerrillas that resulted in the death or mortal wounding of all four men involved. This gave the pilot an opportunity to head again toward the middle of the river, and the other guerrillas jumped overboard to swim to shore.[15]

Confederate agents continued to burn civilian steamers on the Mississippi throughout 1864. While some boats at Louisville, Cairo, and Memphis became targets, the boat burners concentrated on the large number of steamers that did business at St. Louis, destroying five of them on July 15 alone. The provost marshal of the Department of the Missouri used detectives to gather information about them and managed to arrest a few. The Confederates smuggled gold through the lines near Memphis to pay the agents. Senator Williamson S. Oldham of Texas told Jefferson Davis that he thought civilian agents were more effective in this mode of operation than military personnel. In addition to undercover work, the Federal authorities responded to the incendiary threat by increasing security measures along the levees. Sherman bluntly expressed his view of the boat burners when he exclaimed, "It is not war." Any boat captain who caught incendiaries should "drop them overboard and let them find the bottom in their own way." Despite their spectacular mode of operation, the boat burners accounted for only 8.8 percent of the total number of boats lost during the war. Ironically, accidents accounted for the highest percentage of loss—at 47.4 percent.[16]

Trade

Trade remained one of the most difficult problems for Federal occupiers in the West during 1864. In March Sherman wanted to encourage it as much as possible, hoping to make civilians dependent on the Yankees for needed goods and "shake their love for the impoverished rebel concern." Sherman was "willing to use commerce as a means of war to corrupt and demoralize an enemy."[17]

But the always-thorny problem of keeping contraband goods out of the flow of material could never be solved. The army could not do so even when it was responsible for issuing trade permits earlier in the war. Now, the U.S. Treasury Department did not seem to exercise that authority with any better luck. Steamboats left Memphis with Treasury permits and headed south, often landing where Federal troops were not stationed, to trade with Confederate sympathizers and guerrillas and take cotton back to Memphis for sale. The Federals could only reiterate orders prohibiting boat landings at any place other than army posts and step up patrols of the river by armed craft. But these methods only limited the contraband trade; they did not stop it.[18]

Similar difficulties existed on land, forcing Federal occupiers in Vicksburg to allow only visibly loyal citizens to enter and exit the city. In addition, they permitted no more than thirty days' worth of supplies per family to leave Vicksburg and prohibited stores to be established in towns that were not garrisoned by Federal troops. Farther north, Union officers clamped down more firmly. Mason Brayman, tired of the large volume of trade in contraband goods out of Columbus, Kentucky, cut off all commerce into and out of the town. C. C. Washburn did the same thing at Memphis in May. He continued to allow citizens to enter the city by land but prohibited any movement out of the place except by steamboat. Such draconian measures encouraged Unionists and Federal soldiers alike, but they could not last long. Loyalists and neutral elements in the population suffered along with the guilty. The Federals at Columbus eased restrictions on trade, relying on post commanders to decide whether individual citizens could be trusted. It was an imperfect policy that nevertheless gave opportunities to a wide variety of civilians to engage in commerce.[19]

Cotton

Cotton continued to attract a great deal of attention. A Union gunboat captain complained that "many in high places and in low have been unable to withstand the alluring temptations held out to them by enormous cotton gains." He believed it created an "atmosphere of the whole Mississippi valley reeking with . . . corruption." In August Sherman issued general orders setting forth army policy on cotton within the Military Division of the Mississippi. The troops were to seize all cotton within reach and claim it for the government. No private claims of ownership would be entertained. The bales were to be shipped north, if that did not interfere with the shipment of supplies to the army, and Treasury agents would take charge of the confiscated cotton. Sherman also authorized that trade in all articles of commerce be shut down in areas where guerrillas were active, permitting commerce only in noncontraband goods with peaceful citizens elsewhere. Federal commanders overwhelmingly agreed with Sherman. "It is utterly impracticable for cotton and efficient war, loyalty and traitorous traffic to grow together and thrive equally in the same crop," wrote Napoleon J. T. Dana. Officers like Dana supported the idea of the Federal government confiscating all the cotton it could and using it to reimburse owners of steamers destroyed by guerrillas.[20]

The Confederates understood the allure of cotton all too well and suffered from it. They viewed the trade as demoralizing their own citizens and weaning them from Southern loyalty. "I have found that those who associate much with Yankees adopt very many of their opinions," wrote a Confederate scout who reported on the sale of cotton at Memphis. Another observer deplored the fact that cotton had become a weakness of the Confederate cause in Mississippi: "Yankee gold is fast accomplishing what Yankee arms could never achieve." Leonidas Polk did not have enough troops to curtail the transportation of cotton to Union posts on the Mississippi River, and he suggested the army confiscate, buy, or burn it as the only solution. That policy was not prudent, or even feasible, so Polk began to seek ways to manipulate the cotton trade to achieve Confederate objectives. By allowing some of it to be sold, he might prevent Federal raids into disputed territory that seemed to the Confederates to be motivated mostly by a desire to confiscate cotton. Also, by controlling the sale, the Confederate army could acquire gold with which to purchase needed military supplies. It was a delicate game Polk wanted to play, but he never fully implemented his program.[21]

Blacks

John Eaton returned to Vicksburg from a trip to Washington, D.C., in late August 1863 to find that the black refugee problem had grown to immense proportions following the Union conquest of the Mississippi Valley. Thousands of former slaves, now free under the provisions of the Emancipation Proclamation, flocked to Federal camps in unprecedented numbers. Eaton rolled up his sleeves and began to expand the preexisting system of army support for black refugees to encompass the newly garnered territory. He later characterized the new refugees as "to all intents and purposes barbarians," because they were lacking in all material, intellectual, and cultural attributes necessary for comfort. Five thousand freedmen followed Sherman's return from the Meridian raid, and 2,500 trailed the Federal army as it retreated from the Red River expedition in April 1864. Banks had to take care of 150,000 blacks in the Department of the Gulf, while Eaton was responsible for 113,650 in the Department of the Tennessee.[22]

Eaton created more contraband camps to accommodate as many refugees as possible, putting the able-bodied males to work and feeding the rest with army rations. The civilians who hired them had to register with local provost marshals and proffer bonds to ensure their good treatment of the refugees. Thousands of black workers were employed to cut wood for the dozens of wood yards located along the banks of the Mississippi, providing ready supplies of fuel for steamers. Grant worked out an arrangement whereby two-thirds of the wages would be paid directly to the workers, while the rest would go into "a fund for the benefit of the Contrabands" to be managed by Eaton.[23]

Eaton also sought to provide some education for refugee children. A number of Northern teachers volunteered their services, but Eaton initially could do nothing more than offer them government transportation. By September 1864, Lorenzo Thomas gave Eaton authority to control and direct educational endeavors, and Eaton appointed superintendents in every district of the department. Moreover, he opened orphan asylums for black children. By the end of the summer of 1864, 13,320 students took lessons in Eaton's school system.[24]

Eaton could congratulate himself on accomplishing a great humanitarian feat. He estimated that out of 113,650 refugees his subordinates had processed since the fall of Vicksburg, more than 36 percent were working for the army, 54 percent were employed by others, and nearly 9 percent received food from the government. Visiting Grant at City Point, Virginia, in mid-August 1864, Eaton toured the freedmen's camp at Fortress Monroe and admired the fine condition of the place. He noted that the black refugee problem was "far more easily dealt with [in Virginia] than in the Mississippi Valley," due to the enormous number of refugees in the West.[25]

Black Troops

Some black regiments raised along the Mississippi River during 1863 continued to be overused as laborers in early 1864. Officers at times warned superiors that they could not adequately train their men. When Brigadier General John P. Hawkins wrote of "fatigue duty and dirty work," Sherman countered with a report that his white troops did just as much, if not more, fatigue duty and rarely complained about it. Yet Company B, 47th U.S. Colored Troops (USCT), was unable to drill at all during May and June 1864 because it performed so much labor and guard duty at Vicksburg, a record rare among white regiments. Lorenzo Thomas took up this concern with Secretary of War Stanton, noting that prejudice against black soldiers in the Mississippi Valley continued to exist well into 1864. Stanton supported the promulgation of a general order prohibiting the use of black recruits as laborers beyond their share compared to white troops. Nevertheless, Sherman continued to denigrate blacks as soldiers, calling them "a doubtful element" in April 1864. He believed they would make but "a poor quality of soldiery" and avoided using them in the Atlanta campaign.[26]

Slowly and uncertainly, Federal officers in the Mississippi Valley used their black troops less as laborers and more as soldiers, although there were few opportunities to meet the enemy in combat. Black regiments often conducted expeditions into disputed territory, rounding up more recruits and escorting shipments of cotton for private individuals. The new regulations regarding cotton trading, based on permits to private individuals issued by Treasury agents, failed to eliminate controversy. Colonel Charles A. Gilchrist of the 12th Louisiana of African Descent complained that his men conducted an expedition in the Grand Gulf region that accomplished nothing but to help greedy speculators obtain 1,515 bales of cotton, none of which went to benefit the Federal government. Gilchrist was unable to find any able-bodied black males in the area. It seemed impossible to create a clean system of obtaining cotton in the occupied South for Northern markets, and there was no way to completely stop speculators from using the army for their personal gain.[27]

Black troops came into conflict with whites in nonbattle scenarios. When a group of African American soldiers killed a white civilian on the streets of Vicksburg as redress for a personal grievance, the post commander issued orders for everyone to remain calm and not to take the law into their own hands. Now and then, patrols sent out by black units stumbled across guerrillas and firefights ensued. In late August 1864 a company of the 13th USCT fought a skirmish during a scout near Huntingdon, Tennessee, acquitting itself well by wounding the guerrilla leader. A private in the 50th USCT, captured in early February 1864, was sold by the Confederates to a man named Jessie Lee in Georgia. When word of the sale reached the regiment, anxious recruits realized that they could not expect to be treated as soldiers if they fell into enemy hands.[28]

Kentucky constituted an anomaly among the slave areas under Federal control. Exempted from the Emancipation Proclamation, Kentucky slaveowners were extremely jealous of their property even as they continued to tentatively support the Union or remain neutral. They did not want their slaves to come into contact with contraband laborers from other states, afraid they "would become demoralized and worthless" by the association. Consequently, Federal officials had to separate Kentucky slave laborers from contrabands in different work groups. There was no support for enlisting blacks as soldiers among the slave-owning elite of Kentucky.[29]

But black Kentuckians sensed the pivotal change in the institution of slavery and acted, when possible, on their own. In early 1864 Lorenzo Thomas discovered that up to seven thousand African American men in Kentucky had traveled to Northern states as well as Tennessee to enlist in the U.S. Army, and that "the entire slave population of the State was in a state of ferment." Thomas attempted to persuade Unionist governor Thomas E. Bramlette and the state legislature to allow the recruitment of blacks to be credited to Kentucky. He waited for their approval until June 1864. Then, receiving no response, Thomas opened recruiting stations without the support of state officials. His recruiting officers had to contend with a great deal of hostility, which resulted in sporadic beatings of blacks, even though many determined loyalists in the state supported the move. Gradually, as blacks flocked to the colors, white attitudes changed to resigned acceptance. By the time Atlanta fell, Thomas reported that fourteen thousand blacks had enlisted in Kentucky.[30]

Recalcitrant Unionists in the state continued to fulminate about the obvious breakdown of the institution of slavery. Governor Bramlette made his position clear in a letter to President Lincoln. "We are for preserving the rights and liberties of our own race and upholding the character and dignity of our position," he pronounced in September. "We are not willing to sacrifice a single life or imperil the smallest right of free white men for the sake of the negro." Bramlette professed continued support for the Union, regardless of what happened to slavery. Ironically, reports of abuses in the Federal mobilization of Kentucky blacks surfaced as well. Recruiters reportedly coerced some reluctant, able-bodied men into the ranks, and the Federals established a commission to settle loyal owners' claims for compensation when their slaves signed up without permission. As it turned out, most of Kentucky's black regiments wound up being transferred to a different theater of operations. In October 1864 Lorenzo Thomas began to send many of them to Virginia. Several thousand black Kentuckians were assigned to serve in the newly created Twenty-fifth Corps, an all-black unit in the Army of the James.[31]

The mobilization of black soldiers by the Union had attained massive proportions by the end of the war, and the Western theater accounted for a huge portion of the total. The Federals raised at least 158 regiments of infantry, heavy artillery, and cavalry for which we have records to indicate exactly where they were organized. Of that number, 37.9 percent were raised in the Mississippi Valley, immediately along the banks of the great river. Another 28.4 percent came from the Eastern theater—mostly Virginia, Maryland, and North Carolina. The East plus the Mississippi Valley accounted for exactly two-thirds of the black regiments organized by the Federals.[32]

Guerrillas

The guerrilla problem worsened in 1864. Irregulars grew more active across the Western theater, seemingly unafraid of the small Union garrisons left behind as Sherman maximized troop strength on active fronts. The guerrillas struck at defenseless targets, firing into passing trains, cutting telegraph wires, and burning small, undefended bridges and culverts. They lay stones and rails on tracks to disrupt locomotives and burned piles of wood used to fuel the engines. Marauders raided towns to secure supplies, singling out loyalists for ill treatment. They often took hostages and demanded ransom, only to brutally murder the victims after receiving payment. Federal garrisons sent out patrols that sometimes encountered the guerrillas, killing a few and scattering the rest. One Union patrol of only 11 men was ambushed by 110 guerrillas near Fort Donelson and overwhelmed. The marauders mercilessly beat their captives, then pumped up to four bullets into each one.[33]

Guerrillas were more lethal in Kentucky than anywhere else. Federal officials reported that nearly all the towns and counties on the south bank of the Ohio were disloyal, as well as many on the north bank. A great deal of trade in contraband goods was the result. The counties along the Mississippi River were equally disloyal. An officer at Columbus clamped down on the shipment of goods of all kinds to inland towns because they were wide open to guerrillas who ransacked stores.[34]

Efforts to crack down on irregular activity in Kentucky failed to curtail its increase. When ten soldiers were captured by marauders near Mayfield, officials sought to take Confederate sympathizers as hostages to ensure their safe return, but there is no indication if the strategy worked. The Federal commander in the state, Stephen G. Burbridge, canceled all government contracts at the end of May 1864 so he could thoroughly weed out Rebel sympathizers who were growing fat on government funds. He intended to give contracts only to those who were demonstrably loyal. Burbridge also stopped the sale of a book entitled *Life, Services, and Campaigns of Stonewall Jackson* because it was "stirring up discontent and sedition" by "representing the crime of treason in false and alluring colors." He threatened to confiscate the book and arrest anyone who continued to sell it.[35]

Burbridge became controversial because of his extremely active role in trying to suppress guerrillas and all others who professed sympathy with the South. He labeled guerrillas as "wild beasts unknown to the usages of war" and began arresting Rebel sympathizers, intending to ship them down the Mississippi to some foreign country. Such an attitude fully suited Sherman's views as well as those of many officials in Washington. Joseph Holt, judge advocate general of the army, complained to Stanton that large areas of Kentucky were "completely overrun with guerrillas" who normally operated in bands of four to twenty, with one reportedly consisting of three hundred men. Kentucky's Federal commander believed that Lincoln's amnesty proclamation of December 1863 was the chief cause, as hundreds of Union enemies took the loyalty oath but failed to honor its intent. The oath became a cover for those who sought to disrupt Federal control. Burbridge began to execute guerrilla captives as a retaliatory measure, as well as to arrest all Rebel sympathizers within five miles of an incident involving irregulars and transport them out of Union lines. All refugees from Missouri, forced out by Union occupiers for uttering antigovernment sentiments, were to leave Kentucky as well. Lincoln supported these efforts by suspending the writ of habeas corpus in Kentucky in early July 1864. He also suspended the state's amnesty policy. Burbridge meant business. "Have the men been shot that I ordered?" he asked a subordinate. "If not, have them shot at once."[36]

A subordinate of Burbridge caused even more trouble than the Federal commander himself. Eleazar A. Paine, in charge of western Kentucky, was a West Pointer who happened to be a strong abolitionist. He had already executed more than two hundred guerrillas when he commanded at Gallatin, Tennessee, before arriving in Burbridge's district, and he continued that policy in Kentucky, executing forty-three men in fifty-one days. This might not have caused trouble with his superiors, but Paine also allowed his men to confiscate the property of Union and Confederate sympathizers alike. To many neutral Kentuckians, his policies seemed to represent a reign of terror authorized by the Lincoln government. Thus Paine was removed from his command in September 1864.[37]

Although Judge Advocate Holt believed Burbridge's strategy helped to suppress guerrilla activity, it created a firestorm of protest among Kentuckians. Governor Bramlette declared that his "outrageous and indiscriminate arrests" were "menacing the civil authorities and officers of the State." Grant and Lincoln became sensitive to such criticism. Grant believed that "a sensible soldier, one perfectly free from prejudice and party influence," ought to replace Burbridge. Lincoln wanted to hear both sides of the controversy, but he also feared that Burbridge was too freely assessing the property of the disloyal to compensate Unionists who suffered at the hands of guerrillas. Defending his actions to the president, Burbridge argued that a "vigorous policy against rebel sympathizers in this State must be pursued." If he made any mistakes, it was by not making enough arrests, rather than too many. When the Atlanta campaign ended and John Schofield toured his Department of the Ohio, he discovered evidence of widespread corruption in the administration of Burbridge's District of Kentucky; the Federal commander seemed to have participated in at least some of it.[38]

Although Burbridge eventually was relieved of his command, Sherman continued to support the kind of vigorous policies his controversial subordinate had espoused. He again urged wholesale depopulation of the disloyal as the final solution to the problems of Kentucky, for the civil courts could not be trusted. Kentucky was such "a bundle of inexplicable family and State factions" that anyone who was arrested could provide evidence of upright character. "Joe Johnston would never sanction such dogs as call themselves guerrillas in Kentucky," Sherman contended, "nor would Lee or Bragg or any other man who thinks he is fighting to establish a new and independent government better suited to their interests and honor." Sherman tried to cut to the heart of the matter, arguing that in the end all arguments about Union occupation policies in Kentucky were irrelevant. "The only principle in this war is, which party can whip."[39]

14 } Fall Turning Point

The Union war effort in the West reached a turning point in the fall of 1864. After spending a year and eight months advancing from Nashville to Atlanta, Federal troops now found themselves at the end of an increasingly problematic supply line while lodged only halfway across the wide expanse of the Deep South. The Confederate commander was deeply distressed by his failure to hold Atlanta and was ready for a desperate move to redeem his fortunes. Sherman had called off his offensive at Lovejoy's Station for good reasons, but the lull that ensued gave his enemy an opportunity to seize the strategic initiative, as Bragg had done two years before, with disruptive results for the Unionists. The time seemed ripe for another advance that could upset Federal victory.

Strategy

After the fall of Atlanta, Grant had contemplated little more than Sherman's joining Canby at or near Mobile, assuming, of course, that Canby had moved toward capturing the Alabama port city by then. But the need to send two divisions of the Nineteenth Corps to reinforce the Federal troops in Virginia caused a long delay in the strike against Mobile. Grant wanted Sherman to start another campaign as soon as possible, but exactly which point should be the target was now the question. Sherman did not want to continue supplying his large army group by the railroad; he had to detail too many men to guard it, and even then small squads of Wheeler's cavalry or independent guerrillas broke the track at isolated places. Sherman reported that he could live off the land but only if he continued moving, identifying Augusta and Macon as possible targets. He contemplated being ready to start with sixty thousand men to devastate the interior of Georgia sometime in October, but wanted to have an ultimate objective in mind—probably somewhere on the Atlantic or Gulf Coast. The thought of simply staying in Atlanta and "fighting for the safety of its railroad" was not attractive to the restless commander.[1]

To prepare for the move, Sherman set out to "make Atlanta a pure military garrison or depot, with no civil population to influence military measures." He was haunted by the previous examples of Memphis, Vicksburg, Natchez, and New Orleans, where large civilian populations caused a great deal of trouble for occupying troops. He refused to allow civilian businessmen to come to Atlanta, and he tried to eject residents from their homes. "Atlanta is no place for families or non-combatants," he informed Hood on September 7 as he sought to make arrangements with the Confederate commander to receive the refugees. Hood was forced to comply, but he engaged in a fierce exchange of letters with Sherman to protest the policy. "War is cruelty and you cannot refine it," Sherman told Mayor James M. Calhoun when that official also protested. With most of the civilians gone, Sherman constructed a new, shorter line of defense for the city and took control of many buildings for army use. He refused to open trade in and out of Atlanta. All cotton was to be confiscated and shipped to Nashville for government use.[2]

Hood moved from Lovejoy's Station to Palmetto Station, located on the Montgomery and West Point Railroad about twenty-four miles southwest of Atlanta. Jefferson Davis visited the Army of Tennessee at Palmetto, but he was not well received by the soldiers, who were generally disgruntled with the result of their hard campaign for Atlanta. The Confederate president authorized Hood's plan for an advance northward before he left the army on September 29. Discussion was already afoot to consider replacing Hood with P. G. T. Beauregard or some other commander. In the end, the controversial figure was retained at the head of the army and Beauregard was named commander of the Western Confederate forces to give some direction and support to his efforts. On his way to Palmetto, Davis had given a speech at Macon in which he predicted that Sherman would be turned back from Atlanta much like Napoleon had been forced to abandon Moscow and conduct a retreat that nearly destroyed his army in 1812. When Sherman read this comment in the newspaper, he became angry and more determined than ever not to let Confederate moves dictate his own actions. In more speeches at Goldsboro and Greensboro, North Carolina, Davis sought to bolster Confederate morale by further predicting that Hood would soon smash Sherman's railroad and then advance all the way to the Ohio, recruiting thousands of Confederate soldiers along the way. It was a dream as old as Bragg's Kentucky campaign and, by any objective measure, even less likely to succeed.[3]

There was a stark difference between the public picture Davis sought to create and the reality. The president confided that, when he left Hood, he was under the impression that the Army of Tennessee would plant itself squarely on Sherman's supply line somewhere between Atlanta and Chattanooga and then fight a defensive battle. Presumably Davis thought that only then, after a battlefield victory, would Hood go northward. The reality of Hood's northern Georgia campaign played out quite differently. Hood removed the rails for many miles along the railroad linking Macon and Augusta to Atlanta, to hamper any Union effort to continue advancing deeper into Georgia. In early October, the Confederate War Department appointed Beauregard to his new command in the West to help coordinate the coming offensive move. But Hood had already started from Palmetto before Beauregard had any chance to offer advice or control events. The Army of Tennessee was off with little more than a vague understanding between its commander and his superiors as to exactly what he was planning to do.[4]

Hood's Northern Georgia Campaign

Sherman sent George Thomas back to Nashville to deal with Nathan Bedford Forrest, who had begun operating in middle Tennessee by late September 1864. About the same time, intelligence indicated that Hood had left Palmetto and crossed the Chattahoochee River without Federal detection. Sherman was much more concerned about Hood's threat to his supply line than about Forrest, and he initially thought to move east of Atlanta in order to draw the Army of Tennessee after him. That risky move was soon scrapped in favor of taking nearly his entire army group toward the Confederates, leaving the Twentieth Corps to hold Atlanta. Sherman knew that Hood had no secure supply line of his own, that the Army of Tennessee could not stay in one place for very long. He also was aware that Allatoona was the major supply depot between Atlanta and Chattanooga. While fortified to resist a small attack, the post might be overwhelmed if pressed by a larger force. Sherman was determined to hit Hood if he dallied long enough to take on Allatoona.[5]

Despite plans to deal with the immediate threat that Hood posed to his supply line, Sherman did not forget overall Union strategy. As early as October 1 he informed Oliver Otis Howard that, if Hood ultimately headed for Tennessee, he would let Thomas deal with him and strike out from Atlanta for other points in the Deep South. If Hood stayed near the Union supply line, Sherman would be forced to "turn on him."[6]

Hood did strike at Allatoona, but not with his entire force, dispatching only Major General Samuel G. French's division. On October 5 the Confederates threw 3,276 men against John M. Corse's garrison of 2,000 troops, some of whom were armed with repeating rifles. French nearly took the fortified post in some of the most vicious fighting of the war in the West.

Allatoona Station. General John Bell Hood's effort to take this important Federal supply depot while marching northward demonstrated the effectiveness of Union defense measures to guard Major General William T. Sherman's supply line. (Johnson and Buel, *Battles and Leaders*, 4:323)

French lost 799 men, while Corse suffered 706 casualties. The rest of Hood's army continued marching northward, parallel to the railroad, as French retired from Allatoona. Stephen D. Lee partially invested the post at Resaca on October 12, but the small garrison refused a request to surrender. Lee did not think it worthwhile to attack because the Federals could have escaped if pressed. But the 800-man garrison at Dalton, consisting largely of black troops, gave in to Hood's demand to surrender. The African Americans were verbally abused by division commander William B. Bate, whose men stole their shoes and then forced the blacks to tear up the railroad. The Federal commander reported that one of his black soldiers was killed in cold blood when he refused to wreck the track, and five others were shot when they could not keep up with the marching column due to illness. At Villanow, many of his men were turned over to their former masters. By October 13, Hood's army reached Snake Creek Gap, skirmished with the van of Sherman's force, and successfully headed westward toward the Tennessee River Valley in northern Alabama.[7]

Frustrated by the disruption of his strategic plans, Sherman pushed his army corps northward in a futile effort to deal Hood a crippling blow. He was determined not to fall into Hood's game. "We must follow Hood till he is beyond reach of mischief and then resume the offensive," Sherman advised Schofield. It was evident that, traveling lightly, the Confederates could stay a couple of days' march ahead of the Federals. Sherman insisted that his men live off the land, not only to increase their mobility but also because the

Confederates had broken the railroad in several places. But this area had already been scoured of provisions during the Atlanta campaign; only when members of Sherman's van followed Hood into Alabama, stopping near Gadsden, did they find ample supplies of food.[8]

By October 20 Hood had reached Gadsden, where Beauregard—now commander of the Military Division of the West—joined his army. The two conferred on the next move. Hood wanted to make a quick strike at Bridgeport, but he did not have enough cavalry to screen the difficult crossing of the Tennessee River. Beauregard was willing to let Hood divide his army between Thomas and Sherman, but Hood thought it unwise to split his already small force. Instead, he continued moving westward to Florence, threatening the 1,800-man garrison of Decatur with 35,000 hardened veterans as he passed that point on October 26–30. The Federals refused to give up and Hood had no desire to waste manpower in an attack, so he spared Decatur.[9]

It was clear that Hood had no intention of staking everything on a major battle in northern Georgia, and it was equally clear to Sherman that it would be counterproductive to continue chasing him into northern Alabama. Sherman called off the pursuit and began to prepare to defend Tennessee and, at the same time, continue the offensive through Georgia. He sent the Fourth Corps to Chattanooga on October 26 and the Twenty-third Corps under Schofield four days later, delegating to Thomas full responsibility for controlling all the troops he would need in the Military Division of the Mississippi, except the four corps Sherman planned to lead out of Atlanta. Grant approved Sherman's plans and began to arrange for supplies to be shipped to the Savannah area to be ready for his men. Savannah fell into place as the natural objective because Canby's long-anticipated campaign against Mobile was still not under way, but Sherman held open the possibility of diverting his march toward Selma or the mouth of the Appalachicola River in the panhandle of Florida if circumstances called for it.[10]

"This movement is not purely military or strategic," Sherman explained to Halleck, "but it will illustrate the vulnerability of the South." He wanted to make the wealthy planters of the Deep South, who had not yet seen a blue uniform, emotionally feel the impact of war as a way to break the will to resist Union authority among die-hard Southerners. "If we can march a well-appointed army right through his territory," Sherman continued, "it is a demonstration to the world, foreign and domestic, that we have a power which Davis cannot resist. This may not be war, but rather statesmanship."[11]

There was much to be done before Sherman could strike out on his innovative campaign. He wanted to tear up the railroad between Chattanooga and Atlanta, having given up all previous ideas about making Atlanta a major military base. Ironically, before the railroad could be destroyed, crews had to repair the damage Hood's army had done in order to ship all wounded and sick men back to Chattanooga. Sherman also ordered that all supplies, except 1.5 million rations, be shipped from Atlanta. The Twentieth Corps had been busy scouring the region south of the city while Sherman chased Hood. Several forage trains of five hundred wagons, escorted by entire brigades, harvested the ripening corn near Covington and other places. Sherman encouraged this wholesale example of living off the land, arguing: "If Hood breaks our road Georgia must pay for it." As Sherman's men made their way back to Atlanta, they found the countryside along the railroad utterly devastated by both the Atlanta campaign and Hood's northern Georgia offensive. Cassville, a town of about fifteen hundred people, had only a couple of families left. Houses within several miles of the track were burned, and refugees were allowed to ride the trains northward as a corridor stretching between Chattanooga and Atlanta was stripped of signs of civilization. For Sherman's men, the chase after Hood had involved a march of some three hundred miles during the course of one month, with little to show for it except a determination to continue the offensive southward at the earliest moment.[12]

Franklin

Hood's drive northward was delayed three weeks at Florence as the Confederate commander tried to gather supplies to support his invasion of middle Tennessee. He could not establish a cordial working relationship with Beauregard, even though his superior made every effort to rebuild the railroads in the region to supply him. The logistics never really worked, for there was insufficient material or time to get the railroads operating before the end of November. Beauregard even sought to reoccupy and refortify Corinth as a major base of operations, since the Federals had evacuated the town the previous January. Hood promised to set out by November 5 anyway, a promise he could not keep due to the lack of food. His quartermasters tried to round up all the provisions they could find near Florence, but the entire Tennessee Valley had already been stripped of resources by this late period of the war.[13]

Hood also waited for Forrest, who was striking at the Federal supply system by attacking Johnsonville, a depot on the east bank of the Tennessee River about seventy-five miles west of Nashville. Union quartermasters had accumulated a vast amount of material at Johnsonville after a railroad had been opened up linking it with the capital to supplement boat traffic on the Tennessee. Forrest got the drop on Union defenders and managed to destroy four gunboats, fourteen transports, twenty barges, and twenty-six guns at the depot. His men destroyed an estimated $2.2 million worth of government property and took 150 prisoners in one of the most destructive Rebel raids of the war.[14]

By November 17, Hood had accumulated only seven days of provisions for his army, much less than the targeted twenty days' supply he felt he needed before setting out. News of Sherman's departure from Atlanta on November 15 prompted a consultation with Beauregard, and both officers agreed that it would be useless to chase his command across central Georgia. Only a quick strike into middle Tennessee was possible, but Hood delayed several more days as President Davis lost patience with his young commander, desperate for some move to compel Sherman's recall. On November 21 the Army of Tennessee set out from the Florence area with inadequate supplies.[15]

Anticipating Hood's offensive, the Federals had adopted a defensive posture to meet it. On November 5 Schofield moved his Twenty-third Corps to Nashville sending some men temporarily to Johnsonville on news of Forrest's raid there. By November 13 the corps assembled by rail at Pulaski, about seventy miles south of Nashville near the Tennessee-Alabama border, where Schofield assumed command of the Fourth Corps as well. Schofield watched and waited for the expected Confederate advance.[16]

With signs of Hood's movement, Schofield pulled out of Pulaski on November 24 and retired to Columbia, thirty miles north. His men dug in as Hood sought to flank them out of town, setting up a pattern to be followed for the next several days. The Army of Tennessee aimed for Spring Hill, a village located ten miles north of Columbia, and nearly got there in time to block Schofield's retreat. Hood's vanguard arrived on the evening of November 29 and attacked two Federal brigades holding the area, but they were stopped by Fourth Corps artillery. A variety of factors wrecked Confederate plans to concentrate at Spring Hill and trap the Federals, including the lack of precise information about enemy positions, the lack of communication among Hood's subordinates, and the coming of darkness. A certain degree of poor judgment among corps and division commanders, and poor work by their staff, seem to have been the key elements in the Spring Hill disappointment. At any rate, Schofield's two corps managed to march past the Confederates that night, saving a vital element of the Union defense force in middle Tennessee by the narrowest of margins.[17]

"The best move in my career as a soldier, I was thus destined to behold come to naught," Hood complained in his memoirs. Again, he blamed the army's reluctance to take the tactical offensive, stemming from the defensive policy pursued by Johnston during the Atlanta campaign. "In my inmost heart I questioned whether or not I would ever succeed in eradicating this evil." Frustrated and seemingly bent on teaching his men how to fight, Hood moved north to find that Schofield had taken a defensive position at Franklin, only thirty miles south of Nashville, because the wagon bridge over the Harpeth River needed to be rebuilt. The Federals had improved the earthworks guarding the southern approach to the town, fronted by a wide, open slope that presented a good killing field for the defender. Hood was determined to strike the enemy with nearly twenty thousand men, even before most of his artillery had reached the field. The Federals, seventeen thousand strong, could not have guessed that the Confederates would risk such a fight on these terms.[18]

When the Army of Tennessee began its attack at about 4:00 P.M., the entire battlefield was open to clear view from the Federal side. Two Union brigades, however, remained in a forward, isolated position one mile before the main line. This was the only fault in Union dispositions, for the Confederate line overwhelmed these Federals and forced them to retreat in disorder along the Columbia Pike. It caused confusion in the main line along the pike as well, and the Confederates temporarily held the Union works until a reserve brigade commanded by Colonel Emerson Opdycke moved forward and sealed the breach. The battle of Franklin centered at this spot, where seven of eighteen Confederate brigades were engaged.[19]

The battle of Franklin was among the bloodiest engagements of the war. On the far Federal left, the Yankees waited until their enemy was fifty to seventy yards away before they "rose as a blue wave & a wall of fire rose that swept our ranks like hail," as a member of the 35th Alabama described it. Also on the Union left, Federal officers could see their counterparts in gray "frantically rushing at the head of their commands right up to the Cannons Mouth—where they would disappear." On many parts of the line, thousands of Confederate troops crowded close in to the Federal works and held there for several hours, exchanging fire with their opponents well after darkness in a vain effort to break through. The slaughter continued for approximately five hours, but, after their initial and limited success along the Columbia Pike, Hood's men failed to accomplish anything.[20]

It had been a terrible battle with an unsupportable cost for the Army of Tennessee. Hood lost about 7,000 men, including 13 out of 28 general officers. A total of 65 Confederate division, brigade, and regimental commanders fell at Franklin. Schofield lost 2,326 men and pulled his command out of the works that night as he completed his withdrawal to Nashville. The Confederates surveyed the field the next morning with astonishment. It had the "appearance of a *slaughter-pen*," wrote a member of the 19th Louisiana. The ditch in front of the Union earthworks was "filled with dead, dying and wounded Confederates." In places, the casualties seemed to lay four feet deep, and horses mingled with men in their death agonies.[21]

Nashville

Despite everything, Hood's invasion of middle Tennessee had taken the Confederate army all the way to Nashville. Grant was deeply disturbed that his subordinates in the West did not attack the Army of Tennessee after the bloodletting at Franklin rather than retreat northward. He worried that Hood might disrupt the railroad to Chattanooga if left alone. Grant admitted that he did not have a complete understanding of the situation from City Point, but it seemed to the general in chief that George Thomas was taking a great risk in not moving against Hood as soon as possible.[22]

The view of Hood's campaign from the Confederate side was equally desperate. Beauregard feared that Sherman was headed for Petersburg with the intention of driving Lee out of his fortified lines; he hoped that any success Hood could achieve in Tennessee would counterbalance the moral effect of the Confederate capital's fall. Several officials in Richmond continued to argue that Kentucky was ripe for the picking, urging the authorities to push Hood past Nashville and into the border state to liberate Southern partisans from Federal oppression and recruit thousands of fresh troops.[23]

The view from the ground, just south of Nashville, was quite different from these distant perspectives. Hood's army was in no shape to bypass Nashville and attempt a risky invasion of Kentucky, nor did it seem to have much hope of holding its ground in the face of the large concentration of troops from all across the Western theater that Thomas was masterminding. Hood did what Bragg had done after Chickamauga—assume a defensive position and await developments. His men worked to fortify a pretty strong position on the hills south of the state capital, acquiring the materials to make shoes for those men who were unshod and trying to find enough food to keep body and soul together. The situation did not escape the attentive. Douglas Cater of the 19th Louisiana was reminded of what had happened at Missionary Ridge. "I would not say this if the battle of Franklin had not taken place," he admitted.[24]

Thomas prepared well for the final attack against Hood, but his delays wore on the patience of Grant and other authorities in the East. The Virginia-born general had a widespread reputation for slowness and extreme caution, and Grant naturally distrusted his judgment in this situation. As early as December 9, he was ready to replace Thomas with Schofield. Thomas was about to strike on December 10 but was thwarted by "a terrible storm of

Federal line of defense near Nashville. This view shows a section of the Union line opposing Hood's army. (Library of Congress, LC-DIG-cwpb-02087)

freezing rain." He was fully aware of Grant's anxiety and primed to step aside for another commander of Grant's choosing but argued that all delays were unavoidable. Grant canceled plans to replace him as the hills around Nashville remained covered with ice throughout December 11–13. It began to warm up on December 14, and Thomas promised to attack the next day. Grant, however, continued to worry about what he called the "mortifying spectacle" of Hood racing toward the Ohio River, though how he expected the Confederates to move across the ice when the Federals could not was never explained. He made arrangements to send John A. Logan, who had been on a leave of absence to campaign for Lincoln in the North during the fall, to go to Nashville and take charge of affairs. After Logan was on his way, Grant decided to go to Nashville himself.[25]

Grant's anxiety was ill-placed and based on his lack of trust in Thomas as an independent commander. When he reached Washington, a message arrived from Nashville indicating that the long-anticipated attack against Hood had begun. Grant canceled the rest of his trip. Logan also declined to take control of affairs when he learned that Thomas had started, and the ponderous commander of the Department of the Cumberland had a chance to end Hood's invasion of Tennessee.[26]

The result was everything that could be expected of any general. The Federals, who outnumbered Hood with about fifty-five thousand men, including a large force of cavalry and black infantry, struck on December 15. They punished the Army of Tennessee—approximately twenty-three thousand men strong—and forced Hood to retire about two miles south to a more compact defensive position anchored on two hills. Here, the Confederates were soundly defeated on December 16. Many of Hood's men fled in panic once their line broke in what Douglas Cater had feared: a repetition of Missionary Ridge. Casualties in the two-day battle amounted to 3,000 Federals and 6,500 Confederates.[27]

Although Thomas mounted a pursuit of the flying enemy, Hood's men managed to evade their worst fate. Yet they suffered enormously in their headlong retreat. A staff officer reported seeing bloody footprints in the snow as the weather worsened in late December. Some fifteen thousand members of the Army of Tennessee made it to Tupelo by early January, but probably less than half that number were in any condition to fight. Douglas Cater called the remnant "a demoralized wreck. Nearly all without shoes & with worn out garments and added to this a *ear of corn* in each man's haversack to check the awful *epidemic—hunger*." The weather had done its worst for Hood; "Rain, snow, wind, *mud*," as Cater expressed it.[28]

Hunger, combined with demoralization, led Hood's survivors to impose themselves on the civilians around Tupelo to such an extent that officers were forced to take drastic measures. The perpetrators often used their guns, in what amounted to armed robbery by Confederate soldiers of Southern civilians. Instructions went out to Forrest to use reliable cavalrymen to chase deserters as infantry commanders were enjoined to keep their men busy with camp chores so they could not slip away.[29]

The result of Hood's Tennessee campaign was, of course, demoralizing to Confederate partisans. Isham G. Harris, who accompanied Hood, had been unable to recruit Confederate troops from among the population of middle Tennessee. For the Federals, the sound defeat at Nashville had "operated like a charm. Every body seems submissive." As soon as the Confederates retreated across the Tennessee River, Federal forces reclaimed areas of south-central Tennessee and northern Alabama that they had given up in the early stages of the campaign. The time seemed ripe to reconstruct the civil government of the state, and Andrew Johnson was ready. "The effect of the great victory over Hood's army at Nashville is being seen and felt in every part of the State," he told Thomas. "Its withering influence upon rebels is more decided than anything which has transpired since the beginning of the rebellion." Johnson's call for a state constitutional convention to meet early in January began the process of reconstructing Tennessee before the president or Congress could agree on a national policy for that important task. Johnson himself prepared to leave Nashville to become Lincoln's new vice president. For George Thomas, another dividend of Hood's defeat was the opportunity to send troops out of Tennessee to operate against scattered Confederate forces in the Deep South.[30]

March to the Sea

One of the greatest ironies of the Civil War took place in late October and early November 1864 as the two main concentrations of Federal and Confederate strength in the West worked assiduously to gather supplies for a major campaign, one in northern Georgia and the other in northern Alabama, with the intention of driving in different directions instead of toward each other. Sherman relied heavily on Thomas and Schofield to handle affairs against Hood as his men accumulated food and tore up the logistical network around Atlanta in preparation for abandoning the city they had suffered so much to capture. The tracks and all garrisons south of the Etowah River were broken up and the important buildings in Atlanta that were useful for military purposes were destroyed. Twentieth Corps troops, under the direction of engineer Orlando Poe, worked from November 13 to 16 to destroy and to prevent flames from spreading promiscuously throughout the city. Sherman had twenty days' worth of rations for his troops and five days' worth of forage for his animals by the time he was ready to set out from Atlanta on November 15, six days before Hood left Florence for middle Tennessee. "This Army is now ready to march to Mobile, Savannah or Charleston," Sherman told his wife. "We wont starve in Georgia."[31]

When they left Atlanta his men had "a 'devil-may-care' feeling," generally believing that "we were marching for Richmond, and that there we should end the war." Making about fifteen miles per day, Sherman's expectations of finding food were proved right. As soon as his sixty thousand men cleared the Atlanta area, everything from corn to molasses, bacon, sweet potatoes, and beef were available for the taking. Central Georgia had never been traversed by hostile armies before, and the farmers had just harvested their crops. The ease with which the Federals conducted this march proved Sherman's point that raiding the Deep South with large, mobile columns of infantry was the best strategy to follow.[32]

The Federals entered the state capital of Milledgeville on November 23, but they engaged in no widespread destruction of its buildings. Sherman's host lingered only two days before moving on. The only pitched battle of the campaign took place near Griswoldville, about twenty miles southwest of

Railroad depot at Atlanta, the end of the line for the long Union supply system that stretched from Louisville, Kentucky. (Library of Congress, LC-DIG-cwpb-02223)

Milledgeville, where 2,300 Georgia State Line troops, Georgia Militia, and Georgia Reserves confronted a detached brigade of the Fifteenth Corps on November 24. The local troops conducted an attack on the Federals and were mauled, losing 472 men compared to only 51 Union casualties.[33]

With the full confidence of his troops, Sherman demonstrated throughout the March to the Sea that the Confederacy was unable to protect its heartland. "'Pierce the *shell* of the C. S. A. and it's all hollow inside,'" he told one of his staff officers. The Federals devoured food as they moved steadily across the Georgia piedmont toward the sea, and Sherman could only say to

Sherman leaves Atlanta. The Federals begin their March to the Sea by leaving Atlanta on November 15, 1864. (Johnson and Buel, *Battles and Leaders*, 4:666)

complaining civilians that it was not his fault. If "Jeff Davis expects to found an empire on the ruins of the South," he reported telling residents, "he ought to afford to feed the People."[34]

The Confederates struggled to marshal strength to oppose Sherman. Beauregard cogently explained to Jefferson Davis that, with the rail system so poor and an additional distance of 275 miles to march the poorly shod men, it was useless to try to shift Hood's army back to Georgia. He believed reports that thirty thousand other troops could be assembled to oppose Sherman's march were exaggerated. It was impossible for Robert E. Lee to provide men for this purpose without giving up Petersburg and Richmond. Moreover, Grant was fully alert to the possibility that Lee might send help and was ready to pursue any detachment of strength that left Petersburg. Confederate political leaders tried to rouse the populace to arms. "Every citizen with his gun, and every negro with his spade and axe, can do the work of a soldier," proclaimed Senator B. H. Hill to the people of Georgia. Beauregard issued a similar call to the citizenry.[35]

The only force that could be assembled to oppose Sherman, other than the militia, was Joseph Wheeler's cavalry division. Although it had no hope of stopping sixty thousand men, Wheeler's horsemen could relay information about Federal movements and harass Sherman's van. Wheeler attempted a scorched-earth policy by telling civilians they had to drive their

Federal method of destroying railroads. In this previously unpublished photograph, Federal troops burn ties to heat rails and render them useless. (Library of Congress, LC-DIG-cwpb-01332)

stock away if they were in the path of the Federal advance. If they refused, his troopers were responsible for moving the animals. The cavalrymen also burned what corn and fodder they could not consume, even in areas not traversed by the Federals, contributing to the suffering of civilians. These residents' food stocks were depleted and farm animals taken away, making a grim prospect for the next growing season. A general impression emerged among Confederates and Southern civilians that "Wheelers cavalry—are far more terrible to Confederates—than to Yankees." Wheeler sought to defend his command's reputation by reporting that many plunderers only claimed to belong to his command. He issued orders to clamp down on pillaging, appealing to his troopers' sense of pride in their unit.[36]

Two-thirds of the way from Atlanta to Savannah, the Federals left the piedmont and entered the coastal plain. Sherman reported that the terrain became "more sandy and barren," and "food became more scarce." Like Wheeler's men, the Federals wantonly pillaged at times—enough to elicit an order from Howard threatening to shoot anyone found doing so. In general, however, the Federals resisted the worst temptations to throw discipline to the winds. "The nature of the march was calculated to relax discipline," commented division commander Alpheus Williams, yet "comparatively little trouble" occurred and mostly by those men who were always "disorderly and vicious."[37]

The only other pitched battle associated with the March to the Sea, besides that at Griswoldville, occurred at Honey Hill near Grahamville, South Carolina. Brigadier General John P. Hatch struck at the Charleston and Savannah Railroad to prevent the possibility of reinforcements from reaching Georgia from points farther north and was met by a force of Confederates in a fortified position on November 30. The Federals were repulsed with a loss of 750 men, but the results of the engagement at Honey Hill had no effect on the course of Sherman's progress.[38]

After the Federals left Atlanta and moved far away, Confederate authorities reentered the city and evaluated the damage. They reported the rail network around Atlanta to be devastated: forty-six miles of track from the Etowah River to the city and all bridges along the way had been destroyed. Repairs to this stretch were begun by December 16. Along the Georgia Railroad east of Atlanta, thirty-eight miles of track had to be rebuilt and the best estimate was that it could be done by mid-February 1865. The same was true of the lines toward West Point and Macon. Atlanta could not become a significant factor in the Confederate war effort for some time to come, if ever. Meanwhile, the authorities found some citizens still in Atlanta who had cooperated with the Federals during the occupation. About ten of them were arrested and sent to Macon, where a civilian judge was appointed to try them.[39]

The Federals, who had done so much damage to Atlanta, neared the end of their campaign as they approached Savannah in mid-December 1864. The city was ringed with a strong system of earthwork defenses, as well as numerous forts guarding the approach by sea up the Savannah River. Sherman wanted to make contact with the Union fleet offshore as soon as possible, so he assigned his old division of the Fifteenth Corps, now commanded by Major General William B. Hazen, to seize Fort McAllister. Located seven miles up the Ogeechee River and twelve miles from Savannah, the strong fort had repelled a Union gunboat attack early in 1863. The garrison was small and its guns were not pointed inland, yet dozens of torpedoes added to the obstacles faced by Hazen's attacking column. The Federals conducted a quick strike on December 13 with three thousand men, losing many to the torpedoes and to the surprisingly stiff fighting inside the work by the garrison, which was outnumbered fifteen to one. After an hour of combat, the Confederates were overwhelmed and Sherman opened up communications with the outside world for the first time since leaving Atlanta.[40]

McAllister was an isolated post located outside the system of defenses that ringed Savannah. Lieutenant General William J. Hardee and about ten thousand Confederates held the main works, which in places were fronted by flooded rice fields and swamps. But it was possible that Sherman would not need to capture the city. A dispatch from Grant awaited his arrival in the area, instructing him to bring his infantry to Petersburg as soon as possible by sea transport, leaving his cavalry, wagons, and artillery in an entrenched camp. Sherman was disappointed that he could not have the satisfaction of capturing Savannah, but he began to prepare an entrenched camp at Fort McAllister. It was estimated that the navy would need a hundred ships to transport his infantry. By December 18, however, Grant changed his mind after being told that it would take two months to move Sherman's sixty thousand men by sea. Grant allowed him to operate against Savannah for the time being, but Sherman tried to win the city by maneuver rather than by assault. His efforts to cut Hardee off and invest Savannah forced the Confederates to evacuate the city on the night of December 21. Sherman had the town, even though he could not trap the garrison. "I beg to present you, as a Christmas gift, the city of Savannah," he informed Lincoln the next day, with 150 guns and 25,000 bales of cotton.[41]

The fall of Savannah completed the eventful March to the Sea, but immediately after taking up residence in the city Sherman's mind was on his next move. He relished the opportunity to continue his march northward, through the Carolinas, confident that Lee would abandon Petersburg and Richmond as soon as his men reached Weldon or Raleigh. Sherman felt certain his troops could handle the Army of Northern Virginia, especially with Grant hounding its tail. If worse came to worse, Sherman could fight his way back to the coast for safety. "I think the time has come now when we should attempt the boldest moves," he informed Halleck. He viewed his March to the Sea and his future moves "as much a direct attack upon Lee's army as though I were operating within the sound of his artillery."[42]

In addition, Sherman felt that his army was "burning with an insatiable desire to wreak vengeance upon South Carolina. I almost tremble at her fate, but feel that she deserves all that seems in store for her." Sherman considered making war against the recalcitrant element in Southern society as an important objective of his campaigns. "We are not only fighting hostile armies, but a hostile people," he continued while explaining his motives to Halleck, "and must make old and young, rich and poor, feel the hard hand of war, as well as their organized armies."[43]

Sherman had already administered similar treatment to Georgia. He estimated that his men had taken ten thousand horses and mules, destroyed

$80 million worth of property, and consumed $20 million worth of resources. "We have left nothing but desolation behind us," wrote Poe to his wife. "The rebel state of Georgia will long have cause to remember the march of Sherman's Army!" The impact of his campaign, combined with the defeat of Hood, led Federal observers to feel that "we shall see daylight this coming spring." The March to the Sea had "almost disemboweled the rebellion," thought division leader John Geary, but Sherman continued to think of it primarily "as the transfer of a strong army" from the interior of the South to the coast, from where it could move on to a vital theater of operations in Virginia.[44]

Lincoln had approved Sherman's move only reluctantly, but he was impressed by the fact that the Federals had the strength to divide their forces in the West in order to deal with Hood in one sector and conduct the campaign to Savannah in another area simultaneously. He insisted that Thomas's victory be seen as a component of Sherman's March to the Sea; in fact, the Federals in middle Tennessee had made it possible for Sherman to move to Savannah. Lincoln made the most of these thoughts by expressing them in his annual message to Congress on December 6. Sherman seemed ignorant of the details attending Thomas's battle at Nashville, writing his subordinate after reaching Savannah that he was relieved at the outcome. "Had any misfortune fallen you I should have reproached myself for taking away so large [a] proportion of the army and leaving you too weak to cope with Hood. But as events have turned out my judgment has been sustained." In fact, Schofield waited until writing his memoirs, long after Sherman had died, before publicly voicing criticism of his former commander for taking so many troops on a campaign where they were opposed by so few Confederates, while the Federals had to scramble and fight bloody battles to retain control of middle Tennessee. He cogently offered many alternatives to Sherman's course of action, albeit all of them offered with the benefit of hindsight.[45]

Confederate morale was severely affected by the results of Sherman's march and the defeat of Hood, as Southerners could see little light in these events. Birkett D. Fry, commander of the post at Augusta, informed President Davis that Sherman's operation "has had a paralizing effect upon the people." The fact that he treated the citizens of Savannah leniently, in contrast to his policy in Atlanta, also weakened civilian morale to resist Federal occupation. Many citizens "are almost prepared to abandon the struggle and submit to the Yankee yoke," Fry moaned.[46]

Fry was correct in his interpretation of Sherman's occupation policy in Savannah, but the main reason for leniency was that the city was useful to the Federals as a logistical point. The large amount of cotton in Savannah was an object of concern for the Washington authorities as well. Secretary Stanton anxiously told Grant to order its seizure immediately and to disregard any ploys by civilians to retain ownership of even one bale. The difference was that Stanton did not want to turn the cotton over to Treasury agents but use it instead for the benefit of the War Department. Sherman initially allowed the Treasury representative to move it to New York, but he canceled that order on learning of his superior's wishes. The total amounted to thirty-one thousand bales rather than twenty-five thousand. When Stanton personally traveled to Savannah on January 11, 1865, he took charge of the lot.[47]

Sherman was now in the Department of the South, but he was given administrative authority over all the ground his Western troops traversed. He therefore implemented the same general policy regarding trade and cotton as existed in the Military Division of the Mississippi, working through the commander of the Department of the South, Major General John G. Foster. "We should assume a tone of perfect contempt for cotton and everything else in comparison with the great object of the war—the restoration of the Union," he informed Stanton. To counter Confederate harassment of civilians, Sherman also encouraged area citizens to organize militia forces and promised to track down and punish perpetrators of crimes. He also opened up the cities within the department for the sale of locally grown produce. Stanton urged Foster to deport recalcitrant families outside the Union line, "so that they may enjoy the society and share the fortunes of their husbands and fathers," as Halleck put it.[48]

The relatively good conduct of Sherman's men in Savannah, and the general's comparatively gentle policies there, helped a great deal to reconcile residents to Federal occupation. Stories of Union pillaging had frightened the residents until they "regard[ed] us just as the Romans did the Goths and the parallel is not unjust," Sherman thought. The "rather vandalic march" contrasted sharply with the benign occupation of Savannah, demonstrating in Federal eyes commendable discipline. Savannah itself impressed nearly every Yankee who had a chance to tour its sights. "The City beats any thing we have seen in the south yet," effused Edward W. Allen of the 16th Wisconsin.[49]

The discipline exhibited by the Federals was even more commendable when one considers that the men suffered for want of food while at Savannah. Alpheus Williams reported that his troops fared much worse near Savannah than while marching through Georgia. Not only were there too few coastal transports available to move Sherman's host to Virginia in a timely manner, but there also were too few vessels to haul food for men and forage for animals, and local farms were not productive enough to take up the slack. Sherman did not have the luxury, or the inclination, to stay long in Savannah.[50]

The March to the Sea had produced a huge problem involving black refugees, for it traversed an untouched area with a heavy population of slaves. Federal officers could only estimate how many of them tagged along with Sherman's column. Henry W. Slocum, who commanded half of Sherman's force, believed that 17,000 slaves accompanied his wing for at least part of the distance. Alpheus Williams estimated that up to 8,000 followed his division, with 2,500 of them sticking to the end of the campaign. Sherman himself placed the number at 20,000 when he reached Savannah. The Department of the South already had a large complement of black refugees before Sherman arrived, and John Eaton estimated that a total of 82,000 were on Foster's hands by early January 1865.[51]

Controversy dogged Sherman's handling of the refugee problem, and not without some justification. Though remaining sympathetic to the plight of the blacks, he viewed military considerations of paramount importance. Halleck warned him of rumors in Washington that Sherman's men had abandoned a large group of refugees on the march, and soon afterward they were slaughtered by Wheeler's cavalry. In fact, the primary reason for Stanton's visit to Savannah had been to quietly investigate these charges. Sherman defended himself and his command by explaining that the incident had occurred when Fourteenth Corps commander Jefferson C. Davis had to take up a pontoon bridge over Ebenezer Creek to use it for bridging other streams ahead of his column, isolating a group of refugees who were attacked by the Confederates.[52]

In truth, Sherman cooperated in an enlightened policy of trying to settle the refugees on productive land along the coast. The sea islands south of Charleston held many abandoned rice plantations, and Brigadier General Rufus Saxton was placed in charge of overseeing the shipment of refugees to work those lands. Many abandoned farms and plantations for thirty miles up the major rivers in South Carolina and Georgia could be used as well. According to Alpheus Williams, seventeen hundred of the twenty-five hundred refugees who had accompanied his division to Savannah wound up on Coleraine Plantation along the Savannah River. Nearly five hundred more were employed by the army as teamsters and servants. Able-bodied males also were recruited for the Union army. Initial plans to ship them to City Point for organization into units were dropped, probably due to the scarcity of transports, so they were organized at Savannah. But Sherman suggested that black troops not be used to garrison the city. "It seems a perfect bugbear to" the citizens, he wrote.[53]

By the end of 1864, then, the war in the West had taken a dramatic turn compared to the previous twelve months. The main Confederate army had dwindled from nearly sixty thousand men to a mere shell of its former self, and large Federal forces had traversed interior sections of the Confederacy without hindrance. "Where is our Western Army under Genl. Hood[?]," complained a doctor in South Carolina to President Davis. "What has he accomplished . . . on the bleak hills of Tenn.[?]." The crushing defeat of still another Confederate offensive had a more depressing effect on Southern morale, thought Howell Cobb, than Sherman's March to the Sea. The twin events nearly brought major operations to a close in the West, although there were many smaller Confederate forces left and much territory for the Federals yet to penetrate and control.[54]

15 } The Last Campaigns

After receiving authorization to march through North Carolina and South Carolina on January 2, 1865, General William T. Sherman prepared for a move that would be far more difficult and complex than his march across Georgia. He playfully informed his wife that he intended to "dive again beneath the Surface to turn up again in Some mysterious place." Sherman admitted that Robert E. Lee would probably "not let me walk over the track without making me sustain some loss," but he had a clear idea of what he intended to do and how he meant to do it. "We will be along soon," he wrote David D. Porter, "and the braggart Carolinians will find in our Western boys a different kind of metal."[1]

Keeping sixty thousand men supplied as they marched across the Carolinas was Sherman's biggest worry. He gambled that they could find enough food along the way until the army reached Goldsboro, North Carolina, where it could make contact with a rail system to bring in supplies from coastal shipping. Grant planned to funnel all the provisions he could to meet Sherman's command. He even contemplated shipping these troops from any port held by Union forces the rest of the way to Petersburg, though the lieutenant general preferred that Sherman march all the way to the rear of Lee's position. Sherman planned to "gradually close in" on Lee, "cutting all communications" much as he had treated Hood at Atlanta. He even offered to send a good division or corps commander to replace Major General Benjamin F. Butler at the head of the Army of the James, which was cooperating with the Army of the Potomac along the Petersburg lines. He had several "new and fresh men, able to handle large armies." As for John Bell Hood, Grant assumed that, after the defeat at Nashville, the Army of Tennessee would be shifted to the Carolinas to oppose Sherman. This was "just where we want him to go," Grant informed Henry Halleck.[2]

Unlike Sherman's departure from Atlanta, the start of the Carolinas campaign involved a difficult movement across the Savannah River, with Henry W. Slocum and Oliver O. Howard moving their commands in different directions. Sherman left Savannah in charge

Marching through the Carolinas. This sketch illustrates the difficulties encountered as Sherman's large army group struggled through the lowlands of South Carolina in winter. (Johnson and Buel, *Battles and Leaders*, 4:681)

of John Foster and took his staff on a steamer headed for Beaufort, South Carolina, on January 21. Howard shifted the Seventeenth Corps from Savannah to Beaufort by February 10, using only a handful of available boats. From Beaufort, Frank Blair marched his Seventeenth Corps twenty-five miles to Pocotaligo, where a Confederate fort had secured control of the vital Charleston and Savannah Railroad since early in the war. The Federals occupied the fort without opposition. Meanwhile, Slocum crossed the Savannah River at Sister's Ferry, encountering land mines planted by the Confederates. Though rain delayed all movements, Sherman was able to reunite his command along the railroad linking Charleston with Augusta by mid-February. The Federals tore up fifty miles of track while accumulating food in the region, then advanced north toward Orangeburg to hit the rail line linking Charleston with Columbia.[3]

The weather and terrain became a worse enemy than the Confederates, at least during the early part of the Carolinas campaign. Twentieth Corps commander Alpheus Williams referred to the "devilish nature of the country," with rivers that ran in "six to ten channels with the worst entangled swamps between, often three miles wide." Small Confederate forces dug in on the opposite side of these streams, and "it took a good deal of skirmishing in water waist-deep to get them out." Between the crossings of each river lay roads that stretched across sandy, soft ground. With several days of winter rains,

Federals destroying a railroad. A dramatic illustration of how a brigade could tear up a railroad quickly and effectively. (Johnson and Buel, *Battles and Leaders,* 4:684)

these roads seemed to lose their bottom. "Corduroy would sink, again and again," Williams continued. "But we became expert road-makers, first piling on all the fence rails and then cutting the young pines." A member of Williams's corps reported that his feet seemed to weigh fifty pounds each from accumulated mud and water after crossing the wide lowland of one river.[4]

Although many Federals had a desire to teach South Carolina a lesson for starting the war, others tried to curb overly destructive tendencies. A division commander in the Seventeenth Corps called on his troops to remember their own families and leave "a fair share of provisions" for the Carolinians. Howard also tried to clamp down on pillaging, and John A. Logan, who resumed command of the Fifteenth Corps just before the onset of the march through South Carolina, called plundering "disgraceful in the extreme." Efforts were made to organize a better system of foraging so officers could more easily control their men and to protect foragers from attacks by scattered Confederates. In many ways, the journey through the Carolinas proved to be more dangerous than the comparatively easy passage through Georgia.[5]

The mission to wreck Confederate logistical systems remained the same, however. Sherman's chief engineer, Captain Orlando M. Poe, issued instructions for the systematic destruction of railroads so everything from ties to rails could be made unusable. "Tell [Alpheus] Williams I have inspected his work here," Sherman wrote Slocum from Graham's Station, "and the bars are not twisted; better do half the quantity, but do it thoroughly."[6]

Columbia, the capital of South Carolina, felt the impact of Sherman's march more than any other city, though not necessarily through the Federals' intention. Confederate forces evacuated the city on the night of February 16–17, setting a few fires before leaving. The Yankees who first entered Columbia the next morning found many citizens eager to please; they offered a considerable amount of alcohol to the soldiers, inadvertently creating trouble. Federal commanders assigned 4,500 men to provost duty by the afternoon of February 17 as more soldiers entered town. Fires began to spread, especially among several hundred bales of cotton that the Confederates had lined along the streets but had not had time to burn before they evacuated. A strong northwest wind swept across the area and spread sparks from the burning cotton everywhere that evening, creating a firestorm that nearly destroyed all of Columbia.[7]

There is no doubt that some Federals helped the blaze along; in fact, about forty Yankee soldiers perished on the night of February 17 because they were too drunk to evade the flames or were shot by provost guards. Escaped civilian convicts also contributed to the disaster by burning and looting. But the true culprit in the destruction of Columbia was nature, and thousands of Federals risked their lives in trying to contain the fires. They were able to gain control of the situation only after the wind abated about 3:00 A.M. on February 18, but by then 265 private residences had been destroyed.[8]

At dawn, the residents of Columbia seemed "stupefied by the terror of last night," according to Thomas Osborn, Howard's artillery chief. Nearly three-fourths of the city was gone, replaced by "a forest of chimneys." The burning of Columbia created a big refugee problem for Sherman, as families of all classes and political sympathies were now homeless and without food or clothing. He offered the mayor five hundred head of cattle and recommended he urge the citizens to find charitable families in the countryside who were willing to take them in. Sherman even suggested the refugees organize foraging parties like his own men did to scrounge up food. During the remainder of their brief stay in Columbia, the Federals destroyed material of potential usefulness to the Confederate war effort, including one thousand bales of cotton, nineteen locomotives, the railroad depot and warehouses, and powder mills.[9]

Leaving the ruined city behind, Sherman again concentrated on wrecking the railroad system as his columns continued toward Petersburg. He considered the occupation of major cities as of secondary importance to the "utter demolition of the railroad system of South Carolina." In addition to denying the Confederates the use of these facilities, Sherman valued the emotional impact of destroying vital resources deep in the heart of the Confederate nation, in areas once "regarded as inaccessible to us." It demonstrated that there was "now no place in the Confederacy" that was "safe against the Army of the West."[10]

Several of Sherman's subordinates tried to restrain their troops as they approached North Carolina, reminding them that it was one of the last states to secede and that many of its inhabitants were loyal to the Union. They called for "a marked difference" in the manner of treating its citizens compared to those of South Carolina. Whether such appeals had any effect is doubtful. Howard wrote Blair about a particularly bad incident of soldiers stealing watches, jewelry, and cash from civilians, and then rescuing one of their number with guns when he was arrested. "I am inclined to think that there is a regularly organized banditti who commit these outrages," Howard concluded, "and who share the spoils."[11]

The Federals tried to more tightly control the system of foraging as they neared North Carolina, for they were encountering more Confederates all the time. Every forager captured by the enemy became a potential source of information for the Rebels, and Federal commanders worried about the "bummers'" habit of wantonly torching mills that the army needed to grind grain for its sustenance.[12]

Sherman's only mounted force, a division of cavalry led by Hugh Judson Kilpatrick, bore the brunt of confrontation with Confederate forces along the line of march. On February 21 Kilpatrick lost eighteen men, some of whom had their throats cut. On the same day, eight infantrymen on a foraging detail were caught and shot in cold blood. Their bodies were mutilated, and a paper pinned to their chests read "'Death to foragers.'" Sherman authorized retaliation for this incident. He thought it was justified to kill Confederate prisoners and leave their bodies behind the marching column with an explanation attached to them. But he also wanted to impose greater discipline on his own foragers so they would not be caught, and to prevent them from wantonly destroying private property.[13]

Sherman wrote to Lieutenant General Wade Hampton, commander of Confederate forces in the area, warning him that he, Sherman, had a thousand prisoners and was willing to play the deadly game of an eye for an eye. The Union commander assumed Hampton had not authorized the cold-blooded killing and hoped his warning might avert a repetition. Hampton indeed professed no knowledge of the incident but reminded Sherman of outrages by Federal foragers. He held fifty-six prisoners as hostages, awaiting developments. Both sides squared off in a tense stalemate, but there is no evidence that further executions took place.[14]

To give foragers more mobility, both for gathering food and evading Confederates, a mounted foraging party of twenty men was allowed for each brigade and sixty for each division in the Army of the Tennessee. Howard also ordered that the provost marshal send troops ahead of the marching columns to guard all private houses and prevent senseless destruction.[15]

After the burning of Columbia, eight hundred white citizens and "thousands" of blacks tagged along after Sherman's men when they left the city on February 20. The motivation of the black refugees was assumed, but that of the whites varied. Major Osborn listed the reasons: "To escape starvation, to escape the [Confederate] draft, those who have been kind to our men, to escape the vengeance of the people, and to get what little traps they had where it could be used or sold." Howard assigned an officer to take charge of these civilians and organize a refugee train. The officer was authorized to send troops to forage food for them.[16]

Schofield

As Sherman approached the border between South Carolina and North Carolina, Grant was marshaling a new force to meet him near the coast. Actually, the move was initiated by John Schofield. Only eleven days after Hood's crushing defeat at Nashville, Schofield proposed to Grant that he take the Twenty-third Corps—over twenty thousand strong and mostly veterans of the Knoxville, Atlanta, and Franklin-Nashville campaigns—to assist in operations against Robert E. Lee. He admitted that he had little faith in George Thomas's views on the next step in Western strategy. Thomas's only idea was to operate southward out of Tennessee in the spring, but Schofield thought that moving northward out of Mobile (assuming it could be captured soon) was better. At any rate, Schofield chafed under Thomas's command and wanted to take his corps where it could contribute to victory in a decisive theater of operations. Grant quickly agreed and authorized Schofield's transfer to the East. He viewed Thomas as a stalwart commander on the defensive but too sluggish to conduct a slashing offensive deep into enemy territory.[17]

The transport of the Twenty-third Corps was another case study in the superiority of Union logistics during the Civil War. Starting at Eastport, Mississippi, Union quartermasters shipped 20,000 men and 800 animals 1,400 miles in eleven days, arriving at Washington, D.C. on February 2. The job was made much worse by a spell of winter weather; ice clogged the upper Ohio River, forcing the troops to take cars earlier than planned for the rail trip through the mountains. Only one soldier lost his life when he jumped off the train, fearing an accident was about to happen. Quartermaster Lewis Parsons called it the hardest work of his life, "the most remarkable movement of a large body of Troops in the Annals of warfare."[18]

Rather than add Schofield's men to the forces confronting Lee at Petersburg, Grant shifted the Twenty-third Corps to the North Carolina coast to prepare for Sherman's arrival. Two divisions of the Army of the James, under Major General Alfred H. Terry, had already captured Fort Fisher in a hard-fought battle on January 15. That massive Confederate work guarded the mouth of the Cape Fear River, protecting the port city of Wilmington more than twenty miles upstream. Terry's men closed this most important blockade-running port in the Confederacy, impairing Lee's supply system. Schofield joined his command with Terry's and took overall charge of operations to advance on Wilmington as commander of the newly created Department of North Carolina.[19]

Schofield reached the mouth of the Cape Fear River on February 9 and moved against Wilmington two days later. He advanced along the south side of the stream, flanking the strong Confederate earthworks in his way, until the small Rebel force evacuated the city on February 22. Schofield lost only two hundred men and estimated Confederate losses at one thousand in the capture of the place. He took seventy-five guns as well.[20]

Schofield instituted similar policies for the citizens of his occupied area as those already in place in the West. Trade was opened, according to Treasury Department regulations, but the quantity of goods on hand was restricted to the minimum in order to supply the needs of the demonstrably loyal families of Wilmington. Any one suspected of Confederate sympathies was to be deposited outside Union lines or tried "before a military commission." Terry took charge of shipping forges, shoes, and coffee to Sherman's men to tide them over before they reached the coast.[21]

Sherman's men needed the supplies, but they also needed to lose the black and white refugees who had tagged along since the Federals left Columbia. Sherman told Terry that he had 20,000 to 30,000 "useless mouths" to feed. Each division was responsible for their share; John Corse had to find food for 1,100 refugees who had latched onto his division of the Fifteenth Corps. As soon as Sherman reached Fayetteville, North Carolina, on March 11, he organized shipments of refugees by boat and wagon train to Wilmington. Brigadier General Joseph R. Hawley, commander of the post at Wilmington, already had many local residents on his hands who were indigent and pleading for assistance from the army. At Sherman's suggestion, Hawley began to ship the white refugees to New York so government officials could settle them with jobs and places to live.[22]

Sherman's heavy columns continued plodding along terrible roads and crossing innumerable streams as the men tightened their belts against hunger. The weather continued to offer more trouble than the scattered Confederate horsemen hovering around the van. Federal draft animals were giving out under the stress and inadequate forage; division commanders sometimes took horses from their foraging parties to replace those worn out from hauling ordnance. Sherman maintained a hearty attitude toward his prospects, confident of the endurance of his veterans. "We have swept the country well from Savannah here," he told Terry when communications between Wilmington and his roving army were opened. "The people of South Carolina, instead of feeding Lee's army, will now call on Lee to feed them." Having heard that Joseph E. Johnston had replaced John Bell Hood, and that the Army of Tennessee was heading to North Carolina, Sherman was confident he could handle his old adversary from the Atlanta campaign. But he knew that he would have to move his columns "in compact form" to prevent Johnston from attacking him at a disadvantage.[23]

The Confederates grew increasingly desperate in their attempts to find a way to stop Sherman. Jefferson Davis recognized the terrible strain on Southern morale produced by the inexorable March to the Sea and could think only of shifting what was left of the Army of Tennessee to North Carolina to bolster the garrison troops along the coast. Davis was forced to accede to Johnston's replacement of Hood—if for no other reason than by popular demand. "The cry from the camp and the country is 'Restore General Johnston!'" proclaimed Thomas H. Watts, a civilian, to Davis. "It is manifest now, that a great mistake was made in removing him." Hood was relieved in late January 1865, and a month later Johnston was named his successor. It was nothing short of miraculous that the Confederates could move several thousand troops from Mississippi to North Carolina, bypassing Sherman's moving columns, on the wretched railroads available to them. It was an unheralded logistical feat comparable to Schofield's move to the North Carolina coast. Even William Hardee, who was in charge of the garrison forces assembling in the field, complained that the wretched management of the rail system hindered the movement of his men, and they had far shorter distances to travel than did Johnston's troops.[24]

Meanwhile, P. G. T. Beauregard called on South Carolina citizens to use their slaves to obstruct the roads in front of Sherman. He hoped to assemble up to thirty-five thousand troops and crush the Federals, "then to concentrate all forces against Grant, and then to march on Washington to dictate a peace." It was a bombastic and utterly unrealistic strategic plan, based on Beauregard's mistaken intelligence that Sherman had only thirty-five thousand men.[25]

Robert E. Lee, who assumed the post of general in chief of all Confederate armies on February 6, had a more realistic approach to stopping Sherman. He agreed that concentrating all available forces was the only solution, advocated a scorched earth policy in front of the Federals, and suggested the abandonment of all major cities in the theater of operations. Lee had some hope of success if Sherman could be stopped before he joined Schofield at Goldsboro. He rejected Johnston's suggestion to hold Petersburg with only half the men in the Army of Northern Virginia, sending the rest south to meet Sherman. Lee's troops already were being stretched painfully thin along the thirty-five-mile line of earthworks that covered Petersburg and many of the roads to Richmond. In fact, Lee cautioned his subordinate that, if Sherman reached the Roanoke River, he would have to evacuate Petersburg altogether and try to bring the Army of Northern Virginia south to join the Confederate forces in North Carolina.[26]

Johnston's role in Confederate strategy was to delay the Federals and prevent them from reaching Goldsboro. He saw hope in the report that Sherman was moving his two wings on such an extended front that they would need a day to help each other if attacked. It was a slim chance but all the Confederates could find. Only about seven thousand men under Braxton Bragg barred the advance of Schofield's twenty thousand troops from Wilmington toward Goldsboro. Nevertheless, on March 8 Bragg attacked the Federals near Wyse's Cross Roads and captured some seven hundred Federals who constituted an outpost. The Confederates nearly broke through the Union position at the junction of two divisions, but reserves blocked them. No significant fighting took place the following day. On March 10 Bragg renewed the offensive with another attack, one that achieved nothing but cost him fifteen hundred casualties. Admitting defeat, the Confederates retreated, and Schofield crossed the Neuse River on March 14 to occupy Kinston. He began to repair the railroad and continued to move forward on March 20 to occupy Goldsboro the next day, after the Confederates evacuated the town without a fight.[27]

During the period when Schofield was carefully advancing toward Goldsboro, Hardee evacuated Fayetteville on the night of March 10–11, allowing Sherman's column to thoroughly destroy the state arsenal and other public property in the city. Hardee then positioned his eight thousand men to slow down Sherman's left wing under Slocum in order to separate it even more from the right. The Confederates placed themselves along the road in front of Slocum near Averasboro, where a sharp fight took place between Hardee and the Union's Twentieth Corps on March 16. The Confederates lost 500 men in this delaying action while Slocum suffered 682 casualties. Hardee issued an order congratulating his garrison troops for inflicting "the first serious check" on Sherman since the fall of Atlanta.[28]

Two days after Averasboro, Johnston was able to assemble all the available Rebel troops in North Carolina to meet Sherman in a larger battle. With 7,500 men under Hardee, 6,500 under Bragg, and about 4,000 from the old Army of Tennessee, he struck Slocum's column near Bentonville on March 19, taking the Federals by surprise. Advance units of the Fourteenth Corps ran headlong into Bragg's waiting infantrymen and were driven back when the Confederates counterattacked. Johnston then stepped up the offensive with troops from the Army of Tennessee, nearly isolating Brigadier General James D. Morgan's division of the Fourteenth Corps which held against attacks from several directions. Counterstrikes by other Fourteenth Corps troops helped to save Morgan, whose division turned the tide with its heroic stand to allow Twentieth Corps units to reach the battlefield and extend the Union line. More Confederate attacks later in the day failed to drive the Unionists.[29]

Johnston had come close to achieving a stunning victory on March 19 by marshaling almost as many troops as the Federals on a battlefield of his own choosing. Hard fighting turned the tide; by the end of the day the two forces stared at each other in a tactical stalemate. From that point on, Johnston had little hope of accomplishing any good, for Sherman rushed the rest of his command toward Bentonville as fast as possible. When Howard's right wing closed in to extend the Union position to the right, Johnston was forced to extend his own manpower to confront him. Little more than skirmishing took place on March 20, but the next day the Federals launched an attack that held the potential to crush Johnston's now-outnumbered command. It started as a reconnaissance in force by Joseph Mower's division of the Seventeenth Corps that went so far as to nearly capture a key bridge Johnston relied on as a line of retreat across Mill Creek. In fact, Mower's men forced Johnston to evacuate his own headquarters, and Hardee had to throw troops into a hasty counterattack to save the Confederate left flank. Howard wanted to support Mower and turn this into a battle-winning advance, but Sherman chose the more cautious approach and ordered Mower's recall. The Confederates evacuated the field on the night of March 21, bringing the losses at Bentonville to 1,500 Federals and 2,606 Confederates.[30]

Sherman later regretted that he did not support Mower's attack, as Howard suggested, and try to punish Johnston more severely before the Confederates escaped. But he knew that his supply wagons held little food, and he was desperate to make contact with Schofield at Goldsboro as soon as possible. Logistical needs overrode his battle sense on March 21, but in the long run Bentonville has to be counted as a Federal victory, despite Johnston's initial success.[31]

On entering Goldsboro on March 21, Schofield already had instructions from Sherman to destroy all public property in the city and collect the cotton. Sherman arrived on March 23 to join his force with Schofield's, making a mighty host of 80,000 Western veterans planted only 130 miles south of Petersburg. Even if the Confederates could assemble as many as 45,000 men by combining the troops of Lee and Johnston, Sherman was confident he could handle that number. The railroad link between Goldsboro and the coast was not up to fully supplying 80,000 men, but Sherman felt his troops could continue living off the land when they resumed their march. "We can live where the people do," he told Schofield, "and if anybody has to suffer let them suffer." But Sherman realized that his men needed a rest after their hard march across the Carolinas in midwinter. They needed a resupply of clothing and shoes, and it was impossible to rest for any period of time once they resumed their march. "As long as we move we can gather food and forage," he reported to Grant, "but the moment we stop trouble begins." Sherman set April 10 as the earliest date he could start from Goldsboro. He would have to deal with Johnston, who was covering the roads to Raleigh.[32]

During the march from Savannah to Goldsboro, a distance of 425 miles, Sherman's men had crossed five major rivers and broken up miles of railroad. They had also captured several major cities. The Federals made this march in only fifty days, including ten days of rest. It was a remarkable campaign, equal in Sherman's view to fighting "a dozen successful Battles." The experience of John Logan's Fifteenth Corps perhaps was typical of other units in Sherman's command. Logan started the Carolinas campaign with 16,630 men and lost 441 of them during the march. He took 607 Confederate prisoners, received 106 deserters, and took care of 624 white and 3,252 black refugees. His troops released 39 captives from Rebel prisons. The amount of food and other material taken by the corps was astounding; it included almost half a million pounds of bacon, almost 5,000 pounds of tobacco, over 2 million pounds of corn, and nearly 1 million pounds of fodder for animals. The Fifteenth Corps confiscated 1,600 horses, 1,800 mules, and close to 2,000 cattle, plus nearly 100 wagons to add to its transportation. Logan superintended the destruction of 8,290 bales of cotton and almost forty miles of railroad track, but his men constructed over a hundred miles of corduroy roads and thirty-one bridges along their line of march.[33]

The system of foraging that had taken the Federals of Sherman's command across Georgia and the Carolinas was abolished when Sherman reached Goldsboro. That system had kept the men fed, but it also had created problems injurious to military discipline. While most observers praised the Federal "bummers," others condemned the actions of many of these men. James Morgan, only days after his division's important stand at Bentonville, branded many foragers as little more than "highwaymen, with all their cruelty and ferocity and none of their courage; their victims are usually old men, women, and children, and negroes, whom they rob and maltreat without mercy." Morgan understood the necessity of the Federal system of foraging but wanted to protest its abuses now that the campaign was almost over.[34]

The emotional impact of Sherman's march through the Carolinas was mixed. Many Southerners regarded efforts to stop him as hopeless, while others reacted with anger and defiance. Numerous planter women, left alone to tend their family property, stood up to Sherman's men when they tried to take food. Their anger focused on the enemy rather than the Confederate government, which had failed to protect their homes. Cultural restrictions concerning gender relations often helped their cause, for many high-minded Union soldiers could not bring themselves to maltreat women. Overall, however, the destruction of Southern property and the dire effect of that action told as heavily on the Carolinians as on the Georgians. Sherman's host consisted of sixty thousand individuals with varied attitudes toward the civilians they encountered, engendering potentially sixty thousand different ways that civilians of all genders, ages, and races were treated on any given day of this three-month campaign.[35]

The march through the Carolinas had been a challenge of stamina for Sherman's men. It "tested most thoroughly the power of endurance and elasticity of spirit among American soldiers," as division commander John Geary expressed it. The low-lying, swampy terrain and the harsh winter weather were the most trying elements of the march. Twentieth Corps headquarters carefully documented the number of days of rain—twenty-one out of sixty-seven—and reported that the corps train traveled 456 miles during the campaign, three-fifths of that distance on corduroyed roadway newly made by tired infantrymen. "The loss of sleep was exhausting," reported Seventeenth Corps division commander Manning F. Force. Nearly 18 percent of his men were "entirely barefooted." Force issued rations for only three days during a month's time, his troops finding the rest of their food from the countryside. "At times the men were reduced to living on parched corn; at times they feasted upon abundance," Force reported. Yet they remained in good health and "exuberant spirits."[36]

Force was correct in pointing out that the march had not led to an unusual amount of illness among Sherman's men. According to modern estimates, marching cut the rate of sickness almost in half compared to that of troops who remained stationary, for marching kept the men active and focused on a goal. Sherman had insisted that troops in poor health be weeded out before leaving Atlanta, thus eliminating a portion of the force more likely than not to become ill during the march. The appearance of the Federals on their arrival at Goldsboro was a different matter. Alfred Terry's men initially assumed they were African Americans because their faces were "greasy black" from sitting around campfires made of pine wood. In contrast, Terry's black regiments were well fed, suited in new uniforms, and sported well-polished rifles. "What a contrast did they present to Sherman's veterans," recalled a member of the Twentieth Corps.[37]

Grant and Western Strategy

In coordinating the movements of all Union field armies, Grant never had to worry about Sherman lacking ideas about what to do or being slow to implement directives. But Grant could not count on such support from most other army and department commanders across the wide theater of operations in the West. He complained that there were three movements he had tried to get started early in 1865—in part, to divert Confederate attention away from Sherman's march through the Carolinas—but none of them began early enough to achieve much in the way of larger purposes. The first movement involved a major strike against Mobile by forces under Edward R. S. Canby from New Orleans, one that Grant and Nathaniel Banks had contemplated soon after the fall of Vicksburg. Second, Grant wanted George Thomas to push troops south from Tennessee to penetrate the interior of Alabama, capturing important industrial cities like Selma and bringing the war home to areas that had never seen a Yankee soldier before. The third movement Grant envisioned was a small-scale cavalry raid from Knoxville into the mountains of North Carolina. Of the three campaigns, the last would most directly support Sherman's march.[38]

Neither Grant nor Halleck had any confidence that Thomas could take the offensive after his victory at Nashville and carry the war into what was left of the Confederacy. While both commanders admired Thomas's stamina and defensive prowess, they believed he was too cautious to strike out into unknown territory and live off the land. In fact, Thomas had announced his intention of going into winter quarters until the spring of 1865 offered an opportunity to resume operations. Halleck found that plan unacceptable. He cited the immense cost of maintaining the Federal armies and worsening finances in the Treasury Department as proof that all troops should be on the move even during the winter months to hasten the end of the war. Grant fully agreed with Halleck. During his sojourn in Savannah, Sherman instructed Thomas to take Selma and Montgomery with twenty-five thousand infantrymen and a large cavalry force, to strike fear in the hearts of citizens as he had done with his own force in Georgia and as he planned to do in the Carolinas. "They realize that the Confederate armies cannot protect them, and they see in the repetition of such raids the inevitable results of starvation and misery."[39]

But Thomas, claiming that the roads in the Deep South would be too bad in the winter, rejected this call for action. As a result, Grant stripped him of most of his available manpower in Tennessee. Soon after Schofield's Twenty-third Corps went to the coast of North Carolina, Andrew Jackson Smith's wing of the Sixteenth Corps traveled by boat to New Orleans in another impressive example of Union logistical capability. Forty-three steamers and seven towboats with barges transported eighteen thousand infantrymen and five thousand cavalrymen from Eastport, Mississippi. They deposited the troops in New Orleans by February 21, requiring only eleven days to move the men 1,335 miles. That left only the Fourth Corps and James Harrison Wilson's cavalry corps of the Military Division of the Mississippi behind. Thomas wanted to wait until March, then advance from Knoxville eastward to support Sherman's left flank as the Federals headed for Petersburg. Grant eventually allowed Thomas to prepare for such an eventuality, because he worried that Lee might evacuate Petersburg and head for Lynchburg, perhaps even attempt to enter eastern Tennessee. The Fourth Corps advance toward Lynchburg would confront the Army of Northern Virginia while Grant and Sherman pursued Lee.[40]

Mobile

Edward Canby also presented Grant problems in terms of delays and a reluctance to zero in on targets set by higher authorities. Having been appointed commander of the newly created Military Division of West Mississippi, which embraced the Department of the Gulf, on May 7, 1864, Canby puttered about with indefinite plans to attack Mobile that were easily disrupted by any number of issues that cropped up. The only one that justified delay was the transfer of most Nineteenth Corps troops, in midsummer of

1864, to Virginia. Those men played a large role in the Shenandoah Valley campaign of September and October. But Canby still had what was left of the Thirteenth Corps and now Andrew J. Smith's two Sixteenth Corps divisions—more than enough men to overwhelm the small garrison of Mobile. Grant viewed the capture of that city as only the first step in a process of projecting Union power into the interior of Alabama. He wanted Canby to disrupt the planting of spring crops for the Confederate army, to destroy railroad and industrial facilities, and to gather able-bodied black males for Federal use. By midwinter of 1865, the Confederate Congress passed a resolution allowing for the enlistment of black troops in the Rebel army. Grant wanted to deny Southerners the opportunity of pressing slaves into gray uniforms by taking control of them first. All he needed was a general who was not "afraid to cut loose from his base of supplies and who will make the best use of the resources of the Country." Canby did not seem that type of commander, but Smith and Frederick Steele, corps leaders under him, had experience in doing so.[41]

During the previous summer Canby had cooperated with Captain David G. Farragut in closing Mobile as a blockade-running port, but the city itself remained in Confederate hands. Mobile lay on the northwest shore of Mobile Bay, a huge inlet that stretched some forty miles inland and was about ten miles wide. The entrance to the bay was only three miles wide and protected by two prewar masonry forts. The large one, Fort Morgan, lay on the east side of the entrance. Numerous underwater mines also constricted the passage to a narrow space.

Farragut had moved against Mobile with fourteen wooden warships, four monitors, and nine smaller gunboats, supported by 2,400 infantrymen from Canby. He attempted to run past Fort Morgan on August 5, his ships in a tight formation. One monitor, the *Tecumseh*, ran onto a mine and sank immediately. The captain of the leading vessel, the *Brooklyn*, hesitated, and Farragut wanted to take the lead with his flagship, the *Hartford*. It is unclear exactly what he said, but "Damn the torpedoes, full steam ahead!" has been a classic exclamation ever since. The *Hartford* steamed ahead, its captain unconcerned about the torpedoes because of Farragut's optimism, and the fleet made it safely inside the bay despite the heavy fire from Fort Morgan. Later investigation discovered that at least 10 percent of the mines were still operable and ninety of them had been planted only days before; Farragut was lucky.[42]

Inside the bay, the Federals were attacked by one of the Confederacy's most effective ironclad warships, the *Tennessee*. In one of the classic ship-to-ship actions of the Civil War, the Rebel vessel was battered into submission by fifteen-inch naval gunfire and repeated rammings, then captured. Most of the other ships in the small Confederate fleet inside Mobile Bay were also lost. Casualties in Farragut's closing of the port amounted to 226 men, 93 of them on the *Tecumseh*, while the Confederates lost 312. After siege efforts mounted by Federal infantrymen, Fort Morgan fell into Union hands on August 31.[43]

Grant wanted the city of Mobile itself to serve as a base of operations inside Alabama, and late in March 1865 Canby finally mounted a major effort to capture the heavily fortified city. Not only had the Confederates invested four years of work on constructing a ring of fortifications around the city itself, but they had established two fortified points on the eastern shore of Mobile Bay. Canby aimed at those two points first. He assembled 45,200 men to oppose Major General Dabney Herndon Maury, who had positioned 3,000 Confederates on the west side and 6,000 on the east side of the bay. Frederick Steele landed 12,000 men by ocean transport at Pensacola and then marched northwestward toward Mobile, while Andrew J. Smith landed the rest near Fort Morgan and advanced up the eastern shore of the bay. Smith laid siege to Spanish Fort while Steele besieged Fort Blakeley. Neither investment was complete, for the Confederates maintained some degree of contact across the bay due to heavy underwater mines in the area which the Federal naval commanders were loath to challenge.[44]

Smith's men began to dig parallels and siege approaches in front of Spanish Fort by March 27. Artillerymen erected more than fifty heavy guns and thirty-seven field pieces to support the effort. In an attack on the evening of April 8, the infantry captured a portion of the Confederate works. This prompted a full evacuation of Spanish Fort that night. All but 500 of the 3,000-man garrison escaped, leaving behind fifty guns. Steele's men had begun their investment of Fort Blakeley on April 2 and launched an attack of their own on April 9. The Federals broke through the Rebel defenses and captured 3,700 prisoners. Altogether, Canby lost 1,508 men in the campaign, several hundred falling victim to numerous landmines the Confederates had scattered along roads, at watering places, and in front of their fortifications only days before the Yankees approached. Confederate casualties, excluding those captured, amounted to about 500. Three days after the fall of Fort Blakeley, Federal troops entered Mobile itself after Maury evacuated the city. Canby reported a total of 4,924 Confederate prisoners, 12 flags, 231 guns, and nearly 30,000 bales of cotton as the booty from his successful campaign around Mobile Bay.[45]

Wilson's Raid

The second major campaign Grant had wanted in the West also began in March 1865. It was a unique expedition, consisting of nearly fourteen thousand cavalrymen under Brigadier General James H. Wilson, commander of cavalry in Sherman's Military Division of the Mississippi. Wilson assembled the largest mounted force of the war near Eastport, Mississippi, the head of year-round navigation on the Tennessee River. He spread the troops out in temporary camps from Eastport to Gravelly Springs, Alabama. Setting out on March 22, Wilson penetrated Alabama, opposed by a small force under Nathan Bedford Forrest. The two commanders clashed at Ebenezer Church, a dozen miles short of Selma, where, on April 1, the Federals drove Forrest away and captured 300 of his troopers. The next day Wilson attacked the fortifications of Selma and collapsed Confederate resistance. He thoroughly defeated Forrest, taking 2,700 prisoners with the loss of 360 men. The Confederates had already destroyed twenty-five thousand bales of cotton in the city, and the Federals methodically wrecked the valuable war industries located in Selma before leaving the place on April 9.[46]

Wilson was convinced that Mobile would fall without the aid of his command, so he directed his men toward Montgomery. The small Confederate garrison did not contest control of the state capital, which Wilson entered on April 12. He pushed on toward Columbus, Georgia, nestled on the east bank of the Chattahoochee River just across the state line. On the evening of April 16, the Federal troopers staged a mounted attack on the earthworks that guarded Columbus on the west side of the river and managed to cross the stream before the bridge was destroyed. That night they captured Columbus with more than one thousand prisoners, along with the important war industry works in the city and its shipyard.[47]

Columbus was the last battle of Wilson's command, for three days later he learned of Lee's surrender. This did not necessarily mean that the fighting was over, for no one could predict how Confederate commanders in the region would react to the collapse of Rebel resistance in Virginia. While Wilson and his troopers were advancing toward Macon on April 20, word arrived that Johnston and Sherman had negotiated an armistice pending the conclusion of a formal surrender of Confederate forces in North Carolina. Wilson took Macon without opposition, a move Confederate commander Howell Cobb protested as a violation of the Sherman-Johnston agreement. The 2,000-man garrison and some sixty artillery pieces also fell into Federal hands.[48]

During the whole of Wilson's raid, the Federal cavalrymen had traveled 525 miles and taken 6,820 prisoners, 288 guns, and 100,000 small arms, with the loss of 725 men. They destroyed numerous foundries, machine shops, rolling mills, 35 locomotives, and 565 railroad cars.[49]

Stoneman's Raid

Grant had been urging Thomas to send a cavalry force of three thousand men from Knoxville into North Carolina to release Union prisoners of war held at Salisbury and to cooperate with Sherman's command as it swept through the state. Like the move against Mobile and Wilson's cavalry raid, this campaign started in March 1865. By that time Thomas had moved the Fourth Corps to Knoxville, also according to Grant's instructions, in case Lee attempted to escape from Petersburg into southwestern Virginia.[50]

Brigadier General George Stoneman set out from Knoxville with four thousand men on March 21, the last day of Sherman's confrontation with Johnston at Bentonville, and took Boone, North Carolina, seven days later. He hit Salisbury on April 12, three days after Appomattox, the day that Canby entered Mobile, and four days before Wilson took Columbus. The Federals destroyed an immense amount of Confederate property in Salisbury but were prevented from burning the railroad bridge across the Yadkin River by the garrison of a large fort constructed to protect the crossing. Stoneman, nevertheless, cut the Virginia and Tennessee Railroad. On his return trip, at Taylorsville, he learned of Lee's surrender. There was, therefore, no need for Thomas to retain the Fourth Corps at Knoxville.[51]

Grant had been frustrated that these three campaigns in the West had not taken place much earlier, at a time when he thought their strategic impact could have been greater. As it was, there were good reasons to delay them, not the least of which was the difficulty of maneuvering large bodies of troops along the dirt roads of the South in winter. Because all three campaigns took place when the war was rapidly drawing to a close in Virginia, none of them had much of an impact on the course of the larger war. Their effect on Confederate forces in their respective regions, however, was devastating. While Sherman proved that his large army needed little assistance from other forces to make its way through the Carolinas, Canby, Wilson, and Stoneman punctured and deflated Confederate hopes in Alabama, Georgia, and North Carolina. The war ended in those isolated regions by almost completely destroying any spirit of resistance on the part of die-hard Confederate partisans.

E nding a war often proves more difficult than starting or even winning it, and the Rebel government offered no guidance for how its military forces should deal with the many issues involved with bringing peace to the land. Therefore, Confederate commanders in the West were on their own in terms of dealing with Union commanders. For their part, Federal officers had only scant guidelines on how to deal with their Southern counterparts. The war in the West came to a close over the span of a couple of months, concluding a bit differently in different areas. Another problem quickly emerged: how to help the thousands of citizens made destitute by the immediate effects of Union campaigning?

North Carolina

Leaving his massive army under the temporary command of John M. Schofield, Sherman made a quick trip to City Point, Virginia, to consult with Grant and Lincoln on March 27–28, 1865. The three Union commanders met in a cabin on the steamer *River Queen*, and Sherman talked with Grant separately as well. Sherman came away from the conference believing the president's main points were that the Confederates must be disarmed and returned to their homes as soon as possible.[1]

In contemplating the final push toward Petersburg, Sherman advised Grant that he could not start from Goldsboro until April 10. He was certain that Lee would evacuate Petersburg before he got there and attempt to join Johnston. "We must go straight for him and fight him in open ground," Sherman insisted, believing that either he or the general in chief "would have to fight one more bloody battle, and that it would be the *last*."[2]

Grant was unwilling to wait until April 10 for Sherman to leave Goldsboro. He wanted to finish the war in Virginia as early as possible and was persuaded that the combined forces of the Army of the Potomac and the Army of the James could handle Lee's men. Grant therefore started another offensive against the Confederates on March 29—a major drive to turn Lee's right flank. Schofield later explained that Grant and Sherman had divergent views on how to end the campaign at Petersburg: Sherman wanted Lee and Johnston to join forces for a final showdown with his own men, whereas Grant wanted to keep the two Confederate armies separated until the Eastern troops could end the long campaign. In the end, Grant's view of operations won out, and the Eastern veterans did not have to share the glory of Appomattox with their Western counterparts.[3]

Sherman reorganized his force while resting at Goldsboro. Slocum's Army of Georgia would continue to constitute his left wing and Howard's Army of the Tennessee his right, but Schofield's Twenty-third Corps, with Terry's division of the Army of the James, would serve as his center. They planned to set out on April 10, and their immediate objectives would be Raleigh and Johnston's command.[4]

By April 5, rumors began to circulate near Goldsboro of a great battle at Petersburg. The next day, details of Lee's defeat and his evacuation of both Petersburg and Richmond on April 3 were confirmed. The report led to extensive celebrations in the Union camps. Sherman continued to plan for a departure date of April 10 while praising Grant for his final success at Petersburg: the result of his ten-month-long campaign to win the Virginia city had "established a reputation for perseverance and pluck that would make Wellington jump out of his coffin."[5]

Although Lee's defeat at Petersburg cast a pall over the Confederate cause, Jefferson Davis tried to make the best of a bad situation. Just before evacuating Richmond, the president outlined whatever thoughts he had about military movements by expressing the hope that Sherman could be prevented from joining Grant. Only by rapid movement and decisive action could that be effected. "To fight the enemy in detail, it is necessary to outmarch him and surprise him." Yet Davis knew that if Sherman and Grant united, "the enemy may decide our policy." Johnston held little hope of success, telling Lee that "Sherman's course cannot be hindered by the small force I have. I can do no more than annoy him."[6]

General Robert E. Lee's surrender at Appomattox on April 9 was the turning point in the Confederate end game. Twentieth Corps commander Alpheus Williams learned of it on April 12, two days after Sherman's command left Goldsboro and while his own corps was crossing the Neuse River. Williams spied Sherman walking near "a bevy of mules," moving through the herd to meet him. Sherman "grabbed my hand and almost shook my arm off, exclaiming, 'Isn't it glorious? Johnston must come down now or break up!'" Sherman fully expected his opponent to "come down" and give up, assuring Grant that he would offer him the same liberal terms Grant had given Lee at Appomattox. The alternative to a formal surrender was unthinkable—the breakup of Johnston's army into uncontrollable bands of guerrillas. Henry Halleck also worried about that possibility, urging Sherman to offer Grant's terms as an enticement for Johnston to surrender before it became a reality.[7]

A third possibility occurred to Sherman as he was contemplating the end of the war in North Carolina. He began to worry that Johnston might try to bypass his forces and head for Georgia to continue resistance in what was left of the Confederacy. There were reports that Davis was attempting to flee toward the South or Southwest at the same time. It would be quite possible, with a good head start, for Johnston's men to achieve this goal, and he hoped that the large cavalry force commanded by Philip Sheridan, which had been so instrumental in heading Lee off during the Appomattox campaign, could move south to help his lone mounted division do the same to Johnston.[8]

Lincoln's death on the morning of April 15, 1865, at the hands of an assassin affected the end game in North Carolina as well. Secretary of War Stanton informed Sherman of it on the fifteenth, warning him of rumors that another assailant intended to kill Sherman as well. Halleck relayed detailed information about the supposed assassin the same day, but Sherman appears not to have taken it very seriously. He was far more concerned about the effect of Lincoln's murder on the mood of his army, fearful that it would lead to retribution on local civilians. But no unusual activity resulted; the Federal soldiers endured their grief and anger without wrecking vengeance on the innocent. "We have met every phase which this war has assumed," Sherman wrote in an order to his troops, "and must now be prepared for it in its last and worst shape, that of assassins and guerrillas." He worried that Lincoln's assassination might embitter the public mood in the North and affect the process of reconstructing the seceded states and of easing the nation from a wartime environment into peace.[9]

Even before the news of Lincoln's death became generally known, Joseph E. Johnston offered to negotiate surrender terms with Sherman. The Federal commander quickly responded that he would offer Grant's Appomattox terms as the basis of such negotiations. Sherman then ordered that all destruction of railroads and produce stop immediately. He notified subordinates that "the inhabitants will be dealt with kindly, looking to an early reconciliation." Before meeting Johnston, Sherman assured Grant and Stanton that he would "be careful not to complicate any points of civil policy" in his discussions with the Confederate commander.[10]

But Sherman forgot his promise. During their first meeting at Durham Station on April 16, Johnston suggested to Sherman that they negotiate a larger agreement than merely the surrender of his field force. Johnston admitted that the cause was lost and "that it would be murder for him to allow any more conflict." Yet the Confederate officer worried about his army breaking up into guerrilla bands and asked Sherman's help in preventing it. The Federal general was so eager to avoid the outbreak of a large-scale guerrilla movement that he was willing to go along with Johnston's proposal to negotiate a larger settlement embracing all Confederate armies. The conference broke up as both officers returned to their commands. Sherman consulted his subordinates, who all agreed that everything ought to be done to avoid a guerrilla war.[11]

When the conference resumed on the afternoon of April 18, Johnston brought along Secretary of War John C. Breckinridge to add legitimacy to a more general surrender agreement. Sherman was willing to try it. The terms that he offered were far more generous and comprehensive than those Grant had offered Lee. They would permit Confederate soldiers to deposit their arms in state arsenals and return home as soon as possible and covered all Rebel forces across the Confederacy. The agreement called on President Andrew Johnson to recognize existing state governments as soon as the state officials took an oath of allegiance to the U.S. government. Johnson also was to reestablish Federal courts and guarantee political rights to ex-Confederate citizens, with amnesty for everyone. The proposed agreement stepped far beyond the boundaries of Sherman's area of responsibilities, marching boldly into the dangerous landscape of Reconstruction politics.[12]

A trusted staff officer carried the agreement to Washington, D.C., by the evening of April 21. Johnson called a cabinet meeting that night, with Grant present, to discuss it. Everyone disapproved of the terms. Secretary Stanton insisted that a telegram he had sent to Grant on March 3, expressing Lincoln's desire that any surrender negotiations between opposing commanders be restricted to purely military matters, be used as the basis for rejecting the Sherman-Johnston agreement. It was thought best that Grant personally go to North Carolina to break the news to his subordinate and handle the surrender himself.[13]

When Grant reached Raleigh on the morning of April 24, he found that Sherman had rather expected his agreement would be rejected. The general in chief tried to put the best face on the situation by explaining to his colleagues in Washington that Sherman had genuinely thought his agreement comported with the views expressed by Lincoln. The liberal terms Grant had offered Lee at Appomattox, and a call by Major General Godfrey Weitzel for the Virginia legislature to meet, also seemed to support a generous agreement with Johnston along the lines that Sherman had negotiated. Sherman informed Johnston that the agreement was rejected and called on him to surrender on Appomattox terms. Johnston initially preferred to modify the original terms, but that was not possible. Sherman and Johnston met again on April 26 and sealed a surrender agreement based on Grant's terms to Lee. While Johnston told former Confederate officials that he gave up "to avoid the crime of waging hopeless war," Sherman's subordinates tried to clamp down on foraging by their own men to avoid unnecessary suffering among civilians living near army camps.[14]

The surrender controversy would have ended quietly if Stanton had not inflamed public awareness of the original terms through the nation's newspapers. The *New York Times* published Stanton's bulletin, which roundly condemned the terms, on April 24, two days before Sherman and Johnston held their last meeting. Many civilians who read the paper were swayed by Stanton's nine reasons for rejecting the original terms of surrender, and, as a result, some of them called for Sherman's removal from command. Stanton told Grant that the agreement had met with "universal disapprobation. . . . I have not known as much surprise and discontent at anything that has happened during the war." Sherman was "outraged beyond measure" by Stanton's airing of the controversy "and was resolved to resent the insult, cost what it might."[15]

Sherman and other observers assumed that the climate in Washington following Lincoln's assassination had contributed to the spirit of vindictiveness in Stanton's decision to inform the public of the original surrender terms. Even Schofield, who harbored some jealousy toward Sherman, thought it was "utterly inexcusable" to smear Sherman's reputation in that way, even though he also thought Sherman had been unwise to attempt a political negotiation with Johnston. Most officials had known of Lincoln's tendency to craft a lenient Reconstruction policy, but Johnson's views were less well known. In fact, the Federal government had no Reconstruction policy of any kind in April 1865, and there was a decided air of uncertainty about all matters regarding the political relationship of the former Confederate states to the central government.[16]

Putting aside his feud with Stanton until he had a chance to act, Sherman had time to evaluate the effect of his march through the Carolinas. "I believe our southern winter excursions have solved the great problem," he wrote. While Schofield was critical of some of the details of Sherman's movements, he thoroughly praised the ultimate results of the campaign. "If Grant had not captured [Lee's] army, Sherman would," he wrote. The march through the Carolinas "made the end of the rebellion in the spring of 1865 sure beyond any possible doubt."[17]

Giving Up

The overriding concern in Sherman's mind was to avoid the possibility that the Confederate armies might break up into guerrilla bands, "headed by such men as Mosby, Forrest, Red Jackson, and others." He had hoped that a comprehensive agreement with Johnston and Breckinridge might avert that scenario. Fortunately, most Confederate leaders felt the same way as Sherman. Judah P. Benjamin, former secretary of war, thought guerrilla fighting was not "desirable nor does it promise any useful result." Colonel Josiah Patterson of the 5th Alabama Cavalry admitted to Federal general Gordon Granger that irregular warfare "would prove disastrous alike to friend and foe. However much may have been said heretofore of guerrilla warfare as a last resort, yet no good man, however patriotic he might be, would encourage, much less participate in, such a struggle." The commander of the Confederate District of Southern Mississippi and Eastern Louisiana actually proposed a joint expedition with Federal forces to clear out bushwhackers from Warren County, on the west side of the Big Black River. Any ex-Confederate soldiers would be taken into custody by the Rebel forces and ex-Union soldiers by the Federals.[18]

Washington officials urged what was left of the organized Confederate army to lay down its arms, hoping that the guerrilla problem in the West would not grow worse in the meantime. Stanton authorized the offer of Appomattox terms to all Confederate forces in the West and the South. Most Rebel commanders were ready to consider that offer, but Nathan Bedford Forrest held out until the last, grasping any rumor that offered hope of a continuation of the conflict. On April 25 he told his command that Lee had not surrendered after all and that Grant had lost one hundred thousand men through desertion and battle casualties. When George Thomas heard rumors that Forrest had "a desperate scheme" to continue fighting, he wanted the Rebel general to know that "such a reckless and bloodthirsty adventure" could only be met by treating him "as an outlaw, and the States of Mississippi and Alabama will be so destroyed that they will not recover for fifty years."[19]

In fact, a reckless approach such as the one Forrest apparently was contemplating never took place. The primary Confederate commander left in the West was Lieutenant General Richard Taylor, who opened negotiations with Edward Canby in Alabama for his own and those troops who had evacuated Mobile. Taylor was convinced he could not hold out more than two weeks if he continued the struggle, and the Mississippi River was too high to make a crossing and escape west. He hoped to secure liberal terms and desperately wanted his men to understand that staying together as organized units and formally giving up was the best course of action. To break up into bands and continue fighting would only bring ruin down on the land and its women and children. In his talks with Canby at Citronelle, Alabama, Taylor believed that he achieved his purpose, although Canby offered him only the terms Grant had presented Lee. The surrender agreement was signed on May 4, 1865. The Federals sent troops into the last pocket of Confederate territory in Alabama and southern Mississippi to garrison towns, maintain law and order, and repair telegraph lines. Forrest accepted the inevitable. "Reason dictates and humanity demands that no more blood be shed," he informed his soldiers. "That we are beaten is a self-evident fact."[20]

James H. Wilson informed his subordinates near Macon that Johnston's surrender foretold the doom of the Confederacy. "There remains nothing else to be done except to capture the rebel chiefs and their treasure, and break up the forces in Mississippi, Louisiana, and Texas." He dispersed his cavalry corps, sending one contingent to Augusta, another to Tallahassee, Florida, and a smaller force to Atlanta, while keeping a garrison at Macon. All subordinate officers were instructed to accept the surrender of any Confederate troops in their area of control.[21]

The forces under George Thomas also negotiated with Rebel commanders in their area. Confederate brigadier general William T. Wofford, who led what Thomas termed "an insignificant" force in northwestern Georgia, was willing to give up himself but feared that his men would "scatter to the hills and become bushwhackers." Wofford sought to keep them together as long as possible before surrendering in an effort to prevent them from adopting such a course. At Huntsville, Alabama, Robert S. Granger spoke with Confederate cavalry commander Philip D. Roddey about surrendering, but Roddey was concerned that a number of marauders who acknowledged allegiance to neither side were terrorizing civilians in the area. Even a group of men who had once belonged to a Confederate cavalry regiment from Texas were robbing loyalist citizens at Courtland. Thus, in many parts of the West the end of the war did not necessarily mean the end of suffering.[22]

There is no evidence that any appreciable number of regularly organized Confederate troops became guerrilla fighters in the spring of 1865, much to the relief of Union and Confederate officers alike. But there was a preexisting guerrilla force that took orders from no one, and Grant was anxious to curtail its activities as soon as possible by authorizing the extension of Appomattox terms to them. A number of guerrilla leaders were eager to know on what terms they could rehabilitate themselves in a society dominated by their enemy. Grant suggested that a date be set—for example, May 20—by which all guerrillas would appear before the authorities and sign a parole. After that date, those who had not done so would be considered outlaws. It was a generous offer prompted by a desire to end the fighting as quickly as possible.[23]

Except for the commander of the District of West Tennessee, who set April 25 as the date, it is not known if Grant's suggestion for establishing a deadline beyond which guerrillas would be considered outlaws was implemented. But there is evidence that many guerrilla bands came out of the brush to accept Appomattox terms in the West. After some discussion, three of the "chief guerrillas" near Gallatin, Tennessee, gave up on May 9, and local officials paroled them and twenty-five followers. Guerrilla chief Henry L. Giltner negotiated for the surrender of nearly one thousand irregulars at Mount Sterling, Kentucky, but he demanded far more than Appomattox terms. Giltner insisted that his men not be forced to take an oath of allegiance, and he wanted freedom to move anywhere his men chose. Union authorities refused to accede but stalled the negotiations to allow time to shift Union troops near the area. Giltner finally caved in under this show of force and accepted Appomattox terms.[24]

The blanket offer of leniency to all guerrilla bands seemed unjust to some Federal commanders. The guerrillas around Tullahoma, Tennessee, were among the worst in the Western theater. Major General Robert Milroy was reluctant to send a flag of truce to them but had to do so under Thomas's direct order. One of the chief guerrilla leaders, a man named Mead, refused Appomattox terms when offered; Union authorities pronounced him an outlaw to be hunted down as any other criminal.[25]

An interesting problem had developed even before the war ended in the West. As many as three thousand Confederate prisoners refused to be exchanged in the early months of 1865, when the prisoner exchange system was revived. They claimed to be deserters and conscripts and had no desire to be placed in Confederate hands once again. Many of them were willing to join the Union army, and Major General Grenville M. Dodge, commander of the Department of the Missouri, was eager to accept them. Henry Halleck recommended that these men not be returned to the Confederacy, and there is no evidence that they were forced south. The collapse of the Confederacy would have removed all obstructions to their return home.[26]

Another issue involving the repatriation of captives was that some Union soldiers had been taken prisoner and then joined Confederate units to fight the Federals. Dodge knew of 250 such men held in the prison at Alton, Illinois. Some of them had been captured by Union forces in the battle of July

22 east of Atlanta. Others had deserted Confederate ranks but remained in the custody of Federal authorities even though they wished to return to their original Union regiments. Dodge recommended that they be allowed to do so, calling them "good, earnest soldiers," although their final disposition is unknown.[27]

A thornier problem was presented in the case of one hundred Confederate soldiers captured in a battle at Egypt Station, Mississippi, during a Union raid on a railroad useful to Beauregard and Hood during the Tennessee invasion. These men had been Union soldiers who were seized in battle by the Confederates; they had enlisted in the Rebel army to escape prison hardships. Distrusted by their comrades, they had not been given weapons until the night before the battle at Egypt Station on December 28, 1864. At least that was their side of the story. A Union officer, however, reported that these men had been posted on the Confederate skirmish line and had ample opportunity to desert before the battle began. Furthermore, they fired a volley at the start of the engagement, contributing to the loss of one hundred Union soldiers, before they gave up. Rather than receiving clemency, the officer thought, the one hundred men should be listed as deserters and treated accordingly.[28]

It was difficult to process people in this war fairly, for the processors often did not have full information on motives or actions. More often than not, Federal officials ended cases like these simply by releasing the captives when the conflict was over. They also had no control over the fate of black Union soldiers who fell into Confederate hands, many of whom were returned to any white Southerner who claimed that they had owned the man prior to the war. The Confederate government also treated these prisoners of war as laborers, putting them to work on army projects if they had been slaves before enlisting in the Union army. This policy was followed by all officials until the collapse of Confederate authority finally freed the unfortunate captives whose enlistment in the Federal army had not yet ended their exposure to slavery.[29]

Jefferson Davis became a captive barely a month after the fall of Richmond, and it was Wilson's cavalry that found and caught the ex-president of the Confederacy in Georgia. By early May, Davis and his small party of family and staff had made their way across the Carolinas into southwestern Georgia, even though Federal reports alerted all commanders in the Western theater to be on the watch for the group. Wilson spread his troopers out in a wide net to detect Davis's whereabouts, and two columns of cavalry closed in on him at Urwinville in the early morning hours of May 10. Ironically, the troopers fired on each other in the darkness, an exchange that killed two and wounded four Federals. The firing awakened the members of Davis's party, but they could not escape before the Yankees discovered them. When caught, Davis was wearing his wife's shawl over his shoulders. This gave rise to rumors that he had been disguised as a woman to escape detection.[30]

Wilson's men also captured the Confederate postmaster general, John Reagan, with the Davis party. They nabbed Confederate vice president Alexander Stephens, secretary of the navy Stephen R. Mallory, several Confederate senators, cavalry commander Joseph Wheeler, and Georgia governor Joseph E. Brown—all in separate incidents.[31]

Administering the South

Military administration of occupied territory took on a different complexion with the collapse of the Confederate government. Many issues remained the same, such as commerce, the cotton trade, and dealing with the disloyal in a way to encourage them to resume their loyalty to the U.S. government. But there no longer was an organized enemy force with which to contend.

In early May Stanton removed all restrictions on trade in Tennessee and northern Alabama, except in weapons, gray cloth, and railroad and telegraph equipment. By mid-June restrictions on those items were lifted as well, and a general resumption of commerce throughout the country took place by presidential proclamation on June 24. Cotton remained the most difficult trade issue. As soon as the Confederate government ceased to exist, all the cotton that it had owned was open to private claims. Treasury agents had to determine if it was possible to verify these private claims or to exert the claim of the U.S. government on it. There was an upsurge of cotton speculation as Northerners also swooped down on these stashes, which amounted to two hundred thousand bales alone lying east of the Mississippi River and within the jurisdiction of Canby's Military Division of West Mississippi. By late May, Canby ordered a stop to his subordinates' efforts to locate more Confederate-owned cotton and allowed a completely free trade in the white gold.[32]

Modern estimates of the amount of cotton extracted from the war zone show that commercial motives spurred enormous efforts to reap a profit in the crop. It has been calculated that 6 to 7 million bales of cotton were grown in the South during the war years. Southerners themselves destroyed about half that amount to prevent it from falling into Union hands. Northerners and Europeans purchased about 1.5 to 2 million bales of what was left, half a million of that amount in 1864 when cotton prices were plummeting. Following the Purchasing Act of July 1864, U.S. Treasury agents bought 55,000 bales for government use. An additional 450,000 bales were smuggled through the Union blockade by Confederates for Britain. Ironically, it was both easier and more profitable for owners to trade between the lines than to try to smuggle bales through the blockade, especially when they could trade needed goods for the cotton rather than receive cash. It is true, as one historian has put it, that between-the-lines trade tended "to negate the effects of the blockade," but it also benefited Northern textile manufacturers.[33]

In North Carolina, Schofield suggested to Sherman that all restrictions on trade be dropped in early May 1865. Moreover, he complained about the fact that the Federal government had no Reconstruction policy, for the residents in his jurisdiction were beaten and "in a mood to accept almost anything which promises a definite settlement. What is to be done with the freedmen is the question of all, and it is the all-important question." Sherman sympathized with him, noting that he had precious little information on the long-range plans of his government when he negotiated with Johnston at Durham Station. According to Sherman, "Their minds are so absorbed with the horrid deformities of a few assassins and Southern politicians that they overlook the wants and necessities of the great masses. You have seen how Stanton and Halleck turned on me because I simply submitted a skeleton as basis. Anything positive would be infinitely better than the present doubting, halting, nothing-to-do policy of our bewildered Government."[34]

Schofield could, at least, issue a general order to his Department of North Carolina making it clear that Lincoln's Emancipation Proclamation applied to the state, and that all slaves in it were free. Schofield urged former owners to hire their ex-slaves to work the land for wages, and he warned blacks that hanging around army camps would not be a ticket to a free meal.[35]

In the area including Alabama, Georgia, and Mississippi, James H. Wilson reported that the general mood of the people at war's end was based on their disgust with the Davis government's inability to protect them. They accepted Union occupation as a fait accompli, not because they had as yet reverted to loyal U.S. citizens. Nevertheless, the civilians were "completely subjugated and submissive, and only desire to know the will of the Government to execute it." The people seemed to accept the demise of slavery as well as they accepted Federal victory in the war, but they were concerned about developing some new economic relationship with their former slaves. In Wilson's words, they sought "some modified form of controlled labor" to put their lands back into production as soon as possible and wanted some guidance from the government, which, as yet, was not forthcoming.[36]

In Tennessee, many Rebels began to return at war's end to take Lincoln's amnesty oath in order to secure their property and protect themselves from future prosecution. George Thomas therefore declared that all amnesty oaths taken since December 15, 1864, were null and void if they had been administered to anyone other than bona fide members of the Confederate army. He required that any future oaths be approved by his headquarters. He went further than this in his efforts to fill the void created by the government's lack of a Reconstruction policy. Thomas urged county officials in northern Mississippi, Alabama, Georgia, and western North Carolina to resume their work and call elections to fill vacant local offices. He appealed to loyalists everywhere to take the lead in the process, promising military protection as needed. This was already being done on the state level in Tennessee, where Parson Brownlow was elected the state's first postwar governor, packing state offices with other eastern Tennessee loyalists and reconstructing Tennessee along lines consistent with the developing radical Republican trend in the U.S. Congress.[37]

Thomas thought that "military authority should sustain, not assume, the functions of civil authority," but exactly what kind of civil authority was required in the unsettled state of postwar politics was unclear. On May 16 Stanton informed Canby that President Johnson claimed control of "all political subjects," and that commanders everywhere were to prevent the existing state governments from meeting. Obviously he meant to create some sort of policy whereby the former Confederates would be rehabilitated according to a political litmus test to be determined in the near future, rather than rely on Confederate-era state governments to run the ex-Confederate states. Wilson had already refused to allow the Georgia legislature to meet and Godfrey Weitzel's call for the Virginia legislature to convene in April had been rescinded as well, indicating which way the tide was turning in the developing story of Reconstruction.[38]

The collapse of the Confederate war effort now allowed Union commanders to disperse their troops according to convenience and the necessity of protecting citizens against marauders. Thomas was able to strip eastern Tennessee of manpower, for it was still difficult to feed any sizable concentration of troops there, bringing the Fourth Corps back to the Nashville area.[39]

Canby was especially eager "to divest myself as soon as possible of all questions of civil administration" and deal with "purely military" matters in the Military Division of West Mississippi. He lifted all military restrictions and assessments from areas where local civil government operated effectively, maintaining martial rule only where civilians could not keep law and order. While the wartime Reconstruction government of Louisiana was allowed to operate, the Confederate state government of Mississippi was prevented from meeting. Canby instructed his subordinates to find and secure "all judicial, land and other records affecting the title of property and other private interests," for they would be valuable assets in determining a number of issues relating to black-white relations or the possible punishment of ex-Confederates. Rebel deserters who turned themselves in to Union officials after May 15 would not be eligible to take the amnesty oath. Civilians who had worked for the Confederate government or who had lived in rebellious states would not be allowed to enter the limits of the Department of the Gulf, centered around New Orleans, without the permission of its commander.[40]

At Memphis, the center of the District of West Tennessee, C. C. Washburn oversaw the conversion from wartime to peacetime with detailed orders made public to inform all civilians what was expected of them. He felt that the people were "heartily sick and disgusted with the war, and with a little encouragement I think that they may be quieted down and induced to go about their business once more." He stopped providing transportation for those who wished to go north and stopped giving food to all except the truly helpless, announcing that "those that can work must work or starve, black or white." Confederate soldiers in the district had thirty days to find civilian clothes to wear or suffer the consequences, and civilians who had left Federal lines and gone south were now not allowed to return to Memphis. Washburn also encouraged each county in his district to resurrect their county courts and create posses to impose law and order. He offered to sell arms to those posses so they could do their job properly. The army would no longer confiscate horses or mules, and it would give proper vouchers for any provisions taken from civilians. Washburn's superintendent of freedmen offered to arrange contracts for any planter who needed laborers.[41]

Washburn's actions at Memphis mirrored those of many other subcommanders across the West. Everywhere officers sought to remove civilian feeling that the U.S. Army was a burden to them; in fact, that it was a necessity now as the only armed force capable of protecting them from the scattered bands of marauders still roaming some areas. The emphasis was on getting civilians back to work in their shops and on their farms as quickly as possible, taking black-white relations one small step at a time.[42]

Along the Mississippi River, garrisons were alerted to the possibility that Jefferson Davis and members of his government might try to cross the stream and head for Mexico. Although the river was at full flood stage, some officers feared that the presidential party might seize a steamer, or even a gunboat, to make a crossing. Naval commanders forbade steamers from landing anywhere between Helena and Baton Rouge while the alert was in effect, as local commanders gathered up all the small boats they could find along the banks so the Confederates could not use them to cross the broad stream.[43]

In addition to the Davis alert, Halleck received word of another possible threat to river traffic. Confederate operatives who had been developing a range of weapons and craft to defend Charleston, South Carolina, against the Federal blockading fleet might be shifted to the Ohio River valley to destroy steamers and hamper the Union logistical effort in the West. That threat never materialized, but the Confederates made one final foray on the Mississippi when Lieutenant C. W. Read took the gunboat *Webb* from Alexandria, Louisiana, down the Red River and into the stream. He landed parties to cut the telegraph wires every fifteen miles, used Federal flag signals and flew the U.S. colors to confuse observers, and steamed past New Orleans on April 24, 1865. Federal gunboats engaged in a running battle that extended twenty-five miles below the city. When they caught up with the *Webb*, its crew set the boat afire and some of them escaped. It was the last battle of the river war.[44]

Canby moved troops from Mobile into the interior of Alabama to lay claim to territory only traversed briefly by Wilson's men. A large force of infantry and cavalry left for Montgomery on April 14, two days after Wilson had taken the state capital without a battle. The Federals passed through territory that had seen few Union soldiers before; they paroled more than ten thousand Confederate soldiers and discovered about three hundred thousand bales of cotton. Federal commanders distributed Confederate government food to the poor. "The country is filled with bands of armed marauders," reported cavalry commander Benjamin Grierson, "composed mostly of deserters" from the Rebel army. While the poor expressed loyal sentiments, the rich were still bitter toward the central government "and clutch on to slavery with a lingering hope to save at least a relic of their favorite yet barbarous institution for the future."[45]

Wilson reported that the fall of Richmond and Lee's surrender took the heart out of the Confederate war effort within his area of control in Georgia. He clamped down hard on soldier plundering, threatening death to anyone who violated orders not to enter private houses. Provisions could be taken, but in the properly prescribed manner. He ordered division commanders to inspect trains and remove any pillaged material from them. "I am anxious to do all in my power to prevent suffering among the people," Wilson informed the inspector general of the Georgia state government, and he did everything he could to encourage "the resumption of business of every kind, opening of the roads, and a continuance of the mails."[46]

Wilson came to realize that simply feeding people who did not have enough to eat was one of his immediate problems. The areas of Georgia within reach of Sherman's operations from Chattanooga to Savannah, and his own operations from Columbus to Macon, were devastated, "could not possibly be in a worse condition." The areas south of that region were still prosperous, but suffering within the war zones was "fearful." George Thomas responded with orders to accumulate all the tools and supplies required to put the Western and Atlantic Railroad back into operation so food could be shipped to Atlanta for distribution to needy areas. He wanted his quarter-masters to keep detailed accounts so the government could charge the owners of the railroad later for the expense. Wilson worked desperately to help the estimated 25,000 to 50,000 civilians who were "utterly destitute."[47]

As spring began to give way to summer, Atlanta was the epicenter of a developing famine. The previous year's crops had mostly been taken by Sherman's troops, especially during the huge foraging expeditions conducted by the Twentieth Corps in September and October 1864, and the results were now being felt. What little was left of the Georgia state government was powerless to do anything, and county governments were equally weak. The Federal army was the only institution available to meet the crisis. The Chattanooga area was nearly as bad, for the entire Tennessee River Valley from Knoxville, Tennessee, to Eastport, Mississippi, had seen large-scale military operations for a couple of years already. The Federal commander at Chattanooga requested an immediate shipment of five thousand bushels of corn to feed starving civilians, and Thomas's staff began to rush it from Nashville as soon as possible.[48]

At Atlanta, Colonel Edward F. Winslow distributed forty-five thousand pounds of meat and ten thousand pounds of flour during the week ending June 10. Although Thomas was surprised at such largesse, Winslow advised him that it had not been enough to feed even one-quarter of those who most desperately needed help. Even civilians who received the government provisions had enough to last their families no more than a week. "Somebody must act in this matter with such efficiency as to save life, and at once," Winslow lectured his superior. He estimated that eight hundred bushels of corn and thirty thousand pounds of meat would be needed every day to feed the "starving poor" in the area around Atlanta. Given the lack of transportation, most families found it difficult to get to the city to receive the donations, and they needed to pick up as many as ten days' rations to carry their families from one trip to town to the next. The Western and Atlantic Railroad was still not ready for service by early July, further hampering Winslow's humanitarian effort.[49]

Atlanta received the lion's share of attention from concerned Union officials in the West, but the suffering within the Tennessee River Valley was just as acute, if on a smaller scale. "I know of several instances where people have died from starvation," reported Edward Hatch, the Federal commander at Eastport. He distributed all the Confederate stores he could find, which was very little, but needed help from Thomas's headquarters to "feed these people." Another Federal officer estimated that as many as ten thousand civilians were on the point of starvation in northern Alabama by late May 1865. Many of them gathered at the nearest town, hoping to receive anything the Union army could manage to send their way.[50]

Guerrillas

If anything, the guerrilla war in many areas of the West worsened in 1865, at least before the surrender at Appomattox. Kentucky continued to suffer tremendously from irregular warfare. Marauders in the counties that bordered the Ohio River fired on steamboats and committed robberies. They were in contact with sympathetic citizens on the northern side of the river and conducted "a large contraband trade." Joseph Hooker, the Federal commander in the region, believed these guerrillas were not fighting for the Confederate cause but were simply robbing to sustain themselves.[51]

It is difficult to determine what motivated guerrillas in Kentucky, but reports indicate that several areas of the state were almost taken over by them. In the region around Russellville Federal officials estimated that as many as twelve hundred guerrilla fighters, divided into bands of ten to one hundred men, "all well mounted," so terrorized the civilian population that many county courts had ceased functioning. Those loyalists who had not moved to garrisoned towns or fled the state "are in constant fear and suspense." The area commander had too few troops—only four hundred mounted men—which contributed to his inability to curb the rampage. "The State is being overrun," he reported with understandable exaggeration, "depopulated of her best citizens. Insecurity and want of confidence is everywhere predominant."[52]

The fact that the Russellville guerrillas seemed to target loyalists may give some weight to viewing them as Confederate partisans. But elsewhere guerrillas more often took control of isolated towns far from Union garrisons and cleaned out stores, harassed and shot civilians at random, and stole goods landed by steamers at river towns in Tennessee. The guerrillas often disguised themselves as Federal troops to deceive citizens, making their robberies and murders more devastating. While some gangs specifically targeted civilians who had voted for Abraham Lincoln in the November 1864 election, most of them merely looked for victims who had the most possessions and displayed the least resistance.[53]

In February 1865 Washington officials placed John M. Palmer in charge of Kentucky with specific orders to clamp down on guerrilla activity. "All such persons are to be treated as enemies of the human race," Stanton instructed Palmer, giving him carte blanche to deal with the irregulars in any way he saw fit. In addition to his antiguerrilla role, Palmer was to continue enlisting blacks in the Union army and "cultivate a friendly and harmonious spirit" with the sometimes difficult governor of Kentucky, Thomas Bramlette. Although the state's anomalous position within the Union had exempted it from the provisions of Lincoln's Emancipation Proclamation, Congress had passed a law on March 3, 1865, freeing the wives and children of black men in Kentucky who volunteered for service. After Appomattox, some black recruits began to break into county courthouses in order to destroy official records, presumably to eliminate proof of human ownership.[54]

Under Palmer, the Federals mounted additional efforts to track down guerrilla bands and destroy them. These gangs usually put up slight resistance, often losing men and, perhaps more importantly, their horses to pursuing Federal patrols. Mounting more Yankee troops and aggressively pushing them into guerrilla country seemed to be the keys to taking the advantage away from the irregulars.[55]

Tennessee, like Kentucky, continued to suffer from guerrilla depredations in the first half of 1865. The irregulars who operated in central Tennessee carried on a thriving trade in contraband goods across the border with Kentucky. Mounted Union soldiers continued to patrol the area well into the summer of 1865, as several guerrilla organizations refused to give up despite the generous terms offered them. As in Kentucky, these recalcitrants seem to have had no allegiance to the defunct Confederacy but merely sought cash and supplies. Federal officers found some Union soldiers who had deserted their regiments among the guerrillas around Pulaski, Tennessee. By June they reported steady progress in hounding out the irregulars, often killing them on the spot as the quickest way to solve the problem.[56]

In May 1865 Federal commanders in Memphis were able to mount a large movement to quell guerrilla activity in northern Mississippi, sending nine hundred men from different locations through the counties most affected. "People in the country will be kindly treated," orders enjoined, "but must be informed that if they are known to harbor or encourage guerrillas hereafter they shall be utterly destroyed." In early May a gang of starving deserters and disbanded Confederate soldiers ransacked the town of Thomasville, Georgia, looking for food. Though four hundred civilians appealed to them to stop, the ex-soldiers tore the town apart, stealing government stores and civilian property alike. Since the Federal army could not be everywhere at once, Wilson urged local governments to organize their own defense against such actions and to call on his troops only if necessary. As with tracking down and killing guerrillas, there were serious limits to the Federal government's ability to protect Southern citizens against all the dangers inherent in the desperate days that followed Appomattox.[57]

In areas such as northern Florida, which had garnered very little attention from either side during the war, there were scant Federal resources to deal with guerrillas. The border between Florida and Alabama, comparatively unproductive, was riddled with marauders who operated in gangs of more than fifty men each. They seemed to be mostly deserters from the 1st Florida Cavalry, U.S. The area commander had no more than thirty cavalrymen and found it difficult to feed even that many men in the impoverished area. The only good news was that in late May a group of forty armed civilians convinced a gang of one hundred marauders not to ransack Campbellton.[58]

The guerrilla war sputtered to an end during the summer of 1865 as Federal forces tried to clean up the last vestiges of violence engendered by the long, bitter war in the West. Many areas suffered little if at all from the robberies and murders, while other regions were devastated more by the actions of irregulars than by those of regularly organized forces.

The Grand Review

The last public show of the Union armies took place in late May 1865, as authorities sought to display Federal power and celebrate the accomplishments of the rank and file by holding a Grand Review in the nation's capital. Sherman's command conducted a hasty march from central North Carolina to Washington, D.C., in the growing heat, a journey many of his veterans termed "amongst the hardest and most trying of our experance." Reports circulated that several soldiers died of sunstroke during this last march of the Western veterans. Even if the reports were exaggerated, there was little need to push these troops so hard now that the war was over.[59]

Those men of the Twentieth Corps had seen service in the Eastern campaigns as well, and they had a keen interest in viewing the sites of their engagements. When his division marched near the field of Chancellorsville, John Geary was able to locate the remains of a trusted friend who had been

Grand Review of Major General Frank P. Blair's Seventeenth Corps. The Western armies had their day in the sun on May 24, 1865, when they proudly paraded down Pennsylvania Avenue in Washington, D.C., for all to see. (Library of Congress, LC-DIG-cwpb-02816)

killed there. An orderly who received permission to ride across the Chancellorsville battlefield never returned and was presumed killed by guerrillas.[60]

Veterans of the Twentieth Corps found satisfaction in contributing to highly successful operations in the West that eventually brought them back to the scene of their earlier failures in Virginia. They often portrayed the Western troops of Sherman's army as "aghast" when examining the evidence of large-scale battles in the East, the miles of fieldworks and still unburied bones of dead soldiers that littered fields from the Wilderness down to Petersburg. But many of the Westerners downplayed the difficulties of campaigning in Virginia, noting that the rivers and the terrain were not such obstacles as to explain the long delay of the Eastern armies in taking Richmond and defeating Lee's army. John Hill Ferguson of the 10th Illinois examined many battlefields in the East, imagining what his Western commanders would have done to deal with the enemy on them as opposed to what the Eastern commanders had ordered during the actual battles.[61]

The Army of the Potomac conducted its Grand Review down Pennsylvania Avenue on May 23, 1865, to the delight of thousands of civilians who had gathered for the occasion. But the Western armies seemed to garner even more attention. The crowd probably expected "an army of 'bummers,' wild, undisciplined, and unskilled in the precision of military movements," in the words of brigade commander Benjamin Harrison. But they saw an army unexcelled in marching ability, discipline, and vigor, despite its unkempt appearance. Sherman achieved a measure of satisfaction when he snubbed Stanton on the reviewing stand, refusing to shake the secretary's hand in a studied, very public, way. He had also garnered some revenge on Halleck, who had unwisely issued instructions to other officers not to pay any attention to Sherman's draft articles of surrender. When Halleck issued orders barring Sherman's men from visiting Richmond on their way to Washington, Sherman allowed his troops to violate those orders and push past the Eastern guards along the roads to the former Confederate capital.[62]

For Sherman, the Grand Review was a vindication of his men as well. "Many good people, up to that time, had looked upon our Western army as a sort of mob," he recalled in his memoirs, "but the world then saw, and recognized the fact, that it was an army in the proper sense, well organized, well commanded and disciplined; and there was no wonder that it had swept through the South like a tornado."[63]

Following the Grand Review, Sherman's men saw the sights of the capital and often celebrated their pending release from military service with excessive revelry. Sherman's feud with Stanton intensified their feelings, and many Westerners, "especially when a little in liquor," engaged in word duels and fisticuffs with Eastern soldiers. The commander of the Washington garrison refrained from arresting them out of respect, but Grant asked Sherman to maintain a better demeanor among his soldiers. Moreover, the Westerners committed so many depredations on the citizens of the District of Columbia that the civilians established a committee and met with Grant to discuss compensation. The general in chief suggested they form a commission to assess damages, but he urged them to wait until Sherman's men had been shipped West in order to avoid embarrassment and possible trouble.[64]

Sherman's veterans entered Washington with immense pride in their military accomplishments and a heady sense of their importance to the Union victory. Sherman led the way in these feelings. Still smoldering from the supposed insults of Stanton and Halleck, he wrote to John A. Logan: "If such be the welcome the East gives to the West, we can but let them make war and fight it out themselves. I know where is a land and people that will not treat us thus—the West, the Valley of the Mississippi, the heart and soul and future strength of America, and I for one will go there."[65]

{ Conclusion

The Union won and the Confederacy lost the Civil War largely due to what each side did, or failed to do, in the West. This expansive region, embraced by the Mississippi River, the Ohio River, the Gulf Coast, and the Appalachian Highlands, comprised the arena where critical policies and decisive actions shifted the fortunes of victory and defeat to one side or the other. Despite the fact that most public attention seemed to be focused on the East, where large armies grappled in bloody battles within a constricted corridor between Washington, D.C., and Richmond, Virginia, the destiny of the nation was initially worked out in the Mississippi Valley, then extended to the central theater of operations along the rail line bisecting the southeastern Confederacy. Victory and defeat played itself out in Western climes and on Western topography before a massive column of veteran troops under William T. Sherman bore down on Robert E. Lee's embattled army in the trenches at Petersburg to help bring the war to a close in 1865.[1]

It is ironic that decisive victory should take place in a region containing so many features appearing to give the Confederacy many advantages over its opponent. While the Virginia theater of operations, with its short distances and massive accumulation of Federal resources, seemed to favor the invader, the West was so large and geographically diverse that one might suppose no invader could subdue it even if the Confederates had few resources with which to defend the area.

But the Western Federals did a magnificent job of overcoming all obstacles in their area of responsibility. They defeated the Confederates in nearly every major battle in the West, in contrast to those that occurred in the East, and chewed up Rebel territory with every advance. Distance—the chief geographic aspect of the Western war—did not prevent the Unionists from conquering a territory larger than France, Switzerland, and the Low Countries combined in less than four years of fighting.

The Federal victory in the West was due not only to greater resources of manpower, equipment, and supplies, although that superiority was a necessary component of Northern success. It was also due to the Federals' greater ability to mobilize and manipulate those resources to overcome all difficulties of time and space. It should not be assumed that the Confederate forces offered little resistance; the battles in the West were fought at least as hard as those in the East, although typically not on such a lavish scale. After maneuvering large bodies of troops across long distances, overcoming mountains, swamps, innumerable streams, and often on short rations, the Federals met their opponents man for man on the battlefield and more often than not drove them back to reclaim more territory and reduce the already insufficient Rebel manpower in the West by a few thousand troops. One can forgive the excessive praise Westerners heaped upon themselves, beginning with the Vicksburg campaign and coming to a sometimes annoying crescendo by the end of the march through the Carolinas, for their achievements in the West were astounding compared to the Eastern armies and to previous American military experience.

The Confederates contributed to their own defeat in the West; that defeat cannot be accounted for solely by insufficient resources. History is replete with examples of wars won by the weaker power. The Confederates made poor use of what resources were available to them because of poor management, poor decision making at high levels, and the bad luck of having generals who could not learn how to effectively command. It is ironic that there were pockets of abundant food resources in the West—for example, in central Georgia—which were more easily tapped and made use of by invading Union armies than by Confederate forces. High-level decisions kept generals like Braxton Bragg and John Pemberton in charge of key armies at pivotal periods of the war. Even though both men had admirable qualities as administrators and strategists, neither of them possessed either the fighting ability of Lee or that Eastern general's knack of inspiring his subordinates with confidence. In contrast, the generals who came to dominate Federal operations in the West developed into some of the most impressive commanders in American history. Natural ability accounted for much of the success of Ulysses S. Grant and William T. Sherman, but the nurturing of both generals by President Lincoln and Henry Halleck, who gave them the latitude to develop their skills and prove themselves worthy of trust, was equally important. Jefferson Davis had such a relationship with Robert E. Lee but failed to develop it with his Western generals. He was strangely willing to allow troublesome commanders who had lost the confidence of their subordinates to retain prominent commands in the West. As a Westerner himself, Davis seems to have been unusually out of touch with the Western Confederacy—in direct contrast to his fellow Kentuckian in the White House.

Cogent arguments have already been advanced by previous historians to support the idea that the Confederate leadership allocated far fewer resources to the defense of the West than the East. The Army of Tennessee operated in an area of 225,600 square miles, whereas the Army of Northern Virginia was responsible for less than one-tenth of that amount of ground. The front defended by Lee's army amounted to 125 miles from the Shenandoah Valley to Chesapeake Bay, while the Army of Tennessee was responsible for a front of 400 miles from the Mississippi River to the mountains. Despite this, the Army of Tennessee had on average 20,000 to 25,000 fewer troops at its disposal. In fact, the Western states sent more regiments to fight with Lee than the Eastern states sent units to fight with the Army of Tennessee. Moreover, the corps, division, and brigade commanders in Lee's army tended to have more prewar military experience and training than those in the Army of Tennessee.[2]

Technical Superiority

"The application of steam to land and water transportation has perhaps as much modified the conduct of war as it has the pursuits of peace," concluded Lewis B. Parsons halfway through the war. He thought this should allow an invader the "ability for more rapid concentration of troops and supplies at distant points" and "give greater vigor to a campaign and vast advantage to the party having superiority in this respect." Parsons, of course, was absolutely right. Grant recognized, after inspecting the vast expanse of his Military Division of the Mississippi and returning to Nashville, that "in these days of telegraph & steam, I can command whilst traveling and visiting about as well as by remaining here."[3]

To the extent that the war in the West incorporated new technology, the Federals certainly had a decisive edge over their opponents in all matters regarding the employment of steam, rail, and telegraphy. Many Confederates recognized the superiority of their enemy in these areas. "In every form of contest in which mechanical instruments, requiring skill and heavy machinery to make them, can be used, the Federals are our superiors," concluded William J. Hardee. While retaining for his own side a superior ability in "manly courage, patient endurance, and brave impulse," Hardee also recognized the superiority of Federal artillery, the most highly technical component of combat arms in the Civil War.[4]

Hardee probably would have agreed that the Unionists won any contest involving steam power, too. They had an immense advantage in the fact that most river steamers were in the North when secession occurred. Moreover, the North had an enormous capacity for building more boats as needed. Indeed, The Federals had superior resources for the construction of armored river gunboats, which became the spearhead of victory in combined operations along the conveniently located river system of the West. Parsons noted that it was possible for Union quartermasters to transport a larger army than Napoleon had used from Boston or Baltimore to Cairo, Illinois, by rail in three days, put those troops on river transports, and then move them to New Orleans one thousand miles away in four days. For the average Union soldier, who likely would have scarcely traveled more than a few miles from his birthplace, service in the Western war took him thousands of miles from home and into a variety of different climates, landscapes, and subcultures in the Southern United States. This experience was comparable in its own way to the globe-girdling campaigns of American forces in World War II.[5]

The Confederates were never able to tackle the technical problem of mobilizing an effective rail-based logistics system that could adequately supply their armies, even though rich resources of food grew within their borders. As John E. Clark, a student of Confederate railroads, has argued, Rebel leaders never learned from their mistakes. They did not properly study the logistical problems to find solutions to them, failed to institute central planning, and wound up converting their homeland into a "quagmire" where items ranging from food to equipment could not be properly moved to points where they were needed. "The Confederate leadership . . . neither planned nor efficiently managed the war effort. Rather, it squandered its natural advantages of sheer mass and interior lines." As Clark has bluntly put it, the Confederacy needed, as the weaker belligerent in the war, "to carefully organize and shrewdly allocate its limited resources. It did not do so."[6]

Through their personal experiences, many Confederates realized that their government did less than expected in terms of marshaling and using the resources of the South to fight the war. Thomas B. Wilson, a Confederate cavalryman who served as a courier for various commanders in the West, expressed it well when he wrote: "It is a debatable question with me as to which hurt us worse, the good generalship and unlimited resources of the enemy or the mismanagement and bad generalship on our own side."[7]

Destructive Policies, Repatriation, and Guerrillas

A key aspect of Civil War military operations was the development of destructive policies by the Federals as an aide to winning the conflict. These policies developed first in the West, because it was there that Union forces traversed large areas of Confederate territory, needed additional provisions to support their armies, and encountered serious disturbances by guerrillas. All of the factors that led to the enlarged practice of taking Southern property were more prominent in the West than in the East because of the huge geographic expanse of the western Confederacy. As time went by, the Federals more and more thought in terms of using destruction as a way to punish the recalcitrant, favor the loyalist, and deny the Confederates the opportunity to utilize resources.[8]

The Federals never developed an effective system to repatriate Confederate citizens. All they could do was to separate them from contact with the Confederate government and force them to accept the dictates of war. Most of them, either by preference or by necessity, became quiet if sometimes sullen U.S. citizens again, while others remained openly sympathetic to the Southern cause; still others took to the brush and became guerrillas. Government coercion and conciliation never consistently made loyal citizens out of Rebels, and only time could even out the problems engendered by secession and war.

Likewise, the Federals never really won the guerrilla war in the West. They contained it in some places, crushed it in other places, but could not calm all irregular activity through force of arms. The surrender of Lee at Appomattox was a turning point, leading many bands to give up and rehabilitate themselves. The hard-core guerrillas—the marauders who fought mostly for themselves rather than for a cause—could only be hunted down like animals or intimidated until they disappeared into the civilian population, giving up their depredations. The guerrilla war came to an end in the West not so much by Federal policies or military operations as by the force of circumstances. Efforts by recent historians to portray guerrilla fighting as the key to spurring the Federal army toward punitive measures, thereby creating a harsher war policy, are not convincing. Many factors contributed to the growth of a destructive policy of taking or destroying Southern resources, and most of them had nothing to do with retribution inspired by guerrilla attacks. They had everything to do with the limitations of Union logistical arrangements, the natural tendency for soldiers to want to eat something more than army rations, and the inclination of armed men to take what they want when confronting unarmed civilians.[9]

Contrasting West and East

It became a constant theme: Westerners and Easterners were nearly as different from each other as Northerners and Southerners. "The westerners were strangers in this army," commented Surgeon Harris Beecher of the 114th New York when Thirteenth Corps troops traveled down the Mississippi to help Nathaniel P. Banks in 1863. They "attracted considerable attention from their peculiar habits and singular style of doing duty. They were, evidently, excellent fighting men, and were very proficient in drill; but they had a wonderful disregard of personal appearance, wearing all manner of dirty and outlandish costumes."[10]

The keen sense that Westerners were different from Easterners came about naturally in America, for the Western states and their society were yet fairly new in the 1860s. Except for Kentucky, Tennessee, and Louisiana, all of the states lying west of the Appalachian Highlands had largely been settled only after the War of 1812 had eliminated Native American resistance. Most of these states had been admitted to the Union within half a century before the firing on Fort Sumter. The first Western president, Andrew Jackson, left office only twenty-four years before secession. By 1861 the Western states had grown rapidly in population, industry, and agricultural production, but culturally they were still considered provincial enclaves. There was a natural sense of self-pride and resentment against the older East that often conflicted with an Eastern perception that the West was still a crude frontier region.

Although these common attitudes usually led to criticism, there is evidence that some men admired the differences between the Western and Eastern armies of the Union. When Rice C. Bull of the 123rd New York saw Sherman's Western troops during the buildup to the Chattanooga campaign, he called them "a large fine type of men." Wickham Hoffman, who encountered Sixteenth Corps troops during the Red River campaign, remembered they "boasted that they had been in many a fight, and had never been defeated. I believe it was a true boast. It was partly luck, partly their own courage and partly the skill with which they were handled." Many observers of their march down Pennsylvania Avenue during the Grand Review noted that the Westerners had "more of the swinging independent step, a most natural result of their long unceasing march through the enemy's country."[11]

Many Eastern veterans praised their Western comrades after the war, and some envied their experiences. Chill W. Hazzard assured a meeting of the Society of the Army of the Cumberland in 1881 that he "was an *Army of the Potomac* boy, and yet, when I read over the story of your marches and campaigns, it seems as if all the romance of the war rested within the pages of that story, and while our trials and dangers were mutual, yet the excitement of crossing mountains, bridging rivers, galloping through whole states, and stealing chickens, was never vouchsafed us."[12]

Nevertheless, quite a few Easterners had little regard for Westerners, considering them ill-disciplined braggarts. Lieutenant Charles W. Glaser of the 17th New York called them *"nothing but an organized Mob."* As officer of the guard for a civilian house at one point during the Meridian campaign, Glaser tried to stop some of Sherman's men from pillaging the place. They called him "a 'Son of a Bitch,'" forcing him to summon members of his own regiment to restore order. "These are the Western soldiers!," Glaser informed his brother, "a lot of d–n house burners, Thieves & murderers that's what they are! And the officers are *Pis Pots*!" When Grant became general in chief, Glaser had to put up with "a good deal of '*blagarding* from these Western Soldiers. . . . Gen'l Grant is going to show us how to fight these Western Hoosiers say; is going to take Richmond right away!"[13]

If Eastern men had mixed reactions to their Western comrades, the Westerners rarely voiced anything but complaint about their counterparts in Virginia because they seemed incapable of dealing with Lee. "The Army of the Potomac has never done anything and never will," complained John F. Brobst of the 25th Wisconsin in the Sixteenth Corps. "If they had done half as much as the western army, this war would have been rubbed out before this time. This army will have to go down there and take Richmond for them, poor fellows." William T. Clark more charitably concluded that the East "furnished the capital for that war," while the West provided the most effective soldiers. That, of course, was not literally true, but it seemed that way to the former staff member in the Army of the Tennessee.[14]

When Grenville M. Dodge visited Grant's headquarters at City Point, Virginia, in October 1864, after recovering from a terrible head wound suffered during the Atlanta campaign, he was astonished at the rampant complaining he heard among high- and low-level commanders in the Army of the Potomac. In the West, Dodge had grown used to subordinates who cooperated without complaint, confident in their commander's decisions. But here, everyone seemed to have a harsh word for Grant's handling of the Overland and Petersburg campaigns. He told John A. Rawlins, Grant's chief of staff, about it, and Rawlins laughed. "'General, this is not the old Army of the Tennessee'" was his only explanation. While Dodge admired the stamina of troops in the Army of the James, who took their punishment while standing in the open during a reconnaissance in force on October 13, he noted that Western troops in a similar situation would have taken cover without orders and dug fieldworks, all the time keeping up a heavy skirmish fire with the enemy.[15]

On the surface, the war in the East appears to have been bloodier in some ways than the war in the West, leading some observers to assume the Eastern troops had heavier fighting to do than those in the West. The impression left by large battles with heavy casualty lists can account for that appearance. Engagements such as Second Bull Run, Antietam, Fredericksburg, Chancellorsville, Gettysburg, the Wilderness, Spotsylvania, and Cold

Harbor produced stunning losses when one considers the total number of casualties compared to the losses suffered at Shiloh, Perryville, Stones River, Chickamauga, and Franklin. Advocates of placing the Eastern campaigns in the center of importance could point to the former engagements to prove that Eastern soldiers in both blue and gray bore a greater burden of blood in their respective national war efforts.

But the number of casualties can be misleading when gauging the scale of fighting. One has to consider the ratio of loss, not just the total number of killed, wounded, and missing in action, when comparing the burden of blood between East and West. An analysis of forty battles in the East and forty battles in the West produced an interesting conclusion: that the loss ratio was actually higher in the Western engagements than in the Eastern battles. The loss ratios in the East and the West were 8.4 percent and 10.3 percent respectively. One can be generous and average them out to be about 9.3 percent, but even so the point remains that the Eastern battles were not bloodier or more severe than the Western fights, they were simply bigger.

This comparison of loss ratios included both Union and Confederate casualties, which amounts to eighty loss ratio figures for the East and the same number for the West. If one totals the number of loss ratios that exceeded 10 percent, the East accounted for fewer of those costly battles than did the West. Whereas about 18,000 Union soldiers fell at the battle of the Wilderness and about 4,200 at Perryville, the loss ratio for the Federal army at the Wilderness was only 15 percent compared to the Union loss ratio of 19 percent at Perryville. Grant lost 16 percent of his army and Lee 15 percent of his troops at Spotsylvania, but William S. Rosecrans and Braxton Bragg lost 29 percent of their manpower at Stones River. Thirty-four percent of the Yankee force that defended Allatoona on October 5, 1864, was shot down in one of the smallest but most sanguinary battles of the entire war. In comparison, the grand slaughter of the Federals at Gettysburg, memorable as it was, resulted in a loss ratio of 24 percent of the men involved.[16]

Grant was in a better position to observe the performance of both Western and Eastern Federals than any other officer of high rank. In his general report, filed after the conclusion of the war, he diplomatically assured Secretary Stanton that "there is no difference in their fighting qualities. All that it was possible for men to do in battle they have done." Grant tried to sew together the sections in celebrating the Union triumph: "The splendid achievements of each have nationalized our victories, removed all sectional jealousies (of which we have unfortunately experienced too much), and the cause of crimination and recrimination that might have followed had either section failed in its duty."[17]

Grant spoke above as general in chief. But when called on to respond as the former commander of the Army of the Tennessee, he expressed genuine love for the military force he had created and molded into the Union's most successful field army. Although Grant was compelled to turn down most invitations to attend meetings of its veterans, he always wrote a heartfelt note of appreciation for the army. "Naturally I feel an attachment f[or] it, and have an acquaintance with it, greater than any other person can well feel." It was "my first command in the late terrible rebellion, and with which I felt myself identified to the end of its service." The Army of the Tennessee "never sustained a single defeat during four years of war," he proudly observed.[18]

While the literature is replete with comments on East-West characteristics among Federal soldiers, the same is not true among Confederates. Perhaps because Southerners exchanged troops between the sections on a far less extensive scale, there seemed to be less tension between sectional partners in the Confederate war effort. Theo F. Davidson related a story told about one of James Longstreet's men who went West to fight at Chickamauga, bragging to his comrades in the Army of Tennessee that he "'had come down to teach the Western man how to fight.'" After the stubborn defense of Snodgrass Hill by the Federals on September 20, the veteran of Lee's army sang a different tune: "'Look here! Do you folks have to fight that sort of people all the time? Why, I never saw such a fool lot of Yankees; they don't know when to run.'" Davidson concluded that "the Federal armies in the West were far superior to those in the East not only in the ability of their Generals, but in the personnel of the soldiers."[19]

Morale

One way in which the West and the East seemed to differ markedly lies in the area of morale and the importance of gaining an emotional advantage over the enemy on the battlefield. George B. McClellan informed Lincoln in early August 1861, soon after taking command of the shattered Union forces following their defeat at First Bull Run, that the Federal government needed to exert so much force and power as to overawe and intimidate the Rebels. This would "convince all our antagonists . . . of the utter impossibility of resistance." While the East recognized that significant movements were taking place in the West, most of its major policy makers and newspapers seemed fixed on McClellan's operations, viewing the Army of the Potomac "as the hope of the nation in winning a decisive victory and restoring the Republic to union and peace." It is thus supremely ironic that the morale ascendancy McClellan wanted to achieve completely eluded him and all subsequent commanders in the East until Grant arrived. Lee gained that ascendancy instead of his opponents and held it for two years. As Carl Schurz wrote, Lee's success was based on "the haughty assurance of his men that under him they could not be beaten or resisted."[20]

If the Eastern Federals could not achieve morale superiority over their opponents, the Western Federals proved that they could. Shiloh was the most important single engagement in this development. When Matilda Gresham visited her soldier husband at Memphis in the late summer of 1862, she was impressed with the spirit of confidence among Grant's officers. "Certainly they were going to clean the country to the Gulf of armed resistance," she commented. "There may have been doubt and uncertainty at Washington and in the Army of the Potomac, . . . but the men I met then and afterwards believed that as sure as the sun shone they would succeed. They all believed in General Grant's ability to lead them." Other observers liked to talk of a "true Western courage" that animated the Federals and contributed to their confidence in victory. Grant himself felt the spirit of his army after leading it across the Mississippi River and onto the high ground on the Vicksburg side in early May 1863: "No Army ever felt better than this one does nor more confidant of success. Before they are beaten they will be very badly beaten. They look for nothing of the kind and could not be brought to a realizing sense of such a possibility before the fact." Walter Q. Gresham told his wife during the Vicksburg siege that "the boys have never been whipped and they do not believe they ever can be. On the contrary, the Rebels here have always been whipped."[21]

Members of the Army of the Tennessee carried that confidence throughout the remainder of the war. During the Atlanta campaign, Alexander C. Little wrote of the Rebels: "Wherever they stand they will be beaten,—this army cannot be beaten—I believe it to be the best army in the world." Under Sherman's direction, the army group that drove toward Atlanta took on some of the overriding self-confidence seen in the Army of the Tennessee. A surgeon in the Fourteenth Corps assured his wife that "our entire army has the most perfect confidence in him and will go wherever he tells them—confident that it will be right." James A. Connolly, another officer in the Fourteenth Corps, commented that "no such thing as failure is thought of in this army."[22]

Sherman saw Grant's operations in Virginia as, in large measure, an attempt to establish a similar morale ascendancy over Lee that the Federals had enjoyed in the West ever since early 1862. Even the horrific casualties of the Overland campaign seemed a worthy price to pay for that ascendancy, for it would "be an immense moral power" of greater value than the capture of Richmond. "This moral result must precede all mere advantages of strategic movements, and this is what Grant is doing. Out here the enemy knows we can and will fight like the devil; therefore he maneuvers for advantage of ground."[23]

Sherman keenly valued the morale ascendancy enjoyed by his Western troops over their opponents, writing of the Confederates' "undue fear of our Western men" during the Carolinas campaign. "This was a power, and I intended to utilize it." He wanted "to whip the rebels, to humble their pride, to follow them to their inmost recesses, and make them fear and dread us." At the end of the war, one of Sherman's staff officers marveled at the attitude of the Western troops who had gone to the Carolinas to help Grant end the war: "The *morale* of this army is superb; their confidence alike in Sherman and in themselves, is an immense element of success."[24]

Confederate armies did not collapse because they feared defeat on the battlefield, but the consistency of Rebel defeat in the West was remarkable. That consistency had its emotional effect on the troops, taking away a certain edge of aggressiveness in more than one battle. The Western troops won their part of the war with a self-confidence born of repeated successes, nearly as much as they won it through hard fighting and superior utilization of resources.

It must be noted that a handful of successful Western generals went to Virginia in 1862, including Henry Halleck, John Pope, and Franz Sigel, and they did not exactly impress anyone. Part of the problem was that Pope unwisely bragged about what he was going to do even before he began to do it. "Let us understand each other," he wrote in a message to his new command, the Army of Virginia. "I have come to you from the West, where we have always seen the back of our enemies; from an army whose business it has been to seek the adversary and to beat him when he was found; whose policy has been attack and not defense. . . . I presume that I have been called here to pursue the same system and to lead you against the enemy." The utterly dismal results of the Second Bull Run campaign made a hollow mockery of these ill-chosen words, and it would be nearly two more years before Lincoln tried to transport the Western style of warfare to Virginia again. Significantly, he chose in 1864 a man who was the chief organizer of that Western style and gave him supreme command of all Union forces rather than only one field army.[25]

Primacy of the Mississippi Valley

Many Westerners were convinced that their section of the country was the future of America, and no one was more certain of it than William T. Sherman. He urged Grant not to make his headquarters in the East, when Grant was named general in chief, but to stay in the Mississippi Valley. "Here lies the seat of the coming empire and from the West, when our task is done, we will make short work of Charleston and Richmond and the impoverished coast of the Atlantic," he assured Grant.[26]

Thus, after the war, Congressman John A. Logan proposed a bill to move the national capital from Washington, D.C., to the Mississippi Valley. He argued, in January 1870, that a "new republic" was developing out of the ashes of the Civil War, justifying the move to the center of the new nation. Logan and those who supported the bill tended to think of St. Louis, Missouri, as the new capital, but the proposal went nowhere in Congress. Nevertheless, it was indicative of the resurgence of self-pride felt across the Western states in the wake of their great victory over the Southern rebellion.[27]

Ironically, the war had accelerated an economic trend evident before the firing on Fort Sumter: the progressive importance of the railroads in shipping goods across the country, West to East, compared to the steamboat traffic down the Mississippi River. While 46 percent of the cotton crop went down the river in 1859–60, only 33 percent of it did so by 1870–71, and 27 percent in 1876–77. The river became less significant economically even while it retained its symbolic hold on the imagination of the Northwest just as strongly in 1865 as in 1861.[28]

The role played by the reopening of navigation on the Mississippi River has been misinterpreted by some historians over the years. The argument has tended to center on the dramatic concept of splitting the territory of the Confederacy in half—thereby denying Davis's government the opportunity to transfer men and provisions from one embattled sector to another—as a major turning point in the war. A counterargument to that interpretation is centered on the undeniable fact that the Confederates managed to shift some supplies across the river even after the fall of Vicksburg. Because Federal control of the stream was not absolute, the significance of reopening the Mississippi was therefore not as important as once thought.[29]

Union victory in the Civil War began in the Mississippi Valley. Federal control of the river dramatically reduced the shipment of supplies and men from West to East. The same sources that document the ability of the Confederates to ship some food across the river after July 4, 1863, also make it abundantly clear that the volume of supplies and men transferred across the stream was reduced to a trickle because of Union control of the river. Like the naval blockade of the Confederate coast, Federal gunboat patrols along the Mississippi came close to stopping the flow of important goods to places where they were needed. It was a significant factor in the Confederacy's growing inability to feed itself. Moreover, reopening river navigation satisfied one of the most critical public demands of the Northwest, a demand that arguably was second only to the restoration of the Union as a war goal for many people in that part of the country.

But my argument for the primacy of the Mississippi Valley in Union victory lies not in the realm of interregional cooperation within the Confederacy or in the area of Northern public policy, but in how Federal commanders used their advantages against Rebel disadvantages to invade and conquer enemy territory. It involves the ability of Federal armies to conquer space and time while bringing the war to an end in a wide swath of the Confederacy earlier than anywhere else. Jefferson Davis's new nation was a huge geographic entity, and his government was dedicated to protecting all of its major regions. Any area where the North could find a weakness to begin the process of cracking open frontier defenses, and keep the momentum rolling, would witness the beginning of eventual Union victory. That area was the valley of the great river. The stream itself, with its key tributaries, offered a natural route of invasion and supply for Union armies to continue their deep penetration of enemy territory, and Northern superiority in river transport gave Lincoln's people the tools to use it. The Confederates never gave priority to the valley in terms of military resources to sufficiently match Federal advantages there, and the result was that the North created an opening wedge in Rebel defenses that could never be repaired by a growingly desperate Confederate government. Even the marshaling of a field army of thirty thousand men under John Pemberton by 1863 could not stop the Yankees from taking Vicksburg any more than the cannon and earthen forts that provided static defense of the stream.

The key to Federal success in the West was in fashioning a logistical system to transport large armies and supply them along the way, to deeply penetrate the Confederacy. While the river system provided the best venue for this, the rail system linking Louisville with Nashville, Chattanooga, and Atlanta gave the Federals their second best venue to accomplish this essential goal. The rail-based system was not as secure or reliable as the river-based system on the Mississippi and its effectiveness ended at Atlanta, but the rails did allow the Federals to deeply penetrate the Southeastern Confederacy. Moving large numbers of troops through contested countryside without a secure line of communications had also become a major feature of Union military operations by the fall of 1864. Sherman used that raiding strategy to move sixty thousand veterans into the Eastern theater of operations. The Eastern armies barely were able to defeat Lee just before Sherman arrived with those veterans. Otherwise, the West would have won the war in the East and the Western Federals would have had even more reason to brag about the decisive role they played in saving the Union.

{ Notes

Abbreviations

ADAH	Alabama Dept. of Archives and History, Montgomery
AHC	Atlanta History Center, Atlanta
AL	Abraham Lincoln
ALPL	Abraham Lincoln Presidential Library, Springfield, Ill.
BC	Bowdoin College, Special Collections and Archives, Brunswick, Maine
BGSU	Bowling Green State University, Center for Archival Collections, Bowling Green, Ohio
CHS	Chicago Historical Society, Chicago
Conn-HS	Connecticut Historical Society, Hartford
CU	Cornell University, Rare and Manuscript Collection, Ithaca, N.Y.
CWM	College of William and Mary, Special Collections Research Center, Williamsburg, Va.
DU	Duke University, Rare Books, Manuscripts, and Special Collections, Durham, N.C.
EU	Emory University, Manuscripts, Archives, and Rare Books Library, Atlanta
FHS	Filson Historical Society, Louisville, Ky.
GDAH	Georgia Dept. of Archives and History, Atlanta
HQ	Headquarters
IHS	Indiana Historical Society, Indianapolis
ISL	Indiana State Library, Indianapolis
JD	Jefferson Davis
KCPL	Knox County Public Library, McClung Collection, Knoxville, Tenn.
KHS	Kentucky Historical Society, Frankfort
KMNBP	Kennesaw Mountain National Battlefield Park, Kennesaw, Ga.
LC	Library of Congress, Manuscript Division, Washington, D.C.
LMU	Lincoln Memorial University, Abraham Lincoln Library and Museum, Harrogate, Tenn.
LSU	Louisiana State University, Louisiana and Lower Mississippi Valley Collections, Baton Rouge
Mass-HS	Massachusetts Historical Society, Boston
MDAH	Mississippi Dept. of Archives and History, Jackson
MHS	Missouri Historical Society, St. Louis
MOC	Museum of the Confederacy, Richmond, Va.
NL	Newberry Library, Chicago
OR	*The War of the Rebellion: A Compilation of the Official Records of the Union and Confederate Armies.* 128 vols. Washington, D.C.: Government Printing Office, 1880–1901. Unless otherwise noted, citations are to

	series 1. *OR* citations take the following form: volume number (part number, where applicable):page number.
ORN	*Official Records of the Union and Confederate Navies in the War of the Rebellion.* 30 vols. Washington, D.C.: Government Printing Office, 1894–1922. *ORN* citations take the same form as *OR* citations.
REL	Robert E. Lee
SOR	*Supplement to the Official Records of the Union and Confederate Armies.* 100 vols. Wilmington, Del.: Broadfoot, 1995–99. *SOR* citations take the same form as *OR* citations.
SU	Stanford University, Special Collections and University Archives, Stanford, Calif.
TSLA	Tennessee State Library and Archives, Nashville
UA	University of Alabama, William Stanley Hoole Special Collections, Tuscaloosa
UAF	University of Arkansas, Special Collections, Fayetteville
UK	University of Kentucky, Audio-Visual Archives, Lexington
U-Mont	University of Montana, Mansfield Library, Missoula
UNC	University of North Carolina, Southern Historical Collection, Chapel Hill
UND	University of Notre Dame, Rare Books and Special Collections, South Bend, Ind.
UO	University of Oklahoma, Western History Collections, Norman
US	University of the South, Archives and Special Collections, Sewanee, Tenn.
USAMHI	U.S. Army Military History Institute, Carlisle, Pa.
UV	University of Virginia, Special Collections, Charlottesville
UW	University of Washington, Special Collections Division, Seattle
WHS	Wisconsin Historical Society, Madison
WTS	William Tecumseh Sherman

Chapter 1

1. Paludan, "American Civil War," 1019, 1021–25, 1027, 1030; Hess, *Liberty, Virtue, and Progress*, 22–26.

2. Cozzens and Girardi, *Military Memoirs*, 98; J. Sherman, *Recollections of Forty Years*, 242–43; Scribner, *How Soldiers Were Made*, 14; Gresham, *Life of Walter Quintin Gresham*, 1:141.

3. *Chatfield Republican*, April 16, 1861, *Elkhorn Independent*, April 19, 1861, *Indianapolis Daily Journal*, April 27, 1861, *Cincinnati Daily Commercial*, May 6, 1861, and *Daily Chicago Times*, June 12, 1861, all in Perkins, *Northern Editorials*, 2:741, 747, 814–15, 828, 849.

4. Williams, *Wild Life of the Army*, 6; Cox, "War Preparations in the North," 84–85.

5. Hess, "Mississippi River," 188.

6. Saxon, *Father Mississippi*, 213, 249.

7. Ibid., 253–54, 257, 261, 263.

8. Gould, *Fifty Years on the Mississippi*, 431–33, 438.

9. Saxon, *Father Mississippi*, 246–47; Hess, "Mississippi River," 188–89.

10. *Cincinnati Daily Enquirer*, December 28, 1860, in Perkins, *Northern Editorials*, 1:401; Speech on Secession, December 18–19, 1860, in Graf and Haskins, *Papers of Andrew Johnson*, 4:25; *Chicago Daily Tribune*, December 18, 1860, in Perkins, *Northern Editorials*, 2:539–40; WTS to Thomas Ewing Sr., December 1, 1860, and WTS to Ellen, December 23, 1860, in Simpson and Berlin, *Sherman's Civil War*, 13, 25.

11. Hess, "Mississippi River," 189–90; *Cincinnati Daily Gazette*, January 14, 1861, *Daily Wisconsin* (Milwaukee), January 18, 1861, *Burlington Daily Hawk-Eye*, February 8, 1861, and *Chicago Daily Tribune*, February 25, 1861, all in Perkins, *Northern Editorials*, 2:543–45, 554, 558.

12. Hess, "Mississippi River," 194; *Buffalo Morning Express*, December 24, 1860, *Portland Daily Advertiser*, January 29, 1861, *Pittsburgh Evening Chronicle*, January 26, 1861, and *Worcester Palladium*, January 30, 1861, all in Perkins, *Northern Editorials*, 2:540–41, 549, 551–52.

13. Hess, "Mississippi River," 192–93; William C. Rives, *Speech on the Proceedings of the Peace Conference and the State of the Union, Delivered in Richmond, Virginia, March 8, 1861*, in Wakelyn, *Southern Pamphlets on Secession*, 369–70; Robert Jefferson Breckinridge, *The Civil War: Its Nature and End*, and John W. Wood, *Union and Secession in Mississippi*, in Wakelyn, *Southern Unionist Pamphlets*, 30, 133.

14. *Cincinnati Daily Commercial*, January 25, February 20, 1861, in Perkins, *Northern Editorials*, 2:547–48, 593; Annual Message to Congress, December 1, 1862, in Basler, *Collected Works*, 5:528–29; Donald, *Lincoln*, 34, 37.

15. *Daily Chicago Times*, June 12, 1861, in Perkins, *Northern Editorials*, 2:848–49; WTS to David F. Boyd, May 13, 1861, in Simpson and Berlin, *Sherman's Civil War*, 84; Hess, "Mississippi River," 187.

16. McPherson, *Battle Cry of Freedom*, 276–84.

17. Harrison and Klotter, *New History of Kentucky*, 186–89, 194; T. C. Mackey, "Not a Pariah," 33.

18. *Cincinnati Daily Times*, April 26, 1861, and *Providence Evening Press*, May 7, 1861, in Perkins, *Northern Editorials*, 2:878–79, 883–84; Copeland, "Where Were the Kentucky Unionists and Secessionists?," 350; Thompson to Walker, May 11, 1862, *OR* 52(2):94.

19. Harrison and Klotter, *New History of Kentucky*, 189–90; Harrison, "George W. Johnson and Richard Hawes," 8; T. C. Mackey, "Not a Pariah," 36–37; R. W. Johnson, *A Soldier's Reminiscences*, 267.

20. Harris to Pillow, June 13, 1861, *OR*, ser. 4, 1:377; AL to Secretary of War, August 17, 1861, *OR* 4:255.

21. McRae to JD, April 23, 1861, and Mitchell to JD, April 27, 1861, in Crist, *Papers of Jefferson Davis*, 7:121, 134; Walker to Harris, April 19, 1861, *OR* 52(2):56.

22. Gorgas to Secretary of War, April 29, 1861, and W. W. Lee to Walker, May 10, 1861, *OR* 52(2):75, 93–94.

23. Barry, Horne, Moore, and Moss to JD, April 22, 1861, and Tate to Walker, April 23, 1861, *OR* 52(2):62, 67; Anonymous to JD, February 22, May 18, 1861, in Crist, *Papers of Jefferson Davis*, 7:59, 171.

24. Pillow to Walker, May 9, [1861], Tate to Clayton, May 10, 1861, and Pillow to JD,

May 16, 1861, *OR* 52(2):90, 93, 100–101; Moore to Walker, April 10, 1861, Roman to JD, September 15, 1861, and Robinson to Benjamin, September 20, 1861, *OR* 53:669, 739, 742.

25. Walker to Bragg, March 5, 1861, and Twiggs to Walker, August 9, 1861, *OR* 53:621, 722; JD to Polk, May 22, 1861, and Alvord to JD, July 22, 1861, in Crist, *Papers of Jefferson Davis*, 7:174, 260; Pillow to Walker, June 20, 1861, and Trezevant to Polk, November 10, 21, 1862, *OR* 52(2):113, 204–5, 215; Shea and Winschel, *Vicksburg Is the Key*, 4–5.

26. Mansfield to Totten, June 7, 1861, and Totten memorandum, June 3, 1861, *OR* 52:160, 164–5.

27. Scott to McClellan, May 3, 1861, *OR* 51:369–70.

28. WTS to Thomas Ewing Jr., June 3, 1861, in Simpson and Berlin, *Sherman's Civil War*, 98; Yates to Wool, April 30, 1861, Randall to AL, May 6, 1861, and Yates to AL, June 16, 1861, *OR*, ser. 3, 1:147, 168, 273.

29. Drummond and Goodrich to AL, October 1, 1861, *OR*, ser. 3, 1:549–50.

30. Williams, *Wild Life of the Army*, 11–12.

31. AL to Anderson, May 14, 1861, AL to Buckner, July 10, 1861, and AL to Jackson, August 7, 1861, in Basler, *Collected Works*, 4:368–69, 444, 477; Adams to Chase, July 31, 1861, in Niven, *Chase Papers*, 3:83; Cameron to [Scott], June 27, 1861, *OR*, ser. 3, 1:299–300; Nelson to Johnson, July 25, 1861, in Graf and Haskins, *Papers of Andrew Johnson*, 4:596–97.

32. Harrison and Klotter, *New History of Kentucky*, 190–91; Magoffin to JD, August [n.d.], 1861, and JD to Magoffin, August 28, 1861, *OR* 4:378, 396–97; AL to Magoffin, August 24, 1861, in Basler, *Collected Works*, 4:497.

33. Lellyett to Johnson, August 26, [1861], in Graf and Haskins, *Papers of Andrew Johnson*, 4:697–98; Speed to Chase, September 2, 1861, in Niven, *Chase Papers*, 3:92–94.

34. Polk to Walker, July 30, 1861, and Harris to Polk, August 11, 1861, *OR* 4:376, 384; July 28, August 3, 1861, Hardee to Polk, August 4, 1861, Pillow to Polk, August 5, 7, 1861, Gray's report, August 15, 1861, McCown to Henry, August 18, 1861, Thompson to Officer commanding at Camp Sikeston, August 18, 1861, and Thompson to McCown, August 19, 1861, *OR* 3:619, 628–30, 634–35, 652, 661, 664; Hardee to Hindman, August 20, September 2, 1861, *OR* 53:730–31, 735.

35. Pillow to Polk, August 28, 1861, and Polk to JD, August 29, 1861, *OR* 3:685–86, 688; JD to Polk, September 2, 1861, in Crist, *Papers of Jefferson Davis*, 7:318; Polk to Magoffin, September 1, 1861, *OR* 4:179; Parks, *General Leonidas Polk*, 1–152.

36. Jacob Thompson to JD, September 6, 1861, in Crist, *Papers of Jefferson Davis*, 7:329; Roland, *Albert Sidney Johnston*, 6–258.

37. Frémont to Thomas, August 25, 1861, Oglesby to Frémont, August 23, 1861, Anderson to Chase, September 1, 1861, General Orders No. 57, Adjutant General's Office, August 15, 1861, Morton to Scott, August 29, September 2, 1861, and Boyle and Speed to AL, September 2, 1861, in *OR* 4:177, 254–56.

38. Grant, *Memoirs*, 172–73; Perret, *Ulysses S. Grant*, 3–113; Grant to Smith, September 1, 1861, Grant to McClernand, September 1, 1861, and Grant to Frémont, September 1, 1861, *OR* 3:144–46.

39. Waagner to Frémont, September 2, 1861, Grant to Frémont, September 4, 1861, and Frémont to Grant, September 5, 1861, *OR* 3:148–52; Hughes, *Battle of Belmont*, 4.

40. Polk to JD (and Davis endorsement), September 4, 1861, Taylor et al. to Polk, September 5, 1861, McClernand to Frémont, September 5, 1861, Grant to Frémont, September 6, 1861, Hillyer to Paine, September 6, 1861, and Grant to Paine, September 6, 1861, *OR* 4:181–84, 196–98; Special Orders No. [not stated], HQ, District of Southeast Missouri, September 5, 1861, and Frémont to AL, September 8, 1861, *OR* 3:150, 478; Grant, *Memoirs*, 174–76; Hughes, *Battle of Belmont*, 4.

41. T. L. Connelly, *Army of the Heartland*, 64–66.

42. John M. Johnston to Polk, September 9, 1861, Harris to JD, September 4, 1861, Walker to Harris, September 5, 1861, and Buckner to Cooper, September 13, 1861, *OR* 4:185–86, 188–90; Harrison and Klotter, *New History of Kentucky*, 192; T. C. Mackey, "Not a Pariah," 40.

43. Polk to John M. Johnston, September 9, 1861, Polk to JD, September 14, 1861, Henry to JD, September 15, 1861, JD to Polk, September 15, 1861, and Johnston to JD, September 16, 1861, *OR* 4:186–88, 191, 193; Buckner, To the People of Kentucky, September 18, 1861, *OR*, ser. 2, 2:1380–81.

44. Gray to Blake, September 18, 1861, *OR* 3:703–5. Most historians have severely criticized Polk for occupying Columbus, arguing that he made, in Thomas Connelly's words, "probably one of the greatest mistakes of the war." In this view, Polk lost the sentiments of Kentucky to the Union cause. But, as argued in this chapter, there is ample evidence that the state's sentiments had already decisively shifted toward Lincoln's government. Polk and many of his contemporaries saw his incursion as a desperate effort to save what he could of the state for Confederate purposes. See T. L. Connelly, *Army of the Heartland*, 52.

Chapter 2

1. Alcorn to Buckner, October 21, 1861, and Johnston to Benjamin, October 22, 1861, *OR* 4:467, 469; Adams to JD, January 11, 1862, in Crist, *Papers of Jefferson Davis*, 8:12–13; Benjamin to Johnston, December 26, 1861, *OR* 7:796.

2. Harris to JD, October 15, 1861, *OR* 4:449; Cockrill to Walker, May 9, 1861, *OR* 52(2):92; Crist, *Papers of Jefferson Davis*, 7, 177n.

3. Harris to JD, October 15, 1861, *OR* 4:449.

4. Pillow to Weakley, November 20, 1861, and Peoples to Benjamin, November 20, 1861, *OR* 7:684–86; McCown statement, December 1, 1861, *OR* 52(2):223.

5. Polk to JD, November 3, 1861, *OR* 4:505.

6. Gill to L. Thomas, January 17, 1862, *OR*, ser. 3, 1:801; Preston to JD, December 28, 1861, in Crist, *Papers of Jefferson Davis*, 7:445–46.

7. Harrison and Klotter, *New History of Kentucky*, 192–94; Harrison, "George W. Johnson and Richard Hawes," 9; Johnson to JD, November 21, 1861, *OR*, ser. 4, 1:743–44; Stevenson, "Kentucky Neutrality in 1861," 66–67.

8. Hannum to Polk, October 4, 1861, *OR*, ser. 2, 2:1388.

9. Milligan, *Gunboats*, 6–11, 13, 15–17, 22–23, 25.

10. Ibid., xxv, 9–10, 19.

11. Grant to Julia, September 22, 1861, in Simon, *Papers of . . . Grant*, 2:300; Grant, *Memoirs*, 177–78.

12. Hughes, *Battle of Belmont*, 81, 101, 120, 131, 150, 160, 169, 184; Grant, *Memoirs*,

178–79, 184–85; Grant to Father, November 8, 1861, in Simon, *Papers of . . . Grant*, 3:137; Wright, "Battle of Belmont," 70–71, 73–79; Woodworth, *Nothing but Victory*, 47–55.

13. Weakley to Citizens of Northern Alabama and Northern Mississippi, November 23, 1861, and Fontaine to Polk, November 28, 1861, *OR* 7:695–96, 708–9; Polk to Benjamin, October 10, 1861, and Pillow to Thompson, November 16, 1861, *OR* 3:716, 740–41.

14. Thompson to Polk, December 30, 1861, *OR* 8:45.

15. Breckinridge, *The Civil War: Its Nature and End*, in Wakelyn, *Southern Unionist Pamphlets*, 30–31.

16. Groce, *Mountain Rebels*, 1, 39, 41; Johnson to Welles, September 30, 1861 (5:12), and Staples to Johnson, August 16, 1861 (4:681), in Graf and Haskins, *Papers of Andrew Johnson*; Haynes to Walker, July 6, 1861, and Harris to Walker, August 16, 1861, *OR* 4:364–65, 389.

17. "Memorandum for a Plan of Campaign" [ca. October 1, 1861], in Basler, *Collected Works*, 4:544–45; Patton to Johnson, June 27, 1861, in Graf and Haskins, *Papers of Andrew Johnson*, 4:521.

18. WTS to Ewing, December 12, 1861, in Simpson and Berlin, *Sherman's Civil War*, 162, 165n; WTS, *Memoirs*, 1:200–204; Daniel, *Days of Glory*, 19–22; Marszalek, *Sherman*, 1–170.

19. Carter to G. H. Thomas, October 27, 1861, *OR* 4:320; Madden, "Unionist Resistance," 25–26, 28–29.

20. Lewis to JD, November 11, 1861, Graham to JD, November 12, 1861, and Harris to JD, November 12, 1861, *OR*, ser. 2, 1:839, 841; Branner to Benjamin, November 9, 1861, Cannon to Wood, November 10, 1861, Cooper to Leadbetter, November 10, 1861, and Wood to Cooper, November 11, 1861, *OR* 4:231, 233–37; Madden, "Unionist Resistance," 34, 38–39.

21. Carter to G. H. Thomas, November 16, 1861, *OR*, ser. 2, 1:892; WTS to J. Sherman [brother], January 8, 1862, in Simpson and Berlin, *Sherman's Civil War*, 178.

22. Benjamin to Wood, November 25, 1861, *OR*, ser. 2, 1:848; Leadbetter to Benjamin, November 30, 1861, and Benjamin to Carroll, December 10, 1861, *OR* 7:726, 754; Madden, "Unionist Resistance," 38–39.

23. Bryan, "'Tories' amidst Rebels," 9; Leadbetter to Cooper, November 28, 1861, *OR* 7:713; Clark to Benjamin, November 16, 1861, and Brown to Benjamin, November 17, 1861, *OR* 52(2):209.

24. WTS to J. Sherman, January 8, 1862, in Simpson and Berlin, *Sherman's Civil War*, 180; Maynard to Johnson, November 13, 1861, in Graf and Haskins, *Papers of Andrew Johnson*, 5:32; McClellan to Buell, November 7, 12, 1861, *OR* 4:342, 355; McClellan to Buell, November 25, [November 29], and December 3, 1861, *OR* 7:447, 457, 468; Annual Message to Congress, December 3, 1861, in Basler, *Collected Works*, 5:37; Stanton to Hamlin, March 22, 1862, *OR*, ser. 3, 1:942; Engle, *Buell*, 1–126.

25. WTS to J. Sherman, January 8, 1862, in Simpson and Berlin, *Sherman's Civil War*, 175; Buell to McClellan, December 29, 1861, *OR* 7:521.

26. Johnson and Maynard to Buell, December 7, 1861, Buell to AL, January 5, 1862, McClellan to Buell, January 6, 1862, and Buell to McClellan, February 1, 1862, *OR* 7:480, 530–31, 931–32; McClellan to Buell, December 29, 1861, *OR* 1:899; AL to Buell, Janu-

ary 6, 1862, in Basler, *Collected Works*, 5:91; WTS to J. Sherman, January 8, 9, 1862, in Simpson and Berlin, *Sherman's Civil War*, 175, 184; Engle, *Buell*, 154–55; Daniel, *Days of Glory*, 43–44.

27. REL to Mackall, November 6, 1861, Unnumbered order, HQ, Western Dept., November 25, 1861, and Leadbetter to Cooper, January 7, 1862, *OR*, ser. 2, 2:1396–99, 1412.

28. Chase to Mellen, May 29, 1861, in Niven, *Chase Papers*, 3:66; Grant to Cook, September 12, 1861, and Grant to McKeever, October 1, 9, 1861, *OR* 3:490, 511, 529.

29. Grant to Father, May 6, 1861, Grant to Julia, June 6, 1861, and Grant to Mary, September 11, 1861, in Simon, *Papers of . . . Grant*, 2:21–22, 39, 237–38; *Fagots from the Camp Fire*, 183; Grant to Father, November 27, 1861, Grant to Cook, December 25, 1861, and Hillyer to Ross, January 5, 1862, in Simon, *Papers of . . . Grant*, 3:227, 342–43, 373–74.

30. Smith to All Who It May Concern, October 10, 1861, *OR* 4:302.

31. Oglesby to Grant, November 13, 1861, *OR* 3:257; Grant to Kelton, November 28, 1861, *OR* 7:455.

32. Grant to Ross, December 4, 1861, in Simon, *Papers of . . . Grant*, 3:258; Grant to Paine, January 11, 12, 1862, *OR* 8:494–95; Cases of Messrs. Ogden, Perkins, Brady, and Child, n.d., and Oath Signed by 36 Men, February 22, 1862, *OR*, ser. 2, 2:1357–59.

33. Greene to Anderson, September 27, 1861, *OR*, ser. 2, 2:81–82; General Orders No. 5, Dept. of the Cumberland, October 7, 1861, and WTS to Ward, November 2, 1861, *OR* 4:296, 327; Grimsley, *Hard Hand of War*, 61–66.

34. Cases of Charles S. Morehead, Reuben T. Durrett, and M. W. Barr, n.d., Cases of Messrs. Clay, Kearny, Grubbs, and Others, n.d., Coffey to G. H. Thomas, September 25, 1861, and Cases of Richard H. Stanton and Others, n.d., *OR*, ser. 2, 2:805–6, 881–82, 884, 913–15.

35. WTS to L. Thomas, November 6, 1861, *OR* 4:340–41.

36. McClellan to Buell, November 7, 12, 1861, *OR* 4:342, 355; Greene to Henderson, January 10, 1862, *OR*, ser. 2, 2:186.

37. McCook to WTS, November 5, 1861, and WTS to McCook, November 8, 1861, *OR*, ser. 2, 1:776–77; WTS to Turchin, October 15, 1861, *OR* 4:307.

38. Nelson to the People of Northeastern Kentucky, October 17, 1861, and Marshall to Cooper, December 10, 30, 1861, *OR*, ser. 2, 2:106, 1404, 1410; Proclamation, November 5, 1861, *OR* 4:345; Marshall to [not stated], January 14, 1862, *OR* 7:48–49.

39. Carr, "Garfield and Marshall," 253–55, 257, 259–60; Garfield to Citizens of the Sandy Valley, January 16, 1862, *OR* 7:33.

40. Williams, *Wild Life of the Army*, 70; Zollicoffer to the People of Southeastern Kentucky, December 16, 1861, *OR* 7:787.

41. Hafendorfer, *Mill Springs*, 171–73, 177, 181, 289, 421, 425; Prokopowicz, *All for the Regiment*, 68–78.

42. Hafendorfer, *Mill Springs*, 427, 438, 440, 442, 446, 460, 469; Einolf, *George Thomas*, 11–102; William H. Watterson Diary, January 19, 1862, KCPL.

43. Buell to L. Thomas, January 27, 1862, Maynard to Thomas, February 4, 1862, and Haynes to JD, January 27, 1862, *OR* 7:658, 582, 849; Murray to Brothers, January 29, 1862, Murray Papers, USAMHI.

Chapter 3

1. Grant to Halleck, January 29, 1862, in Simon, *Papers of . . . Grant*, 4:103; Grant to WTS, [January 29, 1876], ibid., 27:17; Halleck to McClellan, January 20, 1862, *OR* 8:509; Marszalek, *Commander of All Lincoln's Armies*, 4–104; WTS, *Memoirs*, 1:220; Buell to McClellan, February 5, 1862, *OR* 7:585; Wallace to Wife, February 5, 1862, Wallace Papers, IHS.

2. Cooling, *Forts Henry and Donelson*, 89–90, 98, 102–10; Woodworth, *Nothing but Victory*, 73–78; Grant to Julia, March 1, 1862, in Simon, *Papers of . . . Grant*, 4:307; Grant, *Memoirs*, 190; Carrington Diary, February 6, 1862, Carrington Papers, CHS.

3. Phelps to Foote, February 10, 1862, *OR* 7:154–56; Grant to Julia, February 10, 1862, in Simon, *Papers of . . . Grant*, 4:188.

4. Grant to Cook, February 9, 1862, Grant to Chase, February 9, 1862, and Grant to Mary, February 9, 1862, in Simon, *Papers of . . . Grant*, 4:177–78, 180; General Field Orders No. 5, HQ, District of Cairo, February 9, 1862, *OR* 7:599.

5. Grant to Kelton, February 6, 1862, *OR* 7:125; Grant, *Memoirs*, 196–97.

6. Cooling, *Forts Henry and Donelson*, 140–46, 155–59, 166–71, 177–80, 185–88, 191–95; Grant, *Memoirs*, 198, 201–5.

7. Cooling, *Forts Henry and Donelson*, 200–205, 211–14; Woodworth, *Nothing but Victory*, 87–119.

8. Hillyer to Wife, February 25, 1862, Hillyer Collection, UV; Grant to Cullum, February 19, 1862, *OR*, ser. 2, 3:283; Order relating to Commercial Intercourse, February 28, 1862, in Basler, *Collected Works*, 5:139; General Orders No. 14, HQ, District of West Tennessee, February 26, 1862, in Simon, *Papers of . . . Grant*, 4:290.

9. Halleck to Grant, March 17, 1862, and Grant to Halleck, March 24, 1862, *OR* 10(2):42, 62; General Field Orders No. 16, HQ, Army in the Field, February 16, 1862, Grant to Cullum, February 19, 1862, General Orders No. 12, HQ, District of West Tennessee, February 25, 1862, and Grant to Kelton, March 3, 1862, in Simon, *Papers of . . . Grant*, 4:220, 245, 285, 312–13; Cooling, *Forts Henry and Donelson*, 216; Grant to Cullum, February 17, 1862, and Grant to McClernand, February 17, 1862, *OR*, ser. 2, 3:271–72.

10. Grant to Cullum, February 17, 1862, Mulligan to Halleck, February 27, 1862, Robb to JD, March 6, 1862, Hoffman to Meigs, March 7, 1862, and Jones to L. Thomas, April 6, 1862, *OR*, ser. 2, 3:271–72, 335, 357, 360, 427–29; Lamb to Allison, July 4, 1862, *OR*, ser. 2, 4:128; Allman to Johnson, March 8, 1862, and Bails to Johnson, March 28, 1862, in Graf and Haskins, *Papers of Andrew Johnson*, 5:190, 249–50; Cooling, *Forts Henry and Donelson*, 219–23.

11. Special Orders No. 6, HQ, Dept. of the Mississippi, March 14, 1862, and Cutts to Kelton, March 19, 1862, *OR*, ser. 2, 3:378, 388–89; Hoffman to Fonda, August 30, 1862, *OR*, ser. 2, 4:470–71; [Johnson and Maynard] to Stanton, March 13, 1862, and Johnson to AL, June 5, 1862, in Graf and Haskins, *Papers of Andrew Johnson*, 5:201, 446; Gower and Allen, *Pen and Sword*, 629–30, 672.

12. Grant to Wife, February 16, 1862, in Simon, *Papers of . . . Grant*, 4:229–30; Womack, *Civil War Diary*, 36; Lovell to Johnston, February 12, 1862, Beauregard to Pryor, February 14, 1862, Benjamin to Polk, February 20, 1862, and Maney to Singleton, February 23, 1862, *OR* 7:878, 880, 894, 902; Walker to Beauregard, February 19, 1862, *OR* 52(2):275.

13. Beauregard to Cooper, February 18, 1862, Benjamin to Beauregard, February 19, 1862, Beauregard to Johnston, February 12, 1862, and Pillow to Benjamin, February 26, 1862, *OR* 7:890, 892, 895–96, 908; Walker to Beauregard, February 19, 1862, and Withers to Perkins, February 28, 1862, *OR* 52(2):275, 278–79; WTS to Ewing, February 27, 1862, in Simpson and Berlin, *Sherman's Civil War*, 194.

14. Bragg to Benjamin, February 15, 1862, *OR* 6:826; Johnston to JD, March 18, 1862, and Pillow to Benjamin, February 26, 1862, *OR* 7:260, 909; Johnston to JD, March 7, 1862, *OR* 10(2):302.

15. Johnston to Benjamin, February 25, 1862, *OR* 7:426–27.

16. Trousdale to Committee of Confederate House of Representatives, March 11, 1862, McClellan to Buell, February 24, 1862, and McClellan to Halleck, February 24, 1862, *OR* 432:660–61; Floyd to Benjamin, March 11, 1862, *OR* 10:4.

17. Gwin to Foote, February 23, 1862, *OR* 7:421–22; Gwin to Foote, March 5, 1862, *OR* 10(2):8; Cooling, *Forts Henry and Donelson*, 113–15.

18. Foote to [not stated], February 20, 1862, Foote to Welles, February 20, 1862, *OR* 7:423, 644–45; Cooling, *Forts Henry and Donelson*, 245–47.

19. Scott to Stanton, February 25, 1862, Halleck to McClellan, February 21, 1862, and General Orders No. 13a, HQ, Dept. of the Ohio, February 26, 1862, *OR* 7:424, 647, 669; Buell to Board on Property, March 19, 1862, *OR* 10(2):47–48; Engle, *Buell*, 189–96.

20. Extracts from Col. J. Ammen Diary, February 23–25, 1862, and Buell to McClellan, February 28, March 3, 1862, *OR* 7:660, 671, 679; Maslowski, *Treason Must Be Made Odious*, 20–24, 26.

21. General Orders No. 7, HQ, District of West Tennessee, February 22, 1862, Grant to Cullum, February 23, 1862, and Grant to Julia, February 24, 1862, in Simon, *Papers of . . . Grant*, 4:265, 276, 284; General Orders No. 46, HQ, Dept. of the Missouri, February 22, 1862, *OR* 8:563–64.

22. Halleck to McClellan, February 28, March 4, 1862, Halleck to Grant, March 1, 1862, and Halleck to Buell, March 4, 1862, *OR* 7:672, 674, 682–83; Grant to Julia, March 1, 1862, in Simon, *Papers of . . . Grant*, 4:306.

23. Halleck to McClellan, March 3, 4, 1862, and Halleck to L. Thomas, March 15, 1862, *OR* 7:679–80, 682–83; President's War Order No. 3, March 11, 1862, and Grant to Halleck, March 24, 1862, *OR* 10(2):28, 62; Grant to Washburn, March 22, 1862, in Simon, *Papers of . . . Grant*, 4:409.

24. Grant to Julia, March 11, 1862, in Simon, *Papers of . . . Grant*, 4:349; Daniel, *Shiloh*, 75–77.

25. Ferris, "Captain Jolly," 19; Grant to Halleck, March 11, [13], 1862, Grant to Julia, March 18, 1862, Grant to Smith, March 26, 1862, McClernand to Grant, March 29, 1862, in Simon, *Papers of . . . Grant*, 4:341–42, 351, 389, 425, 438n; General Orders No. 10, HQ, Dept. of the Mississippi, March 28, 1862, *OR* 8:834.

26. Grant, *Memoirs*, 222; Daniel, *Shiloh*, 24–28, 45, 68, 73; T. L. Connelly, *Army of the Heartland*, 20–21; Benjamin to Hebert, February 23, 1862, *OR* 6:830; Beauregard to Cooper, April 11, 1862, *OR* 10(1):385; JD to Johnston, March 26, 1862, *OR* 10(2):365.

27. Marks to Polk, December 2, 1861, and Pettus to [Beauregard], May 1, 1862, *OR* 52(2):225, 309; Gilmer to Wife, March 24, 1862, Gilmer Papers, UNC.

28. Grant to Julia, April 3, 1862, in Simon, *Papers of . . . Grant*, 5:7; Johnston to Soldiers of the Army of the Mississippi, April 3, 1862, *OR* 10(1):396–97; Daniel, *Shiloh*, 128.

29. Daniel, *Shiloh*, 144, 155, 202–14, 218–24; T. B. Smith, "Anatomy of an Icon," 67–74, and *Untold Story*, 34.

30. Daniel, *Shiloh*, 230–37, 246.

31. Ibid., 202–14, 218–24; Woodworth, *Nothing but Victory*, 157–88.

32. Daniel, *Shiloh*, 249, 251, 256, 263.

33. Ibid., 263, 265, 267–92; Prokopowicz, *All for the Regiment*, 101–9.

34. Beauregard to Cooper, April 11, 1862, *OR* 10(1):389; Harrison, "George W. Johnson and Richard Hawes," 25–26; Harrison and Klotter, *New History of Kentucky*, 193–94.

35. Daniel, *Shiloh*, 305; Grant, *Memoirs*, 223, 238–39, 246–47; Grant to Julia, April 15, 1862, in Simon, *Papers of . . . Grant*, 5:47.

36. WTS to Coppee, [January 5, 1865], *SOR* 1(1):642–43.

37. Totten to Beauregard, May [9], 1861, *OR* 10(2):507.

38. General Orders No. 9, 2nd Grand Division, Army of the Mississippi, March 16, 1862, *OR* 10(2):338; Bragg to Jordan, April 30, 1862, *OR* 10(1):469; Bragg to Wife, March 25, April 8, 1862, Bragg Papers, MHS.

39. Daniel, *Shiloh*, 308–9.

40. Doll Reminiscences, 90, 93, ISL; Stanfield to Father, May 1, 9, 1862, Stanfield Papers, IHS.

41. Halleck to Stanton, May 19, 1862, *OR* 10(2):202.

42. Hardee to Beauregard, May 25, 1862, *OR* 10(2):545.

43. Beauregard to Cooper, May 19, 1862, *OR* 10(2):530; Beauregard to Cooper, June 13, 1862, *OR* 10(1):762–64; Fragment of Lockett letter, June 1862, Lockett Papers, box 1, folder 14, UNC.

44. Johnson, *A Soldier's Reminiscences*, 193; Grant, *Memoirs*, 255.

45. Pope to Halleck, June 9, 1862, *OR*, ser. 2, 3:667–68; Gresham, *Life of Walter Quintin Gresham*, 1:188; WTS to J. Sherman, [May 31, 1862], in Simpson and Berlin, *Sherman's Civil War*, 231.

46. Stoker, *Grand Design*, 137.

Chapter 4

1. WTS, *Memoirs*, 1:254, 257; Grant, *Memoirs*, 214, 256; Cozzens and Girardi, *Military Memoirs*, 106–7; Stoker, *Grand Design*, 205.

2. WTS to J. Sherman, [May 31, 1862], in Simpson and Berlin, *Sherman's Civil War*, 231; Halleck to Stanton, June 12, 1862, *OR* 16(2):14; Hess, *Banners to the Breeze*, 5–6.

3. Hess, *Banners to the Breeze*, 3–5.

4. McDonough, *War in Kentucky*, 36.

5. Brown to Stephens, February 25, 1862, *SOR* 1(3):710–11.

6. Hess, *Banners to the Breeze*, 9.

7. Negley to Johnson, June 12, 1862: Hambright to Negley, June 8, 1862, *OR* 10(1):920–21; Fry to Crittenden, June 23, 1862, *OR* 16(2):53–54.

8. Mitchell to Fry, April 11, 1862, *OR* 10(1):641; Bradley and Dahlen, *From Conciliation to Conquest*, 51, 68, 91, 94, 98, 104–25, 217–19, 228; Grimsley, *Hard Hand of War*, 82.

9. Mitchell to Buell, May 2, 1862, *OR* 10(1):876–77; Mitchell to Hunter, May 24, 1862, *OR* 10(2):212–13.

10. Holt to Stanton, March 27, 1863, and Buell to L. Thomas, August 5, 1863, *OR* 10(1):630–34; Brown et al. to JD, June 18, 1862, *OR*, ser. 2, 4:780.

11. Mitchell to Buell, May 2, 1862, *OR* 10(1):877; [Mitchell] to Chase, April 30, 1862, Extract of Mitchell to Stanton, May 13, 1862, and Paul to Sharp, May 4, 1862, *OR* 10(2):293, 637–38.

12. Carter to Fry, March 9, 1862, and Kirby Smith to Cooper, March 13, 23, 1862, *OR* 10(2):23, 320–21, 355–56.

13. Kirby Smith to Cooper, April 2, 1862, General Orders No. 21, Adjutant and Inspector General's Office, War Dept., April 8, 1862, Kirby Smith to REL, April 16, 1862, and Proclamation, April 18, 1862, *OR* 10(2):386, 402, 424, 641; Bryan, "'Tories' amidst Rebels," 11–14.

14. Clay to Rhett, April 23, 1862, and Ashby to Kirby Smith, April 26, 1862, *OR* 10(1):649–50; Kirby Smith to Morgan, August 1, 1862, *OR*, ser. 2, 4:322.

15. Bryan, "'Tories' amidst Rebels," 15–18, 21.

16. Buell to McClellan, March 3, 1862, *OR* 7:679; Johnson to Morgan, June 2, 1862, in Graf and Haskins, *Papers of Andrew Johnson*, 5:434–35; Morgan to Stanton, June 24, 1862, *OR*, ser. 2, 4:60.

17. Daniel and Bock, *Island No. 10*, 4, 6, 30, 33–34.

18. Ibid., 39–40, 42, 50–51, 57, 61, 64, 72–73, 91; Preface to Pope's report of March 14, 1862, *OR* 8:80; Cozzens and Girardi, *Military Memoirs*, 45, 47–50.

19. Cozzens and Girardi, *Military Memoirs*, 51–52; Daniel and Bock, *Island No. 10*, 104–6, 108; Neal, *Illustrated History*, 36, 38.

20. Daniel and Bock, *Island No. 10*, 108, 124, 126, 128, 136, 144–45; Cozzens and Girardi, *Military Memoirs*, 53–57.

21. Pope to Townsend, September 14, 1876, *SOR* 1(1):721; Cozzens and Girardi, *Military Memoirs*, 57, 62.

22. Cozzens and Girardi, *Military Memoirs*, 61–62; Milligan, *Gunboats*, 63–67; Shea and Winschel, *Vicksburg Is the Key*, 10.

23. Milligan, *Gunboats*, 70–71, 73–77; Shea and Winschel, *Vicksburg Is the Key*, 11; Jones to Ruggles, June 3, 1862, *OR* 10(2):579.

24. AL to Seward, June 28, 1862, *OR*, ser. 3, 2:179–80.

25. Stanton to Halleck, June 28, 30, 1862, Halleck to Stanton, June 30, July 1, 1862, AL to Halleck, July 4, 1862, and Halleck to AL, July 5, [1862], *OR* 17(2):42–43, 52, 59, 70–72; AL to Halleck, July 4, 1862, in Basler, *Collected Works*, 5:305.

26. Halleck to AL, July 11, 1862, *OR* 17(2):90; Halleck to Buell, July 12, 1862, *OR* 16(2):128.

27. Cozzens and Girardi, *Military Memoirs*, 118, 120–23, 173.

28. Halleck to WTS, July 16, August 25, 1862, and WTS to Halleck, July 16, 1862, *OR* 17(2):100, 186; Halleck to Butler, August 7, 1862, *OR* 15:544.

29. Ash, *When the Yankees Came*, 18–19, 77.

30. [Hurlbut] to McPherson, October 26, 1862, *OR* 17(2):297; Grant, *Memoirs*, 258, 261.

31. Halleck to Johnson, June 22 [21], 1862, Mundy to Johnson, June 22, 1862, and Johnson to Mundy, June 23, [1862], in Graf and Haskins, *Papers of Andrew Johnson*, 5:494, 496, 504; Johnson to AL, July 26, 1862, *OR*, ser. 2, 4:289; Maslowski, *Treason Must Be Made Odious*, 76–77; Ash, *When the Yankees Came*, 115–20.

32. WTS to Park, July 27, October 1, 1862, and General Orders No. 90, HQ, First Division, Army of the Tennessee, October 25, 1862, *OR* 17(2):127, 252, 294–95.

33. Logan to Wallace, July 7, 1862, Special Orders No. 133, HQ, District of West Tennessee, July 9, 1862, and Logan to Nevins, July 24, 1862, *OR* 17(2):80, 87, 115; General Orders No. 14, HQ, Army of the Mississippi, June 3, 1862, *OR* 10(2):580.

34. Orders No. 44, 54, and 72, HQ, Fifth Division, Army of the Tennessee, June 18, July 19, August 14, 1862, *OR* 17(2):16, 106, 173; W. G. Smith, *Thomas Kilby Smith*, 225.

35. Maslowski, *Treason Must Be Made Odious*, 53–55; Ash, *When the Yankees Came*, 60; W. G. Smith, *Thomas Kilby Smith*, 226; Special Orders No. 21, HQ, Central Division of the Mississippi, July 7, 1862, General Orders No. 25, HQ, District of the Mississippi, July 25, 1862, and Special Orders No. 144, HQ, District of West Tennessee, July 25, 1862, *OR*, ser. 2, 4:147, 286; Mundy to Johnson, June 15, 1862, in Graf and Haskins, *Papers of Andrew Johnson*, 5:480.

36. Maslowski, *Treason Must Be Made Odious*, 56; Ash, *When the Yankees Came*, 44–45; Negley to Johnson, August 13, 1862, in Graf and Haskins, *Papers of Andrew Johnson*, 5:614; Johnson, *A Soldier's Reminiscences*, 193–94.

37. Proclamation concerning Guerrilla Raids, Nashville, May 9, 1862, and Negley to Johnson, June 23, 1862, in Graf and Haskins, *Papers of Andrew Johnson*, 5:374, 499; Special Orders No. 123, HQ, District of West Tennessee, June 29, 1862, WTS to Halleck, July 14, 1862, and General Orders No. 11, HQ, Central Division of the Mississippi, July 26, 1862, *OR*, ser. 2, 4:102, 211, 290–91; Grant, *Memoirs*, 265–66; Ash, *When the Yankees Came*, 64–67.

38. General Orders No. 60, HQ, District of West Tennessee, July 3, 1862, and Grant to Rosecrans, August 11, 1862, in Simon, *Papers of . . . Grant*, 5:190, 285–86; WTS to Fitch, August 7, 1862, *OR* 17(2):157; [Fry] to Alloway, July 20, 1862, *OR* 16(2):229; Ash, *When the Yankees Came*, 53–54.

39. WTS to Grant, August 17, 1862, *OR* 17(2):178.

40. Parsons to Mother, May 25, 1862, Parsons Papers, box 31, folder 4, ALPL; Ash, *When the Yankees Came*, 21–22, 49.

41. Dodge to Rochester, July 20, 1862, Halleck to Grant, August 2, 1862, and McPherson to Halleck, August 24, 1862, *OR* 17:(2):107, 150, 185; Mason to Grant, August 20, 1862, and General Orders No. 115, War Dept., Adjutant General's Office, August 22, 1862, *OR* 16(1):863, 865; Sutherland, *Savage Conflict*, 109–11; Mountcastle, *Punitive War*, 56–84.

42. Richardson to commander of post, Bolivar, January 6, 1863, *OR*, ser. 2, 5:159; Sutherland, *Savage Conflict*, 67, 71, 93–94, 118, 156–57.

43. Grant to Halleck, July 10, 1862, Halleck to Grant, July 10, 1862, General Orders No. 92, HQ, Army of the Mississippi, July 14, 1862, and WTS to Rawlins, July 25, 1862, *OR* 17(2):88, 97, 122; Cooper to Johnson, May 22, 1862, in Graf and Haskins, *Papers of Andrew Johnson*, 5:409–10.

44. "List of Boats Destroyed on the Mississippi River and Its Tributaries from May 1st

1861 to the Surrender of Genl. Kirby Smith's Army and the Cessation of Hostilities, June 2d 1865," oversize folder 7, Parsons Papers, ALPL; Quinby to Grant, August 23, 1862, WTS to Grant, October 4, 1862, *OR* 17(2):184, 261; WTS to Ellen, August 20, 1862, in Simpson and Berlin, *Sherman's Civil War*, 282.

45. WTS to Carr, October 17, 1862, and WTS to Hindman, October 17, 1862, *OR* 13:742–43; WTS to Hurlbut, November 6, 1862, and WTS to Stanton, December 16, 1862, in Simpson and Berlin, *Sherman's Civil War*, 321–22, 347; WTS to Grant, October 4, 22, 1862, *OR* 17(2):260–61, 289.

46. WTS to Grant, October 4, 1862, *OR* 17(2):260–61; WTS to Ellen, June 10, 1862, and WTS to J. Sherman, August 13, 1862, in Simpson and Berlin, *Sherman's Civil War*, 240, 273.

47. Campbell and Stokes to Johnson, April 23, 1862, and Peart to Johnson, June 5, 1862, in Graf and Haskins, *Papers of Andrew Johnson*, 5:322, 443–44; Grant to Washburn, June 19, 1862, in Simon, *Papers of . . . Grant*, 5:146.

48. W. G. Smith, *Thomas Kilby Smith*, 226.

49. WTS to Ewing, August 10, 1862, and WTS to J. Sherman, August 13, October 1, 1862, in Simpson and Berlin, *Sherman's Civil War*, 263–64, 272–73, 312.

50. Elliott to Morgan, August 6, 1863, *OR* 17(2):154.

51. Grant to Halleck, June 27, 1862, and General Orders No. 69, HQ, District of West Tennessee, August 6, 1862, *OR* 17(2):41–42, 155; Halleck to Grant, July 5, 1862, and Grant to Quinby, July 26, [1862], in Simon, *Papers of . . . Grant*, 5:196n, 238.

52. Ferris, "Captain Jolly," 22; Grant to Chase, July 31, 1862, in Simon, *Papers of . . . Grant*, 5:256; WTS to Rawlins, July 30, August 14, 1862, WTS to Kelton, September 4, 1862, and WTS to Grant, October 9, 1862, *OR* 17(2):140–41, 169–70, 200, 273; WTS to Halleck, August 18, 1862, *OR*, ser. 3, 2:402.

53. WTS to Taylor, August 25, 1862, *OR* 52(1):276; WTS to Ellen, October 4, 1862, in Simpson and Berlin, *Sherman's Civil War*, 313; Read to Randolph, October 7, 1862, *OR* 52(2):370–72.

54. AL to Kellogg, June 29, 1863, in Basler, *Collected Works*, 6:307; Ross to McClernand, July 25, 1862, *OR* 17(2):120; General Orders No. 31, HQ, Dept. of the Mississippi, June 6, 1862, *OR* 10(2):632.

55. Grant, *Memoirs*, 266–67; Halleck to Buell, August 25, 1862, *OR* 16(2):417; Elliott to Morgan, August 6, 1862, and WTS to Rawlins, August 14, 1862, *OR* 17(2):154, 171.

56. Special Orders No. 5, 1st Corps, Army of the Mississippi, April 2, 1862, Maury to Johnson, April 27, 1862, Lovell to [Beauregard], May 2, 1862, Lyles to [Van Dorn], May 29, 1862, and Porter to Beauregard, June 6, 1862, *OR* 10(2):385, 455, 481, 558–59, 591–92; Beauregard to Ruggles, June 15, 1862, and Harman to Assistant Adjutant General at Grenada, June 17, 1862, *OR* 17(2):601–2, 605; M. Jeff Thompson to Van Dorn, July 25, 1862, Van Dorn Papers, DU.

57. Halleck to Stanton, June 28, 1862, *OR* 17(2):43; Curtis to Halleck, July 29, 1862, Curtis to Halleck, July 31, 1862, and Phelps to Halleck, October 20, 1862, *OR* 13:519–20, 525, 751; Hess, "Confiscation," 57–63; John Hamilton Trowbridge to Brother and Sister, September 28, 1862, Trowbridge Family Letters, UW.

58. Hess, "Confiscation," 64, 67–70, 72–73; Curtis to Halleck, August 10, 1862, Phelps to Halleck, August 17, September 28, 1862, and Curtis to AL, November 9, 1862, *OR*

13:553, 577, 683–84, 783; Priestly to Father and Mother, August 23, 1862, Thomas Priestly Papers, WHS.

59. Grant to Sister, August 19, 1862, in Simon, *Papers of . . . Grant*, 5:311; Special Orders No. 4, HQ, Dept. of the Tennessee, November 4, 1862, *OR* 52(1):301–2; Chase to Bryant, August 4, 1862, in Niven, *Chase Papers*, 3:244; Special Orders No. 121, HQ, Dept. No. 2, July 16, 1862, *OR*, ser. 2, 4:820–21.

Chapter 5

1. Butler to McClellan, December 2, 1861, *OR* 53:509; Barnard to Colburn, February 7, 1862, and Barnard to McClellan, February 7, 1862, *OR* 6:684–85; Hearn, *Capture of New Orleans*, 129.

2. Phelps to Butler, December 5, 1861, and Phelps to Thomas, February 13, 1862, *OR* 6:465–66, 689; Childe, "General Butler at New Orleans," 176; McClellan to Butler, February 23, 1862, and General Orders No. 20, HQ of the Army, Adjutant General's Office, February 23, 1862, *OR* 6:694–96; Hearn, *Capture of New Orleans*, 125, 135.

3. Seddon to Davie, January 3, 1863, *OR*, ser. 4, 2:281; Benjamin to Moore, October 13, 1861, Lovell to Benjamin, October 18, 1861, January 8, February 27, March 6, 10, 1862, and Benjamin to Lovell, February 8, 1862, *OR* 6:751–53, 799, 823, 832, 842, 850; Hearn, *Capture of New Orleans*, 120–22.

4. General Orders No. 10, 11, HQ, Dept. No. 1, New Orleans, March 15, 18, 1862, and Lovell to Benjamin, March 22, 1862, *OR* 6:857, 860–61, 865; Hearn, *Capture of New Orleans*, 238.

5. Hearn, *Capture of New Orleans*, 184, 209, 218–19, 222, 241, 269–73.

6. Ibid., 237–38.

7. Ibid., 242–45, 252–53; Arnold to Halpine, May 10, 1862, *OR* 6:658.

8. Lovell to Van Dorn, April 30, 1862, Lovell to Randolph, April 15, 1862, and Lovell to Beauregard, May 12, 1862, *OR* 6:884–85, 877, 889; Lovell to [Beauregard], May 2, 1862, *OR* 10(2):481.

9. Battle to Randolph, April 29, 1862, *OR*, ser. 4, 1:1101–2; Randolph to Lovell, April 25, 1862, *OR* 6:883; General Orders No. 17, HQ, Dept. No. 1, May 3, 1862, *OR* 15:459–60.

10. Moore to JD, June 2, 1863, in Crist, *Papers of Jefferson Davis*, 8:213–14; Moore to Randolph, June 1, 13, 1862, *OR* 53:809, 813; Orders No. 682, Louisiana Adjutant General's Office, June 20, 1862, and Huger to Beauregard, August 1, 1862, *OR*, 15:759, 792–93.

11. Special Orders No. 20, HQ, Fort Pillow, April 20, 1862, and Beauregard to Harris, April 21, 25, 1862, Harris Papers, DU.

12. Smith to Kimmel, August [n.d.], 1862, *OR* 15:6–8; Harris to Thomas Jordan, May 20, 1862, Harris Papers, DU; Shea and Winschel, *Vicksburg Is the Key*, 18, 20.

13. Smith to Kimmel, August [n.d.], 1862: Van Dorn to [not stated], September 9, 1862, and Beauregard to Lovell, June 10, 1862, *OR* 15:9, 15, 752; Milligan, *Gunboats*, 79–80; Shea and Winschel, *Vicksburg Is the Key*, 21–22; Stanton to Butler, June 14, 1862, in Butler, *Correspondence*, 1:628.

14. Shea and Winschel, *Vicksburg Is the Key*, 24–26.

15. Porter to Farragut, July 13, 1862, *OR* 15:531; Shea and Winschel, *Vicksburg Is the Key*, 27–28.

16. Smith to Kimmel, August [n.d.], 1862, and Van Dorn to [not stated], September 9, 1862, *OR* 15:10, 16.

17. Bearss, "Battle of Baton Rouge," 73–74, 79, 82; Van Dorn to [not stated], September 9, 1862, *OR* 15:16; Shea and Winschel, *Vicksburg Is the Key*, 29.

18. Bearss, "Battle of Baton Rouge," 84, 92–93; Shea and Winschel, *Vicksburg Is the Key*, 31.

19. Shea and Winschel, *Vicksburg Is the Key*, 31; General Orders No. 57, HQ, Dept. of the Gulf, August 9, 1862, and Breckinridge to Kimmel, September 30, 1862, *OR* 15:42, 79.

20. Bearss, "Battle of Baton Rouge," 96, 98–99, 101–2; Butler to Paine, August 7, 16, 1862, in Butler, *Correspondence*, 2:159, 193; Van Dorn to [not stated], September 9, 1862, Grover to Assistant Adjutant General, December 17, 1862, and Butler to Halleck, August 27, 1862, *OR* 15:17, 191, 555; Shea and Winschel, *Vicksburg Is the Key*, 31.

21. Butler, *Butler's Book*, 374; Silber and Sievens, *Yankee Correspondence*, 31–32.

22. Butler, *Butler's Book*, 370; French to New Orleans S. S., May 14, 1862, in Butler, *Correspondence*, 1:482–83; Blount to Watts, July 8, 1862, *OR*, ser. 2, 4:805; Proclamation, HQ, Dept. of the Gulf, May 1, 1862, *OR* 6:718–20.

23. Butler to Mercer, September 27, 1862, in Butler, *Correspondence*, 2:332–33; Proclamation, HQ, Dept. of the Gulf, May 1, 1862, and General Orders No. 25, HQ, Dept. of the Gulf, May 9, 1862, *OR* 6:720, 725.

24. Proclamation, HQ, Department of the Gulf, May 1, 1862, *OR* 6:720; Pierson, *Mutiny at Fort Jackson*, 22–26, 71, 97, 131, 151, 161–64, 191.

25. Childe, "General Butler at New Orleans," 193; Strong to Weitzel, November 2, 1862, and General Orders No. 76, HQ, Dept. of the Gulf, September 24, 1862, *OR* 15:163, 575; Butler, *Butler's Book*, 521–22.

26. Special Orders Nos. 150, 151, 152, HQ, Dept. of the Gulf, June 30, 1862, and Walker to JD, September 13, 1862, *OR*, ser. 2, 4:105–6, 880; Hearn, *When the Devil Came*, 168–70.

27. Butler to Monroe, May 16, 1862, and Monroe to Butler, May 16, 1862, *OR* 53:527, 626; Butler, *Butler's Book*, 418–19; Butler to Gardner, June 10, 1862 (1:582–83), and "One of Your She Adders" to Butler, December 22, 1862 (2:549;), in Butler, *Correspondence*; Hearn, *When the Devil Came*, 101–6.

28. Seward to Johnson, June 27, 1862, in Butler, *Correspondence*, 2:12; General Orders No. 22, HQ, Dept. of the Gulf, May 4, 1862, and Butler to Seward, May 8, 1862, *OR* 6:722–23.

29. Silber and Sievens, *Yankee Correspondence*, 156; General Orders No. 23, HQ, Dept. of the Gulf, May 6, 1862, *OR* 6:722; Pierson, *Mutiny at Fort Jackson*, 170, 178.

30. General Orders Nos. 19, 20, 21, 25, HQ, Dept. of the Gulf, May 3, 4, 9, 1862, *OR* 6:720–21, 725; Croushore, *A Volunteer's Adventures*, 21; Butler to Stanton, June 28 [July 3], 1862, *OR* 15:503; Butler, *Butler's Book*, 387, 393–94; Butler to Halleck, September 1, 1862, in Butler, *Correspondence*, 2:242–43; Hearn, *When the Devil Came*, 98–99, 177–78.

31. Butler to Mayor and Common Council of New Orleans, May 9, 1862, *OR* 6:723–24; Childe, "General Butler at New Orleans," 191, 194–95; Butler, *Butler's Book*, 396; Pierson, *Mutiny at Fort Jackson*, 166.

32. Croushore, *A Volunteer's Adventures*, 26–27, 31, 39; Hearn, *When the Devil Came*, 96–97.

33. Chase to Butler, July 31, 1862, in Niven, *Chase Papers*, 3:235.

34. Phelps to L. Thomas, February 3, March 12, 1862, *OR* 6:680, 698; Strong to Weitzel, November 2, 1862, and Phelps to JD, June 16, 1862, *OR* 15:162, 487; AL to Johnson, July 26, 1862, *OR* 53:528; Butler to Wife, August 2, 1862, in Butler, *Correspondence*, 2:148.

35. Silber and Sievens, *Yankee Correspondence*, 158; General Orders No. 106, HQ, Dept. of the Gulf, December 15, 1862, in Butler, *Correspondence*, 2:545–46; Childe, "General Butler at New Orleans," 197–98; Pierson, *Mutiny at Fort Jackson*, 187–88.

36. Hearn, *When the Devil Came*, 181, 183, 196.

Chapter 6

1. Hess, *Banners to the Breeze*, 9–10.

2. McDonough, *War in Kentucky*, 43, 45, 102–4.

3. Ibid., 48–54, 57; Hess, *Banners to the Breeze*, 12–13.

4. Fry to Crittenden, July 16, 1862, Buell to Rosecrans, July 28, 1862, Buell to Halleck, August 6, 1862, Buell to Sidell, August 6, 1862, Wright to Miller, August 7, 1862, and Fry to Schoep, August 13, 1862, *OR* 16(2):162, 221–22, 266, 269, 281, 329; Buell statement, May 5, 1863, and Darr testimony, *OR* 16(1):32–33, 602–7.

5. Johnson to AL, September 1, 1862, in Graf and Hoskins, *Papers of Andrew Johnson*, 6:4–5; Buell to Halleck, July 11, 1862, and Halleck to Buell, August 12, 1862, *OR* 16(2):122–23, 314–15; Halleck to WTS, August 25, 1862, *OR* 17(2):186.

6. Grant, *Memoirs*, 257.

7. Letter fragment, June 1862, box 1, folder 14, Lockett Papers, UNC.

8. Hess, *Banners to the Breeze*, 18, 20–21; Bragg to Cooper, May 20, 1863, *OR* 16(1):1089; McWhiney, *Braxton Bragg*, 1–173.

9. Hess, *Banners to the Breeze*, 21–22; T. L. Connelly, *Army of the Heartland*, 197–204; Bragg to Adjutant and Inspector General, July 12, 1862, and Bragg to Cooper, July 23, 1862, *OR* 7(2):645, 655–56; Bragg to JD, July 22, 1862, and Bragg to Beauregard, July 22, 1862, *OR* 52(2):330–31; Bragg to Wife, July 22, 1862, Bragg Papers, MHS.

10. Harris to Randolph, July 30, 1862, *OR* 16(2):740; McDonough, *War in Kentucky*, 74–76, 79–80; Beauregard to Cooper, September 5, 1862, and Crockett et al. to JD, August 18, 1862, *OR* 16(2):544–45, 771–72; Hess, *Banners to the Breeze*, 25 (Davis quotation); AL to Buell, September 7, 1862, in Basler, *Collected Works*, 5:409; Halleck to Curtis, July 19, 1862, *OR* 13:477; Grant to L. Thomas, August 7, 1862, *OR* 17(2):155.

11. Kirby Smith to JD, August 11, 1862, in Crist, *Papers of Jefferson Davis*, 8:332; McDonough, *War in Kentucky*, 113–16; Kirby Smith to Wife, August 21, 24, 1862, and "Notes and Memoranda on the Kentucky Campaign, 1862," Kirby Smith Papers, UNC; Kirby Smith to JD, August 21, 1862, *OR* 16(2):769.

12. Hess, *Banners to the Breeze*, 32, 34, 38–42, 44; Lambert, *When the Ripe Pears Fell*, 57–149, 158; T. L. Connelly, *Army of the Heartland*, 194–96; Allen to W. H. Fairbanks, September 8, 1862, Allen Papers, IHS; Shockley to [not stated], September 7, 1862, Shockley Papers, IHS; Garrett, *Confederate Diary*, 30.

13. Hess, *Banners to the Breeze*, 45–47.

14. Ibid., 47–53.

15. Bragg to Price, August 12, 1862, *OR* 17(2):677; Semple to Wife, August 19, 22, 1862, Semple Papers, UNC; Hess, *Banners to the Breeze*, 57.

16. Buell to Nelson, August 10, 17, 1862, Buell to G. H. Thomas, August 23, 1862, Buell to Wright, September 3, 1862, and Buell to Halleck, September 14, 1862, *OR* 16(2):304, 357, 399, 476–77, 515; Hess, *Banners to the Breeze*, 58, 60–61.

17. Hess, *Banners to the Breeze*, 62; Clayton to Wife, September 14, 1862, Clayton Papers, UA; Bragg to Cooper, May 20, 1863, *OR* 16(1):1089–90; Proclamation to Residents of Kentucky, September 14, 1862, *OR* 16(2):822.

18. Hess, *Banners to the Breeze*, 63–72; McDonough, *War in Kentucky*, 158–87; Daniel, *Days of Glory*, 124; Bragg to Cooper, May 20, 1863, *OR* 16(1):1090; Bragg to Adjutant General, September 25, 1862, *OR* 16(2):876.

19. Testimony of J. B. Steedman, James B. Fry, Gordon Granger, and Marcellus Mundy, Buell Commission Report, *OR* 16(1):133, 228, 432, 640–41.

20. Bragg to Wife, September 18, 1862, Bragg Papers, MHS; Wood to Wife, September 26, 1862, Wood Papers, ADAH; McNeill Diary, September 23, 1862, TSLA; Gilmer to Wife, September 27, 1862, Gilmer Papers, UNC.

21. Special Orders No. 223, Adjutant and Inspector General's Office, September 24, 1862, *OR* 17(2):712; Buckner to the Freemen of Kentucky, September 24, 1862, Bragg to the People of the Northwest, September 26, 1862, and Bragg to the People of Kentucky, September 29, 1862, *OR* 52(2):360, 363–64, 367.

22. Bragg to Adjutant General, September 25, 1862, *OR* 16(2):876; Bragg to JD, October 2, 1862, in Crist, *Papers of Jefferson Davis*, 8:417.

23. Buell to Halleck, September 25, 1862, *OR* 16(2):542–43; Engle, *Buell*, 292–303.

24. Halleck to McKibbin, September 24, 1862, Halleck to G. H. Thomas, September 23, 29, 1862, and Halleck to Buell and Thomas, September 29, 1862, *OR* 16(2):538–39, 555; Daniel, *Days of Glory*, 126–31.

25. Hess, *Banners to the Breeze*, 77–78, 80–83; Harrison and Klotter, *New History of Kentucky*, 194; Harrison, "George W. Johnson and Richard Hawes," 30–35.

26. Harrison and Klotter, *New History of Kentucky*, 194.

27. Hess, *Banners to the Breeze*, 83, 85–91.

28. Ibid., 92–105; Noe, *Perryville*, 181–213, 218–34, 243–61, 296–305, 369, 373; T. L. Connelly, *Army of the Heartland*, 256–71; Engle, *Buell*, 306–11; Junius Gates to David Gates, October 29, 1862, Gates Family Papers, U-Mont.

29. Hess, *Banners to the Breeze*, 111, 113–14; Bragg to Cooper, May 20, 1863, *OR* 16(1):1093; John Euclid Magee Diary, October 16, 1862, *SOR* 3(1):221; Brush Diary, October 17, 19, 1862, MOC; Semple to [not stated], November 28, 1862, Semple Papers, UNC; Kirby Smith to Bragg, October 22, 1862, *OR* 16(2):975.

30. Buell to Halleck, October 16, 17, 22, 1862, *OR* 16(2):619, 622, 637.

31. Halleck to Buell, October 19, 23, 1862, *OR* 16(2):626–27, 638.

32. Buell to Halleck, October 22, 1862, *OR* 16(2):636–37.

33. Buell to Robinson, October 17, [1862], *OR* 16(2):623.

34. Halleck to Rosecrans, October [24], 1862, and Rosecrans to Buell, October 30, 1862, *OR* 16(2):640–41, 653; Engle, *Buell*, 312–18; Daniel, *Days of Glory*, 173–77.

35. Bragg to Cooper, October 19, 1862, and Cooper to Bragg, October 20, 1862, *OR*

16(2):970; JD to Kirby Smith, October 29, 1862, in Crist, *Papers of Jefferson Davis*, 8:469; Bragg to JD, October 23, 1862, *OR* 52(2):382.

36. Seddon to JD, January 3, 1863, *OR*, ser. 4, 2:284; Gilmer to Wife, October 19, 22, 1862, Gilmer Papers, UNC; JD to Bragg, October 17, 1862, and JD to Holmes, October 21, 1862, in Crist, *Papers of Jefferson Davis*, 8:448, 455; Pickens to Beauregard, November 5, 1862, *OR* 14:667.

37. Bragg to Cooper, May 20, 1863, *OR* 16(1):1094; Hess, *Banners to the Breeze*, 5, 232.

38. Seddon to Johnston, December 13, 1862, and Hawes to JD, March 4, 1863, *OR*, ser. 4, 2:236, 417–18.

39. Speed to AL, September 15, 1862, Robinson to AL, September 15, 1862, Stanton to Boyle, September 15, 1862, Boyle to Stanton, September 15, 1862, Wright to Boyle, November 1, 1862, Jones to Hoffman, November 22, 1862, and Hitchcock endorsement, December 3, 1862, *OR*, ser. 2, 4:517–18, 672, 745–46; General Orders No. 49, HQ, Army of the Ohio, October 26, 1862, *OR* 16(2):646; Sipes to Wright, December 18, 1862, and Wright to White, February 26, 1863, *OR*, ser. 2, 5:96–97, 299–300.

40. Bragg to Wright, December 1, 1862, *OR*, ser. 2, 5:2–3.

41. Price to Van Dorn, July 31, August 4, 1862, Bragg to Van Dorn, August 11, 1862, Price to Van Dorn, August 17, 1862, and Van Dorn to Price, September 3, 1862, *OR* 17(2):664–65, 675–76, 687, 691; Beauregard to Cooper, September 5, 1862, *OR* 16(2):545.

42. Hess, *Banners to the Breeze*, 126–30.

43. Ibid., 130–36, 139; Cozzens, *Darkest Days*, 78–82, 87–98, 105–8, 122–23.

44. Hess, *Banners to the Breeze*, 142–53; Cozzens, *Darkest Days*, 140–41, 166–220; Wilcox to Lottie, October 9, 1862, Wilcox Papers, ALPL.

45. Cozzens, *Darkest Days*, 233–70; Hess, *Banners to the Breeze*, 154, 156–65, 167.

46. Cozzens, *Darkest Days*, 282–90; Hess, *Banners to the Breeze*, 168–71; George R. Elliott Diary, October 3–6, 1862, TSLA; August Mersy to Henry Goedeking, October 10, 1862, Engelmann-Kircher Collection, ALPL.

47. Grant, *Memoirs*, 271; Grant to Julia, September 14, 1862, and Grant to Sister, October 16, 1862, in Simon, *Papers of . . . Grant*, 6:44, 154; WTS to Grant, October 9, 1862, *OR* 17(2):273; WTS, *Memoirs*, 1:264; Clay to Randolph, October 24, 1862, *OR*, ser. 4(2):142.

Chapter 7

1. Milligan, *Gunboats*, 94, 96, 98–99, 102.

2. Ibid., 97.

3. JD to Holmes, December 21, 1862, and Speech to Legislature of Mississippi, December 26, 1862, in Crist, *Papers of Jefferson Davis*, 8:561–62, 577.

4. Harris to Secretary of War, December 1, 1862, and Dahlgren to JD, December 3, 1863, *OR* 52(2):394, 569–70.

5. Johnston to JD, December 22, 1862, *OR* 17(2):801; Pemberton to Cooper, December 5, 1862, Johnston to Cooper, November 24, December 4, 6, 1862, and Johnston to JD, December 22, 1862, *OR* 20(2): 424, 436, 440–41, 460.

6. Grant, *Memoirs*, 282–83.

7. Ibid., 281–82, 284, 286; Grant to Hamilton, November 1, 1862, Grant to WTS, No-

vember 1, 1862, and Grant to Davies, November 2, 1862, *OR* 17(2):312, 315, 319; Grant to Halleck, November 2, 1862, *OR* 17(1):466–67.

8. Pride to Parsons, November 17, 1862, *OR* 17(2):352–53.

9. Grant, *Memoirs*, 286; Grant to Hudson, November 15, 1862, in Simon, *Papers of . . . Grant*, 6:320; Shea and Winschel, *Vicksburg Is the Key*, 38.

10. Grant to Halleck, December 4, 1862, *OR* 17(1):472; Woodworth, *Nothing but Victory*, 253–60.

11. Grant to WTS, November 10, 1862: Grant to Commanding Officer at Friar's Point, December 8, 1862, *OR* 17(2):335–36, 394.

12. Coulter to [not stated], n.d., *OR* 17(1):301; General Field Orders No. 2, HQ, Left Wing, Army of the Tennessee, November 5, 1862, Special Field Orders Nos. 1, 2, 6, HQ, Dept. of the Tennessee, November 7, 9, 16, 1862, *OR* 17(2):321, 326, 331–32, 350.

13. WTS to Halleck, November 17, 1862, General Orders No. 2, HQ, Right Wing, Army of the Tennessee, December 6, 1862, *OR* 17(2):351, 390; WTS to Stanton, January 25, 1863, in Simpson and Berlin, *Sherman's Civil War*, 376.

14. Order concerning the Confiscation Act, November 13, 1862, in Basler, *Collected Works*, 5:496; White, *Life of Lyman Trumbull*, 176–77.

15. Grant to Quinby, November 18, 1862: General Orders No. 10, HQ, Dept. of the Tennessee, November 26, 1862, *OR* 17(2):354, 363.

16. Grant to Stanton, December 6, 1862, in Simon, *Papers of . . . Grant*, 6:397–98; Starring to Ada, December 17, 1862, Frederick A. Starring Papers, CHS; Dana to Stanton, January 21, 1863, *OR* 52(1):331.

17. Grant to Sullivan, December 9, 1862, *OR* 17(2):396; Grant to Du Bois, December 9, 1862, in Simon, *Papers of . . . Grant*, vols. 7, 8.

18. Dana to Stanton, January 21, 1863, *OR* 52(1):331; Grant to Halleck, November 9, 1862, Grant to Webster, November 10, 1862, and General Orders No. 11, HQ, Dept. of the Tennessee, December 17, 1862, *OR* 17(2):330, 337, 424; General Orders No. 12, HQ, Dept. of the Tennessee, December 17, 1862, in Simon, *Papers of . . . Grant*, 7:50–55.

19. Harris to Sullivan, November 28, 1862, Sullivan to Commanders at All Posts in District of Jackson, December 3, 1862, *OR* 17(2):365–66, 380–81; Brayman to Buchanan, December 31, 1862, *OR* 17(1):482.

20. Special Field Orders No. 21, HQ, Dept. of the Tennessee, December 12, 1862, *OR* 17(2):405.

21. Eaton, *Grant, Lincoln and the Freedmen*, 2, 4–5, 12–13, 15, 20, 26–27, 31; Grant, *Memoirs*, 284.

22. Grant, *Memoirs*, 285; Eaton, *Grant, Lincoln and the Freedmen*, 32–33, 36; Special Field Orders No. 18, HQ, Dept. of the Tennessee, December 9, 1862, *OR* 17(2):396.

23. Eaton, *Grant, Lincoln and the Freedmen*, 37.

24. To the People of West Tennessee, December 9, 1862, in Simon, *Papers of . . . Grant*, 7:3–5.

25. WTS to Halleck, November 17, 1862, WTS to Porter, December 8, 1862, Grant to Steele, December 8, 1862, and Grant to Pride, December 19, 1862, *OR* 17(2):351, 392–93, 434; Grant to Halleck, December 8, 1862, and Grant to WTS, December 8, 1862, *OR* 17(1):474, 601; Grant, *Memoirs*, 288.

26. Grant, *Memoirs*, 287–89.

27. Chase Journal, August 3, 1862, in Niven, *Chase Papers*, 1:359–60.

28. Chase Journal, September 26–27, 1862, in ibid., 1:403–4; Kiper, *McClernand*, 1–25; McClernand to Stanton, October 10, 1862, McClernand to AL, September 28, 1862, *OR* 17(2):274–75, 849–50, 853; Kiper, *McClernand*, 133–40.

29. Stanton to McClernand, October 29, 1862, and Unnumbered order by Stanton, October 21, 1862, *OR* 17(2):282, 302; Woodworth, *Nothing but Victory*, 248–53.

30. Hillyer to WTS, October 29, 1862, *OR* 17(2):307–8; Halleck to Grant, November 10, 11, 1862, and Grant to Halleck, November 10, 1862, *OR* 17(1):468–69; Grant, *Memoirs*, 285–86; Kiper, *McClernand*, 142–44.

31. Stanton to McClernand, December 17, 1862, and McClernand to Stanton, January 3, 1863, *OR* 17(2):420, 528; Kiper, *McClernand*, 145–47.

32. Grant to Mary, December 15, 1862, in Simon, *Papers of . . . Grant*, 7:44; Grant, *Memoirs*, 289; Shea and Winschel, *Vicksburg Is the Key*, 44; Woodworth, *Nothing but Victory*, 264–65.

33. McPherson to Grant, December 20, 1862, *OR* 17(2):446.

34. Grant to Kelton, December 25, 1862, in Simon, *Papers of . . . Grant*, 7:105; Grant, *Memoirs*, 290–91; O. B. Clark, *Downing's Civil War*, 88–89; Throne, *Diary of . . . Boyd*, 97–98.

35. Allen to Grant, December 11, 1862, WTS to Gorman, December 13, 1862, Parsons to Halleck, December 15, 20, 27, 1862, and WTS to Rawlins, December 18, 1862, *OR* 17(2):99, 409, 413, 426, 441, 496; Parsons to Mother, December 21, 27, 1862, box 31, folder 4, Parsons Papers, ALPL; Milligan, *Gunboats*, 106.

36. Lougheed to Jennie, December 20, 22, 1862, Lougheed Papers, UW; Ferris, "Captain Jolly," 22–23.

37. WTS, *Memoirs*, 1:289; Grabau, *Ninety-eight Days*, 16, 40; Shea and Winschel, *Vicksburg Is the Key*, 52.

38. Shea and Winschel, *Vicksburg Is the Key*, 52; Drennan to Wife, December 25, 1862, Drennan Papers, MDAH; Vandiver, "Louisiana Confederate Letters," 971.

39. Shea and Winschel, *Vicksburg Is the Key*, 54–55; Woodworth, *Nothing but Victory*, 261–63, 266–84.

40. WTS to Rawlins, January 4, 1863, *OR* 17(1):612; A. F. Boyd to Father, January 9, 1863, Boyd-Sitton Family Civil War Letters, GDAH; Speech at Richmond, January 5, 1863, in Crist, *Papers of Jefferson Davis*, 9:12.

41. Grant, *Memoirs*, 289; McClernand to Grant, January 8, 1863, *OR* 17(2):546–47; Shea and Winschel, *Vicksburg Is the Key*, 55; Chipman to Curtis, December 30, 31, 1862, *OR* 22(1):886–87; Bearss, "Battle of the Post of Arkansas," 237, 244–45.

42. Bearss, "Battle of the Post of Arkansas," 238–39, 243, 247–49, 252, 256, 258; Milligan, *Gunboats*, 113–16; Shea and Winschel, *Vicksburg Is the Key*, 56–57.

43. Shea and Winschel, *Vicksburg Is the Key*, 57–58; Bearss, "Battle of the Post of Arkansas," 260–64, 266–67, 274–75; Milligan, *Gunboats*, 116–18; Porter to Grimes, January 24, 1863, *ORN* 24:194.

44. Grant to Halleck, January 11, 1863: Grant to McClernand, January 11, 1863, in Simon, *Papers of . . . Grant* 7, 209–11; Grant, *Memoirs*, 293; Bearss, "Battle of the Post of

Arkansas," 277–78; General Orders No. 3, HQ, Fifteenth Corps, January 12, 1863, and WTS to Scates, January 17, 1863, *OR* 17(2):556–57, 572.

45. Grant, *Memoirs*, 292–93; Grant to McPherson, December 21, 1862, *OR* 17(2):451; Grant to McClernand, January 13, 1863, and Grant to McPherson, January 13, 1863, in Simon, *Papers of . . . Grant*, 7:218–20; Curtis to Loan, December 28, 1862, *OR* 22(1):881.

46. Throne, *Diary of . . . Boyd*, 111–12; [McPherson] to Officers and Soldiers, Seventeenth Corps, February 10, 1863, *OR* 24(3):43–44.

47. Johnston to JD, January 2, February 12, 1863, in Crist, *Papers of Jefferson Davis*, 9:4, 59.

48. Rosecrans to L. Thomas, February 12, 1863, *OR* 20(1):189; Daniel, *Days of Glory*, 183.

49. Speech to Mississippi legislature, December 26, 1862, in Crist, *Papers of Jefferson Davis*, 8:579.

50. General Orders No. 10, HQ, Army of the Tennessee, December 11, 1862, *OR* 20(2):446.

51. Halleck to Rosecrans, December 4, 5, 1862, and Rosecrans to Halleck, December 4, 1862, *OR* 20(2):117–18, 123–24.

52. Rosecrans to AL, August 1, 1863, *OR* 52(1):427; Wright to Cullum, December 18, 1862, *OR*, 20(2):198–99.

53. General Orders No. 19, HQ, Dept. of the Cumberland, November 19, 1862, *OR*, ser. 2, 4:737.

54. General Orders No. 20, HQ, Dept. of the Cumberland, November 19, 1862, *OR*, ser. 2, 4:738; General Orders No. 23, HQ, Dept. of the Cumberland, November 27, 1862, and General Orders No. 31, HQ, Dept. of the Cumberland, December 4, 1862, Garesche to Boyle, December 5, 1862, and G. H. Thomas to Garesche, December 17, 1862, *OR* 20(2):104, 122–23, 25, 193.

55. Hess, *Banners to the Breeze*, 182, 187, 191.

56. Ibid., 197–201, 204–7, 210–11; T. L. Connelly, *Autumn of Glory*, 52–68.

57. Cozzens, *No Better Place to Die*, 85–92, 101, 109–27, 132, 145–66, 177–98; Hess, *Banners to the Breeze*, 217, 219–25.

58. Hess, *Banners to the Breeze*, 225–27, 229, 232–33; Bragg to Cooper, December 28, 1863, and Bragg to Johnston, January 11, 1863, *OR* 20(2):35, 493.

59. Rosecrans to Wright, January 6, 1863, *OR* 20(2):303.

60. Johnson to AL, January 11, 1863, in Graf and Haskins, *Papers of Andrew Johnson*, 6:114.

61. AL to Chase, September 2, 1863, in Basler, *Collected Works*, 6:428–29; Pillow to People of Tennessee and the Confederate States, January 18, 1863, *OR*, ser. 4, 2:362.

62. AL to Rosecrans, January 5, 1863, and Halleck to Rosecrans, January 9, 1863, *OR* 20(1):186, 187; AL to Rosecrans, August 31, 1863, in Basler, *Collected Works*, 6:424–25.

Chapter 8

1. Grant to Kelton, February 1, 1863, in Simon, *Papers of . . . Grant*, 7:274; Grant, *Memoirs*, 294.

2. Grant, *Memoirs*, 295; Grant to Halleck, January 20, 1863, *OR* 24(1):8; Dana, *Recollections*, 30.

3. Throne, *Diary of . . . Boyd*, 112–14.

4. Grant to Kelton, February 4, 1863, in Simon, *Papers of . . . Grant*, 7:281; Grant to Banks, March 22, 1863, *OR* 24(3):126; Grant, *Memoirs*, 297–98; Milligan, *Gunboats*, 146.

5. Grant to McClernand, January 30, 1863, Grant to Deitzler, February 2, 1863, Grant to Kelton, February 4, 1863, Grant to McPherson, February 5, 1863, and Grant to Julia, March 27, 1863, Simon, *Papers of . . . Grant*, 7:257–58, 278–79, 281, 284, 480; Grant, *Memoirs*, 298–99; Ballard, *Vicksburg*, 173–74.

6. Grant to Banks, March 22, 1863, *OR* 24(3):126; Grant, *Memoirs*, 299–301; Smith to Porter, February 19, 1863, *ORN* 24:256; Milligan, *Gunboats*, 130–35; Ballard, *Vicksburg*, 175–84, 188–90.

7. Porter to Welles, January 18, 1863, and Reeder to Allen, February 20, 1863, *ORN* 24:180, 450; McClernand to Grant, January 18, 1863, in Simon, *Papers of . . . Grant*, 7:232n.

8. Grant to Hurlbut, March 19, 1863, Grant to Farragut, March 23, 1863, Grant to Halleck, March 29, 1863, and Halleck to Grant, March 5, 1863, in Simon, *Papers of . . . Grant*, 7:442, 458–59, 484–85; Halleck to Grant, March 24, 1863, Parsons to Grant, March 16, 1863, and Allen to Halleck, March 18, 19, 1863, *OR* 24(3):22, 115–16, 120–21; Copy of R. E. Clary letter, n.d., box 39, folder 7, Parsons Papers, MHS.

9. Porter to Stevenson, March 2, 1863, *OR*, ser. 2, 5:310; Curtis to Fisk, January 7, 1863, and Halleck to Curtis, January 8, 1863, *OR* 22(2):25–26.

10. Grant to Quinby, March 23, 1863, in Simon, *Papers of . . . Grant*, 7:462–64; Fisk to Ross, March 6, 1863, *OR* 24(3):87; Milligan, *Gunboats*, 136.

11. Grant to Quinby, March 23, 1863, in Simon, *Papers of . . . Grant*, 7:464; Grant, *Memoirs*, 301–2; Milligan, *Gunboats*, 137–40; Ballard, *Vicksburg*, 184–88.

12. Grant to WTS, March 22, 1863, in Simon, *Papers of . . . Grant*, 7:455–56; Grant to Banks, March 22, 1863, *OR* 24(3):126; Grant to Kelton, April 12, 1863, in Simon, *Papers of . . . Grant*, 8:55.

13. Milligan, *Gunboats*, 122–26.

14. Ibid., 127–29.

15. Ibid., 142–45.

16. Fox to DuPont, April 2, 1863, *OR* 14:436.

17. Grant to Julia, February 9, 1863, and Grant to Wood, March 6, 1863, in Simon, *Papers of . . . Grant*, 7:309, 392; WTS Porter, February 19, 1863, Porter Papers, MHS; General Orders No. 10, HQ, Fifteenth Corps, March 7, 1863, *OR* 24(3):89–90; WTS to Ellen, March 13, 1863, in Simpson and Berlin, *Sherman's Civil War*, 417; WTS, *Memoirs*, 1:305.

18. Gorman to Curtis, January 3, 1863, *OR* 22(2):15–16; Porter to Welles, January 17, 1863, *ORN* 24:208; Throne, *Diary of . . . Boyd*, 122; Campbell to Pemberton, January 31, 1863, *OR* 24(3):610.

19. Grant to Father, April 21, 1863, in Simon, *Papers of . . . Grant*, 8:109; General Orders No. 7, HQ, Dept. of the Tennessee, January 20, 1863, *OR* 24(3):3; Porter to Gorman, February 15, 1863, Porter to Selfridge, February 11, 1863, and Yeatman to Porter, March 9, 1863, *ORN* 24:344, 351, 464.

20. Hurlbut to Rawlins, March 7, 1863, *OR* 24(3):92; L. Thomas to Stanton, April 4, 6, 1863, *OR*, ser. 3, 3:116–17.

21. Hanford to Pennock, February 14, 1863, *ORN* 24:358–59; Grant to Hillyer, April 1, 1863, in Simon, *Papers of . . . Grant*, 8:3.

22. Grant to Father, April 21, 1863, in Simon, *Papers of . . . Grant*, 8:109; Van Fossen to Grant, March 14, 1863, and Shermard to McPherson, March 17, 1863, in Simon, *Papers of . . . Grant*, 7:542n-544n; Selfridge to Porter, March 14, 24, 1863, *ORN* 24:471–72, 513.

23. Presidential Executive Order, November 13, 1862, *OR*, ser. 3, 2:765; Porter to Welles, February 20, 1863, and Porter to Pennock, March 4, 1863, *ORN* 24:430, 457; Special Orders No. 51, HQ, Third Division, Seventeenth Corps, March 27, 1863, *OR* 24(3):149.

24. Grant to Father, April 21, 1863, in Simon, *Papers of . . . Grant*, 8:109; Hentig to Porter, February 23, 1863, *ORN* 24:432.

25. AL to Johnson, March 26, 1863, in Graf and Haskins, *Papers of Andrew Johnson*, 6:194; Halleck to Grant, March 31, 1863, *OR* 24(3):157.

26. Halleck to Grant, March 31, 1863, *OR* 24(3):156–57; Stanton to L. Thomas, March 25, 1863, *OR*, ser. 3, 3:100–101.

27. L. Thomas to Stanton, April 4, 6, 9, 12, 1863, *OR*, ser. 3, 3:116–17, 121; Hess, *A German in the Yankee Fatherland*, 93–95.

28. Potter and Robbins, *Marching with the First Nebraska*, 150–52.

29. Hurlbut to AL, March 27, 1863, *OR* 24(3):149–50.

30. Throne, *Diary of . . . Boyd*, 118–19; Special Field Orders No. 2, HQ, Dept. of the Tennessee, February 12, 1863, *OR* 24(3):46–47.

31. Throne, *Diary of . . . Boyd*, 120–21, 132.

32. General Orders No. 25, HQ, Dept. of the Tennessee, April 22, 1863, *OR*, ser. 3, 3:147.

33. L. Thomas to Stanton, May 20, 1863, and General Orders No. 143, War Dept., Adjutant and Inspector General's Office, May 22, 1863, *OR*, ser. 3, 3:214–15.

34. Pillow to Planters of Lauderdale, Lawrence, and Franklin Counties, March 6, 1863, *OR*, ser. 4, 2:421.

35. Transcript, Pemberton to "Dear Sir," [1877 or 1878], Pemberton Papers, MDAH; Seddon to Kirby Smith, March 18, 1863, *OR* 22(2):802; Johnston to Cooper, January 12, 1863, *OR* 20(2):495.

36. Grant to Halleck, January 18, 1863, Grant to Porter, March 29, 1863, and Grant to Allen, March 31, 1863, in Simon, *Papers of . . . Grant*, 7:231, 486, 492; Grant to Porter, April 2, 1863, Grant to McClernand, April 2, and Grant to Father, April 21, 1863, in Simon, *Papers of . . . Grant*, 8:3–4, 56–57, 110; Grabau, *Ninety-eight Days*, 53–54.

37. Grant to Halleck, April 12, 1863, in Simon, *Papers of . . . Grant*, 8:53; Grant, *Memoirs*, 307–9, 314; Milligan, *Gunboats*, 149, 151–52; "List of Boats Destroyed on the Mississippi River and Its Tributaries from May 1st 1861 to the Surrender of Genl. Kirby Smith's Army and the Cessation of Hostilities, June 2d 1865," oversize folder 7, Parsons Papers, ALPL; Ballard, *Vicksburg*, 198–202.

38. Grant to Halleck, April 19, 1863, in Simon, *Papers of . . . Grant*, 8:91; Grant to Allen, July 25, 1863, and Grant to Meigs, August 10, 1863, ibid., 9:121, 162–63; Grant, *Memoirs*, 314.

39. Fox to Porter, February 6, 1863, *ORN* 24:243; Grant to Banks, March 22, 1863, *OR* 24(3):126; Grant to Halleck, April 19, 1863, *OR* 24(1):30–31; Grant to McClernand, April 2, 1863, in Simon, *Papers of . . . Grant*, 8:56–57.

40. Pemberton to Chalmers, April 18, 1863, *ORN* 24:717.

41. Grant to Julia, April 28, 1863, in Simon, *Papers of . . . Grant*, 132; Milligan, *Gunboats*, 152–53, 156–57; Grant, *Memoirs*, 315–18; Ballard, *Vicksburg*, 214–19.

42. Grant to Halleck, April 12, 1863, in Simon, *Papers of . . . Grant*, 8:53; Grant, *Memoirs*, 314; McPherson to Rawlins, May 26, 1863, and Logan to Clark, May 26, 1863, *OR* 24(1):634, 643; "List of Boats Destroyed on the Mississippi River and Its Tributaries from May 1st 1861 to the Surrender of Genl. Kirby Smith's Army and the Cessation of Hostilities, June 2d 1865," oversize folder 7, Parsons Papers, ALPL; Ballard, *Vicksburg*, 221–25, 249–50.

43. Grant, *Memoirs*, 321–22, 325; Ballard, *Vicksburg*, 226–39.

44. Grant to WTS, May 3, 1863, in Simon, *Papers of . . . Grant*, 8:152; Grant, *Memoirs*, 327–29; Grant to Banks, May 10, 1863, *OR* 15:315–16; Hewitt, *Port Hudson*, 174.

45. Grant to Hillyer, May 5, 1863, Grant to Halleck, May 6, 1863, Grant to McClernand, May 7, 1863, Grant to WTS, May 8, 9, 1863, Grant to McPherson, May 11, 1863, and Grant to Halleck, May 24, 1863, in Simon, *Papers of . . . Grant*, 8:162, 169, 172–73, 178, 183, 200, 262; Buckland to Sample, June 8, 1863, *OR* 24(1):761–62; Tourtellotte to Martin, May 23, 1863, *OR* 24(2):61.

46. Ballard, *Vicksburg*, 261–71, 273–79, 289–317.

47. Pemberton to Kirby Smith, May 9, 1863, *OR* 24(3):846; Grant to WTS, May 16, 1863, in Simon, *Papers of . . . Grant*, 8:228.

48. Bearss, *Unvexed to the Sea*, 761–67; Ballard, *Vicksburg*, 327–32.

49. General Field Orders No. [not stated], HQ, Dept. of the Tennessee, May 21, 1863, and General Orders No. 38, HQ, Fifteenth Corps, May 21, 1863, *OR* 24(3):333–35; Grant to Halleck, May 24, 1863, in Simon, *Papers of . . . Grant*, 8:261; Bearss, *Unvexed to the Sea*, 815–52, 875–81; Ballard, *Vicksburg*, 338–48; Kiper, *McClernand*, 267–71.

50. Grant to Halleck, May 22, 1863, Grant to Porter, May 22, 1863, and Grant to Halleck, May 24, 1863, in Simon, *Papers of . . . Grant*, 8:249–50, 261; Chase to Garfield, May 31, 1863, in Niven, *Chase Papers*, 4:46; Ballard, *Vicksburg*, 348.

51. Grant to Osterhaus, May 26, 29, 1863, in Simon, *Papers of . . . Grant*, 8:278, 291.

52. Grant to Hurlbut, May 31, 1863, in Simon, *Papers of . . . Grant*, 8:297; Halleck to Schofield, July 7, 1863, *OR* 22(2):355.

53. REL to Longstreet, April 6, 1863, *OR* 18:966; Sauers, *Journal of . . . Bolton*, 122; Taylor to Jane, June 16, 18, 25, 1863, Taylor Letters, CWM; Ballard, *Vicksburg*, 392–93.

54. Grant, *Memoirs*, 367; Grant to Halleck, May 24, 1863, Grant to Banks, May 31, 1863, and Grant to Father, June 15, 1863, in Simon, *Papers of . . . Grant*, 8, 262–63, 295, 375–76.

55. Grant to Porter, May 23, 1863, *OR* 24(3):343; Ballinger to McClernand, September 7, 1863, *SOR* 4(1):413.

56. Stevenson to Memminger, July 29, 1863, *OR* 24(2):345; Diary, June 10, 1863, Alison Papers, UNC; Reed, "A Woman's Experiences," 923–24; [Loughborough], *My Cave Life*, 60–62; Ballard, *Vicksburg*, 386–87.

57. Bearss, *Unvexed to the Sea*, 907–25, 928.

58. Beauregard to Johnston, May 15, 1863, and JD to Bragg, May 22, 1863, *OR* 23(2):836–38, 847; Johnston to Pemberton, May 29, 1863, and Pemberton to Johnston, May 29, 1863, *OR* 24(3):929–30; JD to Pettus, June 20, 1863, *OR* 52(2):498.

59. Pemberton to Johnston, June 15, 1863, and Adams to Breckinridge, July 4, 1863, *OR* 24(3):964, 987–88; D. M. Smith, *Compelled to Appear in Print*, 146; Seddon to Foster, June 23, 1863, *OR* 52(2):500; Seddon to MacBeth, May 14, 1863, *OR* 14:941; Wiley, *Letters of . . . Hagen*, 17.

60. Johnston to Kirby Smith, June 26, 1863, *OR* 24(3):979; Taylor to Boggs, June 8, 1863, and McCulloch to Maclay, June 8, 1863, *OR* 24(2):459, 467; Record of events, Company C and D, 49th USCT, June 7, 1863, *SOR* 78(2):120, 123; Taylor to Jane, June 16, 1863, Taylor Letters, CWM; Dana to Stanton, June 28, 1863, *OR* 24(1):106; Dana, *Recollections*, 86; Milligan, *Gunboats*, 173; Bearss, *Unvexed to the Sea*, 1177–87.

61. Grant to Father, June 15, 1863, in Simon, *Papers of . . . Grant*, 8:376.

62. Grant to Dennis, June 27, 1863, and Grant to Julia, June 19, 1863, in Simon, *Papers of . . . Grant*, 8:438, 444–45; Comstock to Steele, July 2, 1863, and Many Soldiers to Pemberton, June 28, 1863, *OR* 24(3):459, 983; Grant, *Memoirs*, 373.

63. Grant to Pemberton, July 3, 1863, and Grant to Halleck, July 4, 6, 1863, in Simon, *Papers of . . . Grant*, 8:455, 469, 484–85; Grant to Banks, July 4, 1863, *OR* 24(3):470; Ballard, *Vicksburg*, 397–99; Bearss, *Unvexed to the Sea*, 954–55; Woodworth, *Nothing but Victory*, 447–53.

64. WTS to Ellen, July 5, 1863, in Simpson and Berlin, *Sherman's Civil War*, 499; Roth, *Well Mary*, 21; REL to Stone, August 3, 1863, *OR* 24:(2):245; Wise to Meigs, September 14, 1863, *OR*, ser., 3, 5:477; AL to Grant, July 13, 1863, *OR* 52(1):406.

65. Wills, *Old Enough to Die*, 93; Seddon to JD, November 26, 1863, *OR*, ser. 4, 2:991; Trimmier to Wife, June 7, 1863, Trimmier Papers, TSLA.

Chapter 9

1. WTS to Rawlins, July 3, 1863, and Grant to Banks, July 4, 1863, *OR* 24(3):462, 470; Grant to WTS, July 3, 1863: Grant to Halleck, July 4, 1863, in Simon, *Papers of . . . Grant*, 8:460, 469.

2. WTS to Porter, July 19, 1863, *OR* 24(3):531; Ballard, *Vicksburg*, 407–9.

3. WTS to Rawlins, July 28, 1863, and Benton to Scates, July 27, 1863, *OR* 24(2):536, 609; WTS to Porter, July 19, 1863, *OR* 24(3):531.

4. Ord to Molly, July 17, 1863, Ord Letters, SU; Loving, *Letters of . . . Whitman*, 99; Grant to WTS, July 18, 1863, in Simon, *Papers of . . . Grant*, 9:71; Circular, HQ, Breckinridge's Division, July 4, 1863, *OR* 24(3):988; Wiley, *Letters of Hagen*, 28.

5. Ord to Hammond, July 27, 1863, *OR* 24(2):576.

6. Special Orders No. 180, HQ, Dept. of the Tennessee, July 4, 1863, and Special Orders No. 135, HQ, Seventeenth Corps, July 11, 1863, *OR* 24(3):477, 502.

7. Grant to Halleck, July 18, 1863, in Simon, *Papers of . . . Grant*, 9:70; Ransom to Clark, July 16, 1863, *OR* 24(2):680–81.

8. WTS, *Memoirs*, 1:334; WTS to Wright, September 2, 1863, *OR* 30(3):294; Hurlbut to AL, July 10, 1863, *OR* 52(1):398; "Civil War Letters of . . . Orme," 292.

9. Magruder to People of Texas, July 16, 1863, *OR* 26(2):114; Watkins et al. to Flanagin, July 25, 1863, and Seddon to Johnston, August 19, 1863, *OR* 22(2):946, 971.

10. Forrest to Cooper, August 9, 1863, *OR* 30(4):508–9.

11. Faries to Wade, July 10, 1863, *OR* 26(1):220–22.

12. "List of Boats Destroyed on the Mississippi River and Its Tributaries from May 1st 1861 to the Surrender of Genl. Kirby Smith's Army and the Cessation of Hostilities, June 2d 1865," oversize folder 7, Parsons Papers, ALPL; *St. Louis Daily Missouri Democrat*, September 14, 1863.

13. "License of Commercial Intercourse," March 31, 1863, in Basler, *Collected Works*, 6:157; General Orders No. 88, War Dept., Adjutant General's Office, April 3, 1863, *OR* 18:580–82.

14. Grant to WTS, July 21, 1863, Grant to Taylor, October 6, 1863, in Simon, *Papers of . . . Grant*, 9:89, 269; Grant to Chase, July 21, 1863, *OR* 24(3):538; Grant to Stanton, August 26, 1863, and Grant to Chase, September 26, 1863, *OR*, ser. 3, 3:721, 841; Chase to Grant, July 4, 1863, and Chase to Denison, August 26, 1863, in Niven, *Chase Papers*, 4:75, 176–77.

15. Special Orders No. 138, HQ, Seventeenth Corps, July 15, 1863, *OR* 24(3):514; Greer to Porter, September 14, 1863, *SOR* 3(3):74; Buford to Chase, December 13, 1863, in Niven, *Chase Papers*, 4:216.

16. Grant to McPherson, July 5, 1863, *OR* 24(3):479; Grant to Washburn, August 30, 1863, in Simon, *Papers of . . . Grant*, 9:218.

17. Grant to L. Thomas, July 11, 1863, in Simon, *Papers of . . . Grant*, 9:23; Grant to Halleck, July 24, 1863, and AL to Grant, August 9, 1863, *OR* 24(3):547, 584.

18. Grant to AL, August 23, 1863, in Simon, *Papers of . . . Grant*, 9:196; Grant to Crocker, August 28, 1863, *OR*, ser. 3, 3:735; Bowers to McPherson, July 22, 1863, *OR* 24(3):542.

19. Record of events, field and staff, 50th USCT, *SOR* 78(2):131–32.

20. General Orders No. 50, HQ, Dept. of the Tennessee, August 1, 1863, Grant to Halleck, August 11, 1863, Hurlbut to AL, August 11, 1863, *OR* 24(3):570, 587, 589; WTS to Winslow, August 8, 1863, *OR* 30(1):7.

21. Dargan to Seddon, July 24, 1863, August to Lay, August 15, 1863, JD to Howry, August 27, 1863, and Pettus to Mississippi State Senate and House of Representatives, November 3, 1863, *OR*, ser. 4, 2:664–65, 717, 766, 919; JD to R. Davis, July 20, 1863, and Eiland to JD, July 20, 1863, in Crist, *Papers of Jefferson Davis*, 9:291, 293; Chalmers to Ewell, July 29, 1863, Lamar to Chalmers, August 9, 1863, and Ruggles to Ewell, August 10, 1863, *OR* 24(3):1036, 1051, 1053.

22. WTS to Grant, August 4, 1863, *OR*, 24(3):574; Grant to Stone, July 21, 1863, in Simon, *Papers of . . . Grant*, 9:92.

23. WTS to Ellen, July 15, 1863, and WTS to Ewing, July 28, 1863, in Simpson and Berlin, *Sherman's Civil War*, 503, 508.

24. WTS to Barnard, September 4, 1863, WTS to Hill, September 7, 1863, and WTS to Halleck, September 17, 1863, in Simpson and Berlin, *Sherman's Civil War*, 533, 536–38, 544.

25. Pettus to Mississippi State Senate and House of Representatives, November 3, 1863, *OR*, ser. 4, 2:922; Grant to Hurlbut, August 4, 1863, and Grant to Halleck, August 11, 1863, *OR* 24(3):575, 587; Grant to Halleck, August 23, 1863, in Simon, *Papers of . . . Grant*, 9:198.

26. Memminger to Seddon, July 15, 1863, *OR* 52(2):507; DeBow to Johnston, July 25, 1863, *OR* 24(3):1030.

27. George to Goodman, June 26, 1863, *OR* 24(2):506; WTS to Reed and Anderson, August 3, 1863, *OR* 24(3):571–72.

28. Hewitt, *Port Hudson*, 32; Hollandsworth, *Pretense of Glory*, 3–44; Halleck to Banks, November 9, 1862, *OR* 15:590; Hearn, *When the Devil Came*, 216–17, 230.

29. Banks to Halleck, January 7, 1863, *OR* 15:639–40.

30. Banks to Halleck, September 26, 1863, *OR* 26(1):735–36; Banks to Halleck, October 26, 1863, *OR*, ser. 3, 3:925.

31. Circular, HQ, Dept. of the Gulf, February 16, 1863, *OR*, ser. 2, 5:279; General Orders No. 12, HQ, Dept. of the Gulf, January 29, 1863, and General Orders No. 40, HQ, Dept. of the Gulf, May 1, 1863, *OR* 15:666–67, 717; Halleck to Banks, March 25, 1863, *OR*, ser. 3, 3:102.

32. Chase to Bullitt, April [14], 1863, in Niven, *Chase Papers*, 4:12; Denison to Chase, February 12, 26, 1863, in Butler, *Correspondence*, 3:9, 18; Alexander to Blair, January 13, 1863, Butler, *Correspondence*, 2:577.

33. Chase to Butler, February 24, 1863, and Griffin to Butler, February 26, 1863, in Butler, *Correspondence*, 3:15, 18; Hewitt, *Port Hudson*, 59; Graves to Parents, [before December 18, 1862], Graves Papers, NL; Hearn, *When the Devil Came*, 228–30.

34. Banks to Halleck, December 18, 1862, *OR* 15:614; Butler to Chase, February 28, 1863, in Butler, *Correspondence*, 3:22; Hewitt, *Port Hudson*, 39–40.

35. Hewitt, *Port Hudson*, 60, 62, 65–66, 76–95, 97–98, 101, 103, 109.

36. Ibid., 108; F. H. Kennedy, *Battlefield Guide*, 179.

37. Banks to Grant, May 3, 1863, Banks to Halleck, May 12, 1863, *OR* 15:309, 315; Banks to Halleck, June 4, 1863, *OR* 26(1):535–36; Hewitt, *Port Hudson*, 126.

38. Hewitt, *Port Hudson*, 136, 141–55.

39. Banks to Grant, May 28, 29, 1863, *OR* 24(3):353, 360; Halleck to Banks, June 4, 1863, *OR* 26(1):535.

40. Hewitt, *Port Hudson*, 170–71.

41. Chase to Walker, June 8, 1863, in Niven, *Chase Papers*, 4:58; General Orders No. 47, HQ, Dept. of the Gulf, June 6, 1863, *OR* 26(1):539.

42. Johnston to Gardner, May 19, 1863, and Kirby Smith to Taylor, July 12, 1863, *OR* 26(2):9, 109; Johnston to Gardner, June 15, 1863, *OR* 53:873.

43. Halleck to Gillmore, July 5, 1863, *OR* 28(2):14; Hewitt, *Port Hudson*, 173.

44. Palfrey to Mr. Py, July 12, 1863, Palfrey Papers, Mass-HS; Banks to Halleck, August 28, 1863, and General Orders No. 70, HQ, Dept. of the Gulf, September 28, 1863, *OR* 26(1):700, 740.

45. Weitzel to Butler, August 5, 1863, in Butler, *Correspondence*, 3:102; Croushore, *A Volunteer's Adventures*, 146.

46. Banks to [Halleck], September 15, 1863, and Banks to Dunham, September 17, 1863, *OR* 26(1):724, 727; Banks to Porter, August 28, 1863, Porter Papers, MHS; Banks to Grant, July 18, 1863, and Grant to Halleck, August 11, 1863, *OR* 24(3):527, 587; Goodell to [not stated], August 3, 1863, Goodell Letter, Conn-HS.

47. Grant to Halleck, July 24, 1863, Grant to Dana, August 5, 1863, and Grant to

Banks, August 7, 1863, in Simon, *Papers of . . . Grant*, 9:108–9, 146–47, 157; Grant to Banks, July 11, 1863, *OR* 24(3):499–500.

48. Franklin to Stone, October 30, 1863, *OR* 26(1):781; Ord to Molly, July 17, 1863, Ord Letters, SU; Croushore, *A Volunteer's Adventures*, 156; Edmonds, *Yankee Autumn*, 18, 136–42.

49. H. W. Howe, *Passages*, 144; Edmonds, *Yankee Autumn*, 18–19, 354–57.

50. Halleck to Grant, July 11, 23, 1863, *OR* 24(3):497, 542.

51. Grant to Stone, July 21, 1863, and Parsons to Grant, July 18, 25, 1863, in Simon, *Papers of . . . Grant*, 9:92, 153n; Grant to Banks, October 3, 1863, McPherson to WTS, January 20, 1864, Hurlbut to McPherson, January 20, 1864, and Fort to Clark, January 16, 1864, *OR* 26(1):753, 903–5, 907.

52. Denison to Chase, July 15, 1863, in Niven, *Chase Papers*, 4:86; Ord to Molly, September 25, 1863, Ord Letters, SU.

53. Banks to Halleck, August 15, 1863, and Banks to AL, August 17, 1863, *OR* 26(1):683, 688–89; Andrews to Banks, September 1, 1863, and L. Thomas to Stanton, September 5, 1863, *OR*, ser. 3, 3:756–57, 769–70.

54. Denison to Chase, August 12, 1863, in Niven, *Chase Papers*, 4:99; General Orders No. 12, HQ, U.S. Forces at Port Hudson, July 30, 1863, *OR* 26(1):663; Andrews to Logan, August 5, 1863, and Logan to Ewell, September 3, 1863, *OR*, ser. 2, 6:177–78, 258–59.

55. Beckwith to Banks, October 24, 1863, *OR*, ser. 3, 3:926–97.

56. AL to Banks, August 5, 1863, in Basler, *Collected Works*, 6:365; General Orders No. 66, HQ, Dept. of the Gulf, September 3, 1863, and [Stone] to Herron, September 4, 1863, *OR*, 26(1):715–16.

Chapter 10

1. Rosecrans to Halleck, January 17, 1863, *OR* 20(2):334; Halleck to Rosecrans, January 30, 1863, *OR* 23(2):23.

2. Halleck to Wright, January 15, 1863, *OR* 20(2):332; Rosecrans to Halleck, January 29, 1863, Halleck to Rosecrans, February 3, 1863, and Wood to Garfield, April 6, 1863, *OR* 23(2):20–21, 38, 213.

3. Cozzens, *This Terrible Sound*, 13–17.

4. Rice et al. to Secretary of War, January 6, 1863, General Orders No. 3, January 11, 1863, No. 5, HQ, Army of Tennessee, January 13, 1863, and Circular, HQ, Withers's Division, January 14, 1863, *OR* 20(2):442–43, 494–97 (quotation, 497); General Orders No. 38, HQ, Army of Tennessee, February 16, 1863, *OR* 23(2):636.

5. Johnston to Cooper, January 12, 1863, and General Orders No. 6, HQ, Army of Tennessee, January 14, 1863, *OR* 20(2):495–96.

6. Kundahl, *Confederate Engineer*, 201; *The Press*, July 17, 1863; Fremantle, *Three Months*, 146; Mitchell, "Letters of . . . Newberry," 73; Bragg to Wife, June 20, 1863, Bragg Papers, MHS.

7. Reynolds to Flynt, February 10, 1863, *OR* 23(2):54–57; Reynolds to Flynt, April 30, 1863, *OR* 23(1):269–70.

8. Reynolds to Flynt, February 10, 1863, and Halleck to Rosecrans, March 5, 1863, *OR* 23(2):56, 107–8.

9. Rosecrans to Stanton, March 7, 1863, *OR*, ser. 3, 3:59–60; General Orders No. 63, HQ, Dept. of the Cumberland, March 29, 1863, *OR* 23(2):189.

10. Paine to Goddard, February [1], 1863, *OR* 23(2):33; Maxwell to Semple, July 6, 1863, and Sherwood to Kise, March 21, 1863, *OR* 23(1):149–50, 821; "List of Boats Destroyed on the Mississippi River and Its Tributaries from May 1st 1861 to the Surrender of Genl. Kirby Smith's Army and the Cessation of Hostilities, June 2d 1865," oversize folder 7, Parsons Papers, ALPL.

11. Cropsey to Paine, April 27, 1863, *OR* 52(1):355; Foster to Boyle, March 7, 1863, and Foster to Semple, May 2, 1863, *OR* 23(2):118, 308.

12. General Orders No. 43, HQ, Dept. of the Cumberland, March 8, 1863, and General Orders No. 19, HQ, Dept. No. 2, June 4, 1863, *OR* 23(2):121, 861; Maslowski, *Treason Must Be Made Odious*, 61.

13. Galloway to Turner, April 23, 1863, and Proclamation of Col. Robert V. Richardson, January 25, 1863, *OR*, ser. 2, 5:514, 821–22; Sutherland, *Savage Conflict*, 163, 172–73, 181.

14. Jones to McLean, August 12, 1863, Hoffman to Stanton, August 26, 1863, and Hoffman to Rosecrans, August 29, 1863, *OR*, ser. 2, 6:197, 228, 239–40; Ould to Ludlow, May 22, 1863, Ludlow to Ould, May 25, 1863, and Burnside to Bragg, n.d., in Burnside to Rosecrans, May 29, 1863, *OR*, ser. 2, 5:691, 702–3, 718.

15. Robinson to Wright, March 1, 1863, Wright to Robinson, March 4, 1863, Wright to Rosecrans, March 8, 1863, Rosecrans to Wright, March 13, 1863, Wright to Kelton, March 15, 1863, Wright to Cullum, March 15, 1863, and General Orders No. 53, HQ, Dept. of the Ohio, April 28, 1863, *OR* 23(2):96–97, 104, 121, 143–46, 287.

16. F. H. Kennedy, *Battlefield Guide*, 189; Utley to Coburn, n.d., 1863, *OR* 23(1):109–11.

17. AL to Rosecrans, February 17, 1863, in Basler, *Collected Works*, 6:108; Streight to Garfield, April 9, 1863, *OR* 23(2):224; Streight to Whipple, August 22, 1864, and Bragg to Cooper, May 5, [1863], *OR* 23(1):285–94.

18. Rosecrans to L. Thomas, July 24, 1863, *OR* 23(1):404, and Garfield to Stanley, July 1, 1863, *OR* 23(2):497.

19. Bragg to [Beauregard], July 21, 1863, Bragg to [REL], July 22, 1863, and Polk to JD, July 26, 1863, *OR* 23(2):920, 924, 932.

20. Cozzens, *This Terrible Sound*, 21; Stanton to Rosecrans, and Rosecrans to Stanton, July 7, 1863, *OR* 23(2):518.

21. Rosecrans to Burnside, July 8, 1863, *OR* 23(2):522; Wiles to Garfield, July 25, 1863, and Willich to Howell, July 6, 1863, *OR* 23(1):425, 489.

22. General Orders No. 175, HQ, Dept. of the Cumberland, [July] 28, 1863, Garfield to G. H. Thomas, July 8, 1863, Thruston to Sheridan, July 9, 1863, and Garfield to Stanley, July 10, 1863, *OR* 23(2):184–85, 521, 525, 527.

23. Halleck to Burnside, March 23, 1863, and Seddon to Donelson, February 14, 1863, *OR* 23(2):162–64, 635.

24. Gilbert to Willcox, May 20, 1863, *OR* 23(2):344–45.

25. Maury to Seddon, May 7, 1863, and Maury to Johnston, May 11, 1863, *OR* 23(2):822, 832.

26. General Orders No. 38, HQ, Dept. of the Ohio, April 13, 1863, *OR* 23(2):237.

27. Seymour, *Divided Loyalties*, 73, 75–77.

28. General Field Orders No. 13, HQ, Army of the Ohio, September 17, 1863, *OR* 30(3):718; Campbell, "East Tennessee during the Federal Occupation," 66–67; Coulter, "Parson Brownlow's Tour," 9–25.

29. AL to Johnson, September 11, 1863, in Basler, *Collected Works*, 6:440.

30. AL to Johnson, March 26, 1863, Stanton to Johnson, March 28, 1863, and McCook to Stanton, June 3, 1863, *OR*, ser. 3, 3:103, 106, 249.

31. Stearns to Stanton, September 11, 12, 1863, Stanton to Stearns, September 16, 1863, and General Orders No. 329, War Dept., Adjutant General's Office, October 3, 1863, *OR*, ser. 3, 785–86, 793, 816, 860–61.

32. Halleck to Rosecrans, July 24, 25, 1863, and Rosecrans to Halleck, August 6, 7, 1863, *OR* 23(2):552, 554–55, 594, 597; Rosecrans to AL, August 1, 1863, *OR* 52(1):427–28; Chase Journal, August 31, 1863, in Niven, *Chase Papers*, 1:432; Cozzens, *This Terrible Sound*, 22–23, 29–31.

33. Unnumbered Orders, HQ, First Division, Fourteenth Corps, August 12, September 8, 1863, General Orders No. 200, HQ, Dept. of the Cumberland, August 15, 1863, Rosecrans to Adjutant General, August 16, 1863, and Flynt to Reynolds, September 15, 1863, *OR* 30(3):13, 34–35, 46, 447, 645; Rosecrans to AL, August 22, 1863, *OR* 52(1):439; Cozzens, *This Terrible Sound*, 33.

34. Polk to JD, July 26, 1863, Special Orders No. 42, HQ, Stewart's Division, August 6, 1863, *OR* 23(2):932–33, 954; Bragg to Johnston, August 5, 1863, *OR* 52(2):514; Kundahl, *Confederate Engineer*, 218, 229, 231–33; Record of events, Company H, 10th South Carolina, *SOR* 64(2):64, 814; Brent to Wheeler, August 18, 1863, *OR* 30(4):505.

35. Cozzens, *This Terrible Sound*, 86–99; T. L. Connelly, *Autumn of Glory*, 174–86.

36. Quaife, *From the Cannon's Mouth*, 305; Cozzens, *This Terrible Sound*, 139–279.

37. Cozzens, *This Terrible Sound*, 60, 119, 299; Hood, *Advance and Retreat*, 62–63; Polley, *Soldier's Letters*, 141; Pickenpaugh, *Rescue by Rail*, 27–43; T. L. Connelly, *Autumn of Glory*, 151–53.

38. Baird to Flynt, n.d., *OR* 30(1):277; Bragg to Cooper, December 28, 1863, *OR* 30(2):33; Coleman Diary, September 19, 1863, UNC; Mackall to Darling, September 27, 1863, Mackall Papers, UNC.

39. Hicks and Schultz, *Battlefields of the Civil War*, 157; Cozzens, *This Terrible Sound*, 319–404, 417–62, 471–77, 534; Daniel, *Days of Glory*, 327–29, 332–35; Einolf, *George Thomas*, 172–80.

40. Bragg to Wife, September 22, 27, 1863, Bragg Papers, MHS; Kellenberger to Add, December 19, 1863, Kellenberger Letters, LC; Thomas W. Patton to Mother, September 28, 1863, James W. Patton Papers, UNC.

41. Bragg to Cooper, December 28, 1863, Longstreet to Brent, October [n.d.], 1863, *OR* 30(2):37, 289–90.

42. AL to Rosecrans, October 4, 12, 1863, and AL to Williams and Taylor, October 17, 1863, in Basler, *Collected Works*, 6:498, 510, 525; Cozzens, *Shipwreck of Their Hopes*, 8–11, 29–31.

43. Chase Journal, September 23, 1863, in Niven, *Chase Papers*, 1:450–52; Green, "Movement of the 11th and 12th Army Corps," 115–16; Howard, *Autobiography*, 1:452–58; Pickenpaugh, *Rescue By Rail*, 1–7, 73, 130.

44. Blair, *A Politician Goes to War*, 127, 129; Howard to Brother, December 4, 1863, C. H. Howard Papers, BC; General Orders No. 56, HQ, First Division, Twelfth Corp, October 21, 1863, *OR* 31(1):693; Hooker to Chase, November 3, 1863, in Niven, *Chase Papers*, 4:170–71.

45. Quaife, *From the Cannon's Mouth*, 266–67; Howard to Wife, October 13, 1863, O. O. Howard Papers, BC; Journal, October 4–15, 1863, Meysenburg Papers, MHS.

46. Parsons to Rawlins, October 2, 1863, *OR* 30(4):28.

47. General Orders No. 337, Adjutant General's Office, War Dept., October 16, 1863, Halleck to Grant, October 16, 1863, and Scott to Stanton, October 16, 1863, *OR* 30(4):404; Grant to G. H. Thomas, October 19, 1863, Grant to Halleck, October 26, 1863, and Grant to Julia, October 27, 1863, in Simon, *Papers of . . . Grant*, 9:302, 320, 334.

48. Longstreet to Brent, October [n.d.], 1863, *OR* 30(2):289–90; Bragg to Wife, September 27, 1863, Bragg Papers, MHS; Circular, HQ, Army of Tennessee, November 1, 1863, General Orders No. 212, HQ, Army of Tennessee, November 18, 1863, *OR* 31(3):622, 710–11.

49. Grant, *Memoirs*, 417–18; Cozzens, *Shipwreck of Their Hopes*, 53–100; T. L. Connelly, *Autumn of Glory*, 254–62.

50. Henry to Seddon, October 24, 1863, *OR* 31(3):586; Speech at Missionary Ridge, October 10, 1863, in Crist, *Papers of Jefferson Davis*, 10:21–22; Seymour, *Divided Loyalties*, 86–95; T. L. Connelly, *Autumn of Glory*, 234–53.

51. Seymour, *Divided Loyalties*, 104–12.

52. Grant to Halleck, November 6, 19, 21, 1863, and Grant to Jones, November 17, 1863, in Simon, *Papers of . . . Grant*, 9:364, 406, 416, 428; WTS, *Memoirs*, 1:361–62.

53. Bauer, *Soldiering*, 99; WTS, *Memoirs*, 1:363–64; Duke, *History of the Fifty-third*, 126.

54. Grant, *Memoirs*, 434–35, 439–41; Cozzens, *Shipwreck of Their Hopes*, 128–42, 159–98; Daniel, *Days of Glory*, 371–73.

55. Grant, *Memoirs*, 445–48; Cozzens, *Shipwreck of Their Hopes*, 211–42, 257–360, 370–84; Daniel, *Days of Glory*, 373–77.

56. Dana to Stanton, November 26, 1863, *OR* 31(2):69; Grant to Washburn, December 2, 1863, and Grant to Jones, December 5, 1863, in Simon, *Papers of . . . Grant*, 9:491, 496; Kellenberger to Add, December 19, 1863, Kellenberger Letters, LC; Cozzens, *Shipwreck of Their Hopes*, 389.

57. Poe, "Defense of Knoxville," 734–37, 741–44; Gallagher, *Fighting for the Confederacy*, 322–29; Edward McG. Burruss to Papa, December 10, 1863, Burruss Family Papers, LSU; Seymour, *Divided Loyalties*, 147–64, 170.

Chapter 11

1. Meigs to Seward, n.d., *OR*, ser. 3, 3:603–4.

2. Halleck to WTS, October 1, 1863, *OR* 52(1):717.

3. Boggs to Holmes, November 8, 1863, *OR* 22(2):1063; Faries to French, November 18, 1863, and Faries to Semmes, November 21, 1863, *OR* 26(1)453–55; Wallar to [not stated], October 10, 1863, *OR* 30(4):240; Pool to Proctor, November 7, 1863, Brooks to Foster, December 12, 1863, and Greer to Porter, December 22, 1863, *ORN* 25:536–37, 624–26; Ferris, "Captain Jolly," 24–26.

4. Allen to Halleck, October 5, 1863, *OR* 22(1):607; "List of Boats Destroyed on the Mississippi River and Its Tributaries from May 1st 1861 to the Surrender of Genl. Kirby Smith's Army and the Cessation of Hostilities, June 2d 1865," oversize folder 7, Parsons Papers, ALPL; *St. Louis Daily Missouri Democrat*, October 5, 1863; Halleck to Allen, October 8, 1863, *OR* 22(2):618; General Orders No. 105, U.S. Mississippi Squadron, October 10, 1863, *ORN* 25:463.

5. Seddon to JD, November 26, 1863, *OR*, ser. 4, 2:991–92; Reagan, *Memoirs*, 157; Seddon to Johnston, August 19, 1863, and JD to Johnston, November 14, 1863, *OR* 22(2):971, 1068; Northrop to Johnston, October 27, 1863, Kirby Smith to Johnston, October 29, 1863, Seddon to Johnston, November 19, 1863, and Ross to Holt, December 29, 1863, *OR* 31(3):598–99, 606, 714, 880.

6. Powers to Ewell, November 9, 1863, Dameron to Ewell, November 9, 1863, and Paxton to JD, November 13, 1863, *OR* 31(3):673–74, 690–91; Thompson to JD, December 23, 1863, in Crist, *Papers of Jefferson Davis*, 10:123–24.

7. Ewell to Chalmers, October 20, 1863, Mellon to Dameron, November 6, 1863, Paxton to JD, November 13, 1863, Chalmers to Holt, November 23, 1863, Seddon to Johnston, November 29, 1863, Johnston to Jackson, December 2, 1863, and Chalmers to Thompson, December 15, 1863, *OR* 31(3):572, 643, 690–91, 744, 762, 776, 833–35; General Orders No. 1, HQ, Dept. of Alabama, Mississippi, and East Louisiana, December 23, 1863, *OR* 31(3):858.

8. McPherson to WTS, November 22, 1863, Hurlbut to Buford, December 1, 1863, McPherson to Hurlbut, December 8, 1863, and Stevenson to Hurlbut, December 10, 1863, *OR* 31(3):229, 304, 361, 374; Buford to Harris, December 31, 1863, *OR* 22(2):757; WTS endorsement on Wright to Schenck, March 17, 1864, in Simon, *Papers of . . . Grant*, 10:555.

9. WTS to Porter, November 8, 1863, *ORN* 25:539; WTS to Buckland, September 16, 1863, and WTS to McPherson, September 16, 1863, *OR* 30(3):662; McPherson to Hurlbut, December 8, 1863, *OR* 31(3):361.

10. Yeatman to Pattison, November 6, 1863, *ORN* 25:537; *Memphis Daily Appeal*, December 1, 1863; Hurlbut to Kelton, November 17, 1863, *OR* 31(3):180.

11. WTS, *Memoirs*, 1:388; WTS to Porter, November 8, 1863, *ORN* 25:539; WTS to Hurlbut, October 25, 1863, *OR* 31(1):733.

12. WTS to Banks, January 16, 1864, *OR* 32(2):115; WTS to Porter, November 8, 1863, *ORN* 25:540; Rawlins to McPherson, November 2, 1863, WTS to Logan, December 21, 1863, and WTS to Grant, December 29, 1863, *OR* 31(3):22, 459, 527; WTS to Porter, October 25, 1863, and Porter to WTS, October 29, 1863, *OR* 31(1):737, 780–81; Townsend to Mitchell, October 29, 1864, and General Orders No. 121, U.S. Mississippi Squadron, November 12, 1863, *ORN* 26:704–5.

13. McPherson to Leggett, January 9, 1864, *OR* 32(2):55; Reid to WTS, November 17, 1863, and McPherson to WTS, November 22, 1863, *OR* 31(3):180, 229; WTS to Porter, October 25, 1863, *OR* 31(1):737.

14. WTS to McPherson, November 18, 1863, *OR* 31(3):188; WTS to Sawyer, January 31, 1864, *OR* 32(2):278–81; McPherson to Commanding Officer, 2nd Wisconsin Cavalry, August 14, 1863, and WTS to Asboth, September 11, 1863, *OR* 30(3):527.

15. McPherson to Commanding Officer, 2nd Wisconsin Cavalry, August 14, 1863, *OR*

30(3):26; General Orders No. 10, Military Division of the Mississippi, December 12, 1863, *OR* 31(3):396.

16. Special Orders No. 217, HQ, Sixteenth Corps, September 10, 1863, *OR* 30(3):506; Wolfe to Hough, October 21, 1863, *OR* 31(1):692.

17. WTS to Porter, November 8, 1863, *ORN* 25:540–41; General Orders No. 157, HQ, Sixteenth Corps, November 15, 1863, *OR* 31(3):160; McPherson to WTS, December 2, 1863, *ORN* 31(3):309–10.

18. WTS to Hurlbut, October 24, 1863, *OR* 31(1):719; WTS to Smith, January 6, 1864, and McPherson to Eastman, January 26, 1864, *OR* 32(2):36, 227.

19. WTS to J. Sherman, April 11, 1864, in Simpson and Berlin, *Sherman's Civil War*, 620; WTS to Hill, September 7, 1863, *OR* 30(3):402.

20. General Orders No. 67, HQ, Left Wing, Sixteenth Corps, November 12, 1863, General Orders No. 70, HQ, Left Wing, Sixteenth Corps, November 16, 1863, Circular, HQ, Left Wing, Sixteenth Corps, November 19, 1863, Special Orders No. 296, HQ, Left Wing, Sixteenth Corps, November 24, 1863, Dodge to Mizner, November 27, 1863, Dodge to Grant, December 9, 1863, and Grant to Dodge, December 9, 1863, *OR* 31(3):132, 171, 198, 245, 262, 366–67.

21. McCook to Whipple, December 19, 1863, *OR* 31(3):446.

22. General Orders No. 6, HQ, Dept. of the Cumberland, January 6, 1864, *OR* 32(2):37–38; General Orders No. 4, HQ, Military Division of the Mississippi, November 5, 1863, and Whipple to Crook, December 9, 1863, *OR* 31(3):58, 366.

23. Gillem to L. Thomas, December 13, 1863, *OR* 31(3):399; McConnell to Paine, February 10, 1864, and Stokes to Polk, February 7, 1864, *OR* 32(1):155–56, 162–63.

24. Maxwell to Semple, October 24, 1863, and Boyle to Anderson, October 26, 1863, *OR* 31(1):31–32, 750.

25. Ullmann to Wilson, December 4, 1863, and L. Thomas to Stanton, December 24, 1863, *OR*, ser. 3, 3:1126–27, 1190; Grant to Logan, February 26, 1864, *OR* 32(2):477; Hurlbut to WTS, December 7, 1863, and General Orders No. 173, HQ, Sixteenth Corps, December 17, 1863, *OR* 31(1):577.

26. Grant to McPherson, December 1, 1863, and Grant to Halleck, December 7, 1863, in Simon, *Papers of . . . Grant*, 480, 500; Halleck to Grant, December 3, 13, 1863, and Dana to Grant, December 21, 1863, *OR* 31(3):315, 396, 457–58.

27. Grant to Halleck, December 17, 1863, in Simon, *Papers of . . . Grant*, 9: 534; Grant to Julia, January 2, [1864], ibid., 10:6; Dana to Grant, January 10, 1864,: Grant to Halleck, January 15, 1864, WTS to Banks, January 16, 1864, Halleck to Grant, January 18, 1864, and Grant to Halleck, February 12, 1864, *OR* 32(2):58, 99–100, 115, 127, 375; WTS, *Memoirs*, 1:386.

28. Grant to Halleck, January 15, 1864, and WTS to Grant, January 20, 1864, *OR* 32(2):100–101, 157; WTS to J. Sherman, December 29, 1863, in Simpson and Berlin, *Sherman's Civil War*, 577; Hunter to Stanton, December 14, 1863, *OR* 31(3):402.

29. Meigs to McCallum, December 16, 1863, and Donaldson to Whipple, December 23, 1863, *OR* 31(3):422–23, 474.

30. Carter to Potter, December 19, 1863, *OR* 31(3):447–48; Potter to Granger, January 26, 1864, *OR* 32(2):218.

31. Hardee to the Soldiers of the Army of Tennessee, December 2, 1863, REL to JD,

December 3, 7, 1863, Hardee to Cooper, December 17, 1863, and Henry to Johnston, December 29, 1863, *OR* 31(3):776, 779–80, 792, 840, 878.

32. Beauregard to Soule, December 8, 1863, and Henry to Johnston, December 29, 1863, *OR* 813–16, 878; Lawton to Johnston, January 21, 1864, Johnston to Brown, January 25, 1864, and Johnston to JD, February 1, 1864, *OR* 32(2):591–92, 612, 645; Johnston to Beverly Johnston, February 15, 1864, Joseph E. Johnston Papers, CWM; Johnston to Beauregard, January 13, 1864, JD to Longstreet, March 7, 1864, and Mackall to Ewell, March 22, 1864, *OR* 52(2):596–97, 635, 646.

33. Grant, *Memoirs*, 470, 478; Grant to Banks, March 15, 1864, in Simon, *Papers of . . . Grant*, 10:200–201.

34. Grant to WTS, April 4, 1864, in Simon, *Papers of . . . Grant*, 10;251–52.

35. WTS to Halleck, September 15, 1864, *OR* 38(1):61–62.

36. WTS, *Memoirs*, 2:8–9, 11–12; WTS to Dana, April 21, 1864, in Simpson and Berlin, *Sherman's Civil War*, 624.

37. WTS, *Memoirs*, 2:10, 22, 31; WTS to J. Sherman, April 11, 1864, and WTS to Dana, April 21, 1864, in Simpson and Berlin, *Sherman's Civil War*, 619, 623.

38. Beauregard to Soule, May 19, 1863, *OR*, ser. 2, 5:952; Meigs to Seward, [ca. August 1863], *OR*, ser. 3, 3:604–5.

Chapter 12

1. Elmore to Parents, June 1, 1864, Elmore Papers, CHS; S. Davis, *Atlanta Will Fall*, 34–35; WTS to Schofield, May 9, 1864, *OR* 38(4):98.

2. Castel, *Decision in the West*, 131, 143–44, 151; Longacre and Haas, *To Battle for God and the Right*, 171; WTS to McPherson, May 10, 1864, *OR* 38(4):125; T. L. Connelly, *Autumn of Glory*, 335–40.

3. Castel, *Decision in the West*, 154, 156–66, 173–79, 188.

4. General Orders, unnumbered, HQ, Army of Tennessee, May 19, 1864, *OR* 38(4):728; W. C. Davis, *Diary of a Confederate Soldier*, 127; Castel, *Decision in the West*, 200–204; McMurry, *Atlanta*, 82–83; Johnston, *Narrative*, 322–24; Hood, *Advance and Retreat*, 106; Trask Journal, 252–53, EU; Thomas B. Mackall Journal (McMurry transcript, p. 8), Johnston Papers, CWM; T. L. Connelly, *Autumn of Glory*, 346–53.

5. Howard, "Struggle for Atlanta," 306; WTS, *Memoirs*, 2:42; Special Field Orders No. 9, HQ, Military Division of the Mississippi, May 20, 1864, *OR* 38(4):271–72; Castel, *Decision in the West*, 217–21.

6. Castel, *Decision in the West*, 223, 225–26, 229–30, 233–35, 237–38, 241, 243–47; J. C. Thompson to A. P. Stewart, December 8, 1867, Johnston Papers, CWM; Howard, *Autobiography*, 1:551; N. D. Brown, *One of Cleburne's Command*, 185; Hazen, *Narrative*, 257.

7. Castel, *Decision in the West*, 250–51, 255, 259, 264–66; Webster to Blair, May 21, 1864, WTS to Halleck, June 2, 5, 8, 11, 1864, McPherson to Blair, June 7, 1864, and Special Field Orders No. 22, HQ, Military Division of the Mississippi, June 10, 1864, *OR* 38(4):278, 385, 408, 431, 433, 453–55.

8. Castel, *Decision in the West*, 267, 269, 273, 275, 280, 292–95; WTS to Halleck, June 13, 1864, *OR* 38(4):466; McMurry, *Atlanta*, 103; Johnston, *Narrative*, 338.

9. S. Davis, *Atlanta Will Fall*, 81; WTS to Halleck, June 13, 16, 25, 1864, *OR* 38(4):466, 492, 589; Castel, *Decision in the West*, 303, 305, 307–13, 314–16, 319–20; T. L. Connelly, *Autumn of Glory*, 358–60.

10. WTS to Halleck, June 27, 1864, and WTS to G. H. Thomas, June 27, 1864, *OR* 38(4):607, 611; WTS to Halleck, July 9, 1864, and WTS to Grant, July 12, 1864, *OR* 38(5):91, 123; WTS to Ellen, July 9, 1864, in Simpson and Berlin, *Sherman's Civil War*, 663–64.

11. M, "Battle of Dead Angle," 72; Rogers, *125th Regiment Illinois*, 98–99; Tuttle Diary, June 29, 1864, UK; J. T. Bowden to Editor, December 15, 1902, *Confederate Veteran* Papers, DU; Holmes, *52d O.V.I.*, 187; Poe to Wife, July 1, 1864, Poe Papers, LC.

12. WTS, *Memoirs*, 2:61–62; Castel, *Decision in the West*, 330, 332–35; McMurry, *Atlanta*, 113; Shoup, "Dalton Campaign," 263; Kendall, "Recollections of a Confederate Officer," 1171.

13. WTS to G. H. Thomas, July 3, 1864, and WTS to Halleck, July 5, 7, 1864, *OR* 38(5):30–31, 50, 73; WTS, *Memoirs*, 2:69–70; Shoup, "Dalton Campaign," 264.

14. Whipple to Gleason, July 5, 1864, Whipple to McCook, July 11, 1864, and McCook to Whipple, July 14, 1864, *OR* 38(5):62–63, 116–17, 137–38.

15. WTS to Commanding Officer at Allatoona, July 14, 1864, and Dodge to Scott, August 1, 1864, *OR* 38(5):140–41, 938; Allen to Meigs, May 1, 1864, WTS to Webster, May 4, 1864, WTS to AL, May 5, 1864, McCook to Elliott, June 2, 1864, Special Field Orders No. 24, HQ, Military Division of the Mississippi, June 12, 1864, and Schofield to WTS, June 27, 1864, *OR* 38(4):4, 26, 33, 387, 466, 619; Logan to Clark, [September 13, 1864], *OR* 38(3):112; Goodman to Foye, September 22, 1864, *OR* 38(2):153; WTS, *Memoirs*, 2:391–92.

16. WTS to Andersen, July 1, 1864: Steedman to Whipple, July 10, 1864, and Grant to Halleck, July 15, 1864, *OR* 38(5):4, 113, 143; WTS to Governors of Indiana, Illinois, Iowa, and Wisconsin, May 23, 1864, Van Duzer to Dayton, June 18, 1864, Milward to Moe, June 23, 24, 1864, Steedman to Dayton, June 24, 1864, and Rogers to Cadle, June 27, 1864, *OR* 38(4):294–95, 517, 580–81, 587, 624; WTS to Ellen, June 26, July 9, 1864, in Simpson and Berlin, *Sherman's Civil War*, 657, 664.

17. Blair, *A Politician Goes to War*, 179, 185; Lawson, "Hammontrees Fight the Civil War," 118; Special Field Orders No. 8, HQ, Army of the Ohio, May 20, 1864, Circular, HQ, Dept. of the Cumberland, May 22, 1864, and Hascall to Campbell, May 23, 1864, *OR* 38(4):273, 291, 297–98; Spencer to Parents, June 22, 1864, Israel Spencer Letters, SU.

18. WTS to Steedman, July 10, 1864, *OR* 39(5):112.

19. WTS to L. Thomas, June 21, 1864, *OR* 39(2):132; L. Thomas to WTS, June 20, 1864, *OR* 38(4):542–43.

20. General Orders No. 3, HQ, Wheeler's Cavalry Corps, May 31, 1864, General Orders No. 4, Army of the Mississippi, June 1, 1864, and Circular, HQ, Hood's Corps, June 7, 1864, *OR* 38(4):751, 754–55, 763.

21. WTS, *Memoirs*, 2:25–26; WTS to Comstock, April 5, 1864, and Grant to WTS, April 19, 1864, *OR* 32(3):262, 409; "Personal Recollections: Strategy and Battles of Sherman & Johnston Illustrated in Active Campaigns," unpaginated, box 5, folder 3, O. O. Howard Papers, LMU; WTS to Halleck, May 20, June 11, 1864, 1864, *OR* 38(4):260, 455.

22. Halleck to WTS, June 28, 1864, *OR* 38(4):629; Grant to Halleck, July 15, 1864, in Simon, *Papers of . . . Grant*, 11:256; Grant to WTS, July 16, 1864, and WTS to Halleck, July 16, 1864, *OR* 38(5):149–50.

23. WTS to Stanton, May 23, 1864, *OR* 38(4):294.

24. REL to JD, May 9, 1864, in Crist, *Papers of Jefferson Davis*, 10:403; JD to Johnston, May 13, 1864, Johnston to JD, May 20, 1864, and Ratchford to Men of Hood's Corps, May 24, 1864, *OR* 38(4):705, 728, 741.

25. [Dwight], "How We Fight at Atlanta," 664; Stone, "From the Oostenaula to the Chattahoochee," 413; A. J. Johnson to Folks, July 25, 1864, Johnson Papers, IHS.

26. Johnston to JD, May 21, 1864, *OR* 38(4):736; Johnston to JD, July 8, 1864, *OR* 38(5):869; Grant to Clark, March 28, 1864, L. P. Grant Papers, AHC; Hood, *Advance and Retreat*, 124; Hardee to Wife, June 19, 1864, Hardee Family Papers, ADAH.

27. Johnston to Bragg, June 13, 27, 1864, Johnston to S. D. Lee, June 11, 1864, and Bragg to JD, June 4, 29, 1864, *OR* 38(4):762, 769, 772, 795–96, 805; Brown to JD, June 28, 1864, and JD to Brown, June 29, 1864, *OR* 52(2):680–81.

28. Hood to Bragg, July 14, 1864, Bragg to JD, July 15, 1864, Johnston to JD, July 16, 1864, Seddon to Hood, July 17, 1864, and Johnston to Cooper, July 18, 1864, *OR* 38(5):880–81, 883, 885, 888; Johnston to Cooper, October 20, 1864, *OR* 38(3):618; REL to JD, July 12, 1864, in Crist, *Papers of Jefferson Davis*, 10:516; T. L. Connelly, *Autumn of Glory*, 369–73, 404–23.

29. WTS to Ellen, June 30, 1864, in Simpson and Berlin, *Sherman's Civil War*, 660; WTS to Halleck, July 6, 1864, *OR* 38(5):66; S. Davis, *Atlanta Will Fall*, 95–96; WTS, *Memoirs*, 2:71; Johnston to Cooper, October 20, 1864, *OR* 38(3):618.

30. Castel, *Decision in the West*, 368–73, 375–77, 381; Hynes to Brother, July 29, 1864, Hynes Papers, ISL; J. W. M. to Editor, July 21, 1864, *Indianapolis Daily Journal*, July 26, 1864; McMurry, *John Bell Hood*, 129.

31. Gillmore to Upton, September 12, 1864, Leggett to Alexander, July 25, 1864, and Belknap to Kinsman, July 23, 1864, *OR* 38(3):294, 564, 606; Howard, "Battles about Atlanta," 394; Castel, *Decision in the West*, 383–85, 391, 394–96, 402; Woodworth, *Nothing but Victory*, 543–68.

32. WTS to Halleck, September 15, 1864, *OR* 38(1):73; Castel, *Decision in the West*, 398–99, 405–7, 409–11; T. L. Connelly, *Autumn of Glory*, 444–49.

33. Hood, *Advance and Retreat*, 183–87; General Field Orders No. 7, Army of Tennessee, July 25, 1864, *OR* 38(5):909.

34. WTS, *Memoirs*, 2:85–86; WTS to Halleck, July 27, 1864, and General Field Orders No. 5, HQ, Dept. and Army of the Tennessee, July 27, 1864, *OR* 38(5):272, 277.

35. WTS to Logan, July 24, 1864, and [Shoup] to Hardee, July 28. 1864, *OR* 38(5):242–43, 919; David Allan Jr. to Mother, July 25, 1864, Civil War Papers, MHS; Wills, *Army Life*, 287; S. Davis, *Atlanta Will Fall*, 150–53; Castel, *Decision in the West*, 424–25, 428–34; WTS, *Memoirs*, 2:91.

36. Tower, *A Carolinian Goes to War*, 236–37; [Shoup] to S. D. Lee, July 29, 1864, *OR* 38(5):925.

37. JD to Hood, August 5, 1864, in Crist, *Papers of Jefferson Davis*, 10:586; Castel, *Decision in the West*, 453–56; WTS to G. H. Thomas and Howard, July 31, 1864, WTS

to G. H. Thomas, August 2, 1864, Palmer to G. H. Thomas, August 4, 1864, and G. H. Thomas endorsement, Special Field Orders No. 51, HQ, Military Division of the Mississippi, August 4, 1864, WTS to G. H. Thomas, August 5, 1864, and Schofield to WTS, August 5, 1864, *OR* 38(5):310, 330, 354, 364, 369, 371, 380.

38. WTS to G. H. Thomas and Howard, August 9, 1864, WTS to Schofield, August 9, 1864, and WTS to Grant, August 10, 1864, *OR* 38(5):435, 441, 447; Castel, *Decision in the West*, 459–60.

39. Hardee to Mary, August 18, 1864, Hardee Family Papers, ADAH; Circular, August 13, 1864, *OR* 38(5):962.

40. WTS to Halleck, August 7, 9, 1864, WTS to Grant, August 10, 1864, WTS to Howard, August 10, 1864, and WTS to Schofield, August 11, 1864, *OR* 38(5):408–9, 434, 447, 452, 464; S. Davis, *Atlanta Will Fall*, 159, 342–43.

41. Chamberlin, "Skirmish Line," 192; Partridge, *History of the Ninety-sixth Regiment Illinois*, 387; Tower, *A Carolinian Goes to War*, 253; Hazen, *Narrative*, 420; Speir to Wife, August 14, 1864, Speir Collection, AHC; Diary, August 13, 1864, Seay Collection, UO; Douglas to Fannie, August 4, 1864, Douglas J. Cater and Rufus W. Cater Papers, LC; Bek, "Civil War Diary of John T. Buegel," 526.

42. WTS to Ewing, August 11, 1864, in Simpson and Berlin, *Sherman's Civil War*, 689; WTS to Webster, August 2, 4, 1864, WTS to Halleck, August 17, 1864, and WTS to Howard, August 18, 1864, *OR* 38(5):329, 351, 547, 585.

43. Special Field Orders No. 88, HQ, Army of the Ohio, August 20, 1864, General Field Orders No. 14, HQ, Army of Tennessee, August 12, 1864, General Orders No. 16, HQ, Ross's Brigade, Jackson's Cavalry Division, August 14, 1864, and [Shoup] to Cleburne, August 25, 1864, *OR* 38(5):620, 960, 963–64, 989.

44. WTS to Grant, August 7, 1864, Grant to WTS, August 16, 1864, and WTS to Halleck, August 20, 1864, *OR* 38(5):408, 521, 609.

45. WTS to Schofield, August 11, 1864, and WTS to Halleck, August 13, 1864, *OR* 38(5):463, 482; WTS, *Memoirs*, 2:98.

46. WTS to Halleck, August 17, 1864, *OR* 39(2):262; WTS, *Memoirs*, 2:103–4; WTS to Schofield, August 15, 1864, WTS to Halleck, August 17, 1864, WTS to G. H. Thomas, August 17, 1864, and G. H. Thomas to WTS, August 22, 1864, *OR* 38(5):511, 547–48, 629.

47. Special Field Orders No. 101, HQ, Army of the Tennessee, August 17, 1864, WTS to Halleck, August 28, 1864, WTS to G. H. Thomas, August 28, 1864, and WTS to Howard, August 28, 1864, *OR* 38(5):567, 688, 695; Castel, *Decision in the West*, 489, 491; S. Davis, *Atlanta Will Fall*, 177–78.

48. [Hood] to Hardee, August 31, 1864, *OR* 38(5):1006; Tower, *A Carolinian Goes to War*, 246–47; Phillips, *Reminiscences of a Confederate Soldier Boy*, 54; S. Davis, *Atlanta Will Fall*, 185; Castel, *Decision in the West*, 494–95, 499, 502–4.

49. Schofield to WTS, August 31, 1864, Stanley to Whipple, September 1, 1864, WTS to Halleck, September 4, 1864, Shoup to Hardee, August 31, 1864, and Shoup to Stewart, September 2, 1864, *OR* 38(5):732, 746, 792, 1006–7; Castel, *Decision in the West*, 505–6, 510, 515, 517, 524, 526.

50. Coburn to Speed, September 12, 1864, *OR* 38(2):393; WTS to Halleck, September 3, 1864, *OR* 38(5):777.

51. WTS to Halleck, September 3, 1864, *OR* 38(5):777; WTS to Halleck, September 4, 1864, and WTS to Ellen, September 17, 1864, in Simpson and Berlin, *Sherman's Civil War*, 697, 717; Grose to Mason, September 5, 1864, *OR* 38(1):262.

52. Hood to Bragg, September 3, 4, 5, 1864, Hardee to JD, September 4, 1864, and Hood to JD, September 6, 1864, *OR* 38(5):1017–18, 1021, 1023; Hood to Cooper, February 15, 1865, *OR* 38(3):629; Hood, *Advance and Retreat*, 130, 135.

53. Symonds, *Joseph E. Johnston*, 10–98; McMurry, *John Bell Hood*, 1–24.

54. Woods to Sisters, June 13, 1864, Woods Letters, MOC; McNeil, "Survey of Confederate Soldier Morale," 5–14; McMurry, "Confederate Morale," 232–39; Stephen Cowley to Minor, August 6, 1864, Minor Papers, USAMHI.

Chapter 13

1. WTS to Banks, January 16, 1864, *OR* 32(2):114; WTS to Rawlins, March 7, 1864, *OR* 32(1):174; WTS, *Memoirs*, 1:394.

2. WTS to Rawlins, March 7, 1864, *OR* 32(1):174–77; Foster, *Sherman's Mississippi Campaign*, 44–45, 59, 67, 69, 74, 100, 109, 112, 140, 145, 165, 169, 172–73; WTS to Halleck, February 29, 1864, *OR* 32(2):498; Roth, *Well Mary*, 37; Woodworth, *Nothing but Victory*, 480–85; Mountcastle, *Punitive War*, 85–91.

3. F. H. Kennedy, *Battlefield Guide*, 275; Brayman to Hurlbut, March 26, 1864, *OR* 32(1):505; Hurlbut to Sawyer, April 1, 1864, *OR* 32(3):217.

4. Cimprich, *Fort Pillow*, 82–85; Affidavits by survivors of Fort Pillow, *OR* 32(1):518–40.

5. Chetlain to Washburn, April 14, 1864, *OR* 32(3):364; Brayman to [not stated], May 2, 1864, *OR* 32(1):512.

6. F. H. Kennedy, *Battlefield Guide*, 344, 346–47; Ballard, *Civil War Mississippi*, 90, 94.

7. WTS to Stanton, June 15, 1864, *OR* 38(4):480.

8. F. H. Kennedy, *Battlefield Guide*, 347, 349–50; Ballard, *Civil War Mississippi*, 103–4, 106–7.

9. Ballard, *Civil War Mississippi*, 108; Washburn to Clark, September 2, 1864, *OR* 39(1):468–69, 471.

10. WTS to L. Thomas, April 12, 1864, *OR*, ser. 3, 4:225; Jefferies to JD, December 20, 1864, *OR* 52(2):799–800; Barrows to Commander of U.S. Forces Advancing on Jackson, July 5, 1864, *OR* 52(1):567.

11. McArthur to Rodgers, May 25, 1864, *OR* 39(1):6–8; Dana to Stanton, January 10, 1865, *OR* 45(2):566.

12. WTS to Slocum, July 24, 1864, *OR* 39(2):202; WTS to McPherson, March 7, 1864, *OR* 32(3):34; Grant to Stanton, October 13, 1864, in Simon, *Papers of . . . Grant*, 12:303–4.

13. WTS to Slocum, July 24, 1864, WTS to Halleck, August 20, 1864, Canby to WTS, September 11, 1864, and Howard to Rawlins, September 16, 1864, *OR* 39(2):203, 274–75, 363, 392–93.

14. Clay to REL, June 28, 1864, *OR* 39(2):670; Reagan to JD, January 6, 1865, in Crist, *Papers of Jefferson Davis*, 11:284; Gardner to Levy, December 21, 1864, and Buckner to Belton, January 5, 1865, *OR* 45(2):720, 765.

15. Kay to Polk, January 14, 1864, and Seddon to [not stated], March 14, 1864, *OR*

52(2):599–600, 638–39; Buford to Chase, March 1, 1864, in Niven, *Chase Papers*, 4:312; Moore to Comstock, February 1, 1864, *OR* 32(1):156–57; Ferris, "Captain Jolly," 29; Jameson to Adjutant General, U.S. Army, October 29, 1864, *OR* 39(1):880.

16. "List of Boats Destroyed on the Mississippi River and Its Tributaries from May 1st 1861 to the Surrender of Genl. Kirby Smith's Army and the Cessation of Hostilities, June 2d 1865," oversize folder 7, Parsons Papers, ALPL; *St. Louis Daily Missouri Democrat*, July 16, 1864; Baker to Parsons, March 29, 1865, *OR* 48(1):1291–92; Oldham to DJ, February 11, 1865, in Crist, *Papers of Jefferson Davis*, 11:398; General Orders No. 4, HQ, Military Division of the Mississippi, February 6, 1864, *OR* 32(2):347–48; WTS to Rosecrans, April 23, 1864, *OR* 32(3):463–64.

17. WTS to McPherson, March 7, 1864, and WTS to Chase, March 11, 1864, *OR* 32(3):34–35, 55.

18. General Orders No. 4, HQ, District of West Tennessee, May 14, 1864, *OR* 39(2):27–28; General Orders No. 15, HQ, District of Cairo, April 2, 1864, *OR* 32(3):233–34.

19. General Orders No. 4, HQ, District of Vicksburg, May 5, 1864, *OR* 39(2):30–31; Brayman to [not stated], May 2, 1864, *OR* 32(1):512; General Orders No. 3, HQ, District of West Tennessee, May 10, 1864, *OR* 39(2):22–23.

20. Townsend to Washburn, August 18, 1864, *OR* 39(2):267; General Orders No. 25, HQ, Military Division of the Mississippi, August 29, 1864, *OR* 39(2):314–15; Dana to [Howard], November 12, 1864, *OR* 52(1):655; Special Field Orders No. 25, HQ, Dept. of the Tennessee, March 7, 1864, *OR* 32(3):36.

21. Paxton to Seddon, April 11, 1864, and Harris to Bragg, September 7, 1864, *OR*, ser. 4, 3:282–83, 646–47; Smith to JD, April 4, 1864, and Deloney to JD, May 8, 1864, in Crist, *Papers of Jefferson Davis*, 10:310, 400; Winslow to Denis, March 15, 1864, *OR* 32(3):634; Polk to Memminger, April 29, 1864, *OR* 52(2):663; Polk to Adams, May 6, 1864, *OR* 39(2):584.

22. Eaton, *Grant, Lincoln and the Freedmen*, 104–5, 107–31, 134–36, 216.

23. General Orders No. 51, HQ, Dept. of the Tennessee, August 10, 1863, *OR* 24(3):585; Grant, *Memoirs*, 285; Grant to Crocker, August 30, 1863, in Simon, *Papers of . . . Grant*, 9:215–16.

24. Eaton, *Grant, Lincoln and the Freedmen*, 193–96, 201, 204.

25. Ibid., 134, 188.

26. Record of events, field and staff, 47th USCT, November–December 1863, and Record of events, Company B, 47th USCT, May–June 1864, *SOR* 78(2):53, 61; Hawkins to [not stated], April 4, 1864, and WTS endorsement, April 4, 1864, in Simon, *Papers of . . . Grant*, 10:553; [L. Thomas] to Stanton, November 7, 1864, in Berlin, *Freedom*, 171; Orders No. 21, signed Lorenzo Thomas, June 14, 1864, *OR*, ser. 3, 4:431; WTS to J. Sherman, April 22, 1864, in Simpson and Berlin, *Sherman's Civil War*, 628.

27. Record of events, Company E, 50th USCT, *SOR* 78(2):148; Gilchrist to Clark, March 9, 1864, *OR* 32(1):395–96, 400.

28. General Orders No. 7, HQ, District of Vicksburg, May 18, 1864, *OR* 39(2):38; Record of events, Company G, 13th USCT, August 30, 1864, *SOR* 77(2):495; Record of events, 50th USCT, February 15, 1864, *SOR* 78(2):136.

29. Fry to Burnside, October 24, 1863, *OR* 31(1):723.

30. L. Thomas to Stanton, October 5, 1865, *OR*, ser. 3, 5:121–22; L. Thomas to Stan-

ton, July 3, September 19, 1864, and Bowman to L. Thomas, July 23, 1864, *OR*, ser. 3, 4:467, 541, 733; Dickson to Burbridge, June 6, 1864, and Holt to Stanton, July 31, 1864, *OR* 39(2):81, 213–14.

31. Bramlette to AL, September 3, 1864, *OR*, ser. 3, 4:689; General Orders No. 5, HQ, Dept. of Kentucky, February 27, 1865, *OR* 49(1):782; L. Thomas to Stanton, October 8, 1864, and Burbridge to Holt, October 16, 1864, *OR* 39(3):157, 321; L. Thomas to Stanton, January 3, 1865, *OR* 45(2):503.

32. [L. Thomas] to Stanton, November 7, 1864, Berlin, *Freedom*, 170–71; Record of events for USCT units, *SOR* (2).

33. Hequembourg to Crane, May 10, 1864, Waring to Grierson, May 14, 1864, Hurst to Grierson, May 29, 1864, and Grierson endorsement, May 30, 1864, *OR* 39(2):20, 29, 56–57; Branson to Carter, August 8, 1864, and Brott to Smith, August 25, 1864, *OR* 39(1):460–61, 467.

34. Fitch to Porter, December 1, 1863, *ORN* 25:611; Lawrence to Odlin, March 11, 1864, *OR* 32(1):493.

35. General Orders No. 39 and 41, HQ, District of Kentucky, May 2, 12, 1864, and Prince to Hicks, May 12, 1864, *OR* 39(2):7, 23–24.

36. WTS to Burbridge, June 21, 30, 1864, General Orders No. 59 and 61, HQ, District of Kentucky, July 16, 26, 1864, Burbridge to Ewing, July 25, 1864, General Orders No. 233, War Dept. and Adjutant General's Office, July 19, 1864, and Holt to Stanton, July 31, 1864, *OR* 39(2):135–36, 154, 174, 180–82, 203, 205, 212–14.

37. Sutherland, *Savage Conflict*, 223.

38. Holt to Stanton, July 31, 1864, *OR* 39(2):213; Schofield to WTS, October 3, 1864, Bramlette to Grant, November 9, 1864, and Grant endorsement, November 14, 1864, and Burbridge to AL, November 11, 1864, *OR* 39(3):47, 724–25, 749; AL to Burbridge, October 27, 1864, in Basler, *Collected Works*, 8:78.

39. WTS to Stanton, June 21, 1864, WTS to Coombs, August 11, 1864, and WTS to Guthrie, August 14, 1864, *OR* 39(2):131–32, 240–41, 248–49.

Chapter 14

1. Grant to Halleck, October 4, 1864, *OR* 39(3):63–64; Grant to WTS, September 10, 1864, WTS to Grant, September 10, 20, 1864, and WTS to Canby, September 10, 1864, *OR* 39(2):355–56, 358, 412; WTS, *Memoirs*, 2:129–30.

2. WTS, *Memoirs*, 2:111; WTS to Hood, September 7, 10, 14, 1864, Hood to WTS, September 9, 12, 1864, and WTS to Calhoun, September 12, 1864, *OR* 39(2):414–22; WTS to Slocum, September 3, 1864, WTS to Webster, September 8, 1864, and Special Field Orders No. 67, HQ, Military Division of the Mississippi, September 8, 1864, *OR* 38(5):778, 830, 837–38.

3. Castel, *Decision in the West*, 550–51; REL to JD, September 19, 1864, *OR* 39(2):846; Speech at Macon, [September 23, 1864], and Speeches at Goldsboro and Greensboro, N.C., October 5, 1864, in Crist, *Papers of Jefferson Davis*, 11:61, 91–92.

4. JD to Hugh R. Davis, January 8, 1865, in Crist, *Papers of Jefferson Davis*, 11:286; Hood to Bragg, September 21, 1864, *OR* 39(2):860; JD to Seddon, October 2, 1864, *OR* 39(3):782.

5. WTS to Cox, September 30, 1864, *OR* 39(2):540; WTS, *Memoirs*, 2:144, 146; WTS to Commanding Officer at Allatoona, October 3, 1864, *OR* 39(3):53.

6. WTS to Howard, October 1, 1864, *OR* 39(3):6.

7. F. E. Brown, "Battle of Allatoona," 283, 286, 294; Johnson to Mussey, October 17, 1864, Corse to [Dayton], October 27, 1864, REL to Mason, January 30, 1865, and French to Stewart, November 5, 1864, *OR* 39(1):717–21, 766, 810–11, 818.

8. WTS to G. H. Thomas, October 10, 19, 1864, WTS to Schofield, October 17, 1864, and WTS to Halleck, October 19, 1864, *OR* 39(3):191, 335, 358, 365; WTS, *Memoirs*, 2:157.

9. Granger to Polk, November 6, 1864, and Hood to Cooper, February 15, 1865, *OR* 39(1):694–700, 802; WTS, *Memoirs*, 2:163.

10. WTS to Halleck, January 1, 1865, *OR* 39(1):583; Grant to Halleck, October 13, 1864, Stanton to WTS, October 13, 1864, WTS to Halleck, October 19, 1864, and WTS to G. H. Thomas, October 19, 1864, *OR* 39(3):239–40, 357–58, 365; Schofield, *Forty-six Years*, 165.

11. WTS to Halleck, October 19, 1864, and WTS to Grant, November 6, 1864, *OR* 39(3):358, 660.

12. WTS to G. H. Thomas, October 9, 1864, WTS to Slocum, October 20, 1864, and WTS to G. H. Thomas, October 23, 1864, *OR* 39(3):170, 370, 408; WTS to Cox, September 30, 1864, *OR* 39(2):40; Bryant, *Third Regiment of Wisconsin . . . Infantry*, 273; Blair, *A Politician Goes to War*, 208; Robinson to Robinson, December 28, 1864, *OR* 39(1):659–61; Holmes, *52d O.V.I.*, 263–64; Harwell and Racine, *Fiery Trail*, 34.

13. Sword, *Confederacy's Last Hurrah*, 66–67; Beauregard to Cooper, October 24, 1864, *OR* 39(1):797; Brent to Wade, November 8, 1864, *OR* 52(2):776; Whitfield endorsement on undated letter by Gaston to Grant, in Simon, *Papers of . . . Grant*, 16:467n; Beauregard to Hood, November 15, 1864, *OR* 45(1):1210.

14. Sinclair to Hardie, January 7, 1865, and Forrest to Surget, January 12, 1865, *OR* 39(1):862, 871.

15. Sword, *Confederacy's Last Hurrah*, 68–72, 88; Brent to Hood, November 17, 1864, Hood to Brent, November 17, 1864, and Hood to Beauregard, November 17, 1864, *OR* 45(1):1215; T. L. Connelly, *Autumn of Glory*, 477–87.

16. Schofield, *Forty-six Years*, 165–66.

17. Sword, *Confederacy's Last Hurrah*, 93, 95, 126–54; D. B. Connelly, *Schofield*, 123–32; Stewart Diary, November 30, 1864, Francis R. Stewart Papers, BGSU; T. L. Connelly, *Autumn of Glory*, 494–503.

18. Hood, *Advance and Retreat*, 290; Sword, *Confederacy's Last Hurrah*, 159, 163–64, 179–80, 183; D. B. Connelly, *Schofield*, 133–35.

19. Sword, *Confederacy's Last Hurrah*, 191, 199–207.

20. Joseph N. Thompson, "Battle of Franklin," Thompson Family Papers, UNC; Speed to Horace, December 3, 1864, Speed Letterbook, FHS.

21. Sword, *Confederacy's Last Hurrah*, 269–70; Douglas Cater to Fannie, December 15, 1864, January 12, 1865, Douglas J. Cater and Rufus W. Cater Papers, LC; Speed [to Horace], December 2, 1864, Speed Letterbook, FHS.

22. Grant to WTS, December 3, 1864, in Simon, *Papers of . . . Grant*, 13:57; Grant to G. H. Thomas, December 2, 1864, *OR* 45(2):17.

23. Beauregard to Kirby Smith, December 2, 1864, *OR* 44:919; Clemmons to Marsh, December 3, 1864, *OR* 45(2):504–5.

24. Reynolds Diary, December 5, 10–11, 13, 1864, Reynolds Papers, UAF; Unsigned circular, December 6, 1865, General Orders and Circulars, Hood's Corps, MOC; Douglas Cater to Fannie, December 15, 1864, January 12, 1865, Douglas J. Cater and Rufus W. Cater Papers, LC.

25. G. H. Thomas to Grant, December 9, 11, 1864: Grant to Halleck, December 9, 1864, G. H. Thomas to Halleck, December 11, 12, 14, 1864, and Grant to G. H. Thomas, December 11, 1864, *OR* 45(2):115–16, 143, 155, 180; Maley to Father and Mother, December 13, 1864, Maley Letters, UND; Grant, *Memoirs*, 655–56, 659–60; McDonough, *Nashville*, 149–53; Einolf, *George Thomas*, 263–68.

26. Grant to G. H. Thomas, December 15, 1864, *OR* 45(2):195.

27. McDonough, *Nashville*, 160–208, 225–66; William Dudley Gale to [not stated], January 19, 1865, Polk Papers, US.

28. McDonough, *Nashville*, 270–74; William Dudley Gale to [not stated], January 19, 1865, Polk Papers, US; Douglas Cater to Fannie, December 15, 1864, January 12, 1865, Douglas J. Cater and Rufus W. Cater Papers, LC; Einolf, *George Thomas*, 283–87.

29. Circular, HQ, Army of Tennessee, January 14, 1865, Mason to Stewart, January 14, 1865, Mason to Forrest, January 14, 1865, *OR* 45(2):783.

30. Harris to JD, December 25, 1864, *OR* 45(2):732; Dox to Grant, January 14, 1865, in Simon, *Papers of . . . Grant*, 13:505; Whipple to Wilson, December 29, 1864, G. H. Thomas to Johnson, December 30, 1864, and Johnson to G. H. Thomas, January 1, 1865, *OR* 45(2):411, 421, 471; Fisher, "Definitions of Victory," 104.

31. WTS to Halleck, January 1, 1865, and Cogswell to Perkins, December 26, 1864, *OR* 39(1):584, 652; WTS, *Memoirs*, 2:177; WTS to Ellen, October 21, 1864, in Simpson and Berlin, *Sherman's Civil War*, 738–39.

32. WTS, *Memoirs*, 2:179, 181–82, 184.

33. Ibid., 187; Bailey, *War and Ruin*, 67–69, 73–74; Woodworth, *Nothing but Victory*, 596–97.

34. WTS to Ellen, December 16, 1864, in Simpson and Berlin, *Sherman's Civil War*, 767–68; M. A. D. Howe, *Marching with Sherman*, 89.

35. Hill to People of Georgia, November 18, 1864, Beauregard to People of Georgia, November 18, 1864, and Beauregard to JD, December 6, 1864, *OR* 44, 867, 932–33; Barnwell to Magrath, January 9, 1865, in Crist, *Papers of Jefferson Davis*, 11:298; Grant to Meade, November 15, 1864, in Simon, *Papers of . . . Grant*, 12:423.

36. Circular, HQ, Cavalry Corps, December 4, 1864, Wheeler to Bragg, December 28, 1864, and General Orders No. 7, HQ, Cavalry Corps, December 29, 1864, *OR* 44:928, 998, 1002–3; Lawson to JD, December 27, 1864, *OR*, ser. 4, 3:967; Robert to JD, December 25, 1864, and Chesnut to JD, December 26, 1864, in Crist, *Papers of Jefferson Davis*, 11:252.

37. WTS, *Memoirs*, 2:193; Williams to Rodgers, January 9, 1865, and General Field Orders No. 26, HQ, Army of the Tennessee, November 22, 1864, *OR* 44:212, 521.

38. Bailey, *War and Ruin*, 86–87.

39. Cob to Seddon, December 22, 1864, and Gilmer to Seddon, January 3, 1865, *OR* 44, 977, 1012–13.

40. Bailey, *War and Ruin*, 103–7; Woodworth, *Nothing but Victory*, 604–5.

41. B. W. Frobel to M. L. Smith, February 25, 1865, Jones Papers, DU; Harryman to Maggie, December 18, 1864, Harryman Papers, ISL; Lauren Walcott to Sister, December 21, 1864, KMNBP; F. N. Kellogg to Sister, December 25, 1864, Plessinger Papers, ISL; WTS, *Memoirs*, 2:206–7; Grant to WTS, December 6, 1864, in Simon, *Papers of . . . Grant*, 13:72–73; Grant to WTS, December 18, 1864, and WTS to AL, December 22, 1864, *OR* 44:740–41, 783.

42. WTS to Halleck, December 24, 1864, *OR* 44:798–99.

43. Ibid., 799.

44. WTS to Halleck, January 1, 1865, *OR* 44:13; Poe to Nelly, December 16, 1864, Poe Papers, LC; Barnard to Grant, January 2, 1865, *OR* 47(2):8; Blair, *A Politician Goes to War*, 217; WTS, *Memoirs*, 2:220.

45. Annual Message to Congress, December 6, 1864, and AL to WTS, December 26, 1864, in Basler, *Collected Works*, 8:148, 181–82; WTS to L. Thomas, December 25, 1864, in Simpson and Berlin, *Sherman's Civil War*, 779–80; Schofield, *Forty-six Years*, 302, 305, 309, 313, 333, 338.

46. Fry to JD, January 8, 1865, in Crist, *Papers of Jefferson Davis*, 11:293.

47. Stanton to Grant, December 26, 1864, Foster to Halleck, December 26, 1864, and Grant to WTS, December 27, 1864, *OR* 44:809, 817, 821; WTS, *Memoirs*, 2:231, 243.

48. Special Orders No. 12, 13, HQ, Military Division of the Mississippi, January 14, 15, 1865, and WTS to Stanton, January 19, 1865, *OR* 47(2):50, 52–53, 88; Halleck to Foster, December 31, 1864, *OR* 44:846.

49. WTS to Ellen, January 5, 1865, in Simpson and Berlin, *Sherman's Civil War*, 792; WTS to Halleck, December 31, 1864, *OR* 44:842; Allen to Parents, December 19, 21, 1864, Allen Papers, UNC.

50. Quaife, *From the Cannon's Mouth*, 355.

51. WTS to Chase, January 11, 1865: WTS to Halleck, January 12, 1865, in Simpson and Berlin, *Sherman's Civil War*, 794, 796; Williams to Rodgers, January 9, 1865, *OR* 44, 211–12; Eaton, *Grant, Lincoln and the Freedmen*, 216.

52. Halleck to WTS, December 30, 1864, *OR* 44:836; WTS, *Memoirs*, 2:244–45; WTS to Halleck, January 12, 1863, *OR* 47(2):36.

53. Special Orders No. 15, HQ, Military Division of the Mississippi, January 16, 1865, *OR* 47(2):60–62; Foster to Halleck, January 25, 1865, *OR* 47(1):1005–6; Williams to Rodgers, January 9, 1865, WTS to Halleck, December 31, 1864, and Halleck to Foster, December 31, 1864, 44, 211–12, 842, 847.

54. Gregg to JD, December 27, 1864, and Cobb to JD, December 28, 1864, in Crist, *Papers of Jefferson Davis*, 11:255, 257.

Chapter 15

1. WTS, *Memoirs*, 2:240; WTS to Ellen, January 15, 1865, in Simpson and Berlin, *Sherman's Civil War*, 797; WTS to Porter, January 17, 1865, *OR* 47(2):69.

2. WTS, *Memoirs*, 2:272; Grant to WTS, December 27, 1864, *OR* 44:821; WTS to Grant, January 21, 1865, *OR* 47(2):103; Grant to Halleck, December 30, 1864, in Simon, *Papers of . . . Grant*, 13:187.

3. WTS, *Memoirs*, 2:241, 253, 273–75; Barrett, *Sherman's March*, 47.

4. Quaife, *From the Cannon's Mouth*, 386; Bauer, *Soldiering*, 209, 225.

5. General Field Orders No. 7, 9, HQ, Dept. of the Tennessee, January 30, February 9, 1865, General Orders No. 10, HQ, Fourth Division, Seventeenth Corps, January 30, 1865, Special Orders No. 38, HQ, Fifteenth Corps, February 7, 1865, Special Field Orders No. 14, HQ, Fourth Division, Fifteenth Corps, February 11, 1865, and Special Orders No. 4, HQ, Twentieth Corps, February 13, 1865, *OR* 47(2):171, 173, 331, 360, 388–39, 410.

6. Poe to Logan, February 7, 1865, and WTS to Slocum, February 9, 1865, *OR* 47(2):331, 364.

7. Lucas, *Sherman and the Burning of Columbia*, 65, 68–69, 75–76, 83, 98; Woods to Woodhull, February 17, 1865, *OR* 47(2):457; Howard, *Autobiography*, 2:121.

8. Howard, *Autobiography*, 2:122; Harwell and Racine, *Fiery Trail*, 129; Lucas, *Sherman and the Burning of Columbia*, 102–3, 109, 118, 121–24, 127; Barrett, *Sherman's March*, 71–93; Glatthaar, *March to the Sea*, 143–46; Woodworth, *Nothing but Victory*, 617–24.

9. Harwell and Racine, *Fiery Trail*, 134; WTS to Goodwyn, February 19, 1865, and Yorke to Logan, February 20, 1865, *OR* 47(2):485, 503.

10. WTS to Kilpatrick, February 21, 1865, and WTS to Stanton, March 12, 1865, *OR*, 47(2):519, 793.

11. Howard to Blair, February 20, 1865, General Orders No. 8, HQ, Left Wing, Army of Georgia, March 7, 1865, and Special Orders No. 63, HQ, Seventeenth Corps, March 10, 1865, *OR* 47(2):505–6, 719, 760.

12. Special Orders No. 55, HQ, Seventeenth Corps, March 1, 1865, and Circular, HQ, Army of the Tennessee, March 4, 1865, *OR* 47(2):632, 677.

13. Kilpatrick to Dayton, February 22, 1865, WTS to Howard, February 23, 1865, and WTS to Kilpatrick, February 23, 1865, *OR* 47(2):533, 537, 544.

14. WTS to Hampton, February 24, 1865, and Hampton to WTS, February 27, 1865, *OR* 47(2):546, 596–697; Barrett, *Sherman's March*, 104–6.

15. Hazen to Woodhull, February 22, 1865, Special Field Orders No. 56, HQ, Army of the Tennessee, March 8, 1865, and Special Orders No. 45, HQ, First Division, Fifteenth Corps, March 13, 1865, *OR* 47(2):529–30, 728, 809.

16. Howard, *Autobiography*, 2:127; Harwell and Racine, *Fiery Trail*, 139; Special Field Orders No. 43, HQ, Army of the Tennessee, February 19, 1865, *OR* 47(2):485.

17. Grant to WTS, January 21, 1865, and Schofield to Grant, December 27, 1864, *OR* 45(2):101, 377–78; D. B. Connelly, *Schofield*, 147–48.

18. "Journal and Record of Proceedings of Col. Lewis B. Parsons, Chief of Rail, and River Transportation, under Order of the Asst Secty of War, to transport the Army of the Ohio General Schofield Comd'g, from Eastport, Miss. to *Annapolis, Md.*," box 20, folder 2, Parsons Papers, ALPL; Parsons to Stanton, February 2, 1865, and Parsons to Burr, January 21, 1865, *OR* 47(2):215, 248.

19. Schofield to WTS, April 3, 1865, *OR* 47(1):910–11; Schofield, *Forty-six Years*, 346

20. Schofield, *Forty-six Years*, 346; Anderson to Sale, February 23, 1865, *OR* 47(2):1263.

21. General Orders No. 8, HQ, Dept. of North Carolina, February 27, 1865, and Terry to WTS, March 14, 1865, *OR* 47(2):605–6, 840.

22. WTS to Grant, March 12, 1865, WTS to Terry, March 12, 1865, and Corse to Wood-

hull, March 14, 1865, *OR* 47(2):794–95, 803, 826; WTS, *Memoirs*, 2:300; Hawley to Van Fleet, March 28, 1865, *OR* 47(3):51.

23. Circular No. 5, HQ, Fourth Division, Fifteenth Corps, February 22, 1865, WTS to Grant, March 12, 1865, and WTS to Terry, March 12, 1865, *OR* 47(2):531, 794, 803.

24. JD to Taylor, January 12, 1865, Harrison to JD, January 14, 1865, and Special Field Orders No. [not stated], HQ, Military Division of the West, January 23, 1865, *OR* 45(2):778, 784, 805; Longstreet to REL, February 2, 1865, Special Orders No. 3, HQ, Armies of the Confederate States, February 22, 1865, Hardee to Johnston, February 28, 1865, and Brent to Beauregard, March 4, 1865, *OR* 47(2):1078, 1248, 1290, 1322–23; Schofield, *Forty-six Years*, 335; Watts to JD, February 15, 1865, in Crist, *Papers of Jefferson Davis*, 11:404; T. L. Connelly, *Autumn of Glory*, 517–20.

25. Beauregard to JD, February 21, 1865, Beauregard's appeal, February 23, 1865, and Beauregard to Johnston, March 1, 1865, *OR* 47(2):1238, 1265, 1298–99.

26. REL to Breckinridge, February 19, 1865, and Johnston to REL, March 1, 1865, *OR* 47(1):1044, 1051; Johnston to REL, March 1, 1865, and REL to Johnston, February 23, March 15, 1865, *OR* 47(2):1256–57, 1298, 1395; REL to JD, February 23, 1865, *OR* 53:413.

27. Schofield to WTS, April 3, 1865, Abstract of Jacob D. Cox Journal, March 11, 1865, and Johnston to REL, March 8, 1865, *OR* 47(1):912–13, 933, 1052; Schofield, *Forty-six Years*, 346.

28. M. L. Bradley, *Last Stand in the Carolinas*, 114, 121–33; General Orders No. 16, HQ, March 17, 1865, and Johnston to REL, March 18, 1865, *OR* 47(2):1411, 1426.

29. Johnston to REL, March 18, 1865, *OR* 47(2):1426; M. L. Bradley, *Last Stand in the Carolinas*, 160–300.

30. M. L. Bradley, *Last Stand in the Carolinas*, 309, 318–48, 370–96, 400, 404.

31. WTS, *Memoirs*, 2:304.

32. WTS to Schofield, March 12, 1865, WTS to Grant, March 22, 23, 1865, and Circular, HQ, Dept. of North Carolina, March 11, 1865, *OR* 47(2):800, 950, 969, 1378; Schofield, *Forty-six Years*, 346; Abstract of Jacob D. Cox Journal, March 23, 1865, *OR* 47(1):935.

33. WTS, *Memoirs*, 2:306–7; WTS to Ellen, March 26, 1865, in Simpson and Berlin, *Sherman's Civil War*, 837; Logan to Van Dyke, March 31, 1865, *OR* 47(1):239–40.

34. Special Field Orders No. 69, HQ, Army of the Tennessee, March 23, 1865, *OR* 47(2):972; Morgan to McClurg, March 29, 1865, *OR* 47(1):487; Glatthaar, *March to the Sea*, 122, 141, 148–51.

35. Campbell, *When Sherman Marched*, 43–44, 56, 91–92.

36. Force to Cadle, March 28, 1865, Williams to Dechert, March 31, 1865, and Geary to Perkins, March 26, 1865, *OR* 47(1):409, 588, 695; Bauer, *Soldiering*, 235.

37. Bauer, *Soldiering*, 233; Glatthaar, *March to the Sea*, 19–20.

38. Grant, *Memoirs*, 757.

39. Halleck to Grant, December 30, 1864, Grant to Halleck, January 18, 1865, WTS to G. H. Thomas, January 21, 1865, and G. H. Thomas to Halleck, January 24, 1865, *OR* 45(2):420, 609, 621–22, 627–28; Halleck to WTS, January 1, 1865, *OR* 47(2):4.

40. G. H. Thomas to WTS, February 5, 1865, *OR* 49(1):653–54; Grant to G. H. Thomas, February 27, March 7, 1865, and Grant to WTS, March 16, 1865, in Simon, *Papers of . . . Grant*, 14:64–65, 112, 172–75; Hearn, *Mobile Bay*, 147.

41. Grant to Canby, February 27, March 9, 1865, in Simon, *Papers of . . . Grant*, 14:61–63, 124–25; Grant, *Memoirs*, 676; Grant to Canby, February 9, 1865, in Simon, *Papers of . . . Grant*, 13:397.

42. Hearn, *Mobile Bay*, 75, 81–82, 87, 91–92.

43. Ibid., 102–15, 117, 131.

44. Canby to Halleck, June 1, 1865, *OR* 49(1):92–93; Hearn, *Mobile Bay*, 146–47, 151, 157.

45. Canby to Halleck, June 1, 1865, *OR* 49(1):99; Black to Mary, April 12, 1865, Black Papers, ALPL; Andrew J. Minnick to Parents, April 13, 1865, Federal Soldiers' Letters, UNC; Granger to Canby, April 13, 1865, *OR* 49(2):348–49; Hearn, *Mobile Bay*, 170, 179, 187–88, 191, 199, 200–201, 206.

46. Jones, *Yankee Blitzkrieg*, 9, 14, 28, 70–73, 87–91, 100; Wilson to Whipple, June 29, 1865, and Wilson to Ramsey, February 10, 1865, *OR* 49(1):356, 360–62, 689; Scott, *Story of a Cavalry Regiment*, 447; W. B. Lay Reminiscence, *Confederate Veteran* Papers, DU.

47. Wilson to Whipple, June 29, 1865, *OR* 49(1):362–65; Jones, *Yankee Blitzkrieg*, 100, 111, 135–40.

48. Wilson to Whipple, June 29, 1865, *OR* 49(1):365–66; Jones, *Yankee Blitzkrieg*, 143, 167.

49. Wilson to Whipple, June 29, 1865, *OR* 49(1):369–70; Jones, *Yankee Blitzkrieg*, 168, 185.

50. Grant to G. H. Thomas, January 31, 1865, *OR* 49(1):616.

51. Hartley, *Stoneman's Raid*, 38, 221–66, 284–97; Van Noppen, *Stoneman's Last Raid*, 1, 16–18, 64, 67, 69, 71, 74; Stoneman to G. H. Thomas, April 13, 1865, *OR* 49(1):324.

Chapter 16

1. WTS, *Memoirs*, 2:327.

2. Ibid., 326; WTS to Grant, March 31, 1865, *OR* 47(3):65.

3. Grant, *Memoirs*, 690–91; Schofield, *Forty-six Years*, 347.

4. Barrett, *Sherman's March*, 197–98; Special Field Orders No. 48, HQ, Military Division of the Mississippi, April 5, 1865, *OR* 47(3):102–3.

5. Howard to Commander at Morehead City, April 5, 1865, WTS to Howard, April 7, 1865, WTS to Grant, April 8, 1865, and Abstract of Jacob D. Cox Journal, April 6 and 10, 1865, *OR* 47(3):103, 119, 129, 936.

6. JD to Bragg, April 1, 1865, *OR* 47(3):740; Johnston to REL, March 23, 1865, *OR* 47(2):1454.

7. Quaife, *From the Cannon's Mouth*, 381; Halleck to WTS, April 10, 1865, and WTS to Grant, April 12, 1865, *OR* 47(3):150–51, 177; WTS, *Memoirs*, 2:344.

8. WTS to Kilpatrick, April 14, 1865, *OR* 47(3):215.

9. Stanton to WTS, April 15, 1865, Special Field Orders No. 56, HQ, Military Division of the Mississippi, April 17, 1865, WTS to Halleck, April 18, 1865, and WTS to Johnston and Hardee, April 23, 1865, *OR* 47(3):220–21, 239, 245, 287.

10. WTS to Johnston, April 14, 1865, Special Field Orders No. 55, HQ, Military Division of the Mississippi, April 14, 1865, and WTS to Grant and Stanton, April 15, 1865, *OR* 47(3):207, 209, 221.

11. WTS to G. H. Thomas, May 2, 1865, in Simpson and Berlin, *Sherman's Civil War*, 886; WTS, *Memoirs*, 2:349, 351.

12. WTS, *Memoirs*, 2:352–54; WTS to Grant or Halleck, April 18, 1865, *OR* 47(3):243–44.

13. Stanton to Dix, April 22, 1865, *OR* 47(3):285–86.

14. Grant to Stanton, April 24, 1865, WTS to Johnston, April 24, 1865, Johnston to WTS, April 25, 1865, Grant to Stanton, April 26, 1865, Special Field Orders No. 65, HQ, Military Division of the Mississippi, April 27, 1865, Special Field Orders No. 102, HQ, Army of the Tennessee, April 27, 1865, and Johnston to Brown, April 30, 1865, *OR* 47(3):293–94, 304, 311, 322, 324–25, 855.

15. Barrett, *Sherman's March*, 273–76; Sprague to Johnson, April 24, 1865, Stanton to Grant, April 25, 1865, and WTS to Grant, April 28, 1865, *OR* 47(3):301–2, 335; WTS, *Memoirs*, 2:365, 373.

16. Schofield, *Forty-six Years*, 349.

17. WTS to Dyer, April 22, 1865, *OR* 47(3):279; Schofield, *Forty-six Years*, 344.

18. WTS to Grant, April 25, 1865, *OR* 47(3):303; Benjamin to JD, April 22, 1865, in Crist, *Papers of Jefferson Davis*, 11:555; Tucker to Smith, April 18, 1865, and Patterson to Granger, April 26, 1865, *OR* 49(2):406–7, 505; Henderson to Smith, May 8, 1865, *OR*, ser. 2, 8:540–41; Sutherland, *Savage Conflict*, 267–70.

19. Halleck to G. H. Thomas, April 17, 1865, G. H. Thomas to Hatch, May 2, 1865, and Forrest to Soldiers, April 25, 1865, *OR* 49(2):376, 569, 1263.

20. Canby to Grant, May 7, 1865, Surget to Forrest, April 30, 1865, Taylor to Maury, May 2, 3, 1865, General Orders No. 54, HQ, Dept. of Alabama, Mississippi, and East Louisiana, May 6, 1865, and Forrest to Soldiers, May 9, 1865, *OR* 49(2):658–59, 1270, 1275, 1279, 1283–84, 1289; Canby to Halleck, June 1, 1865, *OR* 49(1):99; Osterhaus to Dana, May 4, 1865, *OR* 48(2):311; Osterhaus to Dana, May 8, 1865, *OR* 46(2):672.

21. Wilson to Grierson, May 2, 1865, Special Field Orders No. 30, HQ, Cavalry Corps, Military Division of the Mississippi, May 4, 1865, *OR* 49(2):580, 601.

22. G. H. Thomas to Grant, April 30, 1865, and Granger to Whipple, May 17, 1865, *OR* 49(2):523, 820.

23. Smith to Polk, April 20, 1865, Grant endorsement, May 5, 1865, and Grant to G. H. Thomas, April 30, 1865, *OR* 49(2):418–19, 522.

24. General Orders No. 45, HQ, District of West Tennessee, April 17, 1865, Benjamin to Butler, April 26, 27, 1865, Butler to Hobson, April 30, 1865, and Gilfallan to Polk, May 10, 1865, *OR* 49(2):389, 478, 493, 528, 710.

25. G. H. Thomas to Steedman, May 1, 1865, Polk to Milroy, May 2, 1865, Milroy to Polk, May 2, 1865, and Cravens to Richman, May 4, 1865, *OR* 49(2):552–53, 570, 608.

26. Halleck to Stanton, February 17, 1865, Dodge to Bell, March 5, 1865, and Richardson endorsement on Allen to Richardson, March 11, 1865, *OR*, ser. 2, 8:239–40, 358–59, 381.

27. Dodge to Bell, March 5, 1865, *OR*, ser. 2, 8:358–59.

28. Grierson to Harris, January 14, 1865, *OR* 45(1):847; Noble to Lytle, January 13, 1865, Extract of Grierson report, December 28, 1864, and Hosmer to Stanton, May 13, 1865, *OR*, ser. 2, 8:125–26, 554.

29. Taylor to Maury, March 6, 1865, *OR*, ser. 2, 8:362.

30. Jones, *Yankee Blitzkrieg*, 171–72, 175–77; Pritchard to Scott, May 11, 1865, *OR* 49(2):721–22.

31. Jones, *Yankee Blitzkrieg*, 179–81; Wilson to Stanton, May 10, 1865, *OR* 49(2):702.

32. G. H. Thomas to Hatch, May 2, 1865, Christensen to Smith, May 29, 1865, and Whipple to Wilson, June 18, 1865, *OR* 49(2):569, 930, 1010; Presidential Proclamation, June 24, 1865, *OR*, ser. 3, 5:104–5; Crosby to Herron, May 12, 1865, Dillingham to Flanders, May 18, 1865, and Canby endorsement, May 30, 1865, *OR* 48(2):415, 503.

33. Surdam, "Traders or Traitors," 303–4; Lebergott, "Through the Blockade," 883–84.

34. WTS to Grant, April 28, 1865, Schofield to WTS, May 5, 1865, and WTS to Schofield, May 5, 1865, *OR* 47(3):335, 405–6.

35. General Orders No. 32, HQ, Dept. of North Carolina, April 27, 1865, *OR* 47(3):331.

36. Wilson to Whipple, May 15, 1865, *OR* 49(2):783–84.

37. General Orders No. 21, 22, HQ, Dept. of the Cumberland, April 13, 17, 1865, G. H. Thomas to Citizens of Morgan, Marshall, Lawrence Counties, Ala., n.d., Whipple to Stoneman, June 23, 1865, *OR* 49(2):342–43, 377–78, 506, 1028–29.

38. General Orders No. 27, HQ, Dept. of the Cumberland, May 2, 1865, G. H. Thomas to Wilson, May 9, 1865, and Stanton to Canby, May 16, 1865, *OR* 49(2):567, 680, 810.

39. Grant to G. H. Thomas, April 17, 1865, *OR* 49(2):375.

40. General Orders No. 51, HQ, Dept. of the Gulf, May 5, 1865, Crosby to Herron, May 15, 1865, Canby to Warren, May 20, 1865, General Orders No. 63, HQ, Military Division of West Mississippi, May 29, 1865, Canby to Governor of Louisiana, June 19, 1865, and Canby to Stanton, June 20, 1865, *OR* 48(2):319–20, 448, 520, 650, 932, 944–45.

41. Washburn to G. H. Thomas, March 4, 1865, *OR* 49(1):828; General Orders No. 40, 52, HQ, District of West Tennessee, March 27, May 8, 1865, and Special Orders No. 120, HQ, District of West Tennessee, May 9, 1865, *OR* 49(2):106, 671, 692.

42. Osterhaus to Banks, May 5, 1865, and Speed to Commanding Officer, 66th USCT, May 5, 1865, *OR* 48(2):318, 321.

43. Grant to Stanton, April 26, 1865, *OR* 47(3):311; Dana to Hoel, May 1, 1865, REL to Herron, May 3, 1865, and Davidson to Miller, May 3, 1865, *OR* 48(2):281, 302–3.

44. Grant to Halleck, March 9, 1865, in Simon, *Papers of . . . Grant*, 14:124; Pinkerton to Wood, April 25, 1865, and General Orders No. 13, HQ, Southern Division of Louisiana, March 15, 1865, *OR* 48(1):203–5, 1177.

45. Canby to Halleck, June 1, 1865, and Grierson to Christensen, June 4, 1865, *OR* 49(1):99, 300–301.

46. Special Field Orders No. 15, 20, HQ, Cavalry Corps, Military Division of the Mississippi, April 6, 11, 1865, Wilson to G. H.. Thomas, April 13, 1865, Wilson to Wayne, April 25, 1865, and Circular, HQ, Second Division, Cavalry Corps, Military Division of the Mississippi, May 22, 1865, *OR* 49(2):250, 319–20, 344, 461, 872.

47. Wilson to Winslow, June 2, 1865, Wilson to G. H. Thomas, June 4, 1865, Wilson to Whipple, May 15, June 9, 1865, and G. H. Thomas to Whipple, June 10, 1865, *OR* 49(2):783, 950, 955, 973, 976–77.

48. Winslow to Griffin, May 31, 1865, Judah to Whipple, June 7, 1865, and Whipple to Judah, June 7, 1865, *OR* 49(2):939, 968.

49. Wilson to G. H. Thomas, June 16, 1865, Wilson to Whipple, June 21, 1865, and

Winslow to [Inhoff], July 3, 1865, *OR* 49(2):1002, 1020, 1061–62; Foster to G. W. Lee, April 25, 1865, Foster Letters, KHS.

50. McArthur to Smith, May 23, 1865, Hatch to Whipple, June 19, 1865, and Randall to Commanding Officer at Montevallo, Ala., July 7, 1865, *OR* 49(2):887, 1015, 1071.

51. Morton to Hooker, January 11, 1865, and Potter to Hovey, January 19, 1865, *OR* 45(2):573, 617.

52. Murray to Harlan, March 29, 1865, *OR* 49(2):126.

53. Ingram to Hobson, May 19, 1865, *OR* 49(2):843; Howes to Lindsey, January 30, 1865, Gross to Butler, January 29, 1865, Alexander to Adjutant General of Kentucky, January 30, 1865, Ewing to Hobson, January 31, 1865, Lawton to Burbridge, February 5, 1865, and Watson to Bryson, February 28, 1865, *OR* 49(1):17–18, 619, 657, 788–89.

54. Stanton to Palmer, February 8, 1865, and General Orders No. 10, HQ, Dept. of Kentucky, March 12, 1865, *OR* 49(1):670–71, 904; Latham et al. to Stanton, May 25, 1865, *OR* 49(2):905–6.

55. Hobson to Alexander, February 9, 1865, and Hobson to Bascom, March 2, 1865, *OR* 49(1):684, 817.

56. Johnson to G. H. Thomas, February 3, 1865, Clift to Wells, February 7, 1865, Johnson endorsement, February 8, 1865, Milroy to Whipple, February 14, 1865, and Hale to Whipple, February 28, 1865, *OR* 49(1):640, 665–66, 714–15, 784; Johnson to Palmer, April 21, 1865, Cravens to Commanding Officer of Detachment, 43rd Wisconsin, May 16, 1865, Johnson to Whipple, June 22, 1865, Roberts to Phelps, June 28, 1865, and Cist to Johnson, July 21, 1865, *OR* 49(2):427–28, 807, 1025–26, 1050–51, 1088–89.

57. Circular, HQ, Cavalry Corps, Military Division of the Mississippi, April 28, 1865, Special Orders No. 113, HQ, District of West Tennessee, May 1, 1865, and Williams to McCook, May 9, 1865, *OR* 49(2):504, 557, 683–84.

58. Hawkins to McCook, May 20, 1865, and Johnson to Hough, June 27, 1865, *OR* 49(2):850, 1044–45.

59. Ellison, *On to Atlanta*, 123.

60. Selfridge to Buttrick, May 27, 1865, Fitzpatrick to Creigh, May 26, 1865, and Harrison to Crawford, May 31, 1865, *OR* 47(1):615–16, 726, 793.

61. Bryant, *Third Regiment of Wisconsin . . . Infantry*, 331–33; Ellison, *On to Atlanta*, 127–28.

62. Harrison to Crawford, May 31, 1865, *OR* 47(1):793; WTS, *Memoirs*, 2:372, 374, 377; Woodworth, *Nothing but Victory*, 638–40.

63. WTS, *Memoirs*, 2:378.

64. Grant to WTS, May 27, 1865, *OR* 47(3):576; Sargent to Grant, May 31, 1865, in Simon, *Papers of . . . Grant*, 15:500n.

65. WTS to Logan, May 12, 1865, *OR* 47(3):478.

Conclusion

1. Woodworth, *Decision in the Heartland*, xi–xiii.

2. T. L. Connelly, *Army of the Heartland*, xi–@xii; McMurry, *Two Great Rebel Armies*, 11–15, 24–28, 30–73, 88–90, 93, 110.

3. Parsons to Meigs, October 6, 1863, *OR* 52(1):459; Grant to Father, March 1, 1864, in Simon, *Papers of . . . Grant*, 10:183.

4. Hardee to Brent, February 28, 1863, *OR* 20(1):778.

5. Parsons to Stanton, February 2, 1865, *OR* 47(2):219; Parsons to Meigs, October 6, 1863, and Allen to Meigs, July 1, 1865, *OR* 52(1):459, 692; Michael, "Mississippi Flotilla," 21.

6. Clark, *Railroads in the Civil War*, 217, 219.

7. *Reminiscences of Thomas B. Wilson*, TSLA, 45.

8. Grimsley, *Hard Hand of War*, 2–5, 212; Cooling, "A People's War," 127.

9. R. R. Mackey, *Uncivil War*, 197; Sutherland, *Savage Conflict*, 160, 277–78; Mountcastle, *Punitive War*, 2, 100.

10. Edmonds, *Yankee Autumn*, 18.

11. Bauer, *Soldiering*, 99; Hoffman, *Camp Court and Siege*, 93–94; S. A. Ranlett, "Jackson, Miss.," November 13, 1884; Wiswell to Father, January 8, 1862 [1863], Wiswell Letters, DU; Copp, *Reminiscences*, 524.

12. Hazzard to Bunker, September 3, 1880, in *Society of the Army of the Cumberland, 1880*, 131.

13. Glaser to Andy, March 10, 22, 1864, Glaser Papers, DU.

14. Roth, *Well Mary*, 37; Charles Kroff Diary, December 25, 1862, Cress Papers, UO; Bennett and Haigh, *History of the Thirty-sixth Regiment Illinois*, 371; Clark interview in *New York Graphic*, ca. 1879, in Dawson, *Life and Services*, 257.

15. Dodge, *Personal Recollections*, 17–18, 76–77.

16. F. H. Kennedy, *Battlefield Guide*, 13–430.

17. Grant to Stanton, July 22, 1865, *OR* 38(1):51.

18. Grant to Hillyer, June 29, 1865, in Simon, *Papers of . . . Grant*, 15:234–35; Grant to Force, November 11, 1866, ibid., 16:377.

19. Davidson, "Thirty-ninth Regiment," 702–3.

20. McClellan to AL, August 4, 1861, *OR* 5:6; McClure, *Recollections of Half a Century*, 469–70; Schurz, *Reminiscences*, 3:131.

21. Gresham, *Life of Walter Quintin Gresham*, 1:195, 220; Logan to Hotchkiss, June [not stated], 1862, *OR* 10(1):761; Grant to Wife, May 9, 1863, in Simon, *Papers of . . . Grant*, 8:189.

22. Little to Lizzie, June 7, 1864, Little Papers, CHS; William Harrison Githens to Wife, June 15, 1864, Githens Letters, CU; Angle, *Three Years*, 223.

23. WTS to Ellen, May 20, 1864, in Simpson and Berlin, *Sherman's Civil War*, 638; WTS to Stanton, May 23, 1864, *OR* 38(4):294; Adams, *Our Masters*, vii–ix.

24. WTS, *Memoirs*, 2:249, 254; M. A. D. Howe, *Marching with Sherman*, 281.

25. Pope to Officers and Soldiers of the Army of Virginia, July 14, 1862, *OR* 12(3):474.

26. WTS to Grant, March 10, 1864, *OR* 32(3):49.

27. Dawson, *Life and Services*, 166–67, 203; Logan, *Reminiscences of a Soldier's Wife*, 276.

28. Saxon, *Father Mississippi*, 250.

29. Parish, *American Civil War*, 291–92; McPherson, *Ordeal by Fire*, 333; Roland, *American Iliad*, 147; Weigley, *Great Civil War*, 259; T. L. Connelly, "Vicksburg," 49–53.

{ Bibliography

Archives
Abraham Lincoln Presidential Library, Springfield, Illinois
    John Charles Black Papers
    Engelmann-Kircher Collection
    Lewis Baldwin Parsons Papers
    John S. Wilcox Papers
Alabama Department of Archives and History, Montgomery
    Hardee Family Papers
    Sterling A. M. Wood Papers
Atlanta History Center, Atlanta
    L. P. Grant Papers
    J. S. Speir Collection
Bowdoin College, Special Collections and Archives, Brunswick, Maine
    Charles Henry Howard Papers
    Oliver Otis Howard Papers
Bowling Green State University, Center for Archival Collections, Bowling Green, Ohio
    Francis R. Stewart Papers
Chicago Historical Society, Chicago
    George Carrington Papers
    Day Elmore Papers
    Alexander C. Little Papers
    Frederick A. Starring Papers
College of William and Mary, Special Collections Research Center, Williamsburg,
    Virginia
    Joseph E. Johnston Papers
    William Taylor Letters
Connecticut Historical Society, Hartford
    Henry Goodell Letter
Cornell University, Rare and Manuscript Collection, Ithaca, New York
    William Harrison Githens Letters, Gail and Stephen Rudin Collection of
        Civil War Letters
Duke University, Rare Books, Manuscripts, and Special Collections, Durham,
    North Carolina
    Confederate Veteran Papers
    Charles W. Glaser Papers
    David B. Harris Papers
    Charles Colcock Jones Papers
    Earl Van Dorn Papers
    James H. Wiswell Letters

Emory University, Manuscripts, Archives, and Rare Books Library, Atlanta
    W. L. Trask Journal
Filson Historical Society, Louisville, Kentucky
    Thomas Speed Letterbook
Georgia Department of Archives and History, Atlanta
    Boyd-Sitton Family Civil War Letters
Indiana Historical Society, Indianapolis
    Edward B. Allen Papers
    Andrew J. Johnson Papers
    David Shockley Papers
    Edward Stanfield Papers
    Lew Wallace Papers
Indiana State Library, Indianapolis
    William H. Doll Reminiscences
    Samuel K. Harryman Papers
    William D. Hynes Papers
    James B. Plessinger Papers
Kennesaw Mountain National Battlefield Park, Kennesaw, Georgia
    Lauren Walcott Letter
Kentucky Historical Society, Frankfort
    Ira H. Foster Letters
Knox County Public Library, McClung Historical Collection, Knoxville, Tennessee
    William H. Watterson Papers
Library of Congress, Manuscript Division, Washington, D.C.
    Douglas J. Cater and Rufus W. Cater Papers
    Peter B. Kellenberger Letters
    Orlando Metcalfe Poe Papers
Lincoln Memorial University, Abraham Lincoln Library and Museum,
        Harrogate, Tennessee
    Oliver Otis Howard Papers
Louisiana State University, Louisiana and Lower Mississippi Valley Collections,
        Special Collections, Baton Rouge
    John C. Burruss Family Papers
Massachusetts Historical Society, Boston
    Francis Carver Palfrey Papers
Mississippi Department of Archives and History, Jackson
    William A. Drennan Papers
    John C. Pemberton Papers
Missouri Historical Society, St. Louis
    Braxton Bragg Papers
    Civil War Papers
    Theodore Augustus Meysenburg Papers
    Charles Parsons Papers
    David D. Porter Papers

Museum of the Confederacy, Richmond, Virginia
  Edward Clifford Brush Diary
  General Orders and Circulars, Hood's Corps
  William Samuel Woods Letters, Soldier Letters Collection
Newberry Library, Chicago
  James Taylor Graves Papers
Stanford University, Special Collections and University Archives, Stanford, California
  Civil War Collection: Israel Spencer Letters
  Edward Otho Cresap Ord Letters
Tennessee State Library and Archives, Nashville
  George R. Elliott Diary, Civil War Collection
  Henry C. McNeill Diary, Civil War Collection
  Reminiscences of Thomas B. Wilson, Civil War Collection
  Theodore Gillard Trimmier Papers
University of Alabama, William Stanley Hoole Special Collections, Tuscaloosa
  Henry Delamar Clayton Papers
University of Arkansas, Special Collections, Fayetteville
  Daniel Harris Reynolds Papers
University of Kentucky, Audio-Visual Archives, Lexington
  John W. Tuttle Diary
University of Montana, Mansfield Library, Missoula
  Gates Family Papers
University of North Carolina, Southern Historical Collection, Chapel Hill
  Joseph Dill Alison Papers
  Edward W. Allen Papers
  D. Coleman Diary
  Federal Soldiers' Letters
  Jeremy Francis Gilmer Papers
  Samuel H. Lockett Papers
  William Whann Mackall Papers
  James W. Patton Papers
  Henry C. Semple Papers
  Edmund Kirby Smith Papers
  Thompson Family Papers
University of Notre Dame, Rare Books and Special Collections, South Bend, Indiana
  Henry H. Maley Letters
University of Oklahoma, Western History Collections, Norman
  Sherry Marie Cress Papers
  Abraham J. Seay Collection
University of the South, Archives and Special Collections, Sewanee, Tennessee
  Leonidas Polk Papers
University of Virginia, Special Collections, Charlottesville
  William Silliman Hillyer Collection
University of Washington, Special Collections Division, Seattle

Samuel D. Lougheed Papers

Trowbridge Family Letters

U.S. Army Military History Institute, Carlisle, Pennsylvania

Hubbard T. Minor Papers

Mungo Murray Papers, *Civil War Times Illustrated* Collection

Joseph Scroggs Diary, *Civil War Times Illustrated* Collection

Wisconsin Historical Society, Madison

Thomas Priestly Papers

Newspapers

Chatfield (Minn.) Republican

Indianapolis Daily Journal

Memphis Daily Appeal

The Press (Philadelphia)

St. Louis Daily Missouri Democrat

Books and Articles

Adams, Michael C. C. *Our Masters the Rebels: A Speculation on Union Military Failure in the East, 1861–1865.* Cambridge: Harvard University Press, 1978.

Angle, Paul M., ed. *Three Years in the Army of the Cumberland: The Letters and Diary of Major James A. Connolly.* Bloomington: Indiana University Press, 1959.

Ash, Stephen V. *When the Yankees Came: Conflict and Chaos in the Occupied South, 1861–1865.* Chapel Hill: University of North Carolina Press, 1995.

Bailey, Anne J. *War and Ruin: William T. Sherman and the Savannah Campaign.* Wilmington, Del.: Scholarly Resources, 2003.

Ballard, Michael B. *Civil War Mississippi: A Guide.* Jackson: University Press of Mississippi, 2000.

———. *Vicksburg: The Campaign That Opened the Mississippi.* Chapel Hill: University of North Carolina Press, 2004.

Barrett, John G. *Sherman's March through the Carolinas.* Chapel Hill: University of North Carolina Press, 1956.

Basler, Roy P., ed. *Collected Works of Abraham Lincoln.* 8 vols. New Brunswick, N.J.: Rutgers University Press, 1953.

Bauer, K. Jack, ed. *Soldiering: The Civil War Diary of Rice C. Bull, 123rd New York Volunteer Infantry.* San Rafael, Calif.: Presidio Press, 1977.

Bearss, Edwin C. "The Battle of Baton Rouge." In *The Louisiana Purchase Bicentennial Series in Louisiana History,* vol. 5, edited by Arthur W. Bergeron Jr., 71–108. Lafayette: Center for Louisiana Studies, 2002.

———. "The Battle of the Post of Arkansas." *Arkansas Historical Quarterly* 18, no. 3 (Autumn 1959): 237–79.

———. *Unvexed to the Sea: The Campaign for Vicksburg.* Vol. 3. Dayton, Ohio: Morningside, 1986.

Bek, William G., trans. and ed. "The Civil War Diary of John T. Buegel, Union Soldier: Part Two." *Missouri Historical Review* 40, no. 4 (July 1946): 503–40.

Bennett, L. G., and William M. Haigh. *History of the Thirty-sixth Regiment Illinois Volunteers, during the War of the Rebellion*. Aurora, Ill.: Knickerbocker and Hodder, 1876.

Berlin, Ira, ed. *Free At Last: A Documentary History of Slavery, Freedom, and the Civil War*. New York: New Press, 1992.

———. *Freedom: A Documentary History of Emancipation, 1861–1867: Series II, The Black Military Experience*. New York: Cambridge University Press, 1983.

Blair, William Alan, ed. *A Politician Goes to War: The Civil War Letters of John White Geary*. University Park: Pennsylvania State University Press, 1995.

Bradley, George C., and Richard L. Dahlen. *From Conciliation to Conquest: The Sack of Athens and the Court-Martial of Colonel John B. Turchin*. Tuscaloosa: University of Alabama Press, 2006.

Bradley, Mark L. *Last Stand in the Carolinas: The Battle of Bentonville*. Campbell, Calif.: Savas Woodbury, 1996.

Brown, Fred E. "The Battle of Allatoona." *Civil War History* 6, no. 3 (September 1960): 277–97.

Brown, Norman D., ed. *One of Cleburne's Command: The Civil War Reminiscences and Diary of Capt. Samuel T. Foster, Granbury's Texas Brigade, CSA*. Austin: University of Texas Press, 1980.

Bryan, Charles F., Jr. "'Tories' amidst Rebels: Confederate Occupation of East Tennessee, 1861–63." *East Tennessee Historical Society Papers* 60 (1988): 3–22.

Bryant, Edwin E. *History of the Third Regiment of Wisconsin Veteran Volunteer Infantry, 1861–1865*. Madison: Democrat Printing, 1891.

Butler, Benjamin F. *Butler's Book*. Boston: A. M. Thayer, 1892.

———. *Private and Official Correspondence of Gen. Benjamin F. Butler during the Period of the Civil War*. 5 vols. Norwood, Mass.: Plimpton Press, 1917.

Campbell, Jacqueline Glass. *When Sherman Marched North from the Sea: Resistance on the Confederate Home Front*. Chapel Hill: University of North Carolina Press, 2003.

Campbell, James B. "East Tennessee During the Federal Occupation, 1863–1865." *East Tennessee Historical Society Papers* 19 (1947): 64–80.

Carr, Joseph D. "Garfield and Marshall in the Big Sandy Valley, 1861–1862." *Filson Club History Quarterly* 64, no. 2 (April 1990): 247–63.

Castel, Albert. *Decision in the West: The Atlanta Campaign of 1864*. Lawrence: University Press of Kansas, 1992.

Chamberlin, W. H. "Recollections of the Battle of Atlanta." In *Sketches of War History, 1861–1865: Papers Prepared for the Commandery of the State of Ohio, Military Order of the Loyal Legion of the United States*, 6:276–86. Cincinnati: Monfort, 1908.

———. "The Skirmish Line in the Atlanta Campaign." *Sketches of War History, 1861–1865: Papers Prepared for the Ohio Commandery of the Military Order of the Loyal Legion of the United States*, 3:182–96. Cincinnati: Robert Clarke, 1890.

Childe, Charles B. "General Butler at New Orleans, 1862." In *Sketches of War History, 1861–1865: Papers Prepared for the Commandery of the State of Ohio, Military Order of the Loyal Legion of the United States, 1896–1903*, 5:175–98. Wilmington, N.C.: Broadfoot, 1991.

Cimprich, John. *Fort Pillow, a Civil War Massacre, and Public Memory*. Baton Rouge: Louisiana State University Press, 2005.

"Civil War Letters of Brigadier General William Ward Orme—1862–1866." *Journal of the Illinois State Historical Society* 23 (1930–31): 246–315.

Clark, John E. Jr. *Railroads in the Civil War: The Impact of Management on Victory and Defeat*. Baton Rouge: Louisiana State University Press, 2001.

Clark, Olynthus B., ed. *Downing's Civil War*. Des Moines: Historical Department of Iowa, 1916.

Connelly, Donald B. *John M. Schofield and the Politics of Generalship*. Chapel Hill: University Of North Carolina Press, 2006.

Connelly, Thomas Lawrence. *Army of the Heartland: The Army of Tennessee, 1861–1862*. Baton Rouge: Louisiana State University Press, 1967.

———. *Autumn of Glory: The Army of Tennessee, 1862–1865*. Baton Rouge: Louisiana State University Press, 1971.

———. "Vicksburg: Strategic Point or Propaganda Device?" *Military Affairs* 34, no. 2 (April 1970): 49–53.

Cooling, Benjamin Franklin. *Forts Henry and Donelson: The Key to the Confederate Heartland*. Knoxville: University of Tennessee Press, 1987.

———. "A People's War: Partisan Conflict in Tennessee and Kentucky." In *Guerrillas, Unionists, and Violence on the Confederate Home Front*, edited by Daniel E. Sutherland, 113–32. Fayetteville: University of Arkansas Press, 1999:

Copeland, James E. "Where Were the Kentucky Unionists and Secessionists?" *Register of the Kentucky Historical Society* 71, no. 3 (July 1973): 344–63.

Copp, Elbridge J. *Reminiscences of the War of the Rebellion, 1861–1865*. Nashua, N.H.: Telegraph Publishing, 1911.

Coulter, E. Merton. "Parson Brownlow's Tour of the North During the Civil War." *East Tennessee Historical Society Papers* 7 (1935): 3–27.

Cox, Jacob D. "War Preparations in the North." In *Battles and Leaders of the Civil War*, vol. 1, edited by Robert Underwood Johnson and Clarence Clough Buel, 84–98. New York: Thomas Yoseloff, 1956.

Cozzens, Peter. *The Darkest Days of the War: The Battles of Iuka and Corinth*. Chapel Hill: University of North Carolina Press, 1997.

———. *No Better Place to Die: The Battle of Stones River*. Urbana: University of Illinois Press, 1990.

———. *The Shipwreck of Their Hopes: The Battles for Chattanooga*. Urbana: University of Illinois Press, 1994.

———. *This Terrible Sound: The Battle of Chickamauga*. Urbana: University of Illinois Press, 1992.

Cozzens, Peter, and Robert I. Girardi, eds. *The Military Memoirs of General John Pope*. Chapel Hill: University of North Carolina Press, 1998.

Crist, Lynda Laswell, ed. *Papers of Jefferson Davis*. 12 vols. to date. Baton Rouge: Louisiana State University Press, 1971– .

Croushore, James H., ed. *A Volunteer's Adventures: A Union Captain's Record of the Civil War*. New Haven: Yale University Press, 1946.

Dana, Charles A. *Recollections of the Civil War with the Leaders at Washington and in the Field in the Sixties*. New York: D. Appleton, 1902.

Daniel, Larry J. *Days of Glory: The Army of the Cumberland, 1861–1865*. Baton Rouge: Louisiana State University Press, 2004.

———. *Shiloh: The Battle That Changed the Civil War*. New York: Simon and Schuster, 1997.

Daniel, Larry J., and Lynn N. Bock. *Island No. 10: Struggle for the Mississippi Valley*. Tuscaloosa: University of Alabama Press, 1996.

Davidson, Theo F. "Thirty-ninth Regiment." In *Histories of the Several Regiments and Battalions from North Carolina in the Great War, 1861-'65*, vol. 2, edited by Walter Clark, 699–725. Goldsboro, N.C.; Nash Brothers, 1901.

Davis, Stephen. *Atlanta Will Fall: Sherman, Joe Johnston, and the Yankee Heavy Battalions*. Wilmington, Del.: Scholarly Resources, 2001.

Davis, William C., ed. *Diary of a Confederate Soldier: John S. Jackman of the Orphan Brigade*. Columbia: University of South Carolina Press, 1990.

Dawson, George Francis. *Life and Services of Gen. John A. Logan as Soldier and Statesman*. Chicago: Belford, Clarke, 1887.

Dodge, Grenville M. *Personal Recollections of President Abraham Lincoln, General Ulysses S. Grant and General William T. Sherman*. Denver: Sage Books, 1965.

Donald, David Herbert. *Lincoln*. New York: Simon and Schuster, 1995.

Duke, John K. *History of the Fifty-third Regiment Ohio Volunteer Infantry*. Portsmouth, Ohio: Blade Printing, 1900.

[Dwight, Henry O.]. "How We Fight at Atlanta." *Harper's New Monthly Magazine* 29 (1864): 663–66.

Eaton, John. *Grant, Lincoln and the Freedmen: Reminiscences of the Civil War*. New York: Longmans, Green, 1907.

Edmonds, David E. *Yankee Autumn in Acadiana: A Narrative of the Great Texas Overland Expedition through Southwestern Louisiana, October-December, 1863*. Lafayette: Center for Louisiana Studies, 2005.

Einolf, Christopher J. *George Thomas: Virginia for the Union*. Norman: University of Oklahoma Press, 2007.

Ellison, Janet Correll, ed. *On to Atlanta: The Civil War Diaries of John Hill Ferguson, Illinois Tenth Regiment of Volunteers*. Lincoln: University of Nebraska Press, 2001.

Engle, Stephen D. *Don Carlos Buell: Most Promising of All*. Chapel Hill: University of North Carolina Press, 1999.

Fagots from the Camp Fire. Washington, D.C.: Emily Thornton Charles, 1881.

Ferris, Ruth, ed. "Captain Jolly in the Civil War." *Bulletin of the Missouri Historical Society* 22, no. 1 (October 1965): 14–31.

Fisher, Noel C. "Definitions of Victory: East Tennessee Unionists in the Civil War and Reconstruction." In *Guerrillas, Unionists, and Violence on the Confederate Home Front*, edited by Daniel E. Sutherland. Fayetteville: University of Arkansas Press, 1999: 89–111.

Foster, Buck T. *Sherman's Mississippi Campaign*. Tuscaloosa: University of Alabama Press, 2006.

Frazer, Persifor. "Reminiscences of the Mississippi Squadron in 1864–65." In *Military Essays and Recollections of the Pennsylvania Commandery, Military Order of the Loyal Legion of the United States*, 1:255–88. Wilmington, N.C.: Broadfoot, 1995.

Fremantle, Arthur James Lyon. *Three Months in the Southern States, April–June 1863*. Lincoln: University of Nebraska Press, 1991.

Gallagher, Gary W., ed. *Fighting for the Confederacy: The Personal Recollections of General Edward Porter Alexander*. Chapel Hill: University of North Carolina Press, 1989.

Garrett, Jill K., ed. *Confederate Diary of Robert D. Smith*. Columbia, Tenn.: Capt. James Madison Sparkman Chapter, United Daughters of the Confederacy, 1975.

Glatthaar, Joseph T. *The March to the Sea and Beyond: Sherman's Troops in the Savannah and Carolinas Campaigns*. New York: New York University Press, 1985.

Gould, E. W. *Fifty Years on the Mississippi*. St. Louis: Nixon-Jones, 1889.

Gower, Herschel, and Jack Allen, eds. *Pen and Sword: The Life and Journals of Randal W. McGavock*. Nashville: Tennessee Historical Commission, 1959.

Grabau, Warren E. *Ninety-eight Days: A Geographer's View of the Vicksburg Campaign*. Knoxville: University of Tennessee Press, 2000.

Graf, LeRoy P., and Ralph W. Haskins, eds. *The Papers of Andrew Johnson*. 16 vols. Knoxville: University of Tennessee Press, 1967–2000.

Grant, Ulysses S. *Memoirs and Selected Letters*. 2 vols. in 1. New York: Viking, 1990.

Green, John P. "The Movement of the 11th and 12th Army Corps from the Potomac to the Tennessee." In *Military Essays and Recollections of the Pennsylvania Commandery, Military Order of the Loyal Legion of the United States*, 1:107–22. Wilmington, N.C.: Broadfoot, 1995.

Gresham, Matilda. *Life of Walter Quintin Gresham, 1832–1895*. 2 vols. Chicago: Rand McNally, 1919.

Grimsley, Mark. *The Hard Hand of War: Union Military Policy toward Southern Civilians, 1861–1865*. New York: Cambridge University Press, 1995.

Groce, W. Todd. *Mountain Rebels: East Tennessee Confederates and the Civil War, 1860–1870*. Knoxville: University of Tennessee Press, 1999.

Hafendorfer, Kenneth A. *Mill Springs: Campaign and Battle of Mill Springs, Kentucky*. Louisville: KH Press, 2001.

Harrison, Lowell H. "George W. Johnson and Richard Hawes: The Governors of Confederate Kentucky." *Register of the Kentucky Historical Society*. 79, no. 1 (Winter 1981): 3–39.

Harrison, Lowell H., and James C. Klotter. *A New History of Kentucky*. Lexington: University Press of Kentucky, 1997.

Hartley, Chris J. *Stoneman's Raid, 1865*. Winston-Salem, N.C.: John F. Blair, 2010.

Harwell, Richard, and Philip N. Racine, eds. *The Fiery Trail: A Union Officer's Account of Sherman's Last Campaigns*. Knoxville: University of Tennessee Press, 1986.

Hazen, William B. *A Narrative of Military Service*. Boston: Ticknor, 1885.

Hearn, Chester G. *The Capture of New Orleans, 1862*. Baton Rouge: Louisiana State University Press, 1995.

———. *Mobile Bay and the Mobile Campaign: The Last Great Battles of the Civil War*. Jefferson, N.C.: McFarland, 1993.

————. *When the Devil Came Down to Dixie: Ben Butler in New Orleans*. Baton Rouge: Louisiana State University Press, 1997.

Hess, Earl J. *Banners to the Breeze: The Kentucky Campaign, Corinth and Stones River*. Lincoln: University of Nebraska Press, 2000.

————. "Confiscation and the Northern War Effort: The Army of the Southwest at Helena." *Arkansas Historical Quarterly* 44, no. 1 (Spring 1985): 56–75.

————. *Liberty, Virtue, and Progress: Northerners and Their War for the Union*. 2nd ed. New York: Fordham University Press, 1997.

————. "The Mississippi River and Secession, 1861: The Northwestern Response." *Old Northwest* 10, no. 2 (Summer 1984): 187–207.

————, ed. *A German in the Yankee Fatherland: The Civil War Letters of Henry A. Kircher*. Kent, Ohio: Kent State University Press, 1983.

Hewitt, Lawrence Lee. *Port Hudson: Confederate Bastion on the Mississippi*. Baton Rouge: Louisiana State University Press, 1987.

Hicks, Roger W., and Frances E. Schultz. *Battlefields of the Civil War*. Topsfield, Mass.: Salem House Publishers, 1989.

Hoffman, Wickham. *Camp Court and Siege: A Narrative of Personal Adventure and Observation during Two Wars, 1861–1865, 1870–1871*. New York: Harper and Brothers, 1877.

Hollandsworth, James G., Jr. *Pretense of Glory: The Life of General Nathaniel P. Banks*. Baton Rouge: Louisiana State University Press, 1998.

Holmes, J. T. *52d O.V.I.: Then and Now*. Columbus, Ohio: Berlin Printing, 1898.

Hood, J. B. *Advance and Retreat: Personal Experiences in the United States and Confederate Armies*. Philadelphia: Burk and McFetridge, 1880.

————. "The Defense of Atlanta." In *Battles and Leaders of the Civil War*. Vol. 4. Edited by Robert Underwood Johnson and Clarence Clough Buel, 336–44. New York: Thomas Yoseloff, 1956.

Howard, Oliver Otis. *Autobiography of Oliver Otis Howard*. 2 vols. New York: Baker and Taylor, 1907.

————. "The Battles about Atlanta." *Atlantic Monthly* 38 (October 1876): 385–99.

————. "The Struggle for Atlanta." In *Battles and Leaders of the Civil War*. Vol. 4. Edited by Robert Underwood Johnson and Clarence Clough Buel, 293–325. New York: Thomas Yoseloff, 1956.

Howe, Henry Warren, *Passages from the Life of Henry Warren Howe*. Lowell, Mass.: Courier-Citizen, 1899.

Howe, M. A. DeWolfe, ed. *Marching with Sherman: Passages From the Letters and Campaign Diaries of Henry Hitchcock*. Lincoln: University of Nebraska Press, 1995.

Hughes, Nathaniel Cheairs, Jr. *The Battle of Belmont: Grant Strikes South*. Chapel Hill: University of North Carolina Press, 1991.

Johnson, Richard W. *A Soldier's Reminiscences in Peace and War*. Philadelphia: J. B. Lippincott, 1886.

Johnson, Robert Underwood, and Clarence Clough Buel. *Battles and Leaders of the Civil War*. 4 vols. New York: Century Co., 1887–88.

Johnston, Joseph E. *Narrative of Military Operations*. New York: D. Appleton, 1874.

Jones, James Pickett. *Yankee Blitzkrieg: Wilson's Raid through Alabama and Georgia.* Athens: University of Georgia Press, 1976.

Josyph, Peter, ed. *The Wounded River: The Civil War Letters of John Vance Lauderdale, M.D.* East Lansing: Michigan State University Press, 1993.

Kendall, John Smith. "Recollections of a Confederate Officer." *Louisiana Historical Quarterly* 29 (1946): 1041–1228.

Kennedy, Frances H., ed. *The Civil War Battlefield Guide.* 2nd ed. Boston: Houghton Mifflin, 1998.

Kennedy, Joseph C. G. *Agriculture of the United States in 1860.* Washington, D.C.: Government Printing Office, 1864.

Kiper, Richard L. *Major General John Alexander McClernand: Politician in Uniform.* Kent, Ohio: Kent State University Press, 1999.

Kundahl, George G. *Confederate Engineer: Training and Campaigning with John Morris Wampler.* Knoxville: University of Tennessee Press, 2000.

Lambert, D. Warren. *When the Ripe Pears Fell: The Battle of Richmond, Kentucky.* Richmond: Madison County Historical Society, 1995.

Lawson, Lewis A., ed. "The Hammontrees Fight the Civil War: Letters from the Fifth East Tennessee Infantry." *Lincoln Herald* 78, no. 3 (Fall 1976): 117–22.

Lebergott, Stanley. "Through the Blockade: The Profitability and Extent of Cotton Smuggling, 1861–1865." *Journal of Economic History* 41, no. 4 (December 1981): 867–88.

Logan, Mrs. John A. *Reminiscences of a Soldier's Wife: An Autobiography.* New York: Charles Scribner's Sons, 1913.

Longacre, Glenn V., and John E. Haas, eds. *To Battle for God and the Right: The Civil War Letterbooks of Emerson Opdycke.* Urbana: University of Illinois Press, 2003.

[Loughborough, Mary Ann]. *My Cave Life in Vicksburg.* New York: D. Appleton, 1864.

Loving, Jerome M., ed. *Civil War Letters of George Washington Whitman.* Durham: Duke University Press, 1975.

Lucas, Marion Brunson. *Sherman and the Burning of Columbia.* College Station: Texas A&M University Press, 1976.

M. "The Battle of Dead Angle on the Kennesaw Line, Near Marietta, Georgia." *Southern Bivouac* 3, no. 2 (October 1884): 71–74.

Mackey, Robert R. *The Uncivil War: Irregular Warfare in the Upper South, 1861–1865.* Norman: University of Oklahoma Press, 2004.

Mackey, Thomas C. "Not a Pariah, but a Keystone: Kentucky and Secession." In *Sister States, Enemy States: The Civil War in Kentucky and Tennessee,* edited by Kent T. Dollar, Larry H. Whiteaker, and W. Calvin Dickinson. Lexington: University Press of Kentucky, 2009: 25–45.

Madden, David. "Unionist Resistance to Confederate Occupation: The Bridge Burners of East Tennessee." *East Tennessee Historical Society Papers* 52 and 53 (1981–82): 22–39.

Manufactures of the United States in 1860: Compiled from the Original Returns of the Eighth Census. Washington, D.C.: Government Printing Office, 1865.

Marszalek, John F. *Commander of All Lincoln's Armies: A Life of General Henry W. Halleck.* Cambridge: Harvard University Press, 2004.

———. *Sherman: A Soldier's Passion for Order.* New York: Free Press, 1993.

Maslowski, Peter. *Treason Must Be Made Odious: Military Occupation and Wartime Reconstruction in Nashville, Tennessee, 1862–1865.* Millwood, N.Y.: KTO Press, 1978.

McClure, Alexander K. *Recollections of Half a Century.* Salem, Mass.: Salem Press, 1902.

McDonough, James Lee. *Nashville: The Western Confederacy's Final Gamble.* Knoxville: University of Tennessee Press, 2004.

———. *War in Kentucky: From Shiloh to Perryville.* Knoxville: University of Tennessee Press, 1994.

McMurry, Richard M. *Atlanta, 1864: Last Chance for the Confederacy.* Lincoln: University of Nebraska Press, 2000.

———. "Confederate Morale in the Atlanta Campaign of 1864." *Georgia Historical Quarterly* 54 (1970): 226–43.

———. *John Bell Hood and the War for Southern Independence.* Lexington: University Press of Kentucky, 1982.

———. *Two Great Rebel Armies: An Essay in Confederate Military History.* Chapel Hill: University of North Carolina Press, 1989.

McNeill, William J. "A Survey of Confederate Soldier Morale during Sherman's Campaign through Georgia and the Carolinas." *Georgia Historical Quarterly* 55 (1971): 1–25.

McPherson, James M. *Battle Cry of Freedom: The Civil War Era.* New York; Ballantine Books, 1988.

———. *Ordeal by Fire: The Civil War and Reconstruction.* New York: Alfred A. Knopf, 1982.

McWhiney, Grady. *Braxton Bragg and Confederate Defeat: Volume 1, Field Command.* New York: Columbia University Press, 1969.

Michael, W. H. C. "The Mississippi Flotilla." In *Civil War Sketches and Incidents: Papers Read by Companions of the Commandery of the State of Nebraska, Military Order of the Loyal Legion of the United States,* 1:21–33. Omaha: Burkley, 1902.

Milligan, John D. *Gunboats Down the Mississippi.* Annapolis, Md.: U.S. Naval Institute, 1965.

Mitchell, Enoch L., ed. "The Civil War Letters of Thomas Jefferson Newberry." *Journal of Mississippi History* 10, no. 1 (January 1948): 44–80.

Mountcastle, Clay. *Punitive War: Confederate Guerrillas and Union Reprisals.* Lawrence: University Press of Kansas, 2009.

Neal, William A. *An Illustrated History of the Missouri Engineer and the 25th Infantry Regiments.* Chicago: Donohue and Henneberry, 1889.

Niven, John, ed. *Salmon P. Chase Papers.* 5 vols. Kent, Ohio: Kent State University Press, 1993–98.

Noe, Kenneth W. *Perryville: This Grand Havoc of Battle.* Lexington: University Press of Kentucky, 2001.

Official Records of the Union and Confederate Navies in the War of the Rebellion. 30 vols. Washington, D.C.: Government Printing Office, 1894–1922.

Paludan, Phillip S. "The American Civil War Considered as a Crisis in Law and Order." *American Historical Review* 77, no. 4 (October 1972): 1013–34.

Parish, Peter J. *The American Civil War.* New York: Holmes and Meier, 1975.

Parks, Joseph H. *General Leonidas Polk, C.S.A.: The Fighting Bishop*. Baton Rouge: Louisiana State University Press, 1962.

Partridge, Charles A., ed. *History of the Ninety-sixth Regiment Illinois Volunteer Infantry*. Chicago: Brown, Pettibone, 1887.

Perkins, Howard Cecil, ed. *Northern Editorials on Secession*. 2 vols. Gloucester, Mass.: Peter Smith, 1964.

Perret, Geoffrey. *Ulysses S. Grant: Soldier and President*. New York: Random House, 1997.

Phillips, Brenda G., ed. *Personal Reminiscences of a Confederate Soldier Boy*. Milledgeville, Ga.: Boyd Publishing, 1993.

Pickenpaugh, Roger. *Rescue by Rail: Troop Transfer and the Civil War in the West, 1863*. Lincoln: University of Nebraska Press, 1998.

Pierson, Michael D. *Mutiny at Fort Jackson: The Untold Story of the Fall of New Orleans*. Chapel Hill: University of North Carolina Press, 2008.

Poe, Orlando M. "The Defense of Knoxville." In *Battles and Leaders of the Civil War*, vol. 3, edited by Robert Underwood Johnson and Clarence Clough Buel, 731–45. New York: Thomas Yoseloff, 1956.

Polley, J. B. *A Soldier's Letters to Charming Nellie*. New York: Neale, 1908.

Pond, Fern Nance. "New Salem's Miller and Kelso." *Lincoln Herald* 52, no. 4 (December 1950): 26–41.

Potter, James E., and Edith Robbins, eds. *Marching with the First Nebraska: A Civil War Diary*. Norman: University of Oklahoma Press, 2007.

Prokopowicz, Gerald J. *All for the Regiment: The Army of the Ohio, 1861–1862*. Chapel Hill: University of North Carolina Press, 2001.

Quaife, Milo M., ed. *From the Cannon's Mouth: The Civil War Letters of General Alpheus S. Williams*. Detroit: Wayne State University Press, 1959.

Ranlett, S. A. "Jackson, Miss." *National Tribune*, November 13, 1884.

Reagan, John H. *Memoirs with Special Reference to Secession and the Civil War*. New York: Neale, 1906.

Reed, Lida Lord. "A Woman's Experiences during the Siege of Vicksburg." *Century Magazine* 61 (April 1901): 922–28.

Rogers, Robert M. *The 125th Regiment Illinois Volunteer Infantry*. Champaign, Ill.: Gazette Steam Print, 1882.

Roland, Charles P. *Albert Sidney Johnston: Soldier of the Three Republics*. Austin: University of Texas Press, 1964.

———. *An American Iliad: The Story of the Civil War*. Lexington: University Press of Kentucky, 2004.

Roth, Margaret Brobst, ed. *Well Mary: Civil War Letters of a Wisconsin Volunteer*. Madison: University of Wisconsin Press, 1960.

Sauers, Richard A., ed. *The Civil War Journal of Colonel William J. Bolton, 51st Pennsylvania*. Conshohocken, Pa.: Combined Books, 2000.

Saxon, Lyle. *Father Mississippi*. Gretna, La.: Pelican Publishing, 2006.

Schofield, John M. *Forty-six Years in the Army*. Norman: University of Oklahoma Press, 1998.

Schurz, Carl. *The Reminiscences of Carl Schurz*. 3 vols. London: John Murray, 1909.

Scott, William Forse. *The Story of a Cavalry Regiment: The Career of the Fourth Iowa Veteran Volunteers, from Kansas to Georgia, 1861–1865.* New York: G. P. Putnam's Sons, 1893.

Scribner, B. F. *How Soldiers Were Made; Or, The War as I Saw It.* Chicago: Donohue and Henneberry, 1887.

Seymour, Digby Gordon. *Divided Loyalties: Fort Sanders and the Civil War in East Tennessee.* 3rd ed. Knoxville: East Tennessee Historical Society, 2002.

Shea, William L., and Terrence J. Winschel. *Vicksburg Is the Key: The Struggle for the Mississippi River.* Lincoln: University of Nebraska Press, 2003.

Sherman, John. *Recollections of Forty Years in the House, Senate and Cabinet.* 2 vols. Chicago: Werner, 1895.

Sherman, William T. *Memoirs of General William T. Sherman, by Himself.* 2 vols. New York: D. Appleton, 1875.

Shoup, Francis A. "Dalton Campaign—Works at Chattahoochee River—Interesting History." *Confederate Veteran* 3 (1895): 262–65.

Silber, Nina, and Mary Beth Sievens, eds. *Yankee Correspondence: Civil War Letters between New England Soldiers and the Home Front.* Charlottesville: University Press of Virginia, 1996.

Simon, John Y., ed. *The Papers of Ulysses S. Grant.* 28 vols. Carbondale: Southern Illinois University Press, 1967–2005.

Simpson, Brooks D., and Jean V. Berlin, eds. *Sherman's Civil War: Selected Correspondence of William T. Sherman, 1860–1865.* Chapel Hill: University of North Carolina Press, 1999,

Smith, David M., ed. *Compelled to Appear in Print: The Vicksburg Manuscript of General John C. Pemberton.* Cincinnati: Ironclad Publishing, 1999.

Smith, Timothy B. "Anatomy of an Icon: Shiloh's Hornets' Nest in Civil War Memory." In *The Shiloh Campaign*, edited by Steven E. Woodworth, 55–76. Carbondale: Southern Illinois University Press, 2009.

———. *The Untold Story of Shiloh: The Battle and the Battlefield.* Knoxville: University of Tennessee Press, 2006.

Smith, Walter George. *Life and Letters of Thomas Kilby Smith, 1820–1887.* New York: G. P. Putnam's Sons, 1898.

Society of the Army of the Cumberland: Twelfth Reunion, Toledo, Ohio, 1880. Cincinnati: Robert Clarke, 1881.

Statistics of the United States (Including Mortality, Property, & c.) in 1860: Compiled from the Original Returns and Being the Final Exhibit of the Eighth Census. Washington, D.C.: Government Printing Office, 1866.

Stevenson, Benjamin F. "Kentucky Neutrality in 1861." In *Papers Read before the Ohio Commandery of the Military Order of the Loyal Legion of the United States, 1886–1888*, 2:44–70. Wilmington, N.C.: Broadfoot, 1991.

Stoker, Donald. *The Grand Design: Strategy and the U.S. Civil War.* New York: Oxford University Press, 2010.

Stone, Henry. "From the Oostenaula to the Chattahoochee." In *The Mississippi Valley, Tennessee, Georgia, Alabama, 1861–1864: Papers of the Military Historical Society of Massachusetts*, 8:397–427. Boston: Cadet Armory, 1910.

Supplement to the Official Records of the Union and Confederate Armies. 100 vols. Wilmington, N.C.: Broadfoot, Publishing, 1995–99.

Surdam, David G. "Traders or Traitors: Northern Cotton Trading during the Civil War." *Business and Economic History* 28, no. 2 (Winter 1999): 301–12.

Sutherland, Daniel E. *A Savage Conflict: The Decisive Role of Guerrillas in the American Civil War*. Chapel Hill: University of North Carolina Press, 2009.

Sword, Wiley. *The Confederacy's Last Hurrah: Spring Hill, Franklin, and Nashville*. Lawrence: University Press of Kansas, 1993.

Symonds, Craig L. *Joseph E. Johnston: A Civil War Biography*. New York: W. W. Norton, 1992.

Throne, Mildred, ed. *The Civil War Diary of Cyrus F. Boyd, Fifteenth Iowa Infantry, 1861–1863*. Baton Rouge: Louisiana State University Press, 1998.

Tower, R. Lockwood, ed. *A Carolinian Goes to War: The Civil War Narrative of Arthur Middleton Manigault, Brigadier General, C.S.A.* Columbia: University of South Carolina Press, 1983.

Vandiver, Frank E., ed. "A Collection of Louisiana Confederate Letters." *Louisiana Historical Quarterly* 26 (1943): 937–74.

Van Noppen, Ina Woestemeyer. *Stoneman's Last Raid*. Raleigh: North Carolina State College, 1961.

Wakelyn, Jon L., ed. *Southern Pamphlets on Secession, November 1860-April 1861*. Chapel Hill: University of North Carolina Press, 1996.

———. *Southern Unionist Pamphlets and the Civil War*. Columbia: University of Missouri Press, 1999.

The War of the Rebellion: A Compilation of the Official Records of the Union and Confederate Armies. 128 vols. Washington, D.C.: Government Printing Office, 1880–1901.

Weigley, Russell F. *A Great Civil War: A Military and Political History, 1861–1865*. Bloomington: Indiana University Press, 2000.

White, Horace. *The Life of Lyman Trumbull*. Boston: Houghton Mifflin, 1913.

Wiley, Bell Irvin, ed. *Confederate Letters of John W. Hagen*. Athens: University of Georgia Press, 1954.

Williams, Frederick D., ed. *The Wild Life of the Army: Civil War Letters of James A. Garfield*. East Lansing: Michigan State University Press, 1964.

Wills, Charles W. *Army Life of an Illinois Soldier*. Washington, D.C.; Globe Printing, 1906.

Wills, Ridley, II. *Old Enough to Die*. Franklin, Tenn.: Hillsboro Press, 1996.

Womack, Walter, ed. *The Civil War Diary of Capt. J. J. Womack*. McMinnville, Tenn.: Womack Printing, 1961.

Woodworth, Steven E. *Decision in the Heartland: The Civil War in the West*. Westport, Conn.: Praeger, 2008.

———. *Nothing but Victory: The Army of the Tennessee, 1861–1865*. New York: Alfred A. Knopf, 2005.

Wright, Marcus J. "The Battle of Belmont." *Southern Historical Society Papers* 16 (1888): 69–82.

Index